CRIME LORDS

Other books by Paul Williams:

The General

Gangland

Evil Empire

… Paul Williams is the outstanding journalist of his generation.
Joe Duffy, *Liveline* RTÉ

Williams continues to be a thorn in organised crime's side.
RTÉ *Guide*

… His work … has made him one of Ireland's best-known journalists
and a hate figure for some of the country's most dangerous criminals.
In Dublin

CRIMELORDS

Paul Williams

MERLIN
PUBLISHING

First published in 2003 by
Merlin Publishing
16 Upper Pembroke Street
Dublin 2, Ireland
Tel: +353 1 676 4373
Fax: +353 1 676 4368
publishing@merlin.ie

Text © 2003, 2004 Paul Williams
Editing, Design and Layout © 2003, 2004 Merlin Publishing
Except
Photographs courtesy of the individuals and institutions noted on each
page of the picture sections.

First Edition published 2003
Reprinted 2003, 2004
This second edition published November 2004

First Edition ISBN 1-903582-51-2
Second Edition ISBN 1-903582-59-8

A CIP catalogue record for this book is available from the British
Library.

10 9 8 7 6 5 4 3 2 1

Typeset by Gough Typesetting Services
Cover Design by Graham Thew Design
Cover Image courtesy of Padraig O'Reilly
Printed and bound in Denmark, by Nørhaven Paperback A/S

Dedication

Dedicated to the memory of my father,

Benny Williams 1927–2001

Contents

Acknowledgements

A book which compiles the stories of several criminal godfathers, their gangs and exploits, would be impossible to write without the help, trust and assistance of a great many people. I would like to thank former and current members of the Gardaí, HM Customs in the UK and the Amsterdam police serious crime squad, all of whom gave of their time so that the stories could be told. My thanks also go to the victims and gang members who shared their, often harrowing, experiences. They know who they are.

My thanks also to Michael Brophy, Managing Director, *Sunday World*, Colm MacGinty, Editor, *Sunday World*, John Shiels, and News Editor John "Bram" Donlon, who as always were very understanding about my long absences from the newsroom. My thanks also go to my picture editor, Gavin McClelland, for his hard work and to Diarmuid MacDermott of the Ireland International News Agency. My gratitude is also due to *Sunday Independent* Crime Correspondent Jim Cusack for his advice and to *Sunday World* crime photographers Padraig O'Reilly and Liam O'Connor, who are responsible for many of the pictures of organised crime bosses who feature in *Crime Lords*. Thanks also to Daragh Keany for his research work.

The cover shot was staged to illustrate the world of the *Crime Lords*. My thanks to the 'gangster' and his 'victim', Kevin McElroy and Damian Boyle, and to photographer Padraig O'Reilly. They almost succeeded in scaring the living daylights out of an innocent passerby! Thanks to my editor in Merlin Publishing, Aoife Barrett, for all her hard work. She got a chilling crash course in organised crime and terrorism. Also to Chenile Keogh, Managing Director, Merlin Publishing.

And as always my special gratitude and love goes to my long-suffering family, Anne, Jake and Irena, who have always been there for me.

Gerard Fanning (1954–2004)

On Sunday, October 24, 2004, the Irish legal, media and publishing world lost Gerard Fanning, a brilliant lawyer, cherished friend and loyal confidant. Gerard was a consummate professional who loved his work. He was the best media lawyer this country has ever seen. Unlike so many of his colleagues in the legal profession, Gerard had no room in his life for superficiality or pomposity. He was an honest, straight talking man who lived by a code of justice and equality. His curriculum vitae of work and achievements proved that he really was the best. For almost ten years Gerard worked as the lawyer for the *Sunday World* and it was through that work that he became my great friend, advisor and mentor. We lovingly referred to him as "The Consiglieri".

Gerard had great insight and an awesome knowledge of every aspect of current affairs, from crime to politics. He was quick-witted, good-humoured and a great raconteur. Gerard was always available to help in any way he could, be it with a story or a book or a personal matter. He was the best friend you could have in your corner and everyone in the *Sunday World* and the publishing business depended on his wisdom.

Gerard is survived by his loving partner Anne, his father and mother Stephen and Kay, his sister Mary and his five nieces and nephews. Kieran Kelly, his partner in the firm of Fanning and Kelly Solicitors which they established in 2000, carries on Gerard's tradition of dedication and diligence. Kieran completed the legal work Gerard had started on this updated version of *Crime Lords*. I thank him most sincerely for that and look forward to working with him for many years to come.

Gerard's passing has left a void in the lives of his loved ones and his many friends and colleagues. In a cruel and cynical world Gerard was a true hero.

None of us will ever forget him.

Paul Williams

Introduction

That momentous day in June 1996 now seems like a lifetime away. The day of Veronica Guerin's murder was a watershed. It terrified and stirred a nation to its very core and led to an unprecedented counter-offensive against organised crime. For a time, the result was a dramatic decline in gangland assassinations – the traditional barometer used to gauge the level of activity in the criminal underworld. But to use a chilling threat once uttered by Sinn Féin leader Gerry Adams when commenting on the IRA: "They haven't gone away you know."

Today in Modern Ireland, the crime gangs, like the Provos, have certainly not gone away. In the first four years of the new Millennium organised crime has seen a dramatic upsurge which seems certain to continue. In the almost two year period between the beginning of 2003 and the end of 2004 twenty-five murders have occurred which could be categorised as gangland executions. The majority of the executions, nineteen in total, happened in 2003. In real terms this means that there was a dramatic drop in underworld murders in 2004. However, this does not mean that organised criminal activity is slowing down or that criminals have become imbued with a new regard for the sanctity of human life. In Limerick the constant pressure from the Gardaí and the imprisonment of several killers has resulted in a dramatic decrease in feud-related murders. In Dublin too, the imprisonment of a number of suspected hit men, has also contributed to the respite. But lulls are perennial. The number of shootings and attempted murders remain high. In a lot of cases poor shooting and good luck has contributed to keeping the death toll down.

In the meantime organised crime has thrived and the godfathers are growing fatter and wealthier all the time. By the end of 2004 a considerable number of major drug lords were running their empires from Alicante on Spain's Costa Blanca. At the time of writing it has become the new European hub for organised crime where Irish hoods do business with gangs from Morocco, Eastern Europe, Columbia and across the EU. It has also, perhaps, become a new graveyard for our ambitious gangsters. In 2004, three gangsters, Shane Coates, Stephen Sugg and Sean Dunne, vanished without trace in the province and are presumed dead.

Crime Lords investigates and exposes the godfathers who have dominated the underworld in recent history and are still doing so today. It tells the story of organised crime by focusing on the exploits of some of the most infamous gangland figures. *Crime Lords* pieces together the stories of gangsters like Mickey Green, the so-called Pimpernel, one of the world's biggest drug traffickers; and Martin Foley, The Viper who has survived more murder attempts than any other hoodlum. The savagery of a dangerous drug dealer called "Cotton Eye" Joe Delaney and the dramatic Garda investigation which resulted, against all odds, in successfully solving the first gangland murder in Ireland are also revealed.

The links between the Republican terror group, the INLA, and that organisation's involvement in serious crime are also investigated and exposed. In recent years the INLA has perpetrated some brutal crimes, including the notorious 'Ballymount Bloodbath'. *Crime Lords* unveils the organisation's flagrant breech of their own cease-fire, under the terms of the Good Friday Agreement and the peace process. The organisations of other gangsters, such as convicted kidnapper John Cunningham's international drugs and arms trafficking business and the secret Dutch and Irish police investigations which brought it to an end, are disclosed. *Crime Lords* tells the inside story of a little-known armed robber called Frank Ward, whose career spanned thirty years, and his involvement in one of the country's largest organised crime gangs led by George Mitchell, the godfather better known as "The Penguin".

The ongoing murderous inter-family feuding in Limerick City between the Ryans and the Keanes dominated the headlines for most of 2003 and 2004. So far it has claimed four lives and has been the source of scores of attempted murders and bomb plots. *Crime Lords* tells the inside story of what started this terrifying warfare which, at the time of writing, is expected to cost more lives and cause more misery. It also tells the story of the Gardai's fight back against the killer drug gangs and how they have successfully prosecuted and jailed at least twenty-five criminals for a myriad of offences ranging from murder, attempted murder, bomb making and possession of firearms to stabbings and violent disorder.

The book also exposes one of the country's most dangerous young criminal gang, The Westies. Since their emergence in the late 1990s these ruthless thugs have been responsible for an appalling catalogue of violent crime. The story of The Westies is a chilling insight into the potential state of organised crime in this country in the years to come. *Crime Lords* also investigates the mysterious disappearance of the Westies from their new home in Alicante and explores their likely fate.

Crime Lords reveals that, in 21st century Ireland, law enforcement is in a state of crisis. No less than three of the victims of gangland violence who feature in this book were actually murdered during the writing process. The need to re-write the stories of Ronnie Draper, John Ryan and Bernard "Verb" Sugg, were stark reminders of the ongoing mayhem on our streets. New crime statistics released at the end of 2004, make chilling reading. Murders have dropped by 20% but there has been a 40% increase in the use of firearms in various crimes. Sexual assault has dropped by 25% but rape has increased by 32%. Most alarmingly reports of aggravated assault have risen by a staggering 75%.

The Government's reaction to the crime situation has been nothing short of criminal. Since its re-election in 2002 the government have been promising more officers and resources for an already over-stretched Garda force. In November 2004 the Government finally announced details of how it intends to deliver on these promises. One idea is to increase the size of the force to 14,000 before the next General Election in 2006. The strategy includes relaxing the age limit for recruits. It is hard to foresee how this plan will succeed. Throughout 2004 the increased trend in the number of senior officers taking early retirement has continued. This is creating a catastrophic brain drain as officers with years of relevant professional experience leave the force. The Garda Síochána is experiencing an unprecedented crisis in morale. More emphasis is placed on cutting costs than on actually patrolling the streets or catching criminals. The lack of personnel combined with cutbacks means that in Dublin, for example, most city stations are under strength. If a station does not have enough officers on the beat then it must use its existing personnel to work extra hours. But because of budgetary restrictions there is simply no money to pay for overtime and thus, there are less officers on the streets and the Irish public suffers. In other areas specialist officers are confined to their offices because there is no money to pay for their participation in vital investigations. As a further reflection of the situation, young recruits to the Garda's training college are being lectured on ways to prioritise the public's calls for help. Officers of the future are been prepared for the reality that they will have to decide which crimes they can respond to and, more disturbingly, which ones they will not be able to deal with.

During the Summer of 2003 morale among the Gardaí plummeted to its lowest level yet – thanks to their own political boss, Minister for Justice Michael McDowell. McDowell's, by now infamous, claims that journalists were bribing Gardaí for stories is an excuse to try to introduce draconian legislation that will effectively criminalise both police officers and journalists because they have shared information. The Minister's claims were based on utterly false allegations made by a columnist in a Sunday newspaper. The spurious allegations were later effectively withdrawn because they were baseless and unfounded but the Minister had already done untold damage to the journalists trying to do their job. As he limply declared, "I know what I know", there was no mention of taking on organised crime or of worrying about the dangers of cops being bribed by criminals.

By the end of 2004 the Government is still working on the legislation which enables the State to arrest and imprison journalists who refuse to co-operate with investigations. The legislation allows the State to have the homes and offices of journalists searched in a bid to uncover their sources. Another disturbing aspect of McDowell's legislation is that it will be an offence for any Garda to assist a journalist in a story that is deemed to "undermine the peace process". Simply put, this means that in the future Sinn Féin representatives in the Dáil will be able to push for investigations into the sources of legitimate journalistic stories about Sinn Féin/ IRA racketeering.

In effect McDowell's legislation will help to cover up scandals and gag the freedom of speech.

The controversial storm kicked up by Michael McDowell's proposed legislation has served another Government purpose. It has provided a smoke screen to divert attention from the real issues. The Government no longer seems to want journalists to expose the reality of serious crime in Ireland. Public awareness of what is really going on results in pressure being exerted, on both the police and politicians to do something about the situation. Michael McDowell is trying to demonise and denigrate journalists as common criminals in his quest to shut them up. In the end it is the people, the voters, who will suffer most. At the time of writing more legislation has been introduced to curtail and restrict the lives of ordinary decent citizens than ever before. An over-stretched and under-staffed police force now have the extra duty of spying on pubs to see who is drunk and who is smoking while drug dealers and gangland murderers seem to be able to do what they like.

And while all this is going on the crime lords are prospering and expanding their operations throughout the country. Veronica Guerin and the circumstances of her death have been conveniently forgotten. In the meantime the seeds of another outrage have been nurtured and have taken root. Soon the bad guys will be justified in feeling untouchable. The future is bleak. *Crime Lords* should be a timely reminder.

The reaction of the criminal underworld to the first publication of *Crime Lords* in November 2003 was another stark reminder that organised crime still poses a major threat to Irish society. Within days of the first serialisation of *Crime Lords* in the *Sunday World* the mob showed their disapproval of the contents of this book. Martin "the Viper" Foley, who is one of the gangsters exposed in this book, ordered a campaign of intimidation against me. It began with an acid attack on my car and culminated a month later with the placement of an elaborate hoax bomb underneath the car I was driving which was parked outside my family home. That incident forced the evacuation of 150 innocent men, women and children, my neighbours, from their homes in the early hours of a cold November morning. It was a callous act of thuggery, designed to silence free speech. For a time last November it appeared that I found myself surrounded by enemies on both sides – the Government on one side and the criminals on the other. Both of them had a common goal – shut up the messengers for their own criminal ends. A huge public outcry after the 'bomb' was discovered illustrated that the Irish people were still deeply concerned about organised crime and wanted to exercise their right to be informed about the criminals' activities. Unfortunately for Foley and his hoodlums, his efforts backfired. His actions brought even more heat down on him and his gangsters from the Gardaí. His exploits and those of the other crime gangs continue to be exposed in the Irish media – reminding them that we have not gone away either.

Paul Williams
2004

One

The Pimpernel

The powerful Bentley Turbo R turned left onto the south side of the quays, beside the River Liffey, and picked up speed. The one-way system, travelling west along the river to the motorway, was empty as the driver put the boot down. It was 4.30am on Sunday morning, April 9, 1995, and Dublin was still sleeping. The middle-aged, grey-haired man behind the wheel turned up the music as the luxury motor surged forward at 100 miles per hour. The driver and his four companions were full of the joys of spring – their collective buzz accentuated by the large quantities of booze and cocaine they'd consumed over the previous fourteen hours. The night had been another long, wild party in Dublin's exclusive restaurants, bars and clubs. Now the group, including two beautiful young women, were returning to the driver's country mansion to continue the party. There would be champagne on ice and a large bag of coke would be sitting beside a warm swimming pool and a bubbling jacuzzi. They intended to spend the early morning in a hedonistic haze of sex, drugs and booze.

On the other side of the river Joseph White had also been out all night. The affable taxi driver, from the working class suburb of Crumlin, had started his shift the previous evening at 10pm. He'd spent six hours ferrying Saturday night lovers and boozers around the city. Saturday was the busiest night of the week and a good opportunity to make some badly needed cash. The father of nine, who had been a taxi driver for a short time, was tired and looking forward to a well-earned sleep. As he crossed the River Liffey at Queen Street Bridge, he saw that the lights were green and continued on south towards his home.

At that same moment the driver of the Bentley ignored the red traffic light on his side of the quays. At the junction of Ushers Island and Bridgefoot Street, just south of the bridge, disaster struck. Joseph

White's car drove into the Bentley's path. The Toyota Corona was no match for the awesome power of the Bentley: the taxi driver didn't stand a chance. The huge car smashed into the side of the taxi with such force that it was squashed like a tin can. The Bentley mercilessly bulldozed the car across the junction and sandwiched it against a telegraph pole. Joseph White, still conscious, lay trapped and dying from horrific injuries in the crumpled wreck. In the confusion that followed, the driver of the Bentley tried to restart his car several times and drive off. While he was doing so his minder walked over to the taxi and looked into the wreck. He walked back to the Bentley and took his boss by the arm. The pair walked briskly away followed by the other three passengers, as they all abandoned the dying taxi man.

It took fire fighters forty-five minutes to cut Joseph White from the wreckage of his car. A passer-by had come on the scene of the crash and phoned for help. White died an hour later from shock and massive blood loss. A uniformed Garda patrol that had responded to the accident stopped the Englishman and his companions a short distance away. The women were hysterical and the middle-aged man was obviously drunk. He admitted to the officers that he was the driver of the abandoned Bentley. He was arrested on suspicion of drunk driving. Later that morning the Englishman was formally charged and remanded in custody to Mountjoy prison. The young Garda had no idea that he had just made one of the most significant arrests of his career. For the drunken Englishman was no ordinary middle-aged millionaire. He was Michael John Paul Green one of Europe's biggest international drug traffickers. The Garda had just arrested the man known to law enforcement agencies throughout the world as the Pimpernel.

Mickey Green, alias Brian Perkins and at least a dozen other names, was the head of an underworld empire estimated to be worth at least Stg£100 million. He earned the sobriquet the Pimpernel because, even though he was one of Europe's most hunted criminals, he had successfully evaded capture for almost two decades. He was wanted in Holland, France, Spain, Belgium and Britain in connection with drug trafficking and gold smuggling rackets worth hundreds of millions of English pounds. The Pimpernel was on the target list of every customs and police force in Europe, the US Drug

Enforcement Agency and the FBI. He had direct links with the US Mafia and the Colombian drug cartels. In terms of a criminal aristocracy, Mickey Green was one of the kings.

Until his arrest, the crime lord had been keeping his head down in Ireland for over two years. Despite his cultivated image of a gentleman, Green was a feared gangster who had no problem resorting to extreme violence, including murder, to get his point across. But the powerful godfather now found himself behind bars for a crime he had not planned or anticipated. The Pimpernel's life as a hard-living playboy had finally driven him into the arms of the law – or so it seemed.

* * * *

Mickey Green was born in Edgware, North London on June 23, 1941, at the height of the Second World War. His parents were Irish. The man, who would later hit the criminal big time, started from humble beginnings. His first recorded crime was at the age of fourteen. Green was convicted at Harrow Magistrate's Court on April 3, 1956, for being drunk and disorderly and stealing. The tough North London teenager was fined Stg£2 and bound over for two years. Three months later he was convicted of housebreaking and stealing at Watford Juvenile Court and again bound to keep the peace. Green went on to receive his first prison sentence, of one month, at the age of eighteen for shop breaking, stealing and possession of housebreaking implements.

The 1950s and 1960s were the golden age of London's gangland. It was the time of the Krays and the Richardsons and the Great Train Robbers. Nightclubs, prostitution and armed robbery became the stock and trade of the London villains. Mickey Green soon became what was known in the gangland parlance of the 1960s as a "Face" or an armed robber. Faces were swaggering playboys who had no interest in territory or turf, just money and a good time. They described their work as being "at it" or "on the pavement". One observer summed up the philosophy of the robbers. "Their only interest was instant cash. Sawn-off shotguns in a Wembley bank followed by a spell of sawn-off jeans on a Marbella beach. When they had spent all the cash on flash cars, nice suits, birds and booze they just went back and robbed some more." The police called them 'blaggers'.

As the years went on Green got steadily more involved in armed robbery and serious crime. In 1963, he was jailed for eighteen months for robbing a warehouse and in 1965 got two years for receiving stolen goods.

On his release Mickey Green became a member of the notorious Wembley Mob – a loose team of ten to fifteen North London villains responsible for a string of big pay roll and bank robberies over a four year period. According to Scotland Yard records, the gang made off with over Stg£1.3 million during that time or an estimated €10 million in current values. Between heists Green was 'working' in Edgware as an Arthur Daly-type used car salesman. In 1970, however, the Wembley Mob hit the national headlines for all the wrong reasons.

At 9.45am on Monday, February 9, 1970, a Security Express van stopped outside Barclays bank on High Road in Ilford, north-east London. Each Monday morning the same security van delivered cash and cheques to the Ilford bank from a chain of Tesco supermarkets in the London area. Security staff removed six bags containing Stg£223,496 in cash from the van. They took them inside the building where they were placed on a lift for transfer to the bank vaults. As the last bag was being delivered a man wearing a black wig and brandishing a sawn-off shotgun suddenly appeared. One of the guards threw the bag at the blagger but a second robber stuck a gun in the guard's back and shouted: "Down on the floor my son or you're a dead man." One of the robbers then pointed his gun along the bank counter and ordered staff to lie on the ground while four other members of the Wembley Mob, wearing stockings and crash helmets over their heads, ran in and grabbed the cash bags. The robbers jumped into a waiting van and escaped. The robbery had taken just ninety seconds to complete.

However, this time, Scotland Yard was hot on their heels. They made an early break in the case when a messenger at the bank recognised Green's picture in a police photo album of suspected blaggers. Green had been hanging around outside the bank earlier that morning as staff arrived. The police also questioned the security guards. They quickly discovered that fifty-three-year-old Edward

McCarthy's story did not add up. McCarthy finally confessed to passing Green information about the delivery in return for a payment of Stg£500. A second security guard also admitted his role in the inside job.

It later transpired that most of the planning for the Ilford job had been done in Green's flat. Green and his Wembley Mob partners, Ronald Dark and Arthur Saunders, were charged with the robbery, as were the security guards and Albert Walker, the gang's 'go-between'. But the police did not get the whole gang. Bobby King who had also been on the Ilford job later described the heist to a reporter: "There were nine of us and the planning took five to six weeks." When he was nicked Green said to the police: "If I go down for this I'll get a lot of bird [time], won't I? I'm in the first division now."

On November 6, 1970, Mickey Green's position in the first division of serious crime was acknowledged by the sentence he received at the Old Bailey. After a five-week trial Green was found guilty of the robbery and jailed for eighteen years. Ronald Dark also received eighteen years and Saunders got fifteen years. The security men got six and three years each and Walker was jailed for four years. The rest of the Wembley Mob, including Bobby King, joined their pals two years later when gang member Bertie Smalls became one of the first ever supergrasses. Smalls was granted immunity from prosecution for his part in an armed hold-up in return for helping to jail twenty-one former associates.

Mickey Green got a brief break from Parkhurst Prison at the height of the Smalls's trials, when he sought a decree of divorce in the family courts from his wife Carol. The couple had married in 1961 when she was sixteen and he was twenty. Green gave his evidence from the witness box while handcuffed to a prison officer. Green said that he and his wife had been living apart for the previous "few years" and that their relationship had broken down. He was granted the divorce. Green would marry again but his relationship with his second wife, Anne, would also end in divorce. The womanising gangster would have three children.

* * * *

On March 26, 1979, Mickey Green was released on licence from prison after serving nine years of his eighteen-year sentence. The condition of his release was that he did not participate in crime and that he be of good behaviour. Green had convinced the parole board that he was a changed character. But the gangster had no intention of going straight.

Shortly after his release Green got involved in a multi-million pound VAT fraud, smuggling large quantities of gold into the UK. The operation, which ran from 1979 to 1981, turned over Stg£9 million but was closed down following an investigation by HM Customs and Excise. Customs officers identified Green as the main financier behind the scam and estimated that he personally made Stg£2 million out of the racket. A number of people were arrested and charged and a warrant was issued for Green's arrest. The former "Face" was determined that he would not return to an English prison: he fled to Spain in 1981. In January 1982 his temporary release licence was revoked and an order made that he serve out the rest of his sentence for the Ilford bank job. The Pimpernel would spend the rest of his life on the run from the law.

Green's decision to flee to Spain in 1981 was a calculated career move. In the summer of 1978, a one hundred-year extradition agreement between Britain and Spain collapsed making Spain particularly attractive to fugitive hoodlums. Marbella and Malaga in the Costa del Sol had quickly become home to scores of runaway English villains. It became known in the British press as the Costa del Crime, the part of Spain that "fell off the back of a lorry". It was the perfect location for Green and other criminals – a paradise in the sun that was a short plane ride away from home and family. Ironically the Costa del Sol also became the preferred retirement location for hundreds of former British police officers.

When Green had come out of Parkhurst Prison in 1979 he'd realised that the underworld had undergone a dramatic change. Former "Faces" had found a new way of making a dishonest crust – drugs. The Costa del Crime was ideally suited for the new stock and trade of organised crime. Morocco was a short boat ride across the Mediterranean with a plentiful supply of cannabis resin. Soon the Costa del Crime followed Amsterdam, as it became Europe's second most important hub for the drug trade. When Mickey Green arrived in 1981 he quickly found himself a nice little earner. Soon the Pimpernel would be in the first division of European drug trafficking.

Operating from a luxury villa in Marbella, Green soon established himself as a major hash supplier to the UK market. Wherever Green travelled in the world he always insisted on living a lavish lifestyle. In Marbella, he bought a Rolls Royce, a convertible Porsche and a number of powerboats. He lived with the daughter of a well-known ex-patriot drug trafficker who opened a lot of doors in the business for him. Later the Pimpernel and his associates moved into the cocaine trade making direct contact with the Colombian drug cartels, who were anxious to establish a new European market. The Pimpernel was joined in his new business ventures by former partners from the Wembley Mob and by Ronnie Knight. Knight was the colourful ex-husband of British 'carry-on' film star and *Eastenders'* actress Barbara Windsor. Knight, a former Soho nightclub owner, arrived in the Costa del Sol in 1983. He was on the run from the police after the Stg£6 million Security Express robbery in London. Another recruit to this nest of infamous thieves was former 'Great Train Robber' Charlie Wilson. The group of former pals and new associates set up a drug trafficking cartel together.

Drugs weren't the new cartel's only criminal interest. In November 1983, three of Green's associates were arrested following the kidnapping of a British financier. They had decided to raise some cash to fund their activities. The man had been abducted in France and brought to a house in Mijas on the Costa del Sol, where he was held for three weeks. A ransom had been demanded for the man's safe return. The Pimpernel escaped the police swoop and went into hiding. He was never charged in connection with the incident.

Over the next three years the cartel concentrated on building up their operation. Then, in 1986, the Spanish police began a major operation to target the English drug cartels on the Costa del Crime. They specifically targeted the crime organisation they called 'El Pulpo', meaning the Octopus, because of its many operational arms. The man identified as leading the Octopus was Mickey Green.

In February 1987, Spanish police arrested six Britons and seized Stg£2 million worth of cannabis, eleven powerboats and yachts and several high-performance cars, including Green's Porsche and his Roller. But, again, the Pimpernel managed to disappear just as the Spanish police came looking for him. Nevertheless Spanish police described the swoop as their "greatest success ever" in breaking the link between the Spanish and British gangs. Both Green and Knight were captured a few weeks later but were released without charge. On March 15, 1987, a magistrate ruled that there was insufficient evidence against them.

In July 1987, Green was again in the frame following the arrest in London of US based drug trafficker Nicholas Chrastny and the seizure of cocaine with a street value of Stg£5 million. During interviews with police Chrastny admitted that he had organised a shipment of 390 kilos of cocaine which had been smuggled by boat directly from Colombia to England. Using sophisticated radio and directional finding equipment, Chrastny had guided the boat, the *Aquilon*, to the mouth of a river on the Cornish coast. From there the shipment was moved to London. Chrastny identified Mickey Green as a member of the UK based cartel and as the man who had arranged the deal for the drugs. In 1986, Chrastny had a number of meetings with Green in Vienna. The pair had agreed a price of $30,000 per kilo for the cocaine or Stg£11.7 million for the entire shipment. By the time the drugs hit the streets they would have been worth ten times more to the Green gang. It looked like Green's run of luck was finally up but then Chrastny escaped from custody and disappeared. When Chrastny vanished there was insufficient evidence with which to make a case against Green. The Pimpernel was off the hook. The British authorities have never been able to locate Chrastny.

In 1988, Green was given yet another reason to never return home to London: two of his associates, Graham Long and Stephen Viner, were arrested by HM Customs after officers intercepted 250 kilos of hashish that had been smuggled from Spain to the UK. The evidence against Green centred on the movement of large sums of cash from the UK to a Swiss bank account that he controlled. He was named on indictment but again the Pimpernel evaded justice. Extradition was never sought because Green's exact location could not be established. Long and Viner were each sentenced to ten years imprisonment.

Following this string of close shaves and setbacks Green quietly moved out of sight to live with his girlfriend in Morocco, but it was still business as usual. The Pimpernel began shipping hash to Holland directly from Morocco. One shipment of 1,100 kilos of cannabis and cocaine was intercepted by French customs in 1990 following a surveillance operation. The French had placed an undercover officer in the middle of the operation. The officer was present at meetings attended by Green in Paris while preparations for the shipment were finalised. The Pimpernel was not in France at the time the drugs were seized but the French issued an international warrant for his arrest on drug trafficking charges. On November 6, 1991, despite Green's absence, a court in Lyons sentenced him to twenty years imprisonment.

The Pimpernel then surfaced in Amsterdam where he established a new base and reorganised his supply routes of hashish and cocaine to the UK market. In the meantime he had flown to Columbia and organised a new supply route for high quality cocaine that was smuggled to Holland and then on to the UK. His cartel included associates from Holland, Spain, Belgium, Denmark and the UK. It wasn't long before the operation came under the spotlight of Green's old enemies, HM Customs.

In 1991, HM Customs arrested two of Green's associates, Victor Lee and Robert Mason, after they took delivery of 40 kilos of cocaine with a street value of Stg£4 million. The two men were subsequently convicted and jailed for twelve years each. The British identified Green as the supplier of the drugs but, again, had insufficient evidence with which to seek his extradition. The Pimpernel was proving to be an impossible foe.

Between 1992 and 1993 HM Customs and the Dutch police set up a joint operation, codenamed Operation Lucrativo, in yet another effort to catch Green. During a three-month surveillance operation in late 1992, three of Green's Dutch associates travelled to London where they deposited a total of Stg£7.5 million at a Thomas Cook exchange bureau. The three associates were also connected to the cocaine trafficking operation between Colombia and Europe. A sum of Stg£2.5 million was then moved from the bureau, through a complex laundering operation, to the USA. Over Stg£1 million of that cash was traced to accounts in the names of Brian Perkins and two companies, Flagship Racing and Chequered Flag. The US Drug Enforcement Agency (DEA), who had also become involved in the investigation, discovered that Green was using a false passport in the name of Brian Perkins. They also uncovered evidence that he had used the two companies to launder drug money. The companies had been set up in the US by Green's money launderer. He was an English accountant living in Miami, Florida, who Green regularly visited.

On November 3, 1992, in a warehouse rented by Green's cartel the Dutch police seized 1,100 kilos of cocaine and 1,000 kilos of cannabis, destined for the UK market. The total street value of the haul was estimated at over Stg£112 million. As part of the swoops the police searched an adjoining warehouse rented by Green for his own personal use. In it they found 126 kilos of gold bars, a BMW, a Bentley, a Porsche, a jeep, a Mercedes and a Ford Mercury. All the vehicles had been registered under the various aliases used by the Pimpernel. Three Dutch nationals were subsequently arrested and convicted for their part in the huge drug operation. However, the Pimpernel's instinct for trouble and freedom paid off, he had fled to the US just before the heat came down.

This time Green surfaced in San Francisco where he rented a mansion formerly owned by the rock singer Rod Stewart. By this stage the French, Dutch and British authorities were hot on his heels. The DEA placed him under constant surveillance and monitored several trips he made to meet with his suppliers in Columbia and his associates in Miami. In February 1993, armed with a Dutch extradition warrant, the DEA arrested Mickey Green as he lay by the pool at his new home.

Green was found in possession of three false British passports and the official Irish passport he had obtained several years previously. The DEA also arrested Green's money launderer and seized 950 bearer bonds with a value of $1.5 million. The Pimpernel of organised crime was remanded in custody while the extradition order was being processed. At the same time the French also made an application to the US courts to have the former London car dealer returned to France to serve his twenty year conviction for drug trafficking offences. But just when it appeared that his luck had finally run out the Pimpernel got an unexpected break.

* * * *

Michael Constantine Michael was the ultimate gangland Mr Fixit. A large man, of Greek-Cypriot extraction, he dabbled in fraud and ran a chain of massage parlours and brothels across London. Michael would eventually become the bagman and logistics manager for over twenty drug syndicates in the UK, organising transport, distribution, cash collection and money laundering. But secretly he was also a professional police informant and would later be described as the most prolific "grass" in the history of Scotland Yard. He was about to become Mickey Green's most trusted lieutenant.

Michael Michael was born on November 25, 1957, to hard-working Greek-Cypriot parents who ran a little fish and chip shop in Islington, North London. When he left school, Michael took the rather unlikely step of enrolling on a fashion course at a local college. He dropped out within the year, after falling in love with a Greek-Cypriot girl from Leicester, whom he subsequently married. The couple lived in the English Midlands with her parents, who also ran a fish and chip shop. However, frying chips was not the life the ambitious young crook in the making wanted. Michael yearned for more excitement and wealth in life and the marriage soon ended.

On his return to London, Michael began dabbling in crime through his new profession as a used car salesman. In 1984, he was charged with selling a Porsche that did not belong to him. Michael was convicted and sent to Brixton jail in south London for four months. On his release, he married another Greek-Cypriot girl but that relationship was also doomed.

In 1987, he met his third wife Lynn Baker, an outspoken Eastender. The attractive blonde was an established Madam, running a number of lucrative brothels around London. Michael had finally found a woman who could satisfy his appetite for corruption and adventure. The couple moved in together and within two years she gave birth to the first of two sons. Michael Michael began working with his wife in the "family business" and soon their prostitution racket was expanding across North London.

In the meantime Michael had also set himself up as an accountant after a stint working for a friend as a bookkeeper. They became partners in a personal finance business and Michael started selling pension schemes and arranging mortgages. But he couldn't resist dabbling in fraud. Michael set up mortgages in bogus names to allow his customers to get more than one loan and to speculate on the property market.

In 1989, he was arrested by the Serious Fraud Office (SFO) and charged with mortgage fraud. His career as an informant had begun. Initially Michael began passing on pieces of information to the SFO relating to other mortgage fraud scams and the famous Guinness trial. His first tip-offs included revealing the names of a group of West Indians who were committing aggravated burglaries. It wasn't long before his police handlers realised that Michael was a potential gold mine. They had found out that he was also familiar with the drugs' underworld – a world they were desperate to penetrate.

Michael got their undivided attention when he told them that he had a connection to an Anne Green, Mickey Green's second wife. Anne Green was the widow of murdered London villain Jack "The Hat" McVitie, a former member of the Krays' gang. McVitie's murder, at the hands of the Krays, was one of the most infamous in British gangland history. Anne Green and Lynn Baxter were long time friends and Lynn had also grown up and gone to school with Mickey Green's son from his first marriage. The smooth-talking fraudster and his wife Lynn had just bought a property from two of Anne Green's associates in the drug trade. Michael had just begun working as an accountant for Anne Green's two associates.

The SFO introduced Michael to two detectives attached to the Regional Crime Squad based at Tottenham Court Road in Central London. The officers ensured he received a much lighter four-month sentence for the mortgage fraud in return for his assistance. The Scotland Yard cops visited Michael twice in Wandsworth and Ford prisons to consolidate their special relationship.

Michael also saw a long-term mutual benefit in the arrangement. His prostitution racket was booming and would soon be turning over an average of Stg£500,000 per year. He needed the cops on his side to ensure that the brothels weren't closed down. He told the officers that he used his brothels to glean vital information from major villains and drug dealers. Men's tongues tended to loosen considerably while enjoying the pleasures of a massage parlour, he told them. Michael had a deal.

Michael Michael became an official Scotland Yard informant and was given two pseudonyms, Andrew Ridgley and Chris Stevens. In 1991, he was introduced to Detective Constable Paul Carpenter. For the next seven years Michael worked for DC Carpenter, a relationship which would later be described by an Old Bailey Judge as "completely corrupt". As a result of this relationship Michael was to become a central player at the highest level of London's criminal drug rackets.

DC Paul Carpenter and his bosses in the Yard were particularly interested in Mickey Green and Carpenter pushed Michael to forge stronger links to Anne Green with a view to getting closer to the Pimpernel. Michael was reluctant to get into bed with the likes of a heavy international player like Mickey Green. His police handler assured him that his information would be used only for intelligence purposes and his identity would be disguised. Michael agreed to try. As a first move in September 1992, Michael went with his wife and family for a short holiday with Anne Green at her villa in the Costa del Crime. At the time Mickey Green was living in Miami.

Michael Michael did not have to wait long before the connection was made with the Pimpernel himself. A few weeks after the DEA arrested Green in the US in 1993, Anne Green visited Michael in London. She asked Michael if he could raise money, if necessary, for bail and lawyers on a property the Pimpernel owned in Wembley.

Michael later flew to Malaga and met Anne Green with three of the Pimpernel's Dutch associates. The seizure of Green's gold in the warehouse in Holland was discussed. One of the associates, a Dutch lawyer, advised Anne Green to swear a false affidavit stating that the gold really belonged to her. The Dutch authorities believed that the gold and cars were the proceeds of crimes that linked the Pimpernel to drug trafficking. When Michael reported this meeting back to his Scotland Yard handlers they were instantly excited. At last they had a conduit to the man they wanted to bust more than any other criminal.

Sometime later Michael received a phone call from Mickey Green himself. The call had been routed through a third party from the US prison where Green was being held on the extradition charges. It was Michael Michael's first contact with Green. The Pimpernel asked Michael to go to Marbella and to remove paperwork and photographs from his villa. Michael agreed to go. At the same time Michael's police handler began giving him information to pass on to Green in a bid to get further into his confidence. DC Carpenter gave Michael the names of three UK criminals who had been reported visiting Green's house in Miami. Michael passed on the information to Green and it had the desired effect. Green was impressed but he was also concerned that he had been so closely monitored by the US authorities.

The Scotland Yard man then gave Michael Michael information that proved to be crucial to Green's extradition case. The Pimpernel's case had been the subject of debate between the Dutch, French and British authorities. At a conference it was decided that the Dutch would drop their case in favour of the French matter, as it was a secured conviction with a twenty-year stretch. In any event the Dutch had decided that they had insufficient evidence with which to prosecute Green. DC Carpenter then revealed that there was a flaw in the French extradition case. The French undercover customs' officer central to Green's case had been arrested and charged with a criminal offence. Michael contacted Green and his American lawyer with the information. The Dutch case was withdrawn. Green's lawyers later successfully won compensation from the Dutch government for the time he had spent in prison on their extradition warrant. Then Green's lawyers argued that based on the arrest of the undercover officer the French extradition case was fundamentally flawed. On October 22, 1993, the US District Court of the Northern District of California dismissed the French case on the grounds that there was insufficient probable cause or insufficient evidence. A District Court in Dordrecht meanwhile ordered the return of the gold and fleet of vehicles to the Pimpernel's representatives in Amsterdam.

In the meantime, Green was also in dispute with the US authorities concerning passport offences, for which he had been fined, and his assets were frozen. Crucially DC Carpenter tipped Michael off that one of Green's associates had just been arrested in Holland and was likely to implicate him in a drug trafficking case. Green, fearing a resumption of the Dutch extradition case, cut his losses and made a deal with the US Government. They took half of the $1.5 million in bearer bonds they had seized at the time of his arrest. The other half was returned to him.

In December 1993, the US authorities ordered Green's release from prison and his immediate deportation to Ireland because he was the holder of an Irish passport. As he boarded the flight to Dublin on December 17, 1993, Mickey Green was a happy man. He had beaten the DEA, the Dutch, French and British authorities. The legend of the Pimpernel was the topic of conversation in law enforcement and criminal circles across the world.

The Pimpernel celebrated his freedom by throwing a lavish party in Dublin's Burlington Hotel on the weekend he arrived in Ireland. The party was attended by several of his criminal associates from London, Spain and Holland. Among them were well-known drug traffickers Steve McGoldrick and Clifford Hobbs, with whom Green had formed a new cartel. Members of the notorious London crime families the Adams, the Rileys and the Arifs, also came to celebrate their old pal's extraordinary run of luck. Michael Michael flew from London, bringing two of his most talented prostitutes with him, to take part in the festivities. It was the first time the two men met face-to-face. Green was greatly impressed with the informant and he immediately began to trust him. After all he owed Michael his freedom.

In the following months the brothel boss became an essential cog in the Pimpernel's new drug cartel, organising everything from the distribution of the drugs to laundering the proceeds. He became the equivalent of a Mafia *consiglieri* to Green's 'Godfather'. Green relied on Michael more and more as the operation grew to become one of the largest and best organised in Europe. The fraudster even organised hotel accommodation, flights and false documentation to enable his new boss to move around the world undetected by the ever-growing number of law enforcement agencies who wanted him behind bars. And all this happened under the watchful eye of New Scotland Yard.

Shortly after Christmas 1993, DC Paul Carpenter gave Michael a document that he had copied from a secret Customs and Excise report detailing Mickey Green's activities and his associates. Michael would later claim in court that he paid Carpenter Stg£4,000 for the report. At the height of their relationship Michael claimed that he was paying the Scotland Yard officer Stg£10,000 per week. The police officer also provided confidential reports to Michael relating to the activities of his other business associates. Each time the information was of use the cop was allegedly paid Stg£4,000. The Customs report was invaluable to Mickey Green. The secret document showed that the Customs had compiled detailed information about the Pimpernel and his associates, including their financial dealings. It detailed the Customs' covert operation to obtain information about one of Green's money launderers by secretly searching his baggage at various airports worldwide. It gave details of a Dutch investigation into a boat called the *Gafion* that was being used to import cocaine into Holland. It named two brothers who had been followed bringing cash into the UK. Their bags had also been secretly searched by Customs and they had been tailed to a Bureau de Change at Marble Arch in London. Green was hugely impressed by Michael's intelligence gathering and began to alter his drug operation to avoid further detection. The leaked report resulted in all the named targets adjusting their habits or pulling out of certain deals altogether.

Around the same time Michael organised the sale of Anne Green's villa in Spain after her death from cancer. Mickey Green had agreed to sell the property to his business partner Steve McGoldrick for Stg£200,000. Michael organised the sale through a complex chain of false companies and off-shore banks. Meanwhile Mickey Green was thoroughly enjoying his new life in Ireland and decided to live there permanently. Green, a charming womaniser, met a beautiful young blonde teenager called Anita Murphy from Coolock, North Dublin. Aged eighteen she was thirty-five years younger than her gangster sugar daddy. Murphy later moved in to live with the Pimpernel and up to ten years later they were still together.

On May 14, 1994, Green organised a champagne reception and party to celebrate his mother's birthday in the Burlington Hotel in Dublin. Apart from friends and family, several gangsters from Spain, England, Holland and the USA, flew in for the weekend long party. Green was becoming a familiar face in Dublin's glitzy clubs and pubs. He was particularly popular with staff as he dished out huge tips wherever he went. The owners and managers of the clubs also loved to see the mysterious Englishman arriving with his large entourage of young women and loud-mouthed, hard-drinking roughnecks. Although they were obviously not very 'kosher' the money Green spent ensured that everyone turned a blind eye. The Pimpernel decided that he had found his perfect home. He was breaking no laws and as long as he kept his head down the police steered clear of him and his associates. At the same time business was booming. Green and his cartel were buying huge quantities of drugs from various suppliers in Morocco, Spain, Holland and Colombia and then transporting them to the UK. From there Michael Michael would organise everything else.

Through his relatives in Dublin Green built up a friendship with a number of people involved with the Fianna Fáil party. His driver and general assistant Paul Boulton, from Baldoyle in north Dublin, was also a member of the political party. In November 1994, Boulton and his other Fianna Fáil friends brought Green to a party fundraiser in the Burlington Hotel in Dublin. To everyone present Green was an immensely wealthy retired UK businessman. During the function he even got to shake hands with the then Justice Minister Maire Geoghegan Quinn. Mickey Green was happy to make a very significant donation to the party coffers that night.

In August 1994, Green paid IR£243,000 for Maple Falls, a magnificent mansion newly built on four acres near the village of Kilcock, in County Meath. At the same time he bought a new three-bedroom penthouse apartment for IR£135,000 in Dublin's upmarket Customs House Docks development. Michael Michael transferred sums of money through a network of false companies to pay for the properties in cash.

Green instantly fell in love with Maple Falls. From there he ran his huge drug empire, organising deals and entertaining some of Europe's biggest criminal godfathers. The single-storey house, situated at the beginning of the M4 motorway, was a convenient twenty-minute journey from Central Dublin. Maple Falls had three reception rooms, a spacious kitchen and breakfast room, five bedrooms, four bathrooms and a gym, complete with a full size sauna. The house also had an indoor heated swimming pool and a snooker room. Green spared no expense decorating his new bolthole from justice. He spent a fortune on antique furniture and ordered hand woven custom-made carpets and the best Italian tiles. He equipped both the penthouse and Maple Falls with the most sophisticated sound systems that money could buy.

The grounds were equally impressive and again the multi-millionaire drug lord spent lavishly. The estate included a stable and paddock where Green kept horses for his grandchildren when they came to visit from London. Next to that was a floodlit tennis court and a large pond was situated in the middle of beautifully manicured gardens. Green spent thousands of pounds stocking the pond with exotic Japanese Ki Carp fish that were valued at up to IR£500 each. Next door to the pond was a fully equipped bar and conservatory for entertaining his many criminal guests. Associates would later recall how Green would literally spend hours on his own gazing into the pond, as he planned his various business deals and scams. A former employee at Maple Falls recalled Green's fascination with his fish: "Mickey had great taste and he loved the fish. He found watching them very relaxing and it helped him work things out. When he sat beside the pool he wanted to be alone and he would not tolerate anyone interupting him. It was his special place."

To the local villagers in Kilcock, Green was an affable retired English businessman. The Pimpernel used a coin box in the village to put various drug deals together. While organising the details of a multi-million pound drug deal, he would casually wave to the locals as they passed the phone box. When Green was first exposed, by the *Sunday World* in April 1996, the villagers finally worked out why he needed to use a public phone so much. "It used to strike you that maybe Mick's phone was always on the blink. When we found out what he was really at then it all made sense," a villager said at the time. On several occasions the Pimpernel hosted parties for his underworld pals with large amounts of booze and food bought in from the village. After Green's arrival in Ireland some of the UK's toughest and most notorious gangsters became regular visitors to Dublin and Kilcock. It was not unusual for 'geezers' who sounded remarkably like *Del Boy Trotter* to pop into the local shop or post office in the quiet village, seeking directions to Maple Falls.

Green's parties were inevitably raucous affairs. The Pimpernel hired prostitutes from one of the country's most exclusive escort agencies to provide entertainment for his low-life guests. His favourite Madam was a beautiful high society hooker called Samantha Blandford Hutton. Hutton was a most unlikely prostitute and Madam. Her family had become immensely wealthy from running a chain of popular toy stores. But for cocaine snorting "Sam" selling flesh to gangsters and rock stars was infinitely more fun than selling kids' toys. One visitor later recalled seeing four London hoods naked in Green's swimming pool with several women. "It was just like the decadent stuff you see in the gangster movies but this was all very real. There were drugs, booze and birds. At Mickey's parties anything went and that's why everyone loved to be invited to Ireland. He was a great host, a right diamond of a bloke," a former associate told this writer. However, a bar worker who was hired to work at one of the gangland soirées witnessed an ugly side to the rowdy guests. She phoned her boss in tears, saying that she had seen two men at the party bundle a third man outside after a row broke out. They had returned later, covered in blood, without the third man.

In early 1995, Green summoned Michael Michael to Dublin for a meeting with two other members of the cartel, Steve McGoldrick and Terry McMullen. Over dinner in the Westbury Hotel, Green asked Michael to make arrangements to receive 200 kilos of 'Pakki Black' cannabis. The shipment was to be concealed in soap powder. It would be typical of hundreds of other deals that Michael would handle on Green's behalf.

By 1995, Michael had a very smooth drug distribution operation worked out, with the alleged encouragement of his police handler. The fraudster had set up his organisation through Green's contacts in the UK and was ready for business. Green had arranged for Michael to meet an associate of his who was a car dealer with plenty of contacts in the drugs' underworld. Mark Hooper, a mechanic in his early forties who worked for the car dealer, was also introduced to Michael. Hooper rented a warehouse on the Lee Industrial Estate in Hatfield, Hertfordshire from where he repaired lorries and cars. When Michael offered Hooper a lucrative deal to collect, store and distribute various drug shipments the mechanic was happy to oblige. Hooper was paid a set price of Stg£15 per kilo of cannabis and

Stg£500 per kilo of cocaine delivered to him and then re-distributed on Michael's instructions.

The drugs were mainly delivered by car, a bus – which Michael described as the "fun bus" – and a chemical tanker lorry. The drugs were sent from Spain, France and Holland, depending on which drug group Michael was dealing with. The men who organised the transport were two Britons, Richard Hannigan and Peter Jones, and a Frenchman, Andre Cadoux, all of whom were in their early fifties. Each of the transport men charged a fixed rate per kilo for the drugs they smuggled into England. Smuggling prices ranged from Stg£145 to Stg£200 per kilo, depending on the frequency of importations and the strength of the pound against the various European currencies. On receipt of each load Michael paid the transport managers on behalf of the syndicate organising the deal.

The transport vehicles would rendezvous with Mark Hooper at prearranged locations and were unloaded or alternatively, driven directly to Hooper's warehouse. Hooper's "handling charges" were paid out of the money Michael charged Green and his other clients. On top of that the bagman earned two per cent profit from laundering the proceeds of each sale. Green's car dealer contact had also introduced Michael to Housam Ali, a high-living Lebanese crook who owned a Bureau de Change in Central London. Ali was recruited to launder the drug money. Michael and Ali eventually set up their own Bureau de Change in Edgware Road to exclusively launder drug cash. The Bureau lasted for six months before they switched to a new system involving a Lebanese-based Bureau de Change. Over the following two years Ali laundered an estimated Stg£30 million. Ali also acted as an interpreter between Michael and the French drug suppliers.

Michael used a large number of couriers including his brother Xanthos, his wife, her two sisters, Jill and Karen Baker, and a former 'Page 3' model from *The Sun*, Tracey Kirby. The couriers delivered several million in cash to the drug gangs in Spain, Holland and France. Michael would later claim in court that he had been advised by DC Carpenter to recruit "pretty girls" in order to get through customs and currency controls at airports. He also claimed that DC Carpenter had advised him how best to move cash around the banking system without setting off alarm bells. Most of the couriers

were kept in the dark about the true nature of what they were involved in and about how much money they were carrying. Michael's trick was to use high-denomination currencies, such as 1,000 Dutch guilder notes that were worth more than Stg£300, which meant that Stg£100,000 could be carried in a package less than two inches thick.

When sending a courier by air to Malaga in Spain, Michael paid the courier Stg£800 plus expenses. If couriers travelled to Spain by car they went in pairs and were paid Stg£3,000 including expenses. Couriers travelling to Dublin, Paris or Amsterdam, were each paid Stg£400 plus expenses. Each courier who travelled by air carried an average of Stg£200,000 in drug money while, on an average delivery, the cars brought Stg£400,000. The money would be hidden in a spare tyre fitted in Mark Hooper's warehouse. Another trick, commonly used by drug traffickers, was to vary points of entry and re-entry when flying. A courier would depart from Heathrow with a return ticket. On arrival at the destination the return ticket would be discarded in the bin and another return ticket purchased for a different UK airport. This prevented Customs or police cross-referencing airline manifests while researching patterns of travel for possible couriers.

As would prove unfortunate for everyone involved in the huge drug smuggling business, Michael Michael kept meticulous records and diaries. The details included codes for the various clients, smugglers and couriers, and the sums collected, paid and laundered. He recorded dates, times, locations and quantities. Then he passed on the information about every deal and transaction in which he was involved to his police handler, for inclusion in his ever-expanding informant's file. "Hap" was his code word for Mickey Green. "I called him 'Hap' which is short for 'happy' because he [Green] was always miserable and in a bad humour," Michael would later reveal to Customs investigators. Michael Michael had established one of the most smoothly running drug rackets in Europe. He was becoming indispensable to the drug cartels.

When Green's 'Pakki Black' shipment was ready for collection in 1995, Michael received a call from the Pimpernel in Dublin telling him where to send Hooper. After Hooper had unpacked the load from the washing powder the 200 kilos were moved to the home of

Janice Marlborough. She helped manage and run Michael's chain of brothels. Michael asked his brother Xanthos to bring a one-kilo bar of the hash to the home of Steve McGoldrick, Green's partner in London. It was the first time Michael Michael had seen a bar of hashish. Steve McGoldrick brought the bar to the back garden and broke it in half with a hammer. He kept one half and gave the rest back to Xanthos Michael. The mobster tested the merchandise and deemed it to be of good quality.

Over the following weeks Green and his partners instructed Michael to organise three deliveries to separate customers around London. The money from the deals was handed to Michael in person. He exchanged it for Dutch Guilders and arranged for the cash to be couriered by his brother and Janice Marlborough to one of Green's associates in Holland. It took four deliveries to change and then move all the cash to Holland.

It was just as the new drug business was taking off that Mickey Green found himself in trouble with the Irish law. On the morning of April 9, 1995, when Green's *Bentley* smashed into Joseph White's taxi, the Gardaí arrested Green on suspicion of drink driving and leaving the scene of an accident. At Kevin Street station a doctor arrived at 5.30am to take a blood or urine sample from Green but the Pimpernel twice refused to co-operate. He was charged with failing to provide a sample of blood or urine and leaving the scene of an accident. Green was brought before the Dublin District Court and remanded in custody to Mountjoy Prison.

Michael Michael claimed that DC Carpenter informed him of the accident within a few hours of the incident and suggested that Green might need Michael's assistance. If this is true it is obvious that the Gardaí in Dublin, possibly the Garda Drug Squad, were aware of Green's presence in Ireland and had contacted the man in charge of the Pimpernel's file in the UK, DC Carpenter. Amazingly, however, as will become clear later in this extraordinary story, the officers who arrested Green were not informed of his true identity or told about his past involvement in organised crime. For some reason, known only to a handful of senior police, Green's existence in Ireland was a closely guarded secret. It is clear that the Gardaí didn't want him to suspect they were keeping a discreet eye on him and on the many gangland luminaries who came to visit him. The

Gardaí then passed intelligence to their colleagues in Scotland Yard. But little did they know that their intelligence work was actually filtering back to Green himself. On one occasion in 1995, DC Carpenter showed Michael a Garda surveillance picture that had been secretly taken by undercover Gardaí as Michael left the Conrad Hotel in Dublin, in the company of Mickey Green and Green's assistant Paul Boulton.

Michael immediately contacted Paul Boulton by phone after getting news of the accident from his police handler. Green's personal aid had only just heard about the incident himself and said he was on his way to see the Pimpernel in Mountjoy prison. On Wednesday, April 12, Michael Michael flew to Dublin and put up the bail money for Mickey Green's release. Michael would later report to DC Carpenter that Green tried to use his Fianna Fáil contacts to quash the case against him.

On October 12, 1995 Mickey Green pleaded guilty to the two charges – failing to provide a sample of blood or urine and leaving the scene of an accident – when he appeared before Dublin District Court number five. Green had retained the services of Mr Barry White, one of the country's most distinguished senior counsels, specialising in the area of criminal law. A charge of causing death by dangerous driving was not preferred on the grounds that the charge was not provable because of the lack of evidence and eyewitnesses. A uniformed Garda gave evidence of attending the scene of the accident and arresting Green. In reply to questions from Mr White the Garda said that in the absence of Green's admission they could not have established ownership of the car because there were four other people in the car at the time of the accident. The Garda said that Green had no previous convictions of which he was aware.

Following submissions from Mr Barry White SC, the judge noted that there was no prosecution for dangerous driving. For the purpose of dealing with the charges before the court he could not therefore take Joseph White's death into consideration. The judge said he accepted that this was a bitter pill for the taxi driver's family. It was clear that the judge was unhappy with the charges before the court and with the way matters had turned out. The judge imposed fines totalling IR£950 and disqualified the Pimpernel from driving for two years. Mickey Green had again walked away a free man. He was also greatly relieved that his case had not attracted any media attention. Green's protective blanket of anonymity was still intact.

The inquest into the death of Joseph White was scheduled for February 1996 in the Dublin Coroner's Court. This writer and a colleague from the *Sunday World* attended the case. We had been tipped off that this would be no ordinary coroner's inquest. When we arrived it was obvious that the tip-off had been justified. At least seven men, all of whom were using mobile phones, were standing around the small Coroner's building. They gave the impression that they were there to protect someone, and, from experience, it was also obvious that these guys were no altar boys. The most noticeable figure was a big man who I would later discover was one Michael Constantine Michael. When we first spotted him we assumed that he was Mickey Green's personal bodyguard. Green himself didn't appear in the court. Behind the scenes he and Michael had been working hard to scupper the proceedings.

Shortly after his court case Green had summoned Michael to a meeting in Dublin. The Pimpernel had suggested that Michael's brothel manager, Janice Marlborough, make a false statement to the Coroner's Court, claiming that she was in a car with her Irish boyfriend and had witnessed the accident. A man from Coolock in north Dublin was produced as the 'boyfriend'. Janice Marlborough had travelled to Dublin by ferry and met Green and his fellow cartel-member Terry McMullen. She was introduced to her 'boyfriend' and had agreed to go ahead with the plan. Michael Michael later claimed that he informed his Scotland Yard handler about the perjury plot. He alleged that DC Carpenter replied that it was not his concern as the crime was in another jurisdiction. It is unlikely that the 'perjury plot' intelligence was ever passed on to the Gardaí in Dublin.

A few weeks later Michael had brought Marlborough back to Dublin where they'd again met Green, McMullen and the 'boyfriend'. They'd dropped Marlborough and her 'boyfriend' at the offices of Green's solicitors where the 'loving couple' had made their false statements about the accident. It is important to point out that the reputable firm of solicitors representing Green had no idea about the perjury plot. That evening Michael and Marlborough had travelled back to the UK. Some time later she was asked to attend Bushey police station in London to corroborate her statement.

During the Coroner's hearing in February a number of witnesses described seeing Green and his minder getting out of the crashed Bentley and walking away. They also recalled how the mobster had tried to restart the car and drive off. The 'boyfriend' was then called to give his evidence. He told the court that he had been driving behind the Bentley at the time of the accident. He claimed that he saw the Bentley drive through a green light at Ushers Quay and saw the taxi drive out in front of it. When he was cross-examined 'the boyfriend' said that he'd failed to stop at the scene because he was in a state of shock. He said he was with his English girlfriend at the time. He claimed that his marriage was going through "difficulties" and he did not want to become involved in the fatal accident. When he was asked why he had come forward with his evidence only after the inquest had begun, the 'boyfriend' claimed that he had been unaware the Gardaí were looking for witnesses. The hearing was adjourned, amid claims from the White family's legal counsel that the 'boyfriend' was perjuring himself.

Mickey Green did not appear in the Coroner's court. Michael, Terry McMullen and Green, held a meeting in the pub next door with friends of the dead taxi driver. The subject of compensation was discussed and Green offered a derisory IR£10,000 for the taxi driver's wife and nine children. The offer was rejected.

On March 28, 1996, the inquest resumed. Green's legal team said that he did not wish to give evidence due to the possibility of a civil liability case. The multi-millionaire gangster seemed adamant in his refusal to compensate a family who had lost their sole breadwinner due to his recklessness. The Dublin City Coroner Brian Farrell said that based on the fact that Green would claim privilege and refuse to give evidence if called to the witness box, he would not require him. The jury returned a verdict that Joseph White died as a result of injuries sustained when his car was involved in a collision with Mickey Green's vehicle. The Pimpernel had again escaped any serious sanction. He did not even have to pay compensation. For the moment, at least, he was still an anonymous Englishman – but not for long.

Following the inquest Green started to receive threatening

letters, culminating in him getting a bullet in the post. He was worried that the IRA had targeted him. He contacted a friend of 'the boyfriend', called Gerry, who claimed to have contacts in the organisation. Green wanted Gerry to find out who was threatening him. Michael Michael travelled to Ireland and stayed with Mickey Green and Anita Murphy at Maple Falls. Green then decided to go to Rome and on to Cyprus until the heat died down. Terry McMullen and his wife were also leaving the country. Michael had arranged the flight tickets and booked hotels in Rome and Limassol. Green also instructed his bagman to collect and pay for a sawn off-shotgun, a revolver and a 9mm pistol which he had ordered from his underworld pals in London. The Pimpernel told Michael to store the weapons and then arrange to have them smuggled to Ireland. Green was preparing for a possible confrontation with whoever was threatening him.

When Michael had collected and paid for the weapons he returned to Maple Falls with a London-based security firm. They installed a state-of-the-art security system around the mansion, including closed circuit TV cameras and motion detectors. Michael stayed in Meath while the work was being done. During the stay he met Green's contact Gerry who informed him that the IRA were not behind the death threats.

At the same time the *Sunday World* published an extensive four-page investigation into the life and times of Mickey Green, under the headline Mr. Big. The Pimpernel had been secretly photographed and followed by the newspaper. His entire past life was laid bare to the world. At last he had been stripped of his protective cloak of anonymity. Astonishingly the Gardaí in Dublin used a number of friendly reporters in the national media to completely trash the story and downplay Mickey Green's significance in organised crime. Stories were spun that the *Sunday World* investigation was blown out of all proportion. At one stage the situation got so ludicrous that one prominent journalist openly jeered this writer about the story, effectively claiming that the *Sunday World* had made the whole thing up. No doubt the Pimpernel enjoyed the row.

As a result of the article and the expected extra heat from the police Green cancelled the plan to smuggle the firearms into Dublin and left for Cyprus. A few weeks later Green returned to Dublin.

Michael flew from London and met Green and Anita Murphy for dinner in the La Stampa restaurant in Central Dublin. Green was clearly disturbed by his outing in the newspaper and announced that he was breaking his partnership with Steve McGoldrick and the others involved in the 'Pakki Black' deal. He was starting a new venture.

Green negotiated a deal through the Adams family to import 2,000 kilos of Thai Herbal cannabis through a Dutch-based contact named Charles. The deal had been done over drinks and dinner in Dublin when Terry Adams, the head of the family, had visited Green in Dublin. The 'grass' would be smuggled into the UK in a double articulated lorry. The Pimpernel had agreed to sell the bulk of the herbal cannabis through the Adams. Michael Michael and Mark Hooper had organised to handle the delivery, distribution and sale of 1,248 kilos through the Adams crime family. The remaining 752 kilos were destined for Frank Fraser Junior, the son of the infamous London gangster "Mad" Frankie Fraser, an old contemporary of the Krays and the Richardsons. According to Michael Michael, Green did not trust young Frank Fraser because he suspected he was an informant. Green told Michael he did not want anything to do with the Fraser side of the deal.

Another reason for Green's reluctance to get involved with the Frasers was their ongoing war with the Pimpernel's powerful gangland friends, the Adams family, who were from Islington in north London. The Adams were one of the most feared criminal gangs in the UK with a reputation for violence which linked them to a string of gangland murders during the 1990s. The Adams family had been responsible for shooting "Mad" Frankie Fraser in 1991. David Fraser, another of Mad Frank's sons, had part of his ear bitten off in a row over a drug deal with another member of the Adams clan. Despite Mad Frankie's one-man show and a 'warts and all' autobiography, the violent killer has never spoken about the Adams family or the shooting incident. The crime family's empire was reputed to be worth an estimated Stg£100 million, as a result of prostitution, drug and protection rackets. They were also linked to a huge Stg£26 million gold bullion heist from Heathrow Airport in the 1980s.

In May 1996, the first consignment of 'Thai Herbal' cannabis arrived in London. Green phoned from Kilcock and gave Michael a description of the truck and the time it would arrive at a lorry park outside London. The Adams family's finance chief, Saul Solomon Nahome, from Finchely, North London, had agreed to sell the cannabis on behalf of Green and Terry Adams. Known as "Solly" the thirty-nine-year-old diamond merchant owned a jewellers shop in Hatton Garden. He was better known to the police, however, as an international criminal who specialised in fraud and money laundering. Nahome had helped launder an estimated Stg£25 million of the Adams' drug money. His partner in the cannabis deal was another Adams family employee, Gilbert Wynter, a thirty-five-year-old drug dealer of Jamaican extraction. Wynter was an enforcer and hit man for the family which was a rather busy occupation. The Adams family were suspected of being responsible for up to twenty-five gangland murders in a three-year period alone.

"Solly" collected a kilo of the cannabis from Michael and took it away to test the quality. A few days later "Solly" met Michael in a pub near the junction of Hedge Lane and Green Lane in North London, to discuss prices. Michael and Nahome went to a bank of public phones and called Green in Kilcock. The Adams' money launderer arranged to visit Green in Dublin that weekend in order to settle on a price per kilo.

After the Dublin meeting, Green rang Michael and authorised him to sell the 'Thai Herbal' cannabis for Stg£1,800 per kilo instead of the original asking price of Stg£2,000 per kilo. Solly Nahome took delivery of 300 kilos and then a few days later a further 200 kilos were delivered to him. Green rang Michael with the phone numbers of other customers with whom he had agreed sales. At the same time a crooked Cypriot police officer, who was already on the Adams family's pay roll, arrived in London. The Pimpernel invited the cop, who Terry Adams had nicknamed the "Captain", for a short holiday at Maple Falls. The "Captain" worked at Larnaca airport as an immigration control officer. He could organise a safe passage through Customs for any courier carrying drug money into Cyprus. The corrupt cop could ensure that the couriers were not scrutinised and that their passports were not stamped. Green wanted to sort out a similar business arrangement with him.

Meanwhile Michael Michael was having trouble collecting the

cash from the deal with "Solly" Nahome. Nahome's bagman had paid only Stg£30,000 and still owed Green a total of Stg£900,000. Michael Michael could not contact Nahome, who had run into trouble with the police after being arrested for an attempted bank fraud. Green was furious when he heard that the cash had not been paid and contacted a representative of the Adams family. Nahome meanwhile eventually made contact with Michael. He explained that the cash flow problem lay with the man who had distributed the cannabis, Gilbert Wytner. Nahome claimed that Wytner had had an accident while on holiday in the West Indies and was suffering from memory loss. When Michael informed Green of this latest development the Pimpernel decided to travel to London to sort out the matter himself. Green risked ending up behind bars if he was caught in the UK.

Green and Anita Murphy arrived in London a few days before Christmas 1996. The Pimpernel was travelling with a false passport in the name of Michael Durrant. Michael Michael had booked them into the luxury Conrad Hotel in Chelsea Harbour. Michael also made arrangements for the couple to fly on to Australia on Boxing Day. Michael would later claim that Scotland Yard were fully aware of Green's presence in London and of his whereabouts.

On Christmas Day, 1996, Michael brought Green around to the home of an old gangland pal in Islington. Green and his friend sat around an open fire and talked over old times. Then Green told his friend about the problems he was having getting payment out of Solly Nahome and asked his old pal to mediate. As an incentive, he offered his friend a ten per cent commission on whatever Nahome paid back. The gangster, who was related by marriage to the Adams family, agreed to make enquiries and said he would contact Michael Michael about developments.

In the New Year, Solly made another payment of Stg£18,000. Green was on holiday on Hayman Island off the Australian coast when Michael phoned him with the latest development. The Pimpernel flew into a rage, as he was still owed thousands of pounds. A few days later Solly phoned Michael and handed the phone over to Gilbert Wytner. The Adams family's enforcer informed Michael that the 'Thai Herbal' cannabis was no good and he threatened to get both Michael and Green. The following day Michael and Hooper took back the grass on Green's instructions. Out of Nahome's and Wyntner's original order of 501 kilos, 202 kilos were returned 79 kilos of which they found to be of poor quality. Michael calculated that, including credit for the returned cannabis, Mickey Green was still owed over half a million pounds.

At this stage Green was back in Ireland. He contacted Michael and asked him to find out where Solly lived because he planned to send someone around to 'talk' to him about the outstanding debt. Michael has since claimed that he obtained the address from his police handler. A few days later Michael and Green met with Charles, their Dutch supplier, at the Westbury Hotel in Dublin, to discuss the shipment. By now the bagman referred to the consignment of drugs as "the headache" because it had caused them so much grief. Eventually Michael managed to sell most of the 'Thai Herbal' cannabis with the exception of 123 kilos. But Solly and Wytner still owed Green a lot of money.

In February 1997, Green contacted Michael Michael and asked him to meet him in Marbella. As usual Michael organised flights and accommodation for Green and Anita Murphy. Michael and his wife and two sons flew in a few days beforehand and checked into the Marbella Beach Club Hotel where he had also booked a suite for Green and his lover. The couple arrived in Malaga on a flight from Madrid. The Michaels later joined Green and Murphy for a meal in the Cypriano restaurant in Marbella to celebrate Murphy's 21st birthday. Also invited to the party was Green's new business partner, a Moroccan hash dealer called Larson, and his girlfriend. Arabic in appearance, Larson was in his early fifties. Apart from business interests he shared the Pimpernel's taste for young women – his girlfriend was much the same age as Murphy.

Later Green told Michael that he had dealt with Larson in the past and would be resuming their arrangement. Larson would produce the product and two other Dutch-based partners in the business would arrange to smuggle it from Spain to a warehouse in Holland. There the cannabis would be re-packaged and loaded into a chemical tanker controlled by Richard Hannigan, and driven to England. Michael would be given ten kilos of hashish per tanker load as payment for storing and distributing each load. Green went with Michael to a villa he had sold the bagman a few years earlier.

In the house Green pointed to an area below the window in the back bedroom floor which he said concealed a buried cash box containing Swiss Francs worth Stg£1 million.

On February 21, 1997, Green contacted Michael and told him to instruct a builder to dig up the hidden treasure under the bedroom floor in the villa. One of Green's men collected the cash and gave it to Larson as a down payment for cannabis. Mark Hooper picked up the first delivery from The Pimpernel's new venture, 498 kilos, outside London on May 3, 1997. On Green's instructions Michael Michael sold the hash on to various customers, at an average price of Stg£1,850 per kilo. The shipment was worth almost Stg£1 million. The money was collected and exchanged into various currencies and sent by courier to Holland and Spain.

Over the next eleven months, up to April 1998, Green's new operation with Larson shipped over 15,500 kilos and turned over Stg£28 million in cash. The cannabis aspect of Green's racket did not include the Pimpernel's cocaine smuggling business that was also worth several million pounds. In February 1998, out of the considerable profits, Michael organised the purchase of a luxury apartment at Monteparaiso in Marbella. He paid for the apartment in cash, through a number of bogus companies. The beneficial owners were Green and his glamorous young mistress.

While Green's new venture was taking off, associates of Solly Nahome and Terry Adams approached Michael with a proposition to distribute more herbal cannabis, this time stuff that had been grown in Sierra Leone in Africa. Michael was extremely reluctant to get involved. He and Green were still trying to recoup the balance of what they were owed from the Thai cannabis fiasco. In his coded ledgers Michael still referred to the cannabis as "the headache". But he was also afraid to decline. An 'offer' from the Adams family was an offer that you could not refuse. Michael agreed to take delivery of 2,000 kilos of the African grass on the understanding that he was helping to facilitate the sale of the stuff and was not accepting liability. But the Adams had other ideas.

Michael gave samples of the African produce to three of his biggest customers. They came back within a few days and told him the stuff was no good. Michael contacted a representative of the Adams family and told him that he would not be able to sell it.

Solly and Wytner, the Adams family's enforcer, began calling looking for payment for the inferior dope. Michael said that he could give them no money because no one would buy it. He told them to take it back. Michael also said that they should pay him and Green the money owed for "the headache" cannabis. They refused to pay.

On several more occasions Michael spoke to an intermediary asking Solly to call him about the Pimpernel's debt. In the end Michael decided to write off the debt rather than incur any further grief with Solly, Wynter and the Adams family. Back in Ireland, however, Mickey Green was still demanding his money.

Solly Nahome did finally return Michael's call. He put Wynter on the phone again. The underworld enforcer came straight to the point. He claimed that Green had tried to con them with "the headache" cannabis. He said that if the Pimpernel was in the UK he would find him and have him "done". He warned Michael that if he didn't watch his step that he would do him, his wife and his children. Michael tried to calm the situation down, claiming that he was only the bagman. If there was no money to collect then he could not collect it. When Michael called Green in Kilcock and told him about the threats, Green dismissed them. The Pimpernel decided to arrange a meeting with Terry Adams. Green was a respected gangster and, as far as he was concerned, he had originally agreed "the headache" deal, personally, with Terry Adams. It was now a matter of honour. In the parlance of London's gangland, Wynter had taken a "diabolical liberty" making threats against the likes of Green. The Pimpernel was going to make some enquiries.

In March 1998, Gilbert Wynter vanished without a trace from his north London home. The word on the gangland grapevine was that the enforcer had been taken away and murdered. His body is rumoured to have been buried in the foundations of the Millennium Dome in east London or eaten up in a car crusher. The one thing that everyone was sure of was that Wynter was "brown bread" – dead. His disappearance coincided with Mickey Green's enquiries about his money and the ongoing threats. When news of the killer's disappearance appeared in the London newspapers Mickey Green was neither sad nor surprised. Michael, on the other hand, was worried about what would happen if the Adams family accused him and Green of taking out the enforcer. The bagman had not been privvy to any meetings between Terry Adams and the Pimpernel about Wynter. The word on the street was that Michael and Green had killed the enforcer. The bagman did not want to end his days as part of the foundations of a motorway bridge. He called Green in a panic. Green laughed and told him not to deny that the Pimpernel had had the job done. The Pimpernel had lost considerable face as a result of the unpaid debt over "the headache" cannabis – he wanted his reputation back.

Eight months later, in November 1998, Wynter's partner, Solly Nahome was shot dead thirty yards from his Stg£300,000 home. A lone gunman hit him four times, at point blank range, before jumping on the back of a motorbike and disappearing. The hit had all the hallmarks of an Adams family 'job'. Police investigating the murder said that they were linking it with Wynter's disappearance. The officer leading the investigation, Detective Chief Inspector David Cater, said both men were involved in a multi-million pound cannabis deal where "£800,000 had gone missing". DCI Cater told local reporters: "Our investigations have established that Mr Nahome was linked to Gilbert Wynter and they were both involved in business ventures. Mr Wynter disappeared and Mr Nahome was subsequently murdered, and the two may be linked." But by the time Solly Nahome met his untimely demise neither the Pimpernel nor his bagman had the time or the interest to celebrate. They had their own problems and Michael Michael for one had a cast iron alibi.

* * * *

On November 25, 1997, Micheal Michael had celebrated his fortieth birthday with a lavish party at London's Dorchester Hotel. The fifty guests had enjoyed an endless supply of vintage champagne and fine wines. The centre piece of the bash had been the unveiling of a cake which reflected Michael's lifestyle: alongside a bright red '40' were icing sugar copies of the three mobile phones he always carried, his cherished silver Porsche, the stacks of Stg£50 notes that bulged in his wallet and the Silk Cut cigarettes he chain-smoked. Gangsters, drug couriers and hookers mingled with celebrities and football stars. There had been messages of congratulations from the great and the bad of organised crime, including Mickey Green. The cards and messages had come from Ireland, Holland, Belgium, France and Spain. The drug barons had wanted to toast their most important business associate, the man who ensured the smooth flow of their ill-gotten millions. Little did any of them know that the good times were about to come to an abrupt end.

To the outside world Michael Michael was the king of the hill, hugely successful with an immense fortune. But behind the scenes the bagman and brothel keeper was heading for meltdown. He had developed a serious cocaine habit that exacerbated his already high stress levels. He had become paranoid and trusted no one. Michael was becoming seriously unstable. Operating the largest drug distribution business in Europe, for some of the world's most dangerous gangsters, would tax the coolest nerves. Add to that a secret double life as a police informant and Michael was an accident waiting to happen. He was doing an extraordinary juggling act and the balls were about to fall.

By his fortieth birthday the business was beginning to go into overdrive. It was starting to overwhelm the bagman. He was handling literally tonnes of drug shipments, for up to twenty-six different crime syndicates at the same time. The warehouse at Hatfield was in full operation seven days a week. His group of couriers, who at first had been travelling with money packages to Europe once a month, were now travelling two and three times a week. When couriers grew suspicious about the real origins of the money and tried to pull out, Michael threatened to shoot them. One courier, who called to Michael's luxury Stg£750,000 home to collect a cash shipment for the Spanish run in January 1998, witnessed one of the bagman's unstable episodes. "He was going berserk, shouting and screaming. He was saying: 'She's no good, I'm gonna' keep the kids and I'll get rid of her [Lynne Michael]. I have no choice, if I don't she'll grass me up.' He had completely lost it," the courier would later recall. The bagman was terrified that his wife would find out about his secret life as a police snout and tell Mickey Green and the rest of the mob. By the time Wynter disappeared in March 1998, Michael Michael was on the verge of cracking up.

For years Michael had considered himself untouchable because of his relationship with Scotland Yard. He had never given HM

Customs and Excise a second thought. In early 1998 Customs officers had intercepted a concealed shipment of cocaine and cannabis in one of the trucks carrying Mickey Green's drugs into the UK. The investigators allowed the truck to travel on to its destination – Mark Hooper's warehouse in Hatfield. They set up a surveillance operation on what they thought was a middle of the road drug smuggling gang. Operation Draft was to last for four months, during which time they realised that this was no ordinary racket. From monitoring the warehouse in Hatfield the investigation team were led to Michael Michael.

On the evening of April 25, 1998, the HM Customs officers made their move. In a raid on the Hatfield premises they found Stg£800,000 in cash, 2.9 tonnes of cannabis and 16 kilos of cocaine with a total street value of Stg£11.6 million. At the same time the investigation team surrounded Michael's home in Hertfordshire. Believing that he was about to be robbed by rival gangsters or shot in revenge for the disappearance of Gilbert Wynter, Michael produced a pistol and threatened to shoot the Customs men. It was the same weapon Mickey Green had originally intended bringing back to Dublin two years earlier. The last people Michael expected were the law.

The drug world's Mr Fixit finally surrendered when the HM Customs officers identified themselves. In a search of the house the investigators were stunned when they discovered a room specially designed for storing drug money. In it they found money counting machines, one million Sterling in cash and a gun. Works of art worth over one million pounds hung on the walls of the mansion. Then they discovered Michael's meticulously detailed records.

After a night in the cells Michael realised that he could no longer hope to have immunity from prosecution. He was facing the prospect of spending most of the rest of his life behind bars. In exchange for his assistance, Michael Michael offered HM Customs a deal. Michael proposed that he and his wife Lynne would get shorter sentences and be given new lives with their sons if he co-operated. HM Customs agreed. Then Michael began to talk, and talk and talk. By the time he had finished he had recorded over two hundred and fifty hours of taped interviews and made fifty-four individual witness statements. The man the gangsters would later describe as a "super-supergrass" implicated everyone from the top down: every gangster, henchman and courier he had ever met was offered up on a plate. Michael Michael was proving to be the arrest of a lifetime.

First on Michael's list was Mickey Green, followed by a procession of the aristocrats of London's organised crime gangs, a veritable 'Who's Who' of the underworld. In all Michael exposed the business dealings of twenty-six crime syndicates. His records showed the amount of drugs they had dealt in, the money they had made and how they had laundered it. The "super-supergrass" even gave up his nearest and dearest: his wife, his brother Xanthos, his two sisters-in-law, his mistress, his trusted brothel manager Janice Marlborough, and his money launderer Housam Ali. He revealed how he had even used his own mother to courier cash out of the country. There were phone numbers, dates, times, quantities, names, addresses and bank accounts. Over sixty people were arrested and questioned. HM Customs soon discovered that the police held an informant's file on Michael with over 2,000 pages of intelligence, which he had passed to them over the past nine years. The former bagman alleged that he had been bribing DC Paul Carpenter for years. He claimed that he had paid Carpenter over Stg£250,000, in return for sensitive information. The allegations immediately sparked a major investigation involving the police internal affairs unit, CIB3 and DC Carpenter was arrested.

For the next forty-two months Michael was held in solitary confinement at a secret location. Lynn Michael and her children were placed under police protection for their own safety and they had to be moved seven times in that period. The London mobs had declared that all the Michaels were now targets for assassination. At one stage Lynn Michael and her two sons were accommodated on a RAF air base. Michael's sons were described as being deeply traumatised by the whole dreadful experience. Michael Michael had earned his reputation as the greatest snout in British criminal history at the cost of his own flesh and blood.

It took a number of weeks before the implications of Michael's arrest fully hit the crime lords. From the day of the HM Customs' raid, on April 25, 1998, a huge chunk of the drug distribution business in the UK suddenly stopped. It was then that it dawned on the godfathers that they had become very dependant on just one man. Everyone started to panic, including Mickey Green. As word began to filter back that the bagman had disappeared, most of his major clients packed their bags and took to their toes.

In Maple Falls, in Kilcock, the Pimpernel and his mistress hurriedly packed and left Ireland within weeks of Michael's arrest. When he'd found his Irish bolthole Green had probably thought that his days of running had come to an end. Now at fifty-seven years of age he was doing what he had always done best – running from the law. The couple travelled to South America and then back into Europe through Italy and into Spain. The Pimpernel used his many passports and identities to keep his head down, while at the same time frantically trying to find out exactly what was happening back in the UK. The courts had imposed a complete reporting ban on the case as gangster after gangster was arrested and charged on Michael's word. Steve McGoldrick, Richard Hannigan and Jerry Coffey, three of Green's closest associates, were arrested and charged. Coffey, a managing clerk in a firm of solicitors in London, was charged with laundering Green's drug money. Things did not look good. An international hunt had been ordered, on foot of an arrest warrant from HM Customs, to try to locate Mickey Green, who had literally vanished. A secret conference was held in Spain, which was attended by Green and representatives of the major crime gangs most affected, including the Adams and Riley families. It was agreed to put a contract on Michael's head for one million pounds. Over the following months, as the situation deteriorated, the figure rose to four million pounds and included Michael's wife and children.

To add to Green's problems, the Criminal Assets Bureau (CAB) in Dublin also began to move against the Pimpernel. The CAB had been established in 1996 following the murder of journalist Veronica Guerin. This new and pioneering squad was made up of personnel from the Gardaí, customs, revenue and social welfare. It was the first of its type in Europe. Under crime legislation the CAB could seize cash and property from individuals suspected of making their fortune from criminality. In June 1997, the CAB had targeted Mickey Green and established his ownership of Maple Falls and the docklands penthouse. Following the arrest of Michael Michael in April 1998, the head of the CAB, Detective Chief Superintendent

Felix McKenna, held a number of secret meetings with the officers heading the Operation Draft investigation. Michael Michael had divulged how he had used Green's drug money to buy the Irish properties. Michael had also revealed how Green had bribed the 'boyfriend' from Coolock to perjure himself at the inquest hearing into the death of Joseph White. The CAB had a strong case with which to take on the Pimpernel.

On July 6, 1998, the HM Customs investigation team invited the CAB officers to a conference in London. The officer directly in charge of the CAB enquiry on the ground, Detective Sergeant Paul O'Brien, and a bureau legal officer, attended the conference during which it was decided that Green's Irish properties should be seized. The CAB set up Operation Damask in Dublin to coincide with the British investigation.

On July 30, the CAB raided four premises in Dublin and Kildare, including Green's two properties and the home of his driver and assistant, Paul Boulton. Detective Sergeant O'Brien had been tipped off about a hidden secret compartment in an item of furniture in Green's bedroom at Maple Falls. The officer found the compartment but it was empty. A secret safe was also uncovered but it too had been emptied. However the searches were to prove crucial to the international search for Green. The CAB officers discovered that Boulton was secretly in direct contact with the Pimpernel.

In December 1999, the Criminal Assets Bureau were ready to make their final move. Armed with affidavits from HM Customs and the information given by Michael Michael, the CAB obtained a High Court order freezing the two properties in Dublin and Kildare. Timing was everything. At the same time the Michael Michael cases were proceeding behind closed doors and amid maximum security at Woolwich Crown Court in east London. The Crown Prosecution Service had issued warrants for the arrest of Mickey Green on charges of drug trafficking and money laundering, but, still, no one could locate him. In a secret memo sent to HM Customs, CAB boss Felix McKenna said that his officers were confident that within days of seizing the elusive gangster's properties they would get a fix on Green's whereabouts. The CAB strategy paid off. Green was extremely agitated when he heard that his beloved Maple Falls was to be taken from him. He decided to fight the CAB tooth and nail and that was his mistake.

Early in January 2000, Detective Sergeant O'Brien and his team discovered that Green was living under a false identity in the Barcelona area of Spain. Later O'Brien pinpointed the Pimpernel to the Ritz Hotel and informed HM Customs.

In the first week of February 2000, Mickey Green was arrested by Spanish police and remanded in custody to a prison in Madrid. It appeared that the Pimpernel's number was finally up. From his jail cell Green began fighting the Customs' extradition case in London and the CAB case in Dublin. For the next sixteen months Green fought his legal battles from his pokey Spanish prison cell.

In the meantime the Michael Michael cases continued. By the time it would all be over a total of thirty-four people would be convicted out of the forty-nine charged – thirty of whom would plead guilty – and sentences totalling one hundred and seventy years were handed down by the court. Lynn Michael, Xanthos Michael and Janice Marlborough all agreed to turn state witnesses in return for shorter sentences. Among those convicted were Mark Hooper who was jailed for twenty-one years. Andre Cadoux, who organised the smuggling operation from France, got thirteen years. Peter Jones, who owned tanker trucks used in the smuggling operation, got twelve years. Housam Ali got seven years. Tracey Kirby, the former 'Page 3' model and drug courier, admitted that she had carried five million pounds out of the country for Michael and got three years. Sue Richards, Michael's mistress, got a year for couriering money. Richard Hannigan, Green's friend who was facing charges of smuggling 13,000 kilos of hash, committed suicide in prison while awaiting trial. During one of six trials, defence counsel accused Michael of being a "polished liar" to which he replied: "Yes, I had to lie even to my family. It is the business of informing and dealing... being disloyal comes with the territory. My friends, family and lover are all awaiting trial because of me."

Detective Constable Carpenter had been investigated by internal affairs but no evidence was found to prove Michael's allegations against him. Despite Michael's claims that he had paid the cop over Stg£250,000 there was no trace of the cash anywhere. Customs then arrested and charged Carpenter with conspiracy to import drugs and he was released on Stg£50,000 bail. In court he was accused of being one of the most corrupt officers ever to serve in the policeforce.

In May 2001, however, after a successful legal challenge by a number of defendants, Michael Michael's life as a supergrass came to a sudden halt when the court ruled that it could no longer rely on Michael's uncorroborated testimony. The Crown Prosecution Service freed Steve McGoldrick who had spent several months on remand awaiting trial. Jerry Coffey, who had been out on Stg£500,000 bail, was also free. The case against DC Paul Carpenter was dropped. But most significantly, in light of the court's decision, the Crown Prosecution Service dropped its charges against Mickey Green. Green celebrated his sixtieth birthday by being released from Spanish custody. Once again the Pimpernel had lived up to his extraordinary reputation.

The incredible story of Michael Michael did not become public until December 18, 2001, when the courts lifted a reporting ban on the case. Michael's case was the last one to come before the courts. He pleaded guilty to one count of conspiracy to import cocaine, to a similar count involving cannabis and three charges of conspiracy to launder the proceeds. He also pleaded guilty to possession of a firearm. Standing in the dock, surrounded by police officers armed with machine guns, Michael Michael was a shattered, grey-faced man. Judge Michael Carroll told him that he would spend the rest of his life as a marked man but said his "instrumental" role in the operation could not go unpunished. He praised the "super-supergrass" for his extensive co-operation. Judge Carroll told him: "You will always be a marked man and the risk to your family will remain a real risk indefinitely. This conspiracy involved drugs of such quantities and value that the figures beggar belief." Michael was sentenced to six years. As a result of the time he had already spent in prison, Michael was released shortly afterwards. He was placed in the Witness Protection Programme with his wife and children.

Commenting on Michael's relationship with DC Carpenter Judge Carroll said: "I have no doubt whatsoever that for the purpose of this sentence you received assistance and encouragement from a corrupt person to carry out and carry on the plan. I am satisfied, however, there were mutual benefits for both of you over that arrangement." Nicholas Loraine-Smith, for the prosecution, said of the corruption allegations: "It remains the case for the purposes of this hearing that the relationship between them became corrupt." Following the trial a Scotland Yard spokesperson said: "Despite a rigorous three year investigation these allegations have not been proved and there was insufficient evidence for criminal proceedings. Potential disciplinary offences were disclosed and the officer remains suspended." Paul Carpenter was eventually sacked from the police as a result of the investigation of disciplinary offences.

Early on in his deal with the Crown Prosecution Service Michael Michael was asked by his minders to draw up a list of names of the gangsters most likely to have him murdered. The "super-supergrass" came up with fourteen names – top of the list was the name Mickey Green. As an act of defiance against his sworn enemy the Pimpernel moved into Michael's villa in Marbella. "Well that bastard is hardly likely to come back and ask me to leave is he?" Green told an Irish visitor to the luxury residence. Today Green still lives there with Anita Murphy and has apparently successfully recovered from a skin cancer complaint. In August 2003, Green was spotted out shopping with his grandson in a department store in Puerto Banus, the playground of the rich, in the Costa del Crime. The Pimpernel looked remarkably fit and relaxed for a man with so many problems.

According to international police and customs sources, Mickey Green is still a major player in worldwide drug trafficking. Many of his old foes in law enforcement agencies now say that they are pessimistic of ever catching the sixty-two-year-old Pimpernel. In the meantime Mickey Green has cut his ties with Ireland. The Criminal Assets Bureau sold off his two properties in Dublin and Kildare for a sum in excess of €1.6 million. The loss of his Irish bolthole, Maple Falls, has been one of the worst blows Green has suffered at the hands of law enforcement.

Two

The Viper

"I'm fuckin' sick of this! This is gettin' fuckin' ridiculous," Martin Foley angrily declared. He was sitting in the office of Terenure College swimming pool waiting for an ambulance to arrive. The hardened criminal had just achieved a national record. It would make him a household name and earn him an almost mystical reputation in gangland. But the notorious villain, better known as the Viper, was not in a celebratory mood. He had good reason to be less than enthusiastic about his 'national record' because it had nothing to do with swimming. Foley now held Ireland's criminal record for surviving more murder attempts than any other gangster. The Viper had just cheated death, at the hands of a hit man, for the third time.

Foley's outburst to the first Gardaí who arrived at the scene on a dark evening in September 2000, was one of the classic understatements of his long and turbulent criminal career. About ten minutes earlier a gunman had opened fire on Foley at point blank range: one bullet grazed his skull while the other shattered his ankle. It was Foley's fitness and his hard-earned experience from previous gun attacks that had enabled him to defy the underworld's grim reaper. Foley had developed a talent for survival like no other criminal in Irish history. As he sat clutching his injured leg the Viper told the arriving cops: "This is getting fuckin' ridiculous. I don't know what I'm going to do."

Many experienced detectives who have known Foley for almost thirty years could provide a simple solution for his pressing dilemma – the Viper could retire from crime and, more importantly, alter his life-threatening propensity for irritating terrorists and criminals alike. But despite his many jousts with death, the charmed Viper has emerged fighting fit each time, determined to embroil himself in even more trouble.

From when he was abducted at gun point by an IRA gang in 1984, to the incident at Terenure swimming pool sixteen years later, the Viper has somehow stayed alive. In three gun attacks in 1995, 1996, and 2000 respectively, Foley had survived a hail of at least thirty bullets fired in his direction. His name was engraved on each one. He has actually been wounded a total of six times. He's lost the top of one finger and a bullet is still lodged in his chest. Foley knows more about being on the receiving end of gun attacks than any other criminal. Many of his friends and associates have not been so lucky. They have not survived to share their experiences at what would be the equivalent of a gangland victim support group. If, like the proverbial cat, the Viper has nine lives, he is now down to his last three.

* * * *

Martin Foley was born on November 24, 1952, in Crumlin, Dublin, where he's lived all his life. The youngest of five children, his only recorded employment was as a tyre fitter in various service stations around Dublin. Foley quickly decided that fixing punctures and replacing bald tyres was not going to be his primary source of income. He became officially unemployed in 1981. Records show that he has only worked a total of twenty-two weeks in his life. His real 'job' was committing crime.

Foley had his first recorded scrape with the law when he was sixteen years old. On that occasion, in 1968, he was given the probation act for being drunk and disorderly. In the Irish criminal justice system, the probation act is intended as a reprimand – a chance for the first time offender to see the error of his ways. However, for Foley, like many of his underworld cronies, it didn't work that way. The probation act was soon forgotten and two months later he was back in front of the courts. This time he was charged with larceny and receiving stolen goods.

From the 1960s onwards Foley's working-class neighbourhood of Crumlin and nearby Drimnagh became the unofficial home of organised crime in Ireland. Most of the young men who would usher in a new era of serious crime, and become infamous gangsters in the process, came from the locality. By the 1970s the area had also become the preferred residence-in-exile of several terrorists on the run from the authorities in Northern Ireland.

In the early 1970s Foley became known to the Gardaí as a member of a loose group of criminals centred on a character known as Martin Cahill. In less than ten years this mob of tearaways would become members of one of the most notorious criminal gangs in the history of the State – the General's gang. Apart from Foley, the mob included the Godfather himself Martin Cahill and his brothers and brothers-in-law. The rest of this nest of dangerous villains included Eamon Daly, Seamus "Shavo" Hogan, Noel Lynch, Joseph "Jo Jo" Kavanagh, Christy Dutton, John and Michael Cunningham and John Gilligan. Other associates operating at the time were the notorious Dunne brothers – Christy "Bronco", Larry, Henry, Shamie, Vianney, Gerry, Robert and Charlie. The Dunnes and the Cahills had a close 'working' relationship.

Foley became a member of Martin Cahill's inner-circle of hoodlums. For many years he would remain totally loyal to the General. A fitness fanatic and body builder Foley soon had a formidable reputation as a hard man to be feared. He could give as good as he got and better. He had no compunction about using violence or intimidation to get his point across – no matter who he was dealing with. Foley had no style or panache and was known as a foul-mouthed ruffian. Like the General, Foley was also considered to be a miser who never displayed the wealth he earned from the gang's many strokes (crimes). A retired detective who dealt with the Viper for almost thirty years described him thus: "Foley has never been anything but a bully boy and a thug. He would beat up a woman as soon as he would another hood. He specialises in throwing his weight around and stepping on toes which is why so many people have tried to kill him. On one hand he is as thick as a plank but he has a street cunning which has helped him stay one step ahead of us. Behind it all he is a coward."

By the mid-seventies Foley had become a full-time armed robber. The General's gang were robbing banks, security vans and factory bank rolls with such frequency that they were pulling off an average of one stroke each week. The cops began to take notice of these ruthless new kids on the block and the gang quickly earned a place at the top of the Garda most wanted list. In one stroke, in

November 1974, Martin Foley and the rest of the gang made off with IR£92,000 when they robbed a security van delivering cash to a shopping centre in Rathfarnham, south-west Dublin. At current values the cash would be worth more than three million Euro. Three members of the gang, Martin Cahill, his brother Eddie Cahill and their future brother-in-law, Hugh Delaney, were subsequently charged with the heist. The charges against the General and his brother were dropped before the trial due to a lack of evidence but Delaney remained before the court. Hugh Delaney had made verbal admissions about the crime while in custody. As part of his defence it was stated that Martin Foley was a crucial witness in the case as he could give Delaney an alibi.

The trial began in July, 1976. On the first day Foley was 'kidnapped' outside the Four Courts in Dublin. The Central Criminal Court issued a bench warrant for Foley's arrest when he didn't turn up for his court appearance. As a result of Foley's absence there was no main defence witness and Delaney was acquitted. It was the first time Martin Cahill illustrated his cunning for thwarting the criminal justice system and Martin Foley was only too happy to assist him.

Once the trial was out of the way and Delaney was free, Foley re-emerged. Two weeks later he handed himself into the Gardaí. When he was brought before the court on the bench warrant, Foley claimed that the Provisional IRA had kidnapped him. He said that he knew the identity of his 'abductor' but refused to identify him. "If I give his name, my life is not worth living," the Viper claimed. Foley denied under oath that he had been paid to go into hiding to "get offside". Mr Justice Gannon released Foley remarking, in reference to the kidnap yarn: "Something should be done about it. I cannot direct what should be done, it is not my function." Foley, the General and his mob had given the two fingers to the law. The arrogant hoodlums would do everything in their power to make fools of the police and a joke of the criminal justice system in the years to come.

The Viper's mother and her family had originally come from County Derry. Martin Foley made no secret of the fact that he was an ardent admirer and supporter of the Irish National Liberation Army (INLA) and he forged important contacts for the General through his association with the organisation's members. Being cast as a 'Republican' also gave Martin Foley added street credit and *gravitas*. But in reality the INLA was nothing but a loose collection of dangerous criminals who used Republicanism as a flag of convenience to cloak their illegal activities.

In the early 1980s, Foley befriended the then self-appointed INLA Chief of Staff, Dominic "Mad Dog" McGlinchey who lived near him on Cashel Avenue in Crumlin. McGlinchey had been responsible for an appalling series of murders and atrocities in Northern Ireland. He had moved to Cashel Avenue while on bail fighting an extradition warrant for his return to the North to face murder charges. Foley and his girlfriend, Pauline Quinn, also from Cashel Avenue, often looked after McGlinchey's young children. Foley kept in touch with the INLA boss after "Mad Dog" went on the run to avoid the extradition order. The Viper loved the glamour attached to his association with the country's most wanted terrorist. He even kept a signed copy of McGlinchey's extradition papers which he showed to friends and associates. The friendship would continue until McGlinchey's assassination in 1994. In fact it later emerged that Martin Foley was the last person ever to speak to McGlinchey. On the night of "Mad Dog's" death in February 1994, the terrorist had just called the Viper from a coin box in Drogheda, County Louth when three assassins appeared and pumped several shots into their target. McGlinchey died minutes later.

Another member of the northern ex-patriot INLA community living near Foley was Thomas "Fingers" McCartan from Belfast. The terrorist moved to live in Cashel Avenue in the early eighties after completing a sentence for firearms offences in Portlaoise. McCartan had been caught as part of a hit squad sent to murder the original founder of the INLA, Seamus Costelloe. Foley introduced McCartan to the General's gang and, for a time, the INLA member took part in various heists with the mob. The most sinister result of the new relationship manifested itself on the morning of January 6, 1982. A car bomb seriously injured the State forensic scientist, Dr James Donovan as he drove to work in Dublin. Martin Cahill had asked McCartan to make the device and plant it under the scientist's car. The General wanted the forensic sleuth murdered to prevent him giving crucial evidence against Cahill and his friend Christy

Dutton in an armed robbery case. Dr Donovan survived the horrific attack and eventually gave evidence in the Cahill/Dutton case. However the two were subsequently acquitted on a legal technicality.

In the early 1980s Foley also took part in a campaign against prison officers in Dublin. Calling themselves the Prisoners' Revenge Group the criminals attacked the homes and cars of several prison officers and threatened to murder them. In some cases prison staff were forced to move their families. Prison officers in Mountjoy changed their routes to and from work as the hoods succeeded in striking terror throughout the prison service. Despite a major investigation at the time none of the hoodlums were actually charged with the offences.

* * * *

On July 27, 1983, ten members of the General's gang, including Martin Foley, held up the staff of the O'Connor's jewellery factory in Harold's Cross, south Dublin. They made off with an estimated IR£2 million worth of jewels, diamonds and gold. It was a meticulously planned heist and the largest ever in the history of the State at the time. The originator of the robbery plot was John Traynor, aka the Coach, the General's adviser and later John Gilligan's partner-in-crime. The gang had hit the big time. They were now the undisputed lords of a burgeoning criminal underworld.

In the months after the heist Martin Cahill and his mob organised the sale of the O'Connor's loot through an east London fence called Les Beavis. But some of the gold disappeared while being transported to England. Cahill nominated one of his couriers as the prime suspect for the disappearance. Cahill cemented his brutal reputation when he crucified the courier by nailing him to the floor of a derelict house in Rathmines, South Dublin. The General drove six-inch nails through the palm of each of the courier's hands to force him to confess to the crime. In the end it transpired that the courier was innocent and someone else had stolen the loot. The notorious incident became known in the criminal underworlds as "The Crucifixion".

In response to the crime wave a special Garda squad was set up to target the General, Foley and the rest of the gang. For several weeks the officers placed the mobsters under intense pressure. Many of them were arrested including Foley and questioned about the heist. With such intense surveillance Cahill and his gangsters were afraid the cops might catch them in possession of firearms while on a 'job'. In case this happened the gang hatched a bizarre plot to discredit the detectives in advance. On October 9, 1983, Martin Foley phoned the newsroom of the *Irish Press* in Dublin. He said he wanted to prove that the Gardaí were trying to frame Martin Cahill. Later that night a reporter met the Viper in a pub car park in Tallaght. Foley was heavily disguised and wearing gloves. He described himself as a petty criminal with no subversive links who was now going straight. In the corner of a nearby field he handed the reporter two guns – a sawn-off shotgun and a pistol – which he claimed two detectives had given him to plant on Cahill. Foley claimed that a story about the weapons might "end the harassment" of himself and his family. It later transpired that the weapons had been part of a large cache stolen by the gang from a Garda depot on St John's Road in south Dublin. At the time the building was used to store illegal firearms seized from criminals and subversives. It was the gang's way of further irritating the police. They had made several 'visits' to the depot but the theft was only discovered in September 1983. In their warped logic, the gangsters reckoned that the story would undermine a criminal case if the detectives ever caught them with firearms. The gang's fears of capture and their bizarre conspiracies would soon prove to be the least of their troubles.

In the criminal underworld a reputation for violence is necessary in order for a gang to stay on top and control its turf. But conversely, the same reputation can also attract the attention of dangerous competitors. The bombing of Dr Donovan, the O'Connor's heist, "the Crucifixion" and the Garda surveillance operations had attracted a lot of unwanted attention on the Cahill gang. This attention would eventually almost cost Martin Foley his life. Within a week of the robbery the Provos met Cahill and told him that they wanted a share of the proceeds. Cahill, reflecting the consensus of his gang members, told the IRA to fuck off. "If you want gold then go out and rob yer own gold like we did. You do your strokes and we'll do ours. Ye're not getting' a fuckin' penny," Cahill replied. The gangsters and the Provos were on a one-way trip to confrontation.

At the same time in the early eighties Dublin's working-class suburbs and inner-city ghettos were being strangled by a heroin crisis. Former armed robbers such as Larry and Shamie Dunne had cashed in on the multi-million pound heroin trade. The profits were prodigious and drug dealing was a much more attractive proposition than holding up a security van at gunpoint. Soon many more hoodlums were investing in the new 'business'. Heroin found a ready market among a generation of miserable teenagers, eager to escape the drudgery of no work and no opportunities. Literally in the space of weeks whole working class areas were in the grip of a devastating heroin epidemic, exacerbating an already depressed situation. Hundreds of young people were reduced to mere zombies, enslaved by the contents of a dirty syringe filled with smack. The merciless plague destroyed dignity, hopes and aspirations. It created havoc and despair. Youngsters who had been reared to respect their own neighbourhoods were now mugging old ladies and burgling the homes of neighbours to get cash for their daily fix. The sense of shock and hopelessness gradually turned to rage. So-called Ordinary Decent Criminals (ODCs) who had traditionally enjoyed the collective blind eye of whole communities, now stood accused of poisoning their own people.

As a consequence of the appalling crisis, and a total lack of State intervention, the residents of the worst affected areas banded together under the banner of the Concerned Parents Against Drugs (CPAD). The CPAD marched in large numbers on the homes of known drug dealers and evicted them. Faced with such people power the pushers could no longer threaten or intimidate objectors with impunity. At night, men patrolled flat complexes and housing estates and set up road blocks to prevent the addicts and dealers getting through. In the background members of Sinn Féin and the IRA were also mobilising in the fight against the drug dealers. Many of their members came from the affected areas and they genuinely wanted to do something about the appalling situation. Others in the Republican movement saw it as an opportunity to build a political power base in Dublin's working-class areas where traditionally there had been little or no support.

It was against this backdrop of social upheaval that Martin Cahill and his mob had pulled off the biggest robbery in Irish history in 1983. Even though the relationship between the Dunnes and the General's gang had ended when Larry and Shamie Dunne moved into drugs and introduced the scourge of heroin into their old neighbourhoods, rumours began to circulate that the General's gang had invested the O'Connor's loot in drugs. The rumours were corroborated by the fact that gang members were still closely associated with families suspected of heroin dealing. Members of Cahill's own family were well-known heroin dealers and addicts. The INLA and the IRA met to share intelligence on Cahill and his gang to ascertain what they had done with the money. One of the INLA contingent was the General's bomb maker Thomas McCartan, who had originally been supposed to take part in the actual robbery. After failing to turn up for the job he had been cut out of the action but he still wanted his share of the loot. Foley, who like Cahill had steered clear of the drug business, had told McCartan there was nothing he could do about getting him the money.

In February 1984, the CPAD organised in Crumlin and immediately found itself on a collision course with the criminal community. The principal organiser of the concerned parents was one John Humphrey, a former convicted criminal with a record for armed robbery and assault. He was also closely associated with the Republican movement. On the night of February 19, the CPAD marched on the homes of suspected drug dealers in Lower Crumlin. The protestors also stopped outside the houses of several criminals suspected of involvement in drugs. One of those visited was Martin Foley's friend and fellow gang member, Seamus "Shavo" Hogan. "Shavo" had a blazing row with Humphrey and the rest of the marchers at the front door of his house on Rutland Grove – known locally as 'Hatchet Grove'. The marchers then made for the home of Thomas Gaffney, whose family were suspected of involvement in heroin pushing in the area. Gaffney was one of the General's friends and he was also Martin Foley's best friend. He had a reputation for violence to match that of his pal. Three members of the Gaffney family were known addicts and Ma Baker, a notorious heroin dealer, was also a close family friend.

A former gravedigger in Mount Jerome cemetery in Harold's Cross, Gaffney and his family were well-known to the police.

Gaffney himself had a string of convictions, mostly for theft and assaults on Gardaí. Immediately after the O'Connor's heist Gaffney had hidden part of the loot under a gravestone in the huge cemetery, which was a conveniently short distance from the jewellery factory. In the follow-up Garda investigation Gaffney was one of a number of gang members arrested for questioning about the heist. His involvement was now well-known on the streets of Crumlin. Gaffney confronted the marchers as they approached his home and warned them not to harass his family. He and Humphrey had an intense dislike for each other and the two men exchanged abuse and threats.

Later that night Gaffney went drinking in Crumlin village with Martin Foley and Foley's girlfriend, Pauline Quinn. "Shavo" Hogan joined them later on in the evening. At closing time Hogan said that he was worried about passing through the pickets the CPAD had set up on the main routes to his home. For moral support Foley and Gaffney travelled with him and the group headed off in two cars. On the way Foley stopped at nearby Sundrive Road Garda Station and asked for a squad car escort to get his friend through the CPAD pickets. They were politely told there were no cars available. At Rutland Avenue the pickets stopped the cars. Foley flew into a rage when one of the CPAD men demanded that he open his boot. A fist-fight broke out and Gardaí had to call in reinforcements to quell the melée. Foley, Gaffney and Hogan were taken into custody for their own protection and to allow things to cool down.

The following day a group of criminals, including Martin Foley and Martin Cahill, met in Hogan's house to discuss the ongoing situation. The so-called Ordinary Decent Criminals were no longer able to go about their 'business' without being harassed by the pickets. They reckoned that they deserved more respect.

Cahill suggested that the criminals set up their own organisation to counteract the CPAD and to stand up for their rights. The Concerned Criminals Action Committee (CCAC) was formally inaugurated. Their first protest march was scheduled for three o'clock that afternoon. The sixty strong CCAC group, who were led by Foley and Hogan, called to the homes of people involved in the CPAD. Faced with menacing hoods like Foley and Hogan, many of those visited denied any involvement in the anti-drug activity. The CCAC moved on to the home of John Humphrey and smashed some of his windows. Later that same evening masked men wrecked the homes of Humphrey and Noel Sillery – a member of Sinn Féin and chairman of a CPAD committee. Then shortly before midnight, two armed and masked men ambushed CPAD activists Joe Flynn and Paddy Smyth in the St Theresa's Gardens flat complex. Flynn was shot in the legs as he tried to get away from the gunmen. The gangsters had declared war.

The following day tensions were running high in Crumlin. A large group of the Concerned Criminals stood outside "Shavo" Hogan's house in Rutland Grove. Foley and Hogan had appointed themselves spokesmen for the group and they agreed to give an interview to the *Irish Press*. The Viper complained that the CPAD had begun reporting the criminals' nocturnal movements to the police. He stressed that none of the members of the CCAC were involved in drug pushing. Foley went on to admit that the Joe Flynn shooting was the result of rising tension in the area. Said Foley: "We admit we are criminals, but we are not drug pushers and we can hardly move in the area at night without being reported to the cops by the Concerned Parents Action Group. We have already protested to the CPAD and we are planning further action, including protest marches around the estate."

A few days later Martin Foley and Thomas Gaffney appeared on the RTÉ current affairs programme *Today Tonight*. They were both heavily disguised and stated that they were spokesmen of the Concerned Criminals Action Committee. Foley, obviously enjoying his new status as a gangland mouth piece, declared that the CCAC were opposed to drugs. However he went on to repeat the warning that the CPAD would not be allowed to jeopardise the livelihoods of local criminals who were engaged in illegal activities which were unrelated to drugs.

Despite the CCAC's warnings and blustering threats the criminals soon decided that agreement on a peace proposal was the way forward. The Concerned Criminals felt that they had softened the Concerned Parents up enough to force peace. As a result of Foley's newly acquired talent as a spokesman and his connections to INLA paramilitaries, it was decided that he would lead the CCAC delegation. The other members of the CCAC team were "Shavo" Hogan and Thomas Gaffney. Representing the CPAD side was John

Noonan, a member of the organisation's central committee and a convicted IRA member. Originally from Finglas and now living in Tallaght, Noonan was a prominent Sinn Féin activist in Dublin. Three meetings took place. In the end it was agreed that in future incidents would be sorted out with each side carrying out its own investigation into the source of the problem. Both sides appeared happy with this outcome. But the IRA had other ideas.

Every Sunday afternoon Tommy Gaffney called to the Park Inn public house in Harold's Cross for a few drinks. On Sunday, March 11, barmen noticed four strangers watching Gaffney. The same men had also been spotted in the bar the previous Sunday evening when the gravedigger was there. The General arrived into the pub to meet Gaffney. They had a brief conversation and the General left. Foley also arrived and talked to his friend for a few minutes. Two of the men sitting in the bar got up and went outside. As Foley was leaving the pub he noticed the two men acting suspiciously beside a red Hiace van, outside the pub. He saw that one of the men had a gun but thought that he was selling it to the other man. Foley got on his motor bike and left. In his book there was nothing wrong with guys dealing in illegal weapons.

Gaffney got up to leave the pub around six o'clock. As he reached the door, the two men, who had remained in the bar, grabbed him and frog-marched him outside towards the van which contained the other two men. Gaffney shouted to the barmen to call the police. One of the IRA men shouted back: "We are the police." Gaffney was handcuffed and bundled kicking and screaming into the waiting van. Inside the gravedigger was gagged and bound. Later he was switched to a second van and driven to a safe house in County Tipperary.

The General, Foley, and the rest of the gang met up within hours of the abduction. They were determined to go to war with the IRA if that was what the Provos wanted. The following day Foley and Hogan met John Noonan to give him a message. If Gaffney wasn't freed at once then there would be reprisals and Noonan would be first on their list. The Sinn Féin man said that he knew nothing about the incident but would make enquiries.

The following morning, Wednesday March 14, Foley was again in the front line of another CCAC protest march heading for St

Theresa's Gardens. On the way to the Gardens the gang stopped outside the homes of CPAD members and issued threats. Shots were fired in the air from the CCAC group. The motley hooded crew marched onto the St Theresa's Gardens flat complex, the scene of the Joe Flynn shooting. The mob demanded the immediate release of Thomas Gaffney. When they arrived at the flat complex a large force of Gardaí stood between them and the residents who had barricaded the entrance. Foley and Hogan had a brief meeting with representatives of Sinn Féin and the CPAD. More threats were issued and the CCAC hoods returned to Crumlin.

The following day the Viper also began his own campaign to rescue his kidnapped friend. He made a number of trips to Limerick where he secretly met with Dominic "Mad Dog" McGlinchey who was in hiding in the area. He also visited contacts in Northern Ireland. McGlinchey agreed to help but he was arrested a few days later. Foley also approached a *Sunday World* columnist, Fr Brian D'Arcy, who was a respected mediator. But the situation was about to deteriorate even further.

On the morning of March 20, Foley and Hogan were arrested by detectives investigating the shooting of Joe Flynn and questioned at Kevin Street station. During their interrogation both men denied any involvement in the shooting. They claimed that they had been visiting a relative of Hogan's in hospital at the time of the incident. They were released at 9pm on the night of March 21, 1984. Ten hours later the Provos decided to strike again.

On the morning of March 22, shortly before seven, Martin Foley and Pauline Quinn were asleep at their home on Cashel Avenue when a postman knocked on the front door. Foley's older brother Dominic saw the postman's uniform through the window and answered the door. As he opened the latch the postman rushed in saying he had a message for Martin Foley – from the IRA. He stuck a handgun in Dominic Foley's chest and pushed him back inside. Three other masked men burst in behind him. Dominic Foley was forced to lie face down on the ground and his hands were tied behind his back. They demanded to know which room was Martin's bedroom. Two members of the IRA unit immediately sprinted up the stairs.

Meanwhile, the Viper had been woken by the noise from the

front hall. When Foley opened his door he met a masked man carrying a sawn-off shotgun who was about to smash his way into the bedroom. Foley was not going down without a fight. He grabbed the weapon by the barrel and tried to wrench it from his attacker, pulling him around the room in the process. The 'postman' and the two other masked men arrived upstairs. The 'postman' went to the window to keep watch and told the others: "Quieten the fucker." They beat Foley with a baton and the sawn-off shotguns before pushing him onto the bed. A handgun and a shotgun were pushed into his face. Pauline Quinn had dived for cover and was sitting on the floor in a corner of the room crying. As one of the Provos tried to put handcuffs on Foley he bounced off the bed. He hit the 'postman' and tried to shove him through the window in the process. Foley was flailed with a baton and forced back on the bed where he was finally handcuffed. But the gangster made another run for it, this time heading for the landing with three of the Provos on his heels. The four men had another scuffle and they all ended up tumbling down the stairs, landing in a heap on top of their victim. Foley was dragged into the kitchen where the kidnappers sat on him. Tape was placed around his legs and over his eyes and mouth. Then they wrapped him in a blanket.

The Concerned Criminal was dragged to a waiting van and dumped inside. Two of the Provos jumped in on top of him and the other two got into the front, before they sped away. The Provo kidnap gang was a rather unusual mix of political revolutionaries. The driver of the van was twenty-four-year-old university graduate and self-employed butcher Sean Hick from upmarket Glenageary Avenue in Dun Laoghaire. Twenty-two-year-old Liam O'Dwyer from Castleknock was also university educated and from a family later described by his defence counsel as being of "impeccable respectability". In contrast the third member of the snatch squad was twenty-two-year old Derek Dempsey, a petty criminal from Raheen Drive in Ballyfermot, who had recently joined the IRA. The leader of the team was thirty-three-year-old bar manager James Dunne from Finglas, north-west Dublin, a long-standing member of the IRA.

As the van took off one of the men sitting on Foley pushed a handgun in under the tape covering his eyes and told him: "If you

don't stay quiet I'll blow the fucking head off you. You'll get the
same as Tommy if you don't stay quiet." Within minutes of the
abduction one of Foley's neighbours called the Gardaí and an alert
was immediately transmitted to all patrols in the area. Units were
already on a heightened state of alert due to the mounting tension
between the Concerned Criminals and the Concerned Parents. At
the junction of Crumlin Road and Kildare Road, the crew of a squad
car driven by Garda Tony Tighe spotted the van. They tailed it down
the Crumlin Road and heard the call about Foley's abduction. The
van stopped at the red traffic light outside the front door of Sundrive
Road Garda station. When the van moved off so did the squad car.

"The police are behind us, take it easy and don't panic," one of
the men sitting on Foley instructed Hick. Another Garda car joined
in the slow procession as the van moved on, at no more than thirty
miles per hour and observing all the rules of the road. But every
time Sean Hick turned a corner he could still see the squad car in
his rear view mirror. The Gardaí then decided to move in. As the
van drove down the South Circular Road towards the Phoenix Park
a third squad car suddenly appeared out of the Con Colbert Road
and swerved to block it. Hick drove the van up onto the pavement
and around the blocking squad car and sped off. The chase began.

Squad cars stayed behind the van as it sped towards the Phoenix
Park. Armed units of the Special Task Force (STF) joined the chase.
Detective units from all over the city were also converging on the
area. The scanner the Provos used to listen in on the Garda radio
network crackled with voices. The IRA men began to panic. "They
are still behind us, brake and we will shoot the two of them dead,"
Foley later recalled one of the IRA men telling his mates. The van
turned from Conyngham Road into the main entrance of Phoenix
Park. One of the Garda cars drove up on the van's right side. Sean
Hick immediately tried to ram it off the road. Garda Tighe's car
also pulled alongside the speeding van. The side door of the Hiace
suddenly slid back and Derek Dempsey took aim with a handgun,
firing a number of shots at the squad car. One of the bullets struck
the base of the windscreen wiper in front of Garda Tighe. In a
subsequent statement to detectives Foley recalled: "One of them
started crying in the van and the van drove on and another one said,
'it's no use they are all around us.' One of them then broke the back

window of the van and a few shots were fired. There was a lot of panic at this stage, and one of them said, 'we will hold this fella as hostage', meaning me."

Outside the van Garda Tony Tighe swerved his car from left to right to avoid the volley of bullets. The IRA gang could see the cops were not going to back off. The rear window of the van suddenly exploded, as Liam O'Dwyer blasted his sawn-off shotgun at Tighe's car, showering it with glass and buckshot. The van turned onto Wellington Road. It was forced to stop near the Forty Steps as other squad cars, coming from the opposite direction, blocked its path. The gang made a run for it down the steps leading onto Conyngham Road. They tried to drag Foley with them but abandoned the idea. By now over one hundred officers had arrived in the area. The gang fired several shots at the pursuing officers. Three of the IRA men, Hick, O'Dwyer and Dunne, were forced to take cover when detectives opened fire with Uzi machine-guns and revolvers. Surrounded, and faced with overwhelming odds, the three came out with their hands up. Moments later Dempsey was arrested on a nearby road when a detective fired a shot over the kidnapper's head.

In the meantime Garda Tighe and a colleague had grabbed Foley and bundled him into their squad car. Twenty-five minutes after it had begun the kidnap drama was over. The Concerned Criminal, still in his underpants, was battered and bloodied but safe. He was brought to hospital and treated for a fractured jaw and several bad cuts and bruises. For the first time in his criminal career Foley was glad to see the cops. For their part the Gardaí were also feeling vindicated by their actions and bravery. An entire IRA active service unit had been caught red-handed.

It was a devastating blow for the Provos and had exposed the links between their organisation and the CPAD. It was later discovered that two of the men arrested had also been directly involved in the abduction of Tommy Gaffney. More importantly, the intervention of the police had prevented a dramatic escalation of the tension between the CPAD/IRA and the Concerned Criminals. An all-out bloodbath had been avoided. Several arrests were made, including leading members of the CPAD and Sinn Féin. The Gardaí were optimistic that the arrests would seriously damage the IRA's operations in Dublin.

Later that night the Provos released Tommy Gaffney. He had been held for twelve days and most of his friends and family had given him up for dead. During his captivity he was handcuffed to a chair and repeatedly questioned about Foley, drug dealing and the Joe Flynn shooting. Their main interest however was the General, Martin Cahill and the O'Connor's robbery. Before they set their hostage free the Provos told Gaffney about the Foley incident. They said they were releasing him on the condition that he told the Gardaí he had been abducted by a group "concerned about the chronic drug problem in Dublin". Shortly after midnight, on the morning of March 23, he was left on a roadside near Abbeyfeale in County Limerick. Gaffney's release, Foley's rescue and the capture of an IRA cell, brought one of gangland's most dangerous episodes to an uneasy end. The Provos had no message for the Viper but they had a personal and prophetic message for the General. They told Gaffney: "Tell Cahill that we will never kidnap him – we'll stiff him on the street."

Later, in an interview with the *Irish Times*, organised by Foley, the General claimed that the crisis had been caused because the Provos wanted a share of the O'Connor's loot: "They can't go out and rob for themselves any longer. They have to rob ordinary criminals who have done the work and taken the chances. There's nothing lower than someone who robs a robber." Cahill said that he was prepared to go to war with the Provos in Dublin.

In the hours following the incident Foley was equally belligerent towards his abductors. After his release from hospital he was brought to a Garda station where he formally identified the four men. The underworld hard man spat at the Provos after pointing them out in an identity parade. He also tried to punch one of the terrorists. Over the following two days Foley made three detailed statements. The four Provos were all charged and remanded in custody. The Gardaí had an open and shut case. The trial was set for July 3, 1984.

Gardaí placed round-the-clock surveillance on Foley for the three months leading up to the trial. He was their most important witness. But Foley managed to throw off his police tail to meet members of the INLA at the organisation's request. He was told that the kidnapping had caused tension between the INLA and the Provos. The Viper was exhorted to withdraw his evidence against the IRA men. The INLA told him that questions would be asked at the trial about drugs and specifically if he, Foley, was a drug pusher. He wasn't expected to answer the question but, if he refused to answer or remained silent in the witness box, the Provos would be happy.

At first Foley refused to retract his evidence or admit to being involved in drugs. The Provos had been out to kill him and now he was going to get his own back on them. Soon after the meeting with the INLA, however, Foley received a less subtle request from the Provos. If he didn't comply with their wishes then he would receive another visit from them. This time they wouldn't be coming to abduct him.

When the trial of the four men before the Special Criminal Court started in July 1984, Foley was called as a prosecution witness on the second day. Prosecuting counsel asked Foley to recall the events at his home on the morning of the incident. Foley replied: "I was half asleep and I can't remember what I did. I don't know if I was standing up or still in bed. I remember some noises in the bedroom. What I remember after that was sitting in a patrol car in dense fog with, I think, a lot of police around me. I was on a tarmac road in dense fog and there were fields and trees and a lot of uniformed Gardaí around." When asked if he recalled making a statement to the Gardaí he replied: "I don't remember. I remember one of the Gardaí telling me that I had been kidnapped or something."

It wasn't long before the court agreed to an application from the prosecution to have Foley declared a hostile witness so that they could then cross-examine him. In criminal trials counsel can not cross-examine their own witnesses unless they have been deemed to be hostile. When pressed again about his signed statements Foley claimed: "I was in court when it was read out and it is completely untrue." It was obvious he had got the Provos message.

In Foley's original statement he had been very clear about what had happened during the incident. Here is how he described his actual rescue: "The van stopped and one of them dragged me on to the roadway and he wanted to bring me with him, but my legs were taped and I fell on the ground. He [one of the Provos] ran away from me, the tape was down from my eyes and I could see everything.

I was in the Phoenix Park. I could see the four men running to the left of the van, going down a hill, towards the wall of the Park. They were firing shots. I could see uniformed guards running after them. There were detectives there with guns in their hands. It was foggy but I could see everything that was happening."

In any event the prosecution had overwhelming evidence with which to prove their case against the Provos. On July 26, 1984, the four men were found guilty of Foley's kidnapping, shooting at Garda Tony Tighe and possessing firearms with intent to endanger life and using them to resist arrest. Derek Dempsey received a nine-year sentence; Sean Hick and James Dunne got seven years each and O'Dwyer got five years.

With the case out of the way an uneasy peace returned to gangland and it was business as usual for the mobsters. Tensions between the CPAD and the CCAC fizzled out as both sides pulled back from the brink. A week after the trial Foley married Pauline Quinn. The couple went to Northern Ireland for their honeymoon. They would have two daughters together.

* * * *

In late 1986 a major Garda report was compiled on organised crime across the Dublin Metropolitan Area (DMA). The purpose of the exercise was to centrally collate information on the major players dominating gangland in the mid-eighties. The document made for fascinating reading. It included the names, addresses and associates of each gangster. It catalogued the long list of crimes for which each criminal had been suspected. There were hit men, armed robbers, and drug dealers on the list. Diagrams were used to illustrate the complex web of connections and associations between individuals and gangs. It also charted the many connections between the paramilitaries and the criminals. It was no surprise that the largest section of the report dealt with the south of the city. The section highlighted the names of twenty hardened villains. Top of the list was Martin Cahill. It also included John Gilligan and George "The Penguin" Mitchell. Martin Foley's name appeared fifth on the list. The police had elevated the Viper to the hierarchy of organised crime.

The report was compiled at a time when serious crime was spiralling out of control. The State had allowed the underworld to thrive while they were preoccupied with the threat from Republican terrorists. Now belatedly, the authorities realised that they had a crisis on their hands. Foley with the rest of the General's gang were now officially members of the largest crime gang in the country. Cahill's gangsters were robbing banks with apparent impunity. John Gilligan's infamous Factory Gang had reached the number two slot. Gilligan's mob was involved in the systematic plundering of warehouses and factories throughout the country. The third most significant outfit on gangland's ugly landscape was centred on the Monk, Gerry Hutch, and his armed robbery mob, based in the north inner-city. It was boom time for the criminals.

In 1985, Paddy Shanahan was released from an English jail and returned home to Ireland. The university-educated, former auctioneer from County Kildare had served almost four years of a stretch for robbery at an antique dealer's home in Staffordshire. Shanahan had been involved with the General's gang from the early 1970s, carrying out armed robberies. With his extensive knowledge and connections in the stolen art and antiquities trade, he began planning what he hoped would be the crime of a lifetime – a crime that would make millionaires of all those involved. Shanahan planned to help himself to the many priceless treasures contained in the stately home of Sir Alfred Beit, at Russborough House in County Wicklow. The centrepiece of the treasure throve was the Beit art collection, one of the finest private collections of Dutch Masters in the world. Many of the works were considered priceless. On the black market they could be worth up to IR£40 million.

In early 1986 Shanahan suggested the 'stroke' to Martin Foley and "Shavo" Hogan. The greedy gangsters were extremely excited at the prospect. The two hoods suggested the job to their boss Martin Cahill and he was also enthusiastic about the idea. The General's gang began planning one of the largest art heists in the world.

On May 21, 1986, they walked into the Palladian-style mansion and took eleven of the most valuable pieces in the collection. But the heist would bring the robbers nothing but bad luck. "Shavo" Hogan would later recall of the Beit robbery: "It was a really simple robbery. Robbing the paintings was the easy bit. Everybody thought they were going to be millionaires. But after that night everything went downhill. There was a curse on those paintings." Hogan was right.

For a start the gang had pulled off the robbery behind Shanahan's back. The furious art lover told Foley and Cahill that the paintings they had taken could never be fenced because they were too well-known. He said they were too hot to handle. There were less valuable paintings in the collection that could have been sold without creating problems. There was also a vast amount of valuable antiques.

The gangsters made several unsuccessful attempts to sell the paintings. In the months that followed Shanahan had several meetings with Foley and "Jo Jo" Kavanagh to discuss a possible deal for the paintings but eventually Shanahan washed his hands of the affair. He realised that he was simply wasting his time. Foley and the rest of the General's mob could not give up so easily. They were determined to make their money. But selling the art was fraught with difficulties.

Every time Cahill's mob made a connection with an interested dealer from the art underworld, it turned out to be an undercover cop. Scotland Yard, Interpol and the FBI were all involved in various efforts to lure the gang into a trap. The closest Foley and Cahill came to being caught with the paintings was in September 1987, in the Dublin Mountains. An undercover Interpol officer, posing as an art dealer, managed to lure the gang and the paintings out into the open. On September 27, 1987, Cahill, Foley, Hogan, Noel Lynch and Eamon Daly arranged a viewing for the 'art dealer' at Killakee Wood in the Dublin Mountains. Unknown to the hoods a large force of Gardaí were preparing to swoop. The main players of the biggest crime gang in the country were within minutes of being nabbed. But it all went horribly wrong for the police when their radio network broke down, causing utter confusion. At the same time, Cahill smelt a rat and became suspicious of the art dealer. The gangsters disappeared with the stolen paintings, leaving the Interpol agent standing alone in the middle of the mountains. Cahill would later openly taunt the police about their botched operation to catch him.

Despite their close shave with the law within a few days it was business as usual for the gangsters. A week after the sting operation Foley, Eamon Daly and Cahill's brother John, they teamed up with

John Gilligan for an armed robbery at Portlaoise Post Office on October 3, 1987. The gang got away with IR£100,000 in cash, cheques and registered letters. None of them were ever charged with the robbery. In a second job, soon afterwards, Foley and Gilligan robbed cattle drench from Raheen Co-op near Abbeyleix, also in County Laois. On another occasion the hoods stole a truckload of sweaters from a factory in Falcarra, in north Donegal. Somehow Gilligan forgot to bring the Viper with him and ended up travelling back to Dublin by himself. The truck was later recovered in Dublin and taken to Crumlin Garda station for examination. Gilligan and Foley stole it back from the station yard and it was never seen again.

It would have been an understatement to suggest that the General, Foley, Gilligan and the rest of the mob were beginning to really annoy the authorities. In August 1987, just before the attempted Garda sting operation in the Dublin mountains, the gang had even broken into the offices of the Director of Public Prosecutions. They had stolen some of the most sensitive crime files in the State. The gang members, including Foley, would later try to use the files to bargain with the police in return for dropping criminal charges. In the following months, the gangsters had continued to take the fight to the police. It was time for pay back.

* * * *

In Garda Headquarters it was decided to play the gangsters at their own game and the famous T (for target) or Tango Squad was formed. Cahill, Foley, Hogan, and other members of the gang were all to be targeted. Cahill was Tango One and Foley was Tango Seven. The Tango squad's plan was pretty simple. They would place constant overt surveillance on the main gang members. Led by experienced serious crime squad detectives, the bulk of the squad consisted of young, enthusiastic officers from all over the city. Many of them had only been in the Gardaí for a few years and were still attached to uniformed branch. But they all had one thing in common – they were not afraid to lock horns with gangland's most dangerous hoodlums.

On January 1, 1988, the Tango Squad went into action. When the seven gangsters woke up on New Year's morning and looked out their bedroom windows the squad was outside waiting for them. When the hoods defiantly stood at their doors and stared at the fresh-faced cops, they were greeted with grins and little waves. Now the police were bringing the fight to the gangsters' doorsteps. Each target had an average of six officers, driving in three cars, watching his every move – twenty-four hours a day, seven days a week. Wherever the gang members went the Tango Squad were there beside them. The mobsters were well used to police surveillance but they had never seen anything like this before. "Shavo" Hogan would later recall: "The first week it started we thought, this is great *craic* but it became a nightmare: beeping horns and shining torches into the house at night. It really fucked up everything. You could not go out for a drink without a cop sitting beside you." Tango One was the only member of the gang to take up the challenge to play the mind games. He once joked to a reporter: "I'm thinking of getting involved in the security business. No one is going to rob me with all these armed police around me."

At the height of the Tango Squad operation the main targets suddenly found themselves in the glare of the TV cameras and the General became a household name overnight. Foley and the other members of the gang typically threatened and punched the photographers or cameramen who came near them. Foley had obviously decided to abandon his earlier CCAC approach to dealing with the media. Cahill however had other ideas. When he was stopped on the street by Brendan O'Brien of the RTÉ *Today Tonight* programme he decided to bluff it out and gave an impromptu interview. When asked was he the General or did he know who the General was, Cahill glibly replied: "I don't know, some army officer maybe. Sure the way the country is goin' these days you wouldn't know what way to think." When questioned about the Beit paintings Cahill claimed that his friend Noel Lynch had appointed him as a private detective to recover the art collection. "I am on standby with Martin Foley and Eamon Daly for a job to get them [paintings] back," said Cahill.

The programme, which was broadcast on February 10, succeeded in turning up the heat on the gang. They even became the subject of debate in the Irish parliament, Dáil Eireann. Foley and the rest of the mob were furious at the amount of exposure they were getting. The miserly Viper was particularly upset when, as a result of Cahill's "private investigator" comment, the Department of Social Welfare queried Foley's unemployment assistance. Foley told the social welfare people that the comments weren't true and that he intended suing Cahill over them. When Foley complained to the General about the repercussions of his TV performance, Cahill smiled and told him: "Ah you can be Magnum and I'll be Cannon, what d'ya think?"

At first, Martin Foley had tried to brave it out. He'd pretended that he wasn't fazed by all the attention. But unlike the smiling, media-friendly Cahill, Foley had trouble controlling his violent temper. On February 19, 1988, Foley and Hogan were driving to Crumlin from the city centre. As usual three Tango Squad cars were in front, behind and alongside them. On Church Street bridge the Tango car in front jammed on its brakes and Foley's car rammed into the back of it. The two gangsters got out and began arguing with the masked Tango Squad officers in the middle of the street. Foley demanded an ambulance be called. The Viper, Hogan and two of the cops were fitted with surgical collars and brought to St James' hospital for further examination. While in the hospital waiting room one of the Tango officers, Detective Garda Gerard O'Connor, went to talk to Foley. The Viper jumped up and punched Detective Garda O'Connor in the face, smashing his jaw and leaving him unconscious. The detective eventually had to leave the squad as a result of his injuries.

Foley was arrested and charged with assault. When he was later released from custody at Kevin Street Garda Station Foley's car suddenly broke down in the middle of the road about 100 yards from the station. Foley discovered that a large quantity of sugar had found its way into his petrol tank. The Tango Squad watched and smiled.

The gangsters soon began fighting back with their most reliable weapon – intimidation and fear. None of the criminals under surveillance were strangers to employing terror tactics. The hoods reckoned that the same tactics used in the early eighties by the Prisoners' Revenge Group would work again. The gang began organising counter-surveillance on the Tango Squad members. By the end of February, the mobsters were already in a position to give some of the officers disturbing details, listing their home addresses, the names of their wives and children, and the schools they attended.

The General would drive into streets where individual officers lived and flash his hazard warning lights as he passed the homes of the detectives tailing him. Squad cars were being ambushed and rammed by young joy riders recruited by the gang. As the intense war of wits escalated, hundreds of car tyres were slashed in middle-class neighbourhoods around South Dublin, whenever there was an altercation between the cops and the robbers. In one incident extensive damage was caused in the Garda golf club at Stackstown when the greens were dug up. One of the more persistent detectives who insisted on sitting beside his target in the pub was told in great detail the difference a bullet makes to a face when shot through the back of the head.

The Tango Squad, however, kept up the pressure and refused to be intimidated. On a number of occasions the tyres on the gangsters' own cars were also slashed. On one occasion the windows were smashed and the four tyres were slashed on Cahill's car outside his house in Cowper Downs. Luckily for the General he could rely on the only honest skill Martin Foley had ever possessed – fitting car tyres – to deal with the problem.

In one incident Foley appeared at his door in Cashel Avenue and aimed a crossbow at the watching Tango Squad officers. One of the officers walked into the middle of the road, produced his revolver and aimed it at Foley: "Now Martin which do you think goes faster? A bullet or an arrow?" The Viper mused over the proposition for a few minutes and, when he had worked it out, quickly retreated inside. A few days later Foley arrived at the squad's base at the Dublin Metropolitan HQ at Harcourt Square. He was wearing a mask and demanded to meet a named officer whom he challenged to a fist-fight. A Tango Squad member dismissed him: "Fuck off Martin or you'll be arrested. You'll have plenty of time to fight."

Foley bred Rotweiller dogs at the time and he made no secret of the fact that he was prepared to set them on the Tango Squad. The police in turn left Foley under no illusion that if that happened they would have no choice but to shoot the dogs. Foley kept his dogs on a lead after that. One evening he brought one of the fearsome animals for a walk and, as usual, was promptly followed by his large entourage of masked policemen. As he went through Poddle Park one of the officers, a larger than life character nicknamed Bridie by his colleagues, walked beside Foley. In a friendly tone of voice the officer enquired if Foley had bred the dog himself. "Yeah I did," replied Foley, falling for the trap. "Oh I thought so alright, he looks the spit of you. A fine looking dog he is too," the cop added, with a smile. When Foley told the cop to go and fuck himself, the officer reprimanded the Viper, as a parent would scold a child: "Language Martin, language. Don't be using language like that. The lads will be offended."

The pressure from the Tango Squad began to get results. They were forcing the gang members to make mistakes. Six days after Foley attacked Detective Garda O'Connor in St James's hospital, John Foy and "Shavo" Hogan were arrested and charged with possession of firearms with intent to endanger life. Gardaí arrested the pair, as they were about to carry out an armed robbery in Walkinstown. They had opened fire on unarmed officers during the chase. Three weeks later Eamon Daly was one of four armed robbers arrested when they attempted to hold up a DIY store.

During the ongoing drama between the cops and the robbers, the Tango Squad also laid siege to Cahill's upmarket residence at Cowper Downs in Rathmines, whenever he was home. The detectives would sit on the walls around the back garden and watch the General. Cahill would regularly appear on the roof of his pigeon loft and taunt the watching cops with offers of money and songs. On the day after Eamon Daly's arrest, Foley joined Cahill on the pigeon loft. A video camera lens was pushed out through the window of Cahill's house and the show began. Cahill shouted abuse in the direction of his neighbour's house. He accused the retired businessman of helping the police. He also shouted sexual obscenities that were aimed at the businessman's invalid wife, who was in her seventies. Cahill got down from the loft and Foley began throwing stones at him shouting: "We will get you Cahill, we will burn you out." Cahill then turned and shouted back at his henchman: "Guard get off me wall." As the Tango Squad took in the show one of them radioed his colleagues: "It's Cahill and Foley they've gone completely fucking mad. The pair of them have gone daft."

In another ploy to fool the police the targeted hoods would regularly meet at Cahill's house. After spending some time inside the seven men, all dressed identical to the General in anoraks and balaclavas, would emerge and walk off in different directions. One former Tango Squad member recalled: "Most of them were cute and if you called out Cahill's name they would all turn around. If you called out their own names they wouldn't respond. But Foley wasn't as quick. We'd be driving after him and call out 'Foley look' and he would suddenly swing around. No matter how many times we did that he always fell for it."

The intense surveillance operation lasted for several months but failed to put Tango One or Tango Seven out of business. At the end of it, however, the General did serve a few months imprisonment for refusing to enter a bond to keep the peace after threatening his neighbours. The surveillance operation had also succeeded in breaking up the powerful collection of villains. Most of the gang, including two of Cahill's brothers, were facing serious charges and they went on to receive long jail sentences. Other gang members, like Lynch and Dutton, decided to go their separate ways. They'd had enough of the game with the police, which had also caused considerable bad feeling and mistrust. In one instance "Shavo" Hogan was accused of giving the Gardaí information, which they used to catch John Foy for a second time. Foy had been nabbed as he collected guns for another robbery. The real target of the operation, Martin Cahill had escaped the bust by minutes. Hogan was also accused of planting a pistol in the General's house that was later found in a search by the Gardaí.

By 1990 most of the gang members had ended up in Portlaoise maximum-security prison. One day "Shavo" Hogan was attacked by his former friends in the exercise yard: they tried to slice off the top of one of his ears. It was the gangland symbol of the rat.

In the meantime Martin Foley decided that prison was just not for him. The Viper went on the run to England while he was out on bail for the serious assault on Detective Garda O'Connor in 1988. He was eventually extradited back to Ireland in March 1990 and placed in custody. In May of the same year he was jailed for two years after pleading guilty to the charge. During the hearing Foley's counsel said that he had been under "extreme Garda surveillance" and had become a "banned person".

Shortly after the Viper's release from prison in 1991 Foley and Cahill became bitter enemies. There was much speculation about what caused the rift. The most likely reason is that Foley was still angry that he had not received the expected windfall from the sale of the Beit paintings. In an interview with this writer in 2001 Foley would not say why the two former close friends had fallen out. He told me: "I walked away from Martin in 1991 because Martin went off the rails. It had nothing to do with money or informing. But the reason me and Martin parted friendship, I will carry that secret to the grave. I don't want to dig up old sores. I walked away because I wasn't happy with something that he done and somebody else went and got involved. No matter what has been claimed Martin never accused me of being an informant or a rat. I wouldn't be friends with his brothers if I was a rat."

For his part Martin Cahill claimed, in a rare interview given to London-based *GQ* magazine in 1991, that Foley had tried to set him up. In one of his bizarre conspiracy theories Cahill maintained that Foley's assault on Detective O'Connor was a "set-up". The General said that Foley had come to him with a plan to "do something" about the injured detective. The idea was that if the plan was carried out then the assault charges against Foley could not proceed. The General claimed that he didn't take the bait. During the *GQ* interview he referred to Foley by the nickname the Viper. It would remain the General's legacy to his former friend.

* * * *

After prison Foley and Hogan remained close friends and business associates. In the short time they were away gangland had changed considerably. For a time Foley and Hogan kept their heads down and faded into the background.

For the next few years they continued to maintain a low profile. This was due in no small way to the repercussions caused by the IRA's murder of the General in August 1994. In September, Foley's old enemies, the Provos, had abducted him for a second time. The IRA questioned him about money and drugs and the likely whereabouts of Cahill's hidden loot. He was released unharmed after a day.

A month later "Shavo" Hogan was arrested for questioning in relation to the murder of his former associate Paddy Shanahan. On the day he was arrested Hogan smeared his own excrement on his face to try to put the police off their jobs. The only effect it had was that in criminal circles "Shavo" had earned himself a new nickname – "Shithead". Hogan was subsequently released without charge.

It wasn't long before Foley and Hogan began to dabble in the drug trade. The Viper took a number of young criminals under his wing and showed them the ropes. It was better to have young enthusiastic thugs taking all the risks. Clive Bolger was his best pupil. Bolger became Foley's constant sidekick. They went everywhere together and shared a passion for body-building. In fact the pair spent so much time together that local police once thought they were both gay. Born in 1970, Bolger had become a career conman by his twentieth birthday. Also known as "Wigsy" – he was prematurely bald and wore a hairpiece – Bolger came from a respectable background. His family owned a supermarket and car dealership in Crumlin. By his own admission, Bolger caused the business to go bust because of a series of car loan frauds and he also ripped off several customers. Bolger and an associate from Rathmines began smuggling stolen cars from Northern Ireland. On one occasion the crooks scammed the wrong people –clients from Northern Ireland with Loyalist paramilitary connections. The pair were abducted and taken for a 'chat'. They were later released in Dundalk.

In an interview with this writer some years later Bolger confessed: "When we lost the business my family was left with nothing. It was devastating. I got involved in crime to make money. I suppose I stroked about one million pounds out of car finance companies in a two-year period. I did everything from fraud to robbery. It was around that time that I started hanging around with Martin. To me he was this big impressive gang boss and we made a lot of money together. Martin and I had a great credit card scam which lasted a few years. No one got hurt except the banks." In the same interview "Wigsy" admitted that he had also been involved in prostitution and drugs but refused to elaborate any further. The pair even tried their hand at a legitimate enterprise for a while – delivering newspapers. Bolger later recalled of the venture: "That fell apart because Martin got lost a few times and couldn't find the shops. On other occasions he delivered the morning newspapers to different shops at 4pm in the evening. I don't think we were cut out for the business."

In 1995, Foley and Bolger began buying relatively small amounts of cannabis from the Gilligan gang. The Viper was one of the gang's smallest customers purchasing one or two kilos at a time. For a while business was going well until the Viper's love life got in the way. At the time he was seeing an attractive young woman who lived in Fatima Mansions. Unfortunately for Foley a prospering drug dealer, Brian O'Keefe, was also vying for the woman's affections. O'Keefe decided to even up the romantic odds. Foley visited his 'girlfriend' like clockwork, around the same time, most evenings. Locals referred to the Viper as "beep beep" because he always honked his car horn to tell her he'd arrived.

On Tuesday evening December 5, 1995, Foley turned up as usual. As he was leaving her flat at around 10.30pm a man emerged from the shadows. He shot Foley twice – in the stomach and in the arm. The gunman, however, could not finish Foley off because he kept twisting and spinning around on the ground to avoid the fatal bullet. When Gardaí arrived on the scene Foley, who was seriously injured, told them he thought he was going to die. He told the officers that the IRA had shot him. Then, when he discovered that he was not going to join his many murdered friends, Foley refused to even tell the police his own name. Despite injuries to his spleen the gangster made a remarkable recovery and was back on his feet in weeks. Clive Bolger later claimed that it was he who discovered O'Keefe was behind the attack. Brian O'Keefe was the only man arrested for questioning in relation to the incident. Detectives categorised the shooting as a "crime of passion".

Around the same time Foley was heading for even more trouble of the life threatening variety. Foley and Hogan had been putting pressure on John Traynor, Gilligan's partner-in-crime, for money they reckoned they were owed from the proceeds of the sale of some of the Beit art collection to the Loyalist terror group the UVF. Traynor was afraid of the General's old henchmen. As part of his campaign against Traynor and the Gilligan gang, Foley began spreading rumours that they were involved in heroin dealing. Criminals are notorious gossips and scandalmongers. In the Dublin underworld Foley is considered to be one of the worst. "An auld woman with a moustache – and an ugly auld woman at that," was how one villain described him.

In January 1996, John Gilligan's lieutenant, and Foley's neighbour, Brian Meehan was called to a meeting with the IRA and questioned about the rumours. The Provos told Meehan the information had come from their old foe, the Viper. Meehan convinced the IRA that the gang were not involved in the smack trade. Later Meehan met with the rest of the Gilligan gang and it was decided that the Viper had to be murdered. Ex-soldier Charlie Bowden was the gang's armourer and general manager who ran the day-to-day business of the gang. He looked after the gang's weapons, collected drug consignments and filled orders for customers. On January 29, 1996, Bowden was called to a meeting with Meehan and another gang member, Paul Ward in Tallaght. The three men went to the Jewish cemetery on the Oldcourt Road where the gang hid an awesome arsenal of automatic weapons and ammunition. Bowden took out an Agram 2000 machine pistol and a .45 automatic pistol. Bowden, a trained army marksman, showed Meehan how to use the deadly machine pistol.

Three days later, on the evening of February 1, 1996, the gang members met at Paul Ward's home in Walkinstown. It was a short distance from Foley's home at Cashel Avenue, Crumlin. The guns were collected and the gang went to work. Meehan had arranged to meet Foley at 7pm on the pretext of collecting drug money from him. At 6.55pm Foley began reversing his car away from the house to turn onto Captain's Road. Meehan and Ward were waiting for him on the corner of Cashel Avenue in a stolen car. Foley spotted them and stopped. Ward, who was driving, pulled out on the road blocking Foley's car. Meehan and Ward then ran towards Foley's car, opening fire with the Agram and the automatic pistol. They peppered Foley's car with bullets. One bullet hit his finger. The Viper reversed back up the road with the two gangsters running after him. Foley abandoned the car and jumped into a garden. Meehan, still firing his machine pistol, ran after Foley. Ward had thrown the automatic pistol to Meehan as a back-up weapon while he returned to the getaway car.

Foley's fitness and his keen sense of survival paid off. He burst through the back door of a house, turning the lights off as he entered. "Call the police! They're after me," Foley yelled at the shocked occupants. The family all ran for the front door. When they opened the door Meehan came racing towards them. "Where's the fucker? Get out of the way!" he shouted, as the family sprinted into the middle of the street. The woman was screaming that someone was being murdered in her home. At the same time Foley spotted Meehan and raced upstairs. Meehan opened fire again, this time hitting Foley in the back. Other bullets went through a bathroom door. Foley jumped through a glass window in a back bedroom, landing on an extension roof outside. He got off the roof and jumped into the garden of the house next door. Meehan climbed onto the roof and fired more shots at the Viper, as he raced through several gardens, in a desperate bid to escape. Foley burst through the back door of another house and bolted it. He ran through the house, locked the front door and, as he lay cowering on the floor, phoned for the police and an ambulance. In the meantime Meehan and Ward made their getaway.

Foley had cheated death for the second time in two months. He was hospitalised for two weeks and again made a remarkable recovery. The top of his injured finger was amputated. Sources close to Foley have claimed that the Viper later found out who had shot him and why. The Viper's keen survivalist instinct told him that there was little he could do to get back at John Gilligan's powerful gang. After that they effectively kissed and made up.

This, however, didn't stop the Viper from trying to capitalise on any trouble involving the Gilligan gang. One of the more bizarre revenge plots dreamed up by Foley and Bolger took place a week after the murder of journalist Veronica Guerin, in June 1996. Meehan, the violent thug who had shot at the Viper only months before, rode the motorbike used in the murder. Bolger called the *Sunday Independent*, the newspaper where Veronica Gurerin had worked, and offered them information on the people responsible for the outrage. Bolger wanted IR£5,000 for his trouble. He also made the same call to the *Sunday World*. Neither newspaper paid him a penny.

A year later Foley did, however, seek revenge of a more concrete kind. He began civil proceedings against Charlie Bowden for the injuries he had received in the February attack. Bowden had become the State's first ever supergrass and had agreed to give evidence against his former partners in the Gilligan gang. As part of his testimony, in the trials of Paul Ward, Brian Meehan and John Gilligan, Bowden had admitted that it was he who had loaded the guns used in the Foley attack. The cheeky Viper decided that it was a good way to get back at the police and the system. "I didn't have to go after Meehan and Ward, the Guards did that for me by putting them in jail," he later told the *Sunday World*.

* * * *

The break-up of John Gilligan's crime empire left a huge vacuum in the cannabis distribution business in Dublin. Hogan, Foley and Bolger were quick to stake their claim. In Holland convicted kidnapper John Cunningham, who had absconded from an open prison in September 1996, had effectively taken over the Dutch end of the operation. And in Dublin, Cunningham's close friend Eamon Daly became one of the new drug lord's biggest customers, moving huge quantities of cocaine, hashish, heroin and ecstasy. In turn Daly supplied Foley, Bolger and Hogan. *(See Chapter 7)* The former members of the General's gang were back in business together. Foley also did business with underworld contacts on the periphery of the paramilitary groups in the North and along the border. One of them was a transport company boss and used car salesman in Derry. In Dublin, Foley began supplying a gang of young thugs from Crumlin and Drimnagh whom he used to do his dirty work.

The Viper's new success soon put him in the firing line again. This time the Viper faced Declan "Wacker" Duffy and his INLA gang. *(See Chapter 3)* Duffy demanded protection money from Foley. When Foley refused, Duffy and his gang went to Crumlin one evening to shoot him. What would have been the Viper's third gun attack was abandoned when the INLA couldn't find him. Apparently Foley later told one of his Garda contacts that he subsequently began paying protection money to the Provos in

Crumlin and the INLA backed off.

In the meantime "Shavo" Hogan was also experiencing difficulties with would-be hit men. In July and August 1998 he survived two gun attacks. In the first incident he was shot at with a handgun from a passing car but the shooter missed. Six weeks later in the early hours of August 30, 1998 he was shot again, this time with a sawn-off shotgun. Hogan was hit by shotgun pellets in the shoulder and was slightly injured but was released from hospital within hours. The shootings were reportedly the result of a row between Hogan and another local villain.

Despite their various problems with other criminals the Viper's gang continued to thrive in the drug trade. Foley, Hogan and Bolger began dealing with thirty-five-year-old Chris Casserly from Beaumont, North Dublin. Casserly, who has never had a serious criminal conviction recorded against him, was also one of John Cunningham's biggest customers. Buying shipments of drugs from Cunningham he became a major supplier of ecstasy, cocaine and hashish in Dublin. He had been a target of the Garda National Drug Unit (GNDU) since 1995 but had proved extremely difficult to catch. Some of his customers however were not so lucky.

On March 3, 1999, Casserly arranged the delivery of 28 kilos of cannabis to "Shavo" Hogan. It was part of a larger shipment he had organised through Cunningham in Holland. But the GNDU had been keeping watch on the operation and moved in to arrest Hogan as he took delivery of the hash from one of Casserly's couriers, Dean McCarney from Artane, North Dublin. Hogan and McCarney attempted to ram their way through a GNDU checkpoint but were arrested at gun point. Both men were later charged with drug trafficking offences. McCarney subsequently pleaded guilty to the charges but tragically committed suicide while he was on bail awaiting sentence. Hogan now found himself facing a very long stretch in prison. Behind the scenes, unknown to the other gang members, he began working to save his own neck. A month later the Viper and his associates experienced another serious setback.

Foley had moved out of his home at Cashel Avenue in late 1998, following the attempts to shoot Hogan. The Viper and Bolger began staying at the home of forty-two-year old Brigid O'Hanlon in Tallaght. A widow from South Armagh, O'Hanlon claimed to have had strong links with the IRA along the border. She was believed to have been Bolger's lover. The two hoodlums began using O'Hanlon as a courier for their drug shipments and on several occasions she travelled to Holland with Bolger.

On April 27, 1999, disaster struck. As O'Hanlon drove a car off the ferry at Harwich International Port she was arrested by English Customs officers. She was returning from Holland and the officers discovered 118 kilos of cannabis and ten kilos of ecstasy hidden in the car boot. The haul had a street value of over IR£1.6 million. Foley and Bolger had stood to make over IR£700,000 from the deal. O'Hanlon was charged with the illegal importation of controlled drugs and remanded in custody. Her trial date was set for September.

A month after O'Hanlon's arrest, in May 1999, Clive Bolger appeared before the Circuit Criminal Court to ask for more time to pay IR£12,000 to a finance company, AIB Leasing. He had been ordered to pay the money after pleading guilty to his role in defrauding the company of IR£60,000. The previous January he'd received a three year suspended sentence for the scam. Detective Sergeant Denis O'Sullivan, of the Garda Bureau of Fraud Investigation, said he believed that if Bolger were given the opportunity to repay the £12,000 it would lead to further crime. However, the court granted Bolger another six months to get the cash. The Garda officer's suspicions were soon proved to be correct.

Twenty-five days, later on July 5, 1999, Detective Sergeant Christy Mangan of the Garda National Drug Unit received information that Foley and Bolger were planning to import a large quantity of cocaine. Mangan was directing a GNDU operation against the two hoods and had already arrested Hogan a few months earlier. This time Mangan had been told that the drugs were to be collected in Holland and smuggled through Dublin port in a container lorry. Bolger and Foley were to meet the truck as it arrived off the ferry on the evening of July 6. They would collect the drugs and hand over the cash. Mangan sent a surveillance team to watch for the handover.

Around 5.30pm, on July 6, the officers spotted Bolger parking his car outside a hotel on Customs Quay. He got into Martin Foley's car and the pair drove towards the East Wall. Two other associates, one of whom was Foley's neighbour, twenty-four-year-old Keith Hastings, drove behind them in a Saab. Foley and Bolger drove around the area changing their direction several times as an anti-surveillance tactic. The crew in the Saab also patrolled the area. A white County Monaghan registered tractor unit was waiting to meet them in the car park of a nearby filling station. Hastings and the other hood in the Saab took up positions near the truck to keep watch as Foley and Bolger drove up to the front of the waiting vehicle. They got into the truck beside the driver and the curtains in the cab were pulled over.

Detective Sergeant Mangan ordered his team to move in and arrest everyone. As the officers opened the truck doors Foley exclaimed: "Fuck we've been set up." The Viper made an attempt to dump a plastic bag but it was too late. The detectives also found him sitting on a second bag. The officers found over Stg£52,000 cash between the two bags. Another IR£34,500 was later found in a search of Bolger's car on Customs Quay. The money was confiscated and the gang members taken in for questioning. The GNDU were disappointed that they hadn't recovered the cocaine. It later transpired that the information had not been entirely accurate. The truck driver was going to bring the cash to Holland to pay for the cocaine and smuggle the shipment back to Ireland on the return journey. Foley and Bolger had narrowly escaped a serious drug importation charge. Nevertheless it had been a very expensive day for the two hoods. The Criminal Assets Bureau (CAB) subsequently confiscated the money as the proceeds of drug trafficking. Foley's criminal associate from County Derry later tried to claim that he owned the cash and that he had been going to buy vehicles for sale in Ireland. He produced documentation, which was deemed to be inconsistent with his claims, and the mobsters lost their cash.

On September 10, 1999, Brigid O'Hanlon was convicted on the drug charges and jailed for twelve years. Following her prosecution members of the GNDU and the CAB, who were anxious to smash Foley's operation, made a number of visits to O'Hanlon in HM Prison, Foston Hall, Derbyshire. She claimed that the two hoods had threatened to harm her child if she did not transport the drugs on the ferry. She described how Foley and Bolger ran a tight

Mickey "The Pimpernel" Green and his girlfriend Anita Murphy on a Dublin street in 1996.

For over four years "The Pimpernel" ran his drug empire from his Irish base.

Maple Falls, Green's estate near Kilcock, County Kildare.

Mickey Green relaxing in the sun, 2003.

Detective Superintendent Felix McKenna, Director of the Criminal Assets Bureau – the only law enforcement agency in the world to successfully track Green down.

The *Sunday World* exposé, April 1996.

Inside Green's luxury penthouse apartment in Dublin's Docklands.

Taxi driver Joseph White who was killed in a collision with Mickey Green's car.

Martin "The Viper" Foley.

Clive Bolger, the Viper's former sidekick.

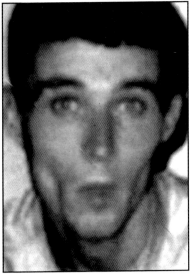

Gilligan gang member Paul Ward.

Hit man Brian Meehan, who tried to murder the Viper.

John Gilligan.

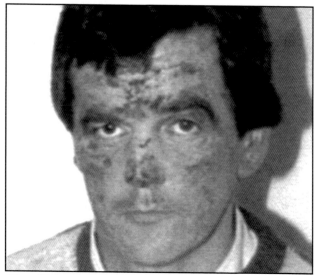

"Shavo" Hogan pictured while in Garda custody in 1994. He had smeared his own excrement over his face.

Martin Cahill – The General.

Patrick Shanahan.

Martin Foley (left) at the funeral of his long-time friend, Seamus "Shavo" Hogan.

©Sunday World

Seamus "Shavo" Hogan shortly before his murder in 2001.

© Collins, Dublin

Dessie O'Hare, the INLA terrorist known as the Border Fox.

Dublin drug dealer Brian O'Keefe whose gang took on the INLA in the notorious Ballymount Bloodbath.

John "The Coach" Traynor who took part in fraud scams with the INLA.

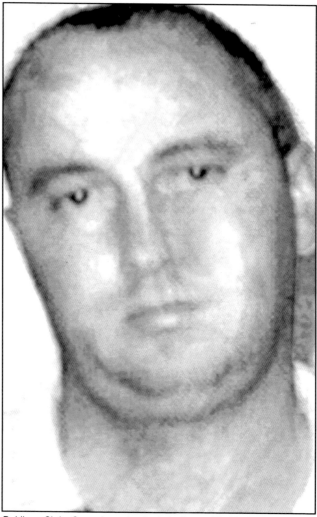

Dubliner Chris Casserley, who had dealings with Martin Foley, Clive Bolger and John Cunningham.

INLA member "Mad Nicky" O'Hare, who was shot dead in 2000.

Derek Lenihan, INLA member shot dead in 2001.

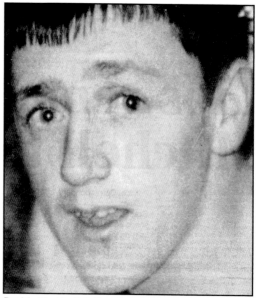

Patrick "Paddy Bo" Campbell, INLA member, murdered during the Ballymount Bloodbath, October 1999.

Declan "Wacker" Duffy one of the INLA's top mobsters in Dublin.

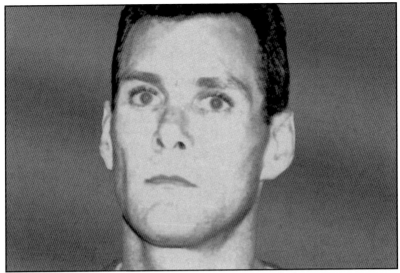
INLA member Colm Peake, who killed himself in a Dublin Garda Station.

Convicted INLA boss Gerard Burns.

International drug-trafficker and former INLA member Mickey Weldon.

Weldon's partner-in-crime, drug-trafficker and ex-INLA member, Tommy Savage.

Dundalk businessman Stephen Connolly who was murdered by Nicky O'Hare in 2000.

Fergal Toal, member of Dessie O'Hare's gang who were responsible for the kidnapping of dentist John O'Grady in 1987.

Members of the Garda team who investigated the INLA and the Ballymount Bloodbath included *from left and back*: Gardaí Denis Nagle and Mick McMahon, *from left and front:* Supt. John Manley, Det. Insp. Tom Mulligan (Now Supt.), Det. Sgt. Joe O'Hara and Det. Supt. Denis Donegan.

operation to avoid capture by the police. "Foley and Bolger trust no one, not even each other that's why they're not caught. They have amassed a fortune but no one except them knows where it is," she told detectives. Foley and Bolger were terrified that O'Hanlon might do a deal with the authorities in return for giving evidence against them. In the end O'Hanlon opted to remain silent and began studying for a degree in psychology. In the meantime it was business as usual for the two gangsters.

On September 16, two weeks after Brigid O'Hanlon's conviction, French police and customs officers at the port of Calais seized a huge haul of cocaine, ecstasy and hashish with an estimated street value of IR£8 million. The polyload of drugs, which had originated in Amsterdam, was concealed in an Irish registered container lorry. The information on the shipment had come from the Irish police. John Cunningham had sourced the consignment that was to be split between the Foley gang and another mob based at Newry, in south Armagh.

At this stage the police did not know about Cunningham's involvement in the racket. This state of affairs wouldn't last for much longer. In the winter of the same year a major international investigation into drugs and arms smuggling involving the Irish and Dutch police swung into operation. As part of that investigation, Dutch phone taps intercepted calls between Casserly, Foley, Bolger and Cunningham. Codenamed Operation Plover, it soon began to hurt the gangsters.

On December 13, Keith Hastings collected a shipment of 30,000 ecstasy tablets that had been organised through Cunningham by Chris Casserly. Hastings picked up the drugs from a truck driver in Northern Ireland. He was bringing them down to Dublin when he was stopped near Ashbourne in County Meath by Detective Sergeant Pat Walsh of the GNDU. Hastings was subsequently convicted of drug trafficking and jailed for seven years. Within a few days the Dutch police heard Bolger calling Cunningham and trying to arrange a replacement load for the lost ecstasy. But there was more bad luck in store for the Viper's mob.

On January 27, 2000, the Dutch phone taps led to the arrest of thirty-eight-year-old Campbell Lunn when he was stopped by police in Hillsborough, County Down, Northern Ireland. He was transporting 200,000 ecstasy tablets and a firearm. The haul was another joint venture between Foley, Bolger and Casserly. Lunn subsequently pleaded guilty and was jailed for six years. The business partners were undeterred by the seizure and quickly arranged another deal from Cunningham for 200,000 ecstasy tablets. Casserly paid truck driver Gary McNulty to collect the drugs from Cunningham in Holland on February 9. The night before the deal Casserly was spotted by the GNDU meeting Foley and Bolger in the Leinster Pub on Harold's Cross Road as they made arrangements for the distribution of the ecstasy. But again the secret police investigation was to cost the gang dearly. Within an hour of picking up the consignment Belgian police were waiting to pull McNulty over as he crossed the border from Holland. The seizure had cost the three gangsters IR£100,000 in cash which they had paid to Cunningham. Foley and Bolger had a bitter falling out with Casserly as a result of the seizures with each side accusing the other of being responsible for the screw-ups.

The Viper and his pal decided to go their own way and later that month a clearly desperate Foley organised yet another shipment, this time through a County Tyrone smuggler the gang had used on previous occasions. The Viper gave the smuggler Stg£90,000 in cash which was to be given to Cunningham as part payment for drugs and guns. Unfortunately for the Viper, the Dutch police swooped and arrested Cunningham a month later, seizing fifteen high-powered firearms and drugs worth IR£8 million. Garda and Dutch police intelligence later revealed that part of the seized haul had been earmarked for Foley and Bolger who had been identified as Cunningham's customers during a three month undercover investigation. After the arrests the Tyrone smuggler hung onto the money feeling safe in the knowledge that the Viper would think his cash had also been seized. Two years later, however, Foley and four associates travelled from Dublin to the man's home in County Tyrone to threaten him in an attempt to get Foley's money back. But the Viper and his pals were forced to flee when they themselves were intimated at gunpoint.

* * * *

In April 2000, an uniformed Garda patrol intercepted two men who had been acting suspiciously in the Crumlin area. When the men were arrested one of them was found to be carrying a firearm. In a follow up operation detectives discovered that the two men were involved in the IRA. In one search of an IRA figure's flat in Dublin officers found what they described as a "hit list" with two prominent names on it – Martin Foley and "Shavo" Hogan. Officers visited Foley and told him that they had picked up information that he may be the target of a shooting.

On Tuesday, September 12, 2000, Foley left his home shortly after 8pm. He was heading to the swimming pool at prestigious Terenure College, a short distance away. He swam every day as part of an impressive fitness-training programme. As Foley drove out of Cashel Avenue he met a blue Toyata Corolla saloon car, similar to a standard detective unit squad car, which had just turned into the Avenue. Foley stopped to allow the car to pass, as there was only enough space for one vehicle at a time on the narrow side road. In any case the cautious Viper wanted to see who was inside. As the car drove past he saw three men. The driver put his hand up to cover his face, while his two passengers immediately looked the other way. Foley watched them for a moment in his rear view mirror and then drove on to his destination.

He spent half an hour at the pool before leaving shortly after 9pm. When he walked outside he stood on the pavement and looked around before opening his car door with his remote control key. He walked around the car to the driver's door, looking around as he went. He opened the door and flipped the lever to open the boot. As he walked back around the car he spotted a man wearing a baseball hat and a jacket zipped up as far as his nose. He was running towards Foley with his hand inside his jacket. When Foley spotted him, the hit man stopped at another car that stood between them. Foley made a dash to get back into the swimming pool building and the would-be assassin followed firing several shots from a powerful handgun.

One of the bullets hit the Viper in the right foot shattering his ankle. The bullet travelled up through his leg, exiting beneath the kneecap. The force of the gunshot knocked Foley to the ground and the hit man aimed his weapon at the Viper's head to finish him off. The drug dealer however had no intentions of giving up. At the very moment the hit man fired the shot Foley ducked his head and the bullet grazed the side of his skull. He grabbed the front wheel of a car, using it to pull himself out of the hit man's line of fire. More shots were fired, some of them hitting a parked car shattering its windows and leaving large, gaping holes in its body work.

Foley waited for a moment before making a second, successful dash for the swimming pool doors. The assassin's weapon appeared to either jam or run out of bullets. The killer abandoned his mission and took off in a waiting getaway van. Foley ordered a pool attendant to call the police.

As police officers arrived at the scene they were astonished to find Foley relatively calm for a man who had just escaped death for the fourth time in his life. "I'm fuckin' sick of this! This is gettin' fuckin' ridiculous," he responded angrily when the officers asked about his injuries as they waited for an ambulance. "This is getting fuckin' ridiculous. I don't know what I'm going to do about it," Foley continued, scolding. He could have been talking about some irritating vandals who had just thrown stones through his windows for the umpteenth time.

Later when detectives visited him in hospital the Viper was in upbeat mood. When the investigators asked him did he know who shot him he laughed and said "oh yeah", but refused to share the good news with them. "They've tried their best and they can't fuckin' get me. I'm too quick for them," Foley bragged, as he sat up in his hospital bed. No one was charged in connection with the incident but sources close to Foley say that he knew who did the shooting. According to them the attack was carried out by associates of Chris Casserly from north County Dublin. Clive Bolger also confirmed the theory to this writer. "Martin fell out with them [Casserly's mob] over something and they decided to kill him," he said.

Two months after the Terenure assassination bid Martin Foley was back in court. This time it was on more agreeable business – his claim for damages against Charlie Bowden. On November 15, 2000, the action to assess damages in the case was heard in the High Court before Mr Justice Dermot Kinlen. Bowden, who was still incarcerated in Arbour Hill prison as a State protected witness in the case against John Gilligan, did not appear. Foley's senior counsel, Mr Ronnie Robbins SC, said the supergrass had been advised the case was proceeding but had not responded. In Foley's statement of claim it was submitted that during proceedings in the Special Criminal Court in 1999 against Brian Meehan, Bowden had admitted that he'd supplied the weapon used to carry out the attack on Foley in 1996. Bowden had provided instructions on how to carry out the attack.

Opening the action, Mr Robbins outlined the events that occurred on the night of the attack on February 1, 1996. Foley's counsel said it had been a terrifying experience for his client. The physical injuries paled to insignificance when compared to the trauma which he had suffered. Foley, he said, had suffered post-traumatic stress disorder. He was afraid when he was outside his own doors and he had to be "hyper-vigilant" at all times. If he heard a car or motor bicycle passing he became agitated.

In his own evidence Foley, who was still walking with the aid of crutches as a result of the September shooting, was un-characteristically forthcoming with information especially when compared to his many previous court appearances. He told Mr Justice Kinlen it had taken months before the physical pain from the 1996 injuries had begun to ease. He was nervous, upset and afraid to leave home. He said he was afraid of being shot and developed panic attacks and always tried to get home before dark. He had attended a GP and a psychiatrist and learned to do relaxation techniques. He suffered nightmares and flashbacks. He had been advised to seek counselling and made several appointments to do so but did not attend any of them. Foley said he had matrimonial problems after the shooting and he became "aggressive and screamed". He felt ashamed at the way he was carrying on, but the situation had improved a lot now. Most of the people involved in the other shootings were now behind bars he claimed.

Foley's long-suffering wife Pauline described problems in their relationship after the shooting. She feared there might be another attack. The shooting had affected her husband's relationship with her and they'd started "rowing". Dr Peter Fahy, consultant psychiatrist, said he saw Foley earlier in the year. Mr Foley was referred to him because of the incident at Terenure College. He was suffering considerable post-traumatic stress symptoms and had significant depression. If he had treatment and psychotherapy he would be doing well to be clear of his condition in twelve months. Asked by the judge what the position would be if somebody else took a shot at the Viper, Dr Fahy said it would have an "exacerbating effect and seriously raise his anxiety levels".

Giving judgement, Mr Justice Kinlen said people were determined to kill Mr Foley and had made three attempts on his life. It was a great compliment to the Gardaí that the assailants were behind bars. The judge added that "in his day" there had been one or two murders a year. Now there were three or four judges dealing with rape or murder cases at any one time. The judge said Irish society now compared with the notorious society of New York and Chicago of the 1930s. Nowadays, he said, individuals could not go about their business because there were people "going around attempting to assassinate other people". The judge added that in the absence of an appearance, judgement had been given against Bowden. The difficulty in the case was that Mr Foley's main injury was his nervous condition, which was perfectly understandable. The court awarded Foley IR£120,000. The publicity-shy gangster was later driven away by Clive Bolger to avoid prying media cameras. But Bolger would not be driving his friend around for much longer.

* * * *

The relationship between Foley and Bolger could probably be best summarised as intense. It was what a romantic would describe as a friendship made in heaven. Both men held each other in the highest esteem and were inseparable But in the latter part of 2000 something went terribly wrong and the passionate friendship was suddenly replaced with an equally passionate hatred. Neither man has divulged the reason for the sudden falling out but it is thought to be connected to the row with Chris Casserly. Foley in particular was totally consumed with his hatred for Clive Bolger. He even later accused Bolger of setting him up for the murder attempt in Terenure. The mutual loathing led to both men plotting to murder each other. Bolger was forced to move address on several occasions out of fear of his former friend. In February 2001, "Wigsy" called the Gardaí to his apartment in Blanchardstown after Foley and a younger gang member called to his door. Bolger told officers that the row began when he'd expressed a wish to get out of the Viper's criminal rackets.

Bolger then moved to a house in Dunboyne, County Meath, to hide from the Viper. It wasn't long before he was forced to move again. On April 3, eight masked men tried to force their way into the house. Bolger managed to keep them out while he called the police. When Gardaí arrived Bolger told them Foley had been behind the attack. "Martin was behind that attack on my house, I have no doubt that I was going to be done that night. I heard later that he bragged that he had trained me too well," Bolger later told this writer.

The feud continued to spiral out of control. In May 2001, detectives arrested Foley in a hotel in Dun Laoghaire when they found a sawn-off shotgun and ammunition in the boot of his car. Foley had slipped off for a weekend with his young mistress. He was in bed when members of the Emergency Response Unit (ERU) burst in on top of him. The Viper had a hood placed on his head and the officers made him put on a forensic suit. Foley later claimed that Bolger had planted the gun and then tipped off the police. Bolger denied this. The Viper was never charged with possession of the firearm. Following the incident he told the *Sunday World*: "I know who planted the gun in my car. It was Bolger. The police had to do their job. They were very fair to me and treated me fine despite our past differences."

Two weeks before the Dun Laoghaire incident Foley had been presented with an even more pressing problem, this time from the dreaded Criminal Assets Bureau. An irredeemable skinflint by nature, Foley's associates say that he would cut his arm off rather than give away his money – especially to the police! His money was well concealed and, because of this, he reckoned himself to be untouchable. But in May 2001 a letter from the CAB dropped on the matt in Foley's house in Crumlin. The CAB had assessed him as owing them IR£172,586 in unpaid taxes based on his criminal activity and social welfare claims. Added to the original sum were interest and penalties which equalled IR£159,000. The CAB had already seized over IR£85,000 cash, that the GNDU had discovered when they swooped on Foley and Bolger in 1999. Foley was still seeking the return of the cash despite the fact that he was claiming that he had no money in the first place. The cheeky gangster even applied for free legal aid to fight the case. The CAB case was based on the belief that the money had been generated through drug trafficking.

The man leading the Criminal Assets Bureau was an old acquaintance of Foley's. Detective Chief Superintendent Felix McKenna was one of the force's most experienced serious crime investigators who had been one of the senior officers attached to the Tango Squad. Throughout the years McKenna had had many encounters with the Viper. McKenna and his men had succeeded in putting several of Foley's old friends behind bars, including John Gilligan. When the CAB was established following the Guerin murder in 1996 McKenna was appointed second-in-command. By the time the large tax assessment dropped through Foley's letterbox, McKenna was in overall command of the most successful police unit of its type in Europe. When Foley phoned the CAB headquarters and asked to speak with his "old friend Felix" he was politely told that the only matter they would be discussing was the method of payment of the tax demand. When this writer asked Foley about the CAB's tax assessments on him he flew into an instant rage. "Where are my criminal assets? Up me fucking arse is where. Just look around me house, this is not the home of a wealthy drug baron." Nevertheless Foley did manage to cough up over IR£21,730 in income tax for the years 1993/94 to 2000 in order to comply with the statutory appeals provisions laid down in the Proceeds of Crime Legislation. The Viper has begun negotiations to settle his affairs with the CAB.

In the meantime, the Viper and "Shavo" Hogan felt that they now needed something with which to bargain their way out of trouble. They needed to steal something that they could later trade off for "Shavo's" freedom and possibly to help them resolve the CAB situation. The two underworld chums decided to revisit Russborough House. This time Foley and Hogan would not take part in the heist. They would confine their involvement to the planning stage. Second time around members of the young gang of loyal hoods Foley had gathered around him would do the actual dirty work.

On the afternoon of June 26, 2001, history repeated itself. The gang drove a stolen jeep through the front doors of the stately home and within three minutes had escaped with two paintings worth an estimated IR£3 million. One of the two works of art, *Madame Baccelli*, was one of the original paintings stolen by Foley and the rest of Cahill's gang back in 1986.

Foley and Hogan made a number of efforts to seek a reward from the insurance company for the return of the paintings. However, just over two weeks later, "Shavo" Hogan had no further need of the money. On the evening of Saturday, July 14, Hogan drove his car to the Transport Club on Clogher Road in Crumlin, accompanied by his wife Lily. Two masked men armed with an automatic pistol and a sawn-off shotgun had been waiting in a stolen car. They rushed over when Hogan arrived. "Shavo" spotted the two men and shouted at his wife to stay in the car. He put his hands up to protect his face as one of the gunmen shot him through the driver's window. The bullet just missed Lily as it travelled through the car, shattering the passenger window. Hogan shoved the car into reverse to get away. Lily Hogan later recalled: "We were bent right down in the car. He screamed at me, 'Lily get out' and I said 'I can't'. The car seemed to be speeding around the car park. There may have been one, two, three more shots, I'm not sure." The gunman followed the car as it lurched around the car park, shooting another five times at the target. As he ran off his accomplice looked into the car to ensure that "Shavo" had been hit. Hogan, one of the country's most infamous criminals and Martin Foley's best friend, was dead before the getaway car left the car park. He had been hit twice in the chest, the bullets ripping through his heart and lungs in the process.

Detectives had some difficulty investigating the case because, like the Viper, Hogan had many enemies. The most likely suspects, however, were members of John Cunningham's gang in Dublin. They had accused Hogan of helping the GNDU seize a large consignment of cocaine a few months earlier. "Shavo" was still suspected of being an informant following his days in the General's gang. His impending drug trial certainly provided a motive for Hogan to try to save his own neck. In the mind of a paranoid criminal that would be enough to justify taking a life. Within an hour of the incident a prisoner in Portlaoise got a telephone message: "Tell him [the prisoner] the job is done." No one has ever been charged with the murder. Martin Foley was one of the pallbearers at his friend's his funeral four days later. He now had another reason to be fearful for his own life.

Foley and his gang of young hoods made several more attempts to off-load the Beit paintings and secure a reward. But at the same time, unknown to them, the Garda National Bureau of Criminal Investigation (NBCI) were secretly watching and waiting to pounce. Catching Foley with the treasures would be a wonderful coup.

In the winter of 2001, at the height of the negotiations, Foley's gang went on a fund raising mission to rob the AIB bank branch in Abbeyleix, County Laois. John Bishop from Clondalkin, Kevin Lynch from Tallaght and Foley's nephews, Ian and Gareth Quinn, all of whom had taken part in the Beit art heist in June, were secretly observed stealing a number of high-powered cars which they intended using in the heist.

On Friday December 7, 2001, a large team of officers attached to the National Surveillance Unit (NSU) backed up by the Emergency Response Unit (ERU) followed the gang, as they travelled to the midlands in three stolen cars.

Shortly before 4pm Inspector Liam King of the NSU spotted the gang moving into a car park at the side of the bank. He contacted his colleagues in the ERU to pass on the information. The officer in charge of the ERU, Detective Inspector John Gantley, ordered two units to intercept the gang. Then everything went tragically wrong. In the confusion that followed the gang made an attempt to escape and the ERU men tried to disable one of the gang's cars. A number of shots were fired and when it was over Det. Sgt. John Eiffe of the NSU lay mortally wounded on the ground. The dedicated officer, a married man with four young children, had been hit in the chest when a round from one of the ERU's powerful shotguns ricocheted off the engine block in the gang's getaway car. The round was specifically designed to disable a vehicle's engine. Det. Sgt. Eiffe died from his injury a short time later. Meanwhile the four hoods were arrested and charged. Following the incident discreet offers were made to return the paintings in return for a possible deal. Foley's mob were told to shove off.

In November 2002, after a six week trial in Portlaoise Circuit Court, Lynch, Bishop and Ian Quinn were convicted of conspiring to rob the bank and jailed for ten years each. A bench warrant had been issued for Gareth Quinn when he failed to turn up for his trial. The curse of the Beit paintings had struck again. In September 2002 the two paintings stolen by the gang in June 2001 were "recovered" by the NBCI in south Dublin. Foley did not realise a penny in profit for his efforts.

Despite his many setbacks and his preoccupation with the law, Foley refused to forget his vicious vendetta with Clive Bolger. Foley and his gang of young hoods plotted to ambush Bolger when he turned up at the Dublin District Court in relation to charges by the GNDU on February 28, 2002. Officers had received information that Bolger was to be shot outside the court. The ERU were drafted into the area, along with other armed units, to prevent a gun attack on the conman. The officers had also been told that Foley's hoods had planned to petrol bomb Bolger as he drove away in his jeep. The large police presence prevented a bloodbath.

A month later, on the night of March 5, 2002 around 11.30pm, Foley spotted a car driving by his door on Cashel Avenue. The three occupants were wearing masks and drove out of the estate. A motorbike then drove into the Avenue. As the motorbike passed Foley's house, the Viper and an associate ran out from the house. Using a handgun they opened fire on the motorbike as it raced off. Foley believed that the two men on the bike were about to assassinate him. The Viper missed his targets and the bullets hit a number of neighbour's homes. When local detectives began to investigate the incident the residents refused to co-operate. They were too scared of the local bullyboy.

Then in June 2002, Clive Bolger arrived in Crumlin Garda station claiming that Foley and his mob had tried to ambush him at the Traders Pub in Walkinstown. He claimed that he saw the Viper brandishing a pistol in the front seat of a waiting car. Bolger however declined to make a formal complaint about the incident. A month later Gardaí from Crumlin uncovered a revolver hidden in a garden near Foley's home. The officers believed that the .38 weapon was there for the Viper's protection. Later it was discovered that the revolver had been stolen from a member of the Police Service of Northern Ireland. Foley was never charged with the find.

In the meantime detectives received intelligence that Bolger had travelled to Spain to meet with Chris Casserly and former members of the IRA who were involved in international drug trafficking operations. One Provo from Belfast, who had been sentenced to death by his former comrades, agreed to murder Foley for a fee. Nothing ever came of the plot. At the same time in Dublin, Foley's Crumlin gang had shot and injured two street drug dealers associated with Bolger and Casserly's operation.

In Autumn 2002, officers received intelligence of another elaborate plot to murder the ever-wary Viper. A dustbin truck had been stolen as a cover for a hit on Foley. It was planned to go down on a Wednesday morning, the collection day for rubbish in the area. Several teams of ERU men, backed up by a surveillance plane staked out the area, to prevent the attack. The murder gang abandoned the plan at the last minute and no arrests were made. Without him even knowing about it, the Viper's luck was still holding.

Around the same time Foley was convicted for criminal damage to a neighbour's car in a row which he claimed was over obscene phone calls and letters which were sent to his teenage daughters, Amy and Rachel. Foley used a steering lock to smash up Tina Doyle's car on August 7, 2001. Ms Doyle told the District Court that Foley walked up to her car and began hitting it with the steering lock. The Viper was after Doyle's nephew seventeen-year-old Paul Hynes who he had accused of harassing his daughters. When Hynes saw Foley he ran for it. "He [Foley] kept banging it and roaring. He was like a raving lunatic," Tina Doyle told the court. In his defence Foley admitted that he had wanted to give Ms Doyle's nephew a "clatter" but denied he had a steering lock. Foley said that his daughters had been subjected to a barrage of obscene phone calls from Doyle's nephew. "They [letters and calls] were saying what they would or wouldn't do to them," said the Viper. "It was so bad that we had to get the phone disconnected from the house. I had wanted to speak to Hynes about the letters and calls and I got me chance when I saw him in Tina Doyle's car. I jumped out of my car and ran at the passenger window – he ran off," Foley claimed.

Foley was given a three-month jail sentence that the court suspended for twelve years. But the court was not told was that the attack on Doyle's car was also the result of an ongoing feud between Foley and Doyle's former partner, INLA man Bobby Tohill. Tohill, a former member of the IRA from Belfast, had been shot in 1994 as punishment for the misappropriation of INLA weapons. He was terrified of Martin Foley. Tohill claimed Foley had originally accused him of being responsible for the 1996 shooting carried out by Brian Meehan. In May 2003, Foley began a court action to appeal the conviction.

In January 2003, Foley's wife Pauline died from cancer. After her death Foley told associates that he regretted the hard life he had given his wife. "You only appreciate them when they are gone," said Foley, in a rare display of grief. His sad loss did nothing to change the Viper's insatiable desire for trouble and crime. Foley's young gang got involved in a bloody turf war with another young mob for control of drug rackets in Drimnagh and Crumlin. By the summer of 2003 the feud had cost the lives of two young men. There have been several other shootings and stabbings in which members of both gangs have been seriously injured. However, as a result of some of the ringleaders being arrested and jailed on other offences, the gang war had effectively ceased by Winter 2004.

At the same time the feud between Foley and his neighbours has intensified. Shots were fired at one house and Ms Doyle received a dead hamster in the post. Foley then received a hoax letter bomb. Clive Bolger and Foley are also still jousting with each other. It would not require a fortune-teller to predict that their feud is likely to lead to further bloodshed and possibly death. Bolger, however, has claimed that he will not be the one to finish off his old pal: "Martin will self-destruct along the way and he won't need any help from me."

Apart from his illegal fundraising activities and sundry wars, the Viper also stepped up pressure on the authorities to get his compensation money from the Bowden case. In 2002, the High Court had ruled that Foley was not entitled to an order to establish what financial arrangements existed between the Gardaí and Bowden in connection with the Witness Protection Programme. On June 23, 2003, the Supreme Court overturned that ruling and directed that the Garda Commissioner or a nominated officer be questioned on the matter. Foley has sought information about Bowden's financial arrangements with the State in a bid to secure payment of the IR£120,000 award made to him in proceedings against Bowden.

The Chief Justice said one had to proceed on the assumption that there may be sums of money that could be the subject of a garnishee order (giving a creditor a lien over funds due to them). If the Gardaí wished to object during oral examination to the production of any documents on the grounds that their disclosure would not be in the public interest, they could do so, the Supreme Court said. The judge conducting the examination could rule on the validity of the objection and if necessary inspect the documents. There should also be no difficulty, the court said, in conducting the examination in a manner that would not disclose the new identity or location of Bowden. If Foley ever gets his hands on the money it is likely that he will have to hand it over to the Criminal Assets Bureau.

****

Despite the brief period Foley spent in the early 1980s as a spokesman for the General's farcical Concerned Criminals group, the Viper has worked hard to avoid publicity. Like most cowardly criminals, he doesn't like being written about in the newspapers. He moans and complains and makes threats about what is written – even though he knows it's the truth. For over fifteen years Foley had been particularly preoccupied by the publicity he received in the pages of the *Sunday World,* many of the articles were written by this writer. Before this book was first published in Autumn 2003, the Viper discovered that a chapter had been written dedicated to his life and crimes. During the summer Garda intelligence had discovered that the Viper's associates were trying to plot some kind of attack on this writer. The conspirators were informed that their plot had been rumbled and it was abandoned. Stories in the *Sunday World* and *The Star* newspapers also exposed the plot. However it was known in the criminal underworld that Foley was still planning to "teach Paul Williams a lesson". He was also apparently furious with the Gardaí who, as a result of the ongoing stories, had been keeping him and his mob under closer scrutiny. The unwanted attention was bad for his drug business.

When *Crime Lords* came out the Viper began to plot a campaign of violence and intimidation. On October 26, 2003, the *Sunday World* published exclusive extracts from this book in a special twelve-page supplement. Four pages of the supplement were dedicated to this chapter. Foley responded with his favourite tool – intimidation. However, as per usual, he was not prepared to do his own dirty work. He left that to the three young thugs who have become his closest associates since his break up with Clive Bolger. The oldest of the three is a thug in his early thirties who grew up in Crumlin. When Foley and Bolger fell out the hood replaced Bolger in the Viper's affections and has been Foley's trusted sidekick for several years. He is described as something of a dimwit, of low intelligence, who allows the Viper to use him to commit crimes that the gangster considers are too risky for his own personal involvement. The second associate is in his early twenties and also from Crumlin. By day he works for a security company but by night he is a violent thug who is constantly in Foley's company. The third associate is also in his twenties and lives with his girlfriend in an apartment in Terenure. Like the other two he is an easy touch whom Foley manipulates and uses at will. The three criminals enjoy the 'hardman' image they think they have gained from associating with one of gangland's most notorious gangsters. The fact that they could easily become targets when the next assassination attempt is made on Foley doesn't seem to worry them.

In the early hours of October 29, three days after *Crime Lords* was serialised, one of Foley's three pals poured acid over my car. It took him a few seconds to complete his task before disappearing into the night. Two days later, in the early hours of October 31, one of the three thugs placed a hoax call to Dublin Fire Brigade informing them that there was a fire at my home. Two fire engines were dispatched on the false call on a night when the fire service is traditionally at its busiest. Martin Foley would not care if someone lost his/her life because of his activities. It later emerged, under investigation, that Foley's associate made the phone call from a coin box on Wellington Lane in Templeogue. A charge was never pressed against the thug despite the fact that six Garda officers could identify his voice.

Foley was determined to continue his campaign of intimidation but this time he was prepared to go one step further and up the stakes. This time a hoax bomb was planted at my home.

Two weeks later, on November 14, one of Foley's henchmen

arrived at my house at 1.12am. He removed an elaborate device from a bag and quickly planted it underneath the rear of the replacement car I had been using following the acid attack on my own car a few weeks earlier. His associate was also in the area, waiting for him and keeping a look out.

At the same time Foley and one of his pals were waiting in Terenure, listening to a radio scanner. They wanted to know the minute the Gardaí found the device. But when the two other thugs got back to the flat the Gardaí still hadn't found it. Foley then instructed the twenty-something, who had planted the hoax bomb, to phone a Garda he knew to tell him that "some device or something had been placed" under the car. When the hoaxer phoned the cop and told him about it the thug claimed he was ringing because he didn't want to see anyone getting hurt in the morning. The hood then sent the Garda a text message that said: "You did not hear from me. I can't say where it came from but its 100 per cent. Text me back let me know you got this." In an attempt to guarantee even more publicity Foley's associate then phoned a Dublin-based journalist who the gang considered would make the bomb hoax headline news.

The Garda received the first call from the Viper's man at 2.45am. As the Garda rushed over to check the car a vigilant passing patrol from Crumlin Garda Station had just spotted the 'bomb'. It was 2.58am. Gardaí Mark Gallagher, Dave Finnerty and Michael Redmond, who were in the unmarked patrol car, immediately cordoned off the area. A major security operation was put in place. Officers were communicating on mobile phones so that the criminals would not hear what was happening by scanning the Garda radio network. An Army Bomb Disposal Unit was mobilised.

I heard the doorbell ring shortly after 3am. When I answered on the intercom it was Detective Garda Gallagher. "Paul can you come down to the door now," he said. I recognised his voice, which was calm but firm. When I opened the door he stepped into the hallway. "We've just found something under the car outside. It looks like a device of some sort. We want you and the family out of the house now while we sort this."

A few minutes later we were being guided out of the house and were brought to a safe distance from the device. Several officers were standing by and there was total silence as they worked. We were driven away to the local Garda station.

While the drama was unfolding Martin Foley and his three henchmen were waiting back in the apartment. According to one of his thugs, who subsequently talked to me and to the Gardaí, the Viper was agitated, hyper and anxiously listening to the Garda radio network. Shortly before 4am a taxi picked up Foley and one of his thugs and brought them to Crumlin. As the cab was driving to Foley's home it met the Army Bomb Squad team, being escorted by the Gardaí under blue lights, making it's way to the 'bomb' site. Foley got agitated and excited and ordered the cab driver to drive down a side road. The cowardly godfather slumped down in the back of the taxi as the convoy of police and military vehicles sped up the road.

Shortly after 4am a specialist X-ray machine, mounted on a Bomb Disposal robot, was deployed to inspect the device. At that stage it appeared to be a genuine bomb and the Army officer in charge ordered the evacuation of the 150 men, women and children living on the road. Forcing the evacuation of my neighbours was nothing less than an act of terrorism against innocent, decent people whose only crime was that they lived beside me. At 4.30am a charge was fixed to the fuse in the device so that a controlled 'explosion' could be carried out to make it safe. It was later discovered that the device had been put together in Foley's associate's apartment in Terenure. It was contained in a tin box with similar component parts, such as circuit boards, to those used in a real bomb. The criminals had used simple dough to show up as real explosives on the bomb squad X-ray machine.

Foley's intention was to create an emergency situation that would result in the maximum disruption to my family and neighbours, as they were forced to leave their homes in the middle of an icy winter's night. The purpose of the plot was to scare me into silence. The following morning the Viper and his associates got what they wanted most – maximum publicity and public fear.

The incident dominated news reports throughout the day and over the following weekend. In the end, however, all the Viper achieved was to focus even more media attention on himself and his gang of dim-witted goons. Within an hour of finding the device the Gardaí knew who their suspect was. In an attempt to save himself in the days that followed Foley and his snouts leaked information to Gardaí naming a number of other criminals who had an interest in intimidating this writer. He particularly singled out members of the INLA who were also featured in this book. Despite these efforts Foley and his three cronies were arrested and questioned as part of the ongoing Garda investigation into the incident. Foley and his thirty-something sidekick were the last to be arrested in February 2004. The night after they were released from custody, fire engines were again sent to my home. On another occasion thugs were sent to a gym I use in an attempt to smash up my car for the second time. Armed members of the Garda Special Detective Unit apprehended them before they could do any damage.

In the final analysis the 'bomb' incident was one of the biggest mistakes Foley has made in his long career as a ruthless thug. Whatever about the effect the incident had on this writer and his family, the fact that the Viper's act of terrorism affected the lives of so many innocent people has assured him his place as Ireland's most reviled criminal figure. At the time of writing a file is being reviewed by the DPP.

* * * *

The story of Martin Foley is far from over. Over his thirty-year career the Viper has amassed almost forty criminal convictions, including convictions for crimes of violence, theft and malicious damage. The Viper continues to be treated with intense suspicion by other members of the criminal underworld who simply don't trust him. The bomb hoax focused a lot of unwanted attention on Foley's activities. He has become a source of embarrassment to the likes of Sinn Féin\IRA who Foley, by his own admissions, has effectively bought off. According to reliable sources the Viper is no longer a target for the IRA's hit men despite the fact that he has been on many of their murder lists in the past. It is widely rumoured in gangland circles that Foley broke the habit of a lifetime and decided to pay some of his drug money into the coffers of Sinn Féin, the IRA's political party who allegedly stand for social justice.

Garda intelligence has consistently categorised Foley as a "dangerous, violent criminal". The Viper's charmed existence in terms of dealing with the IRA and other gun attacks has been reflected in his dealings with the police. He has successfully avoided a long-term stay in prison.

Foley's ability to avoid being caught has caused considerable unease among many police officers, especially amongst those whose job it is to watch the Viper. Several reliable sources, both in the Garda Síochána and in the underworld, believe that the Viper is protected by a senior ranking member of the force. The theory is that Foley passes high-grade information about the activities of other drug dealers to this officer. In the twelve months since the bomb hoax Foley has miraculously managed to avoid at least three major drug busts where large amounts of cocaine and other narcotics were seized. In each case Foley had, astonishingly, left the scene where the drugs were found just a short time before the police came knocking.

The Viper is obviously not the type of hood who will simply retire and fade away into obscurity. A retired detective who has known the colourful gangster for almost thirty years commented: "No, that's not for Martin he doesn't have the cop on to know when to quit and he can't help himself getting into trouble. I have always predicted that Foley will not die in his sleep and have told him this on many occasions. The only thing that amazes me is that he has lived for so long."

Three

The INLA

It is late on an October night. Outside a small factory complex on the edge of a city's industrial hinterland a van stands empty. The complex is deserted and quiet. Sounds of a muffled commotion seep from behind the shuttered doors of one darkened warehouse. Inside agonising screams echo around the walls: cries of pain and pleas for mercy follow loud slaps and thuds against bare flesh. Shouted threats and questions prevent even a momentary respite. This is the sound of torture.

In a corner at the rear of the building, six naked young men lie face down on the cold concrete floor with their hands and legs bound with ties. Blood oozes from freshly opened wounds. Sinister masked figures stand over the six prisoners, kicking, punching and flailing. The crowd of moving bodies cast eerie, muddled shadows that bounce frantically around the walls like some grotesque Chinese shadow theatre.

On October 6, 1999, the Ballymount Road Industrial Estate in west Dublin became the unlikely venue for a savage confrontation involving twenty-four violent men. On one side was a rag tag group made up of the criminal associates and friends of a middle league drug dealer: on the other side was the Republican terror group – the Irish National Liberation Army (INLA).

This monstrous torture chamber was to set the opening scene in one of the most extraordinary showdowns ever witnessed in the Irish criminal underworld. It could have been a scene in a gratuitously violent gangster movie. The 'stage set' bears a chilling resemblance to scenes portrayed in Quentin Tarrantino's ground-breaking movie, *Reservoir Dogs*. But in life, truth is often stranger than fiction. This gruesome episode is as brutally true as it gets – it became known as the Ballymount Bloodbath.

****

The seeds for the Ballymount Bloodbath were sown twenty-five years earlier by a man called Seamus Costelloe, who founded the INLA and the Irish Republican Socialist Party (IRSP). The organisation officially came into existence at a meeting in a Dublin hotel on December 19, 1974. It was formed as a result of a split in the ranks of the Official IRA or the Stickies. The Official IRA had emerged after an earlier split in the IRA that saw the establishment of the Provisional IRA or the Provos.

Costello, a former car salesman, joined the Republican movement when he was a teenager and was a Sinn Féin member for Bray Urban District Council. He was a former Director of Operations of the Official IRA and the vice-president of Official Sinn Féin. He styled the organisation on European Marxist terror groups, such as the Red Brigade and the Bader-Meinhoff. Politically their aim would be the establishment of a socialist united Ireland. However, any pretence of being a political terrorist organisation effectively ended in 1977 with the murder of Seamus Costello by Belfast-based members of the INLA who wanted to seize control. Costello's murder would set a bloody precedent for the future of the organisation he had established.

From its formation in the mid-seventies the INLA went on to become one of the most ruthless paramilitary groups ever produced by Ireland's long history of political violence. The INLA acted as a magnet for the dregs of the Republican movement. It quickly became a wasp's nest of the most extreme elements, who were prepared to strike at the most innocuous and innocent targets.

The INLA earned its reputation for ferocious violence through a series of atrocities carried out in the name of 'the War' and through the murder of a large number of its own members in a string of blood feuds. In fact observers have noted that the INLA seemed more adept at murdering each other than actually fighting British occupation or establishing their version of a socialist Marxist State.

Among the INLA's notably few 'celebrated' acts of war was the murder of the Conservative Party's Northern Ireland spokesman, Airey Neave, in a car bomb at the House of Commons in 1979. Three years later they were responsible for the mass murder of seventeen people, eleven of them off-duty British soldiers, at the Dropping Well disco at Ballykelly, in County Derry. They also blew up a radar station in County Cork that they claimed was being used by NATO. Three INLA members died during the Maze Prison hunger strikes in 1981. One of the INLA's most audacious "Acts of War" was carried out behind the barbed wire fence of the Maze Prison in 1997. Three INLA prisoners somehow managed to smuggle themselves and a firearm into the loyalist area of the prison complex where they killed Billy Wright, the murderous boss of the Loyalist Volunteer Force (LVF).

The history of the INLA's criminal activities is as inglorious and disreputable as the events that unfolded in Ballymount on the night of October 6, 1999. Although they claimed to have a similar military command structure to the IRA, in reality the INLA was a criminal rabble. Their godfathers and gangs styled themselves 'Chiefs of Staff' and 'commanders' of 'the army'. The organisation became a collection of feuding factions where loyalties were betrayed at a whim. Its political wing, the Irish Republican Socialist Party (IRSP), was equally inept and ineffectual with no real political ideological basis. The INLA and the IRSP also maintained some links with extreme left-wing terror groups on the continent. There was constant bickering about funds, leadership and direction. In Belfast, Derry and Dublin the various INLA groups did their own thing and there was no cohesive approach to anything except perhaps criminal activity. Their selective interpretation of Marxist doctrine meant that they had no ethical qualms about immersing themselves in criminal rackets. The ethos of the organisation was more "mé féin" (myself alone) than "sinn féin" (ourselves alone). In essence the organisation was a flag of convenience for a collection of dangerous thugs. The INLA was treated with utter contempt and derision by the rest of the Republican movement. An investigation of its actions in the Irish Republic since 1976 reveals that its members became intrinsically involved in organised crime, while at the same time pretending to fight for the cause of an "Irish socialist republic". The hypocrisy was often quite breathtaking.

The presence of the INLA in Dublin was a direct consequence of the Troubles in Northern Ireland. Several INLA members moved south of the border in the late seventies on the run from the Northern

Ireland security services. The wave of violent 'political' migrants soon spread mayhem throughout the country. They took full advantage of a police force totally unequipped to deal with an upsurge in serious organised crime. The paramilitaries were armed and dangerous and began 'fund raising' for the 'war effort' by armed robbery. In 1969, at the start of the Troubles, there were six armed robberies in the twenty-six counties. A few years later that figure rocketed to an annual average of one hundred and fifty and continued to rise.

One of the INLA's most notorious leaders was Dominic McGlinchey. Born in County Derry in 1954, he had been an IRA member from the age of sixteen. He joined the INLA while serving a sentence in Portlaoise prison in the early 1980s. Upon his release in 1981 McGlinchey declared himself the organisation's Chief of Staff and set-up his power base in the Dundalk area of County Louth. He controlled his mob with an iron fist, quickly earning the nickname "Mad Dog". By his own admission he was personally involved in at least thirty murders and two hundred bombings. McGlinchey and his family moved to live for a time in Cashel Avenue in the working-class suburb of Crumlin in south Dublin from where he directed the INLA's terror campaign.

The 'politicals' had quickly introduced the so-called 'ordinary decent criminal' class to the most lucrative way of turning a dishonest buck in the late seventies. By the time McClinchey moved to Crumlin in the early 1980s gangs like the Cahills, the Cunninghams and the Dunnes were the underworld's new celebrities. The era of the armed robber or the blagger had arrived. Organised crime was here to stay.

McGlinchey was a close friend of Martin "the Viper" Foley. Foley was a prominent member of the General, Martin Cahill's gang and lived a few doors away on Cashel Avenue. The Viper and several of his criminal associates ran with the INLA and gave the impression that they were also 'Republicans'. The relationship was strengthened by the fact that at least six prominent INLA men lived in that corner of Crumlin. "Mad Dog" McGlinchey and his "troops" carried out a string of armed robberies with their underworld sympathisers.

One of McGlinchey's neighbours in Dublin was Belfast INLA man Thomas "Fingers" McCartan. A former Provo from the Turf

Lodge area in Belfast ,Thomas McCartan's father was Jack "Fingers" McCartan who was shot dead by the IRA in Andersonstown in 1976 after he embezzled money from a Provo drinking club. As a result of this Thomas McCartan defected to the INLA. In 1976, he was part of the first assassination squad dispatched to Dublin to murder INLA founder Seamus Costello. McCartan, however, was shot and wounded by Garda Detective Gerry O'Carroll who was lying in wait for him and the rest of his team when they arrived at a safe house in Dublin. McCartan was subsequently jailed by the, non-jury, Special Criminal Court in Dublin for possession of a firearm with intent to endanger life. On his release from prison he moved to Crumlin. His previous 'work' as an INLA killer had introduced him to the Dublin underworld. Like McGlinchey he became a close associate of Martin Foley, who in turn introduced McCartan to the General.

The INLA men were more than happy to offer their particular range of violent services to criminals. McCartan took part in several criminal escapades with the General's gang while continuing to be an active member of the INLA. In January 1982, The General recruited McCartan to make a car bomb which the gang then used in a bid to assassinate the State's forensic scientist, Dr James Donovan.

McCartan was also involved in the General's plot to rob almost IR£2 million worth of diamonds and jewels from the O'Connor's jewellery factory in Dublin in 1983. After the INLA man failed to turn up for the job McCartan fell out with the General over the proceeds of the huge heist. Following the robbery the IRA began putting pressure on Cahill and his gang for a share of the loot. Their threats culminated in the kidnap of one of Martin Foley's closest friends. Foley asked the INLA to help him secure his pal's release but they did nothing. Foley was himself kidnapped by the Provos but rescued by the police. The INLA later 'advised' Foley not to testify against his captors. (See Chapter Two)

Two other Dublin-based INLA members closely associated with the criminal underworld were Tommy Savage and Michael Weldon. Nicknamed the Zombie, Savage had a formidable reputation for violence. Born in Swords in 1950, Savage first got involved with the quasi-Republican group Saor Eire, then with the Official IRA and later with the INLA in the late 1970s. He carried out armed robberies throughout the country for 'the cause'. For his efforts he incurred convictions for armed robbery, theft and violence. On one occasion he was sentenced to nine years in Portlaoise prison for armed robbery. He served his time on the INLA's wing in the jail. He was also arrested on numerous occasions under the Prevention of Terrorism Act for questioning in relation to INLA activities.

Savage's partner-in-crime, Michael Weldon, was the same age and a former neighbour. Weldon joined the INLA in the late-seventies while serving in an infantry battalion of the Irish Defence Forces. Described as a "top class" soldier he was promoted to the rank of Corporal. Weldon was later suspected of stealing weapons, including a rifle and a machine gun, from his army unit for the INLA. He is reputed to have literally thrown the weapons over the wall of his Dublin barracks. He left before Army intelligence had discovered his unsavoury associations with subversives.

Garda intelligence documented INLA members Savage and Weldon as being actively involved in the emerging drug industry as far back as the late 1970s and early 1980s when most criminals were still making a dishonest pound holding up banks. The INLA pair established links and supply routes with cannabis suppliers in Holland, Morocco, and the Middle East. Soon they were becoming major players in the burgeoning drug trade, controlling a substantial portion of the market in Dublin and later in Cork. Savage in particular was feared by practically everyone in gangland. Both men were among the most successful terrorists-turned-drug dealers in the business.

The names of Savage and Weldon also featured heavily in the Garda files relating to the new chilling phenomenon associated with the drug trade – the gangland murder. Several of their associates perished at the hands of the hit man. One associate, Danny McOwen, another INLA member, got involved with the two drug barons in the early 1980s. But he fell out with them and set up his own armed robbery gang, which he called the Gang of Six. He also began moving in on their drug dealing territory. On the morning of June 14, 1983, McOwen was shot four times as he left the Cumberland Street Labour Exchange after collecting his dole money. He was an easy target for assassination as he made the same trip to the city centre every week. The McOwen murder came two months after another associate of Savage and Weldon, Gerry Hourigan from Ballymun, North Dublin, suffered a similar fate. For over two decades the INLA's ruthless mob of extortionists, heavies and drug dealers would continue to be major players in Dublin's criminal underworld.

At the same time as the row between the General and the Provos was coming to a head and Savage and Weldon were establishing their drug operation, McGlinchey's bloody reign as the head of the INLA came to an effective end. While "Mad Dog" McGlinchey and his troops were living in Crumlin he was on bail pending a Supreme Court challenge to an application from the Northern Ireland authorities seeking his extradition to face murder charges in Belfast. In December 1982, he skipped bail just before the Supreme Court ruled that his extradition should go ahead. In November 1983, while still on the run, he copper-fastened his reputation – and that of the INLA – when his gang indiscriminately opened fire into a packed Pentecostal prayer hall at Darkley in South Armagh. Three men, church elders, were murdered and seven others were seriously wounded in one of the worst atrocities to take place during the years of the Northern Ireland Troubles. In a newspaper interview some time later "Mad Dog" McGlinchey admitted that he was linked to the Darkley outrage but denied that he had any direct involvement. He claimed that he had given the murder weapon to one of his men to shoot a UVF member. He said that the INLA man "must have been unbalanced" when he opened fire on the prayer meeting.

"Mad Dog" McGlinchey was eventually captured in County Clare in March 1984, following a shoot-out with Special Branch detectives. One of the officers involved in the incident, Detective Garda Christy Power, was shot and injured by McGlinchey. "Mad Dog" was immediately extradited back across the border and subsequently convicted of murder. The Belfast Appeal Court, however, overturned the conviction in October 1985 on a legal technicality. Mad Dog was extradited back to the south where he received a ten-year sentence for the County Clare shoot out.

With their erratic and violent leader on the run and out of the picture the INLA was leaderless. It began to turn in on itself. At the same time the organisation was thrown into further turmoil in 1983 when INLA man Harry Kirkpatrick agreed to turn state witness against his former comrades. It was the first of the infamous supergrass trials in Belfast. During the trials over 300 members of Loyalist and Republican terror groups were jailed on the evidence of former comrades. In Kirkpatrick's case he implicated thirty-two of his former partners in terrorist crime. In December 1986, however, the Northern Ireland Court of Appeal ruled as "unsafe" all the convictions secured by Kirkpatrick's evidence and all thirty-two men were released. All the other "supergrass" trials suffered the same fate. Several of the freed INLA men then moved to live south of the border, joining many of their comrades who had fled before being arrested on Kirkpatrick's evidence. The "supergrass" trials lit the fuse for a series of INLA blood feuds.

One of the worst feuds began within weeks of the release of the INLA members implicated in the trials. While in prison the INLA had split into two factions. The majority of the inmates supported Belfast man John O'Reilly, who had taken over what was left of the organisation after McGlinchey's arrest. O'Reilly's group styled itself the GHQ faction. On the other side of the split was Gerry Steenson, who had been dubbed "Dr Death" during the Kirkpatrick trials. Also know as "Pretty Boy", Steenson was as ruthless as the rest of his INLA cronies. He committed his first murder, that of a British soldier, when he was just fourteen years old. A year later he shot dead Billy McMillan, the Belfast leader of the Official IRA. By 1987, he had been responsible for at least a dozen other murders. "Dr Death" and his Army Council faction argued for the disbandment of the INLA and the creation of a new organisation that would revitalise republican socialism. The seeds had been sown for an INLA showdown.

Among those prisoners backing O'Reilly was prominent INLA 'commander' Hugh "Cueball" Torney, from Ballymurphy in Belfast. Torney was a founding member of the INLA and a close associate of "Mad Dog" McGlinchey, with whom he shared a passion for extreme violence. Torney's nickname, "Cueball", derived from his prison habit of beating other prisoners with a pool ball wrapped inside a sock. As a terrorist he was equally ham-fisted and brutal. In one incident, in 1982, Torney was responsible for a bomb attack on British soldiers in the Divis Flats in West Belfast that killed two young boys. Both McGlinchey and Torney had already executed a number of INLA men for various infractions of their military rules, including suspected informants. In fact INLA members would later blame Torney and McGlinchey for influencing Kirkpatrick to turn supergrass which he did after the murder of one of his close friends, Gerard "Sparky" Barkley. In the early 1980s, McGlinchey and his wife Mary shot Barkley in the back of the head after they had lured him to a house in Dundalk. The terrorist couple then cut Barkley's throat and drained his blood into a farmyard gutter before disposing of his body.

On December 22, 1986, two days before the release of "Cueball" Torney and his cohorts, Thomas McCartan was shot dead in Andersonstown, in Belfast. When the opening shots of the feud had been fired McCartan had returned to his home town to take part in the action but instead he had become one of its first victims.

On January 20, 1987, Gerard "Dr Death" Steenson's faction ambushed the leadership of O'Reilly's GHQ faction at the Rosnaree Hotel, outside Drogheda in County Louth. Garda Special Branch believed that Weldon and Savage, who supported Steenson, were also at the hotel on the night of the attack. "Dr Death's" plan was for one clean attack that would wipe out the O'Reilly and "Cueball" Torney leadership and force the disbandment of the INLA. INLA members, John O'Reilly and Thomas 'Ta' Power, were shot dead in the ambush but "Cueball" Torney and another leading member of the GHQ faction, Peter Stewart, survived with relatively minor injuries. Weldon was later arrested and questioned about the incident. The GHQ faction immediately began a counter-offensive.

GHQ faction member, Dessie O'Hare was born in County Armagh in 1958. Like "Mad Dog" he was on active service with an IRA unit at the age of sixteen. The youngster quickly acquired a reputation as one of the most ruthless killers produced by the Troubles. In 1979, he switched organisations and joined the INLA. He came to epitomise the organisation's lack of discipline and lethal unpredictability. O'Hare became a truly awesome killing machine. In one of his many atrocities he assassinated a part-time soldier in the notorious Ulster Defence Regiment (UDR), Margaret Hearst, in Keady, South Armagh. O'Hare shot the UDR woman several times, killing her instantly. As he left the scene he also fired a burst of bullets into the baby's cot, miraculously the child survived. Even by INLA standards, O'Hare was one of the worst killers to emerge from its stable of psychopaths.

Later in 1979 Gardaí arrested him just south of the border after a car crash. O'Hare and an associate had been chased into the South by the RUC while moving firearms. He was convicted of possession of a firearm and sentenced to nine years in Portlaoise prison. Described as a loner and general oddball he was a troublesome prisoner and made a number of foolhardy attempts to escape from one of Europe's most secure prisons.

At the time of his release in October 1986, O'Hare told Gardaí that he had become a pacifist after studying the works of Martin Luther King, Mahatma Gandhi and Owen Sheehy Skeffington. But his pacifism did not last long. On New Year's Eve 1986, he attacked a protestant neighbour in Ballymacauley, County Armagh. The neighbour, another part-time member of the Ulster Defence Regiment, was carrying a gun. Obviously out of killing practise O'Hare appeared nervous and wounded the UDR man after firing at point blank range. He did, however, manage to murder his target's seventy-two-year-old mother. Within days he was back to his old ways and up to his neck in the blood feud.

On February 4, 1987, as part of the GHQ faction's counter-attack, Dessie O'Hare abducted Army Council faction member Tony McCloskey from his Monaghan home. McCloskey was suspected of taking part in the Rosnaree attack. Based on first impressions Dessie O'Hare appeared to be a most unlikely killer. Soft-spoken and baby-faced he came across as an inoffensive, gentle soul who would be more at home running a crèche than an INLA unit. O'Hare used bolt cutters to cut off McCloskey's ear and some of his fingers. Then he and a female companion took turns pumping bullets into McCloskey's mutilated body. The man nicknamed the Border Fox would later tell the *Sunday Tribune* that he was happy to give McCloskey a hard death.

Another casualty of the blood feud was Mary McGlinchey, "Mad Dog's" wife. She was gunned down in February 1987, as she bathed her two young sons, in her home near Dundalk, County Louth. McGlinchey's killers shot her in a 'cross of bullets': hitting her once in the chest, once in the forehead and once in each eye, leaving the sign of the cross. O'Hare was blamed for the murder because of the savagery of the attack but he denied any involvement. It was later discovered that 'the cross of bullets' was the hallmark of a hit man closely associated with an IRA criminal family from South Armagh. Mary and Dominic McGlinchey had shot dead two smugglers, one of whom was a member of the IRA family. In the bloodshed that followed O'Hare personally killed another three members of the Army Council faction.

The 1987 feud ended with the ambush and murder of Gerry "Dr Death" Steenson and another man in Ballymurphy two months later on March 14, 1987. The bloody feud had claimed the lives of thirteen INLA members. Immediately following the feud "Cueball" Torney assumed control of the INLA but in the wake of the feud the INLA fell into a state of utter disarray and were almost defunct as a terrorist or criminal organisation. It fragmented into a number of different groups. Torney's opponents left to form up under a new flag of convenience, the Irish People's Liberation Organisation (IPLO). The IPLO eventually destroyed itself in another internal war in 1992.

Even by the INLA standards of depravity the McCloskey murder was a source of concern to "Cueball" Torney and his gang of killers. His GHQ faction held an inquiry into the death which by any standard was an utterly ludicrous action. At a kangaroo court one of O'Hare's representatives said that the account of the murder had been exaggerated. The GHQ mob let O'Hare off with a mild censure and no action was taken against him because they were afraid of the Border Fox.

Over the following eight months O'Hare embarked on a spiral of crime and violence. His gang robbed a string of banks in towns along the south of the border during which he opened fire on unarmed Gardaí. The Border Fox even robbed weapons from a Provo arms dump in South Armagh and attempted to murder Official Unionist MP Jim Nicholson. The Provos were concerned that O'Hare's erratic and unpredictable behaviour was jeopardising their own operations in the border area. They told the INLA that if they did not do something about O'Hare then the IRA killers would do it for them. On September 11, 1987, O'Hare was expelled from the organisation.

In the context of the INLA's erratic and disorganised nature the expulsion meant little. O'Hare continued to operate as before but he was angered by the sacking. He believed that he had personally won the internal feud for the GHQ faction and that this was his thanks. In keeping with the INLA's approach to 'à la carte' terrorism O'Hare renamed his unit The Irish Revolutionary Brigade. Intelligence filtering back from Republican circles was clear – Dessie O'Hare was a catastrophe waiting to happen.

O'Hare had made very little money from his armed robberies and he badly needed cash to run his Revolutionary Brigade. He began plotting a high-profile kidnap. Abduction had been employed as a fund raising tactic by the Provos on a number of occasions in the past but with limited success. There had been thirty-seven kidnap cases in the Republic in 1985 alone. The Border Fox reckoned he could do better than the Provos. However, in the run up to the kidnap drama O'Hare was showing all the signs of a man going completely out of control. When he suggested the kidnapping to several of his old INLA associates they wanted no part in what would surely be a chaotic crime and went into hiding. They were too terrified to refuse O'Hare to his face. Even the man who initially suggested the kidnap fell foul of the Border Fox. Jimmy McDaid, was a Dublin based INLA man who had served time with O'Hare in Portlaoise and was one of the few people with whom he had been friendly while inside. For some unexplained reason McDaid refused to participate in the kidnapping. On the morning of October 4 he was abducted by O'Hare and driven to the border where he was executed on the side of a road. McDaid's refusal to participate in the crime rendered him a traitor in O'Hare's eyes and there was no room for such loose ends.

Rapidly running out of friends and allies, the Border Fox was left to rely on a few loyal terrorists to carry out his plot. O'Hare's gang consisted of fellow INLA men Fergal Toal from Armagh and Eddie Hogan from Cork. Both men were, like O'Hare, violent, reckless thugs who had also served time with the Border Fox and he knew he could rely on them. Another member of the team was Toal's friend, Tony McNeill, a young militant Republican from Belfast. In the early 1980s, McNeill fled to Dublin amid fears that the police were going to kill him and he joined the INLA. McNeill in turn recruited the help of a forty-five-year-old barber called Gerry Wright from Parkgate Street in Dublin. Wright agreed to help organise safe houses in Dublin.

O'Hare eventually chose his target – Dr Austin Darragh, the wealthy owner of a medical research company based in Dublin. He was to be kidnapped from his south Dublin mansion on the night of October 13, 1987. But from the beginning O'Hare's plan was in disarray. Dr Darragh had not actually lived in the house for four years. Instead his daughter Marise and her husband, dentist Dr John O'Grady, lived there.

On the morning of the crime O'Hare and his gang discovered their mistake. They decided to kidnap John O'Grady instead. It was the beginning of a six-week drama during which the Border Fox and the police played a dangerous game of cat and mouse throughout the country. O'Hare demanded a ransom of IR£1.5 million. At one stage he personally chopped off the dentist's two little fingers and left them for his victim's family in an envelope behind a statue in Carlow Cathedral.

Eventually on November 5, 1987, detectives rescued John O'Grady from a house in Dublin. Toal, Hogan and McNeill were with the victim when the detectives arrived on a routine enquiry. O'Hare was away from the house arranging the collection of the ransom money. In the confusion that followed Eddie Hogan shot Detective Garda Martin O'Connor, seriously injuring him. The three kidnappers escaped but were later captured. O'Hare himself was arrested three weeks later on November 27 when he drove into an ambush set up by Irish Army snipers in County Kilkenny. O'Hare was seriously injured and his companion was killed in a hail of high velocity bullets. His survival was nothing short of extraordinary.

On April 13, 1988, the Border Fox and his gang were convicted of the O'Grady kidnapping in the Special Criminal Court in Dublin. O'Hare was given a total of forty years. Eddie Hogan also received a total of forty years for false imprisonment and the attempted murder of Detective Garda O'Connor. Fergal Toal was given twenty years for the kidnapping charge and a fifteen-year concurrent sentence for possession of a firearm with intent to endanger life. Tony McNeill was given fifteen years for kidnapping and possession of a firearm. Gerry Wright got seven years. Handing down sentence Mr Justice

Liam Hamilton described the crime as: "One of the most serious cases to come before the courts of this State."

After they were sentenced O'Hare made a ten-minute statement to the packed court. Standing and reading from typed sheets of paper O'Hare said: "I would like to state that full responsibility for the actions rest with me." O'Hare said that his three accomplices were "carrying out military orders in good faith" and Gerry Wright had been "hoodwinked" into helping them through "threat of death". The Border Fox paid tribute to Toal and Hogan's "...unfailing dedication to the cause of Irish unity." He continued: "My objective as a Republican militant was primarily to attack the free masonry, Unionist ruling classes in the Six Counties. When I was released from Portlaoise Prison I found the means to carry out my objectives deficient and I was forced to go to a source of great wealth in this country."

O'Hare said he made no apology that the source he went to was a " ...legalised drug peddler for mind control in the interests of international capitalism." His only regret he said was that he and his comrades could not fulfil the liberation of the country. He accused the Irish public of "cowardice" and of "an avaricious mentality" that supported British rule.

The most astonishing aspect of O'Hare's speech from the dock was his call to Republican terrorists to attack the Irish establishment "particularly the judiciary, members of the prison service, the Navy, the Army and the Gardaí for carrying out dirty work which will determine their fate in years to come. It is morally wrong for republicans to eschew retribution against figures in the South. It will always be justifiable and morally right for Irish men and women to slay those who collaborate with British rule".

O'Hare denounced the leaders of the Republican movement and called them "quasi-Republicans" and concluded: "Justice for the oppressed of Ireland can only come through the barrel of a gun. Victory to the universal enemies of Britain and especially victory to the Irish Revolutionary Brigade."

O'Hare and his gang gave clenched fist salutes before being led away in handcuffs to begin their sentences in Portlaoise. While in prison O'Hare completely disassociated himself from all other inmates, including members of the INLA, and for several years was incarcerated in isolation in the basement of the maximum security prison. But at the time of writing O'Hare and his INLA cronies have reunited behind bars and are actively campaigning for release under the terms of the Good Friday Agreement. O'Hare and his mob are again using the Republican flag of convenience to achieve their ends.

* * * *

In the period following the supergrass trials and the blood feuds, over thirty INLA members were murdered by former friends and associates. This statistic was all the more astounding for an organisation that, at its peak, had no more than one hundred and fifty active members. Battered and bloodied from the bitter internal war, the membership faded into the background to lick their collective wounds and regroup. But by the early 1990s the INLA's fortunes were about to change.

The INLA underwent a sinister revival in Dublin where it's so-called 'soldiers' again joined forces with organised crime. Members of the INLA and many of the erstwhile blaggers had discovered an even more lucrative industry – the drug trade. In the early- eighties drug barons, and INLA members, Weldon and Savage had shown the INLA how much money could be generated by controlling lucrative drug territories. Weldon and Savage had managed to continue to run their drug operation in the wake of the 1987 feud but in 1991 they hit a major problem. Ex-INLA member and an associate of Savage and Weldon, hairdresser Patrick "Teasy Weasy" McDonald was known as a hard-drinking thug who threw his weight around and stood on a lot of toes in the process. On Christmas week 1991 McDonald was working in his salon in the north inner-city when a gunman walked in and shot him six times with an automatic pistol – once in the head and five times in the body. Savage was forced to flee to Amsterdam within a few months of the McDonald murder. He later claimed he had to emigrate because the Gardaí had let it be known that he was their prime suspect in the case and an IRA hit team from South Armagh had agreed to assassinate him in revenge for McDonald's murder "for old time's sake". Michael Weldon did not stick around for too long either without his underworld pal. He too was on the IRA hit list after the "Teasy Weasy" murder. He was caught on the Canadian Border with a large quantity of US dollars which were believed to be the proceeds of drug trafficking. The money was confiscated and Weldon was deported. When he arrived back in Ireland, the Garda Special Branch arrested him when they found a fully loaded automatic pistol under the seat of his car as he drove through Crumlin. Weldon was released on bail after secretly promising to act as an informant for the Gardaí. A short time later he also fled to Amsterdam where he has remained to this day.

Since their departure to the European home of organised crime Savage and Weldon have become extremely wealthy international drug traffickers, with each running his own individual operation. Weldon features high on the American Drug Enforcement Agency's (DEA) target list because of his links with Colombian cocaine cartels. Despite his criminal and terrorist background Weldon managed to obtain a pilot's licence in the USA and is, at the time of writing, reputed to own his own aircraft which he uses to fly around the world organising drug deals.

Meanwhile with their gangland business partners, the INLA were enjoying a degree of prosperity. The organisation even made a few attempts to get back into the war. Originally from Belfast, INLA member Gerry Burns had typically fled to Dublin in the early-eighties to avoid the attentions of the RUC. In 1984, he had received a three year suspended sentence for possession of heroin and allowing his home in Blanchardstown, West Dublin, to be used for the distribution of the drug. Then in 1990, Gerry Burns, was caught by the Special Branch in Cork after taking possession of an arms cache smuggled in from other ex-patriot INLA members in France. A well-placed mole, on the run from the Irish police in Spain at the time, was secretly working for the Garda Intelligence Services in Dublin and tipped them off about the shipment. Burns was given a six-year sentence for his patriotic efforts.

A new younger breed of violent INLA men also readily embraced the new criminal relationship and the efforts to get back into 'the war'. Among them were Joseph Magee, Declan "Wacker" Duffy and Anthony "Fanta" Gorman – all of whom were from County Armagh. Magee, Duffy and Gorman were on the run from the British police who wanted them in connection with an INLA, so-called 'military', action in the UK. On April 13, 1992, they had been spotted in the vicinity of Liversage Street car park where British army recruiting Sergeant Michael Newman was murdered. The soldier had just left his office and was walking towards his car when two men walked up to him. One of them produced a handgun and shot Sergeant Newman in the head at point blank range. The pair ran to a waiting getaway car driven by the third member of the killer gang.

Within hours of the incident Derbyshire police took the unprecedented step of identifying the three men they believed were responsible for the attack – Magee, Duffy and Gorman. The officer heading the investigation, Assistant Chief Constable Don Dovaston, issued detailed descriptions of the three INLA men and warned the public not to tackle them. "These men are considered to be dangerous," he told the media.

Magee, aged twenty-six, was the oldest member of the team with the most extensive record for terrorist-related crime. He had accumulated fourteen convictions in Northern Ireland, including two for possession of firearms. One of those convictions related to the possession of a handgun and ammunition when he was seventeen. Magee was spared involvement in the 1987 feud when he was jailed for possession of firearms. It was also reported that he had a limp that he'd received as the result of a Provo punishment shooting.

Gorman, who was aged twenty-two at the time, had no terror-related convictions but was known to the security services as an active member of the INLA. Nineteen-year-old Declan "Wacker" Duffy was the youngest of the three. The thug would later boast to a *Sunday World* reporter that he preferred shooting people in the head rather than the kneecaps. He already had a number of convictions including one for an armed robbery using an imitation firearm in Armagh. Duffy came from a staunchly republican background with strong links to the Provos and Sinn Féin. However Duffy's older brother Kevin had opted to join the INLA and had been a member of Dessie O'Hare's unit during the 1987 feud. He was tortured and killed on March 22, 1987 in retaliation for the McCloskey murder. His brother's death did nothing to deter Declan

Duffy and he joined the organisation soon afterwards.

Following the Newman murder the three young INLA members went into hiding in Dublin. The thirty-year-old self-appointed leader of the so-called Dublin Brigade, Michael Kenny from Sandyford, South Dublin, ensured that his new 'recruits' were looked after. The cold-blooded murder had given the organisation a much needed publicity boost in Britain and Ireland. Now considered heroes among their comrades in the criminal underworld, the three thugs exploited their reputations as hardened terrorists.

Their desperado reputations were further enhanced when detectives investigating a series of armed robberies carried out by the INLA in Limerick arrested Magee on January 9, 1993. Magee had been placed under surveillance after being spotted making contact with members of the notorious Keane gang. (*See Chapter 9*.) He was arrested boarding a train for Dublin and held in custody. He was initially charged under the Offences Against the State legislation for refusing to give his name when requested to do so.

At the same time the police in Derbyshire obtained a magistrate's warrant for Magee's arrest and extradition for murder. Members of the investigation team immediately flew to Limerick. On January 14, Magee was formally arrested on foot of the extradition warrant and a District Judge ordered that he be brought back to England. The INLA man appealed the decision and began a lengthy High Court challenge to the order. While the challenge was pending he was remanded in custody. Some months later Sergeant Mark Cheatham of the Derbyshire police told a High Court bail hearing that Magee had been clearly identified by an eyewitness as one of Sgt. Newman's attackers. The officer said there was also fingerprint evidence linking Magee with the getaway vehicle.

Meanwhile Anthony "Fanta" Gorman was also arrested on foot of a similar extradition warrant and was remanded in custody to Portlaoise prison pending a High Court challenge. In January 1994 Magee's appeal was heard in the High Court in Dublin. The INLA man's legal team argued that the charge for which his extradition was being sought fell into the category of a political offence. Under Irish extradition law a person could not be extradited for a politically motivated offence. His lawyers also argued that due to widespread publicity in Britain his client would not get a fair trial. The English press had referred to Magee as "evil", a "mad dog" and a "gun psycho".

On February 14, 1994, Mr Justice Feargus Flood upheld Magee's Appeal stating that Sgt Newman's death had been a political assassination. He also ruled that Magee would not get a fair trial due to the media coverage of the case. After his release Magee told reporters that he would be staying in Dublin and could not go home to the North. A month later on March 13, Anthony "Fanta" Gorman was also freed by the District Court at a remand hearing when the Attorney General offered no evidence against the INLA man in relation to the extradition case. It had been decided that there was no point going through the motions of a High Court Appeal as the case was identical to Magee's. Gorman at first appeared confused by the result and was on his way back to the cells when police told him he was free to go. He gave a clenched fist salute and cheered: "Let's go."

The success of Magee and Gorman in fighting the extradition orders had given the INLA another major morale boost. Together with Duffy, who was now also off the hook, they had gained invaluable street credibility for the INLA. "Wacker" Duffy who would later become another self-appointed INLA Dublin 'commander' had become Michael Kenny's sidekick since his arrival in Dublin and was living with Kenny's niece. The three terrorists were now men you didn't meddle with. People would have to show the new gangsters on the block respect.

Fresh from their extradition victory the INLA forged a relationship with a new criminal friend and benefactor. John Joseph Gilligan was released from Portlaoise prison in September 1993 with an ambitious plan to become the country's most powerful godfather. By 1994, he was ready to put that plan into practice and an essential part of the plan included his friends in the INLA.

In the late 1980s and 1990s the E1 wing in Portlaoise became organised crime's premier training academy. The wing accommodated the elite of Ireland's criminal hierarchy, including the Dessie O'Hare gang. Gilligan used his time inside to nurture the sort of contacts necessary to run a burgeoning drug 'business' on the outside. He established friendships with individual members of the INLA, particularly Fergal Toal who was serving his time on E1 for the O'Grady kidnap and still had a lot of influence with his old INLA cronies in Dublin and Belfast. Another INLA member who would feature in Gilligan's plan for gangland dominance was Gerry Burns. Burns had remained a loyal 'soldier' and was still serving his six-year sentence for smuggling arms in the 1990s. Gilligan was fully aware of the need to have friends with the know-how and violent tendencies of the INLA. They would be formidable allies in a mutually beneficial relationship.

Also resident on the wing was Patrick "Dutchie" Holland who was serving a sentence for possession of explosives. A convicted armed robber and suspected hit man, he was a close friend of Gilligan. Through the years "Dutchie" had 'worked' with members of the INLA and had plenty of important contacts on both sides of the prison walls. Gilligan even managed to strike up a friendship with the normally aloof Border Fox.

On the outside Gilligan's partner in his new criminal venture was John Traynor, a smooth-talking, devious con man, who had begun associating with the INLA as far back as the 1980s. Traynor, known in the media as "the Coach", was gangland's undisputed king of the fixers. For several years Traynor had been an essential cog in Martin Cahill's gang. He was Cahill's adviser on all matters criminal: the Irish underworld's equivalent of a Mafia "consiglieri". Traynor initiated and helped mastermind several of the General's most spectacular crimes, including the 1983 O'Connor's jewellery heist.

After Gilligan's release from prison in September 1993, Traynor helped to establish contact with European drug traffickers and he also secured a large cash loan of around IR£600,000 from the General to finance the first drug shipments. At the same time "the Coach" ensured a smooth working relationship with the INLA, acting as a liaison between the Gilligan gang and INLA boss Michael Kenny and his sidekick Declan "Wacker" Duffy. Kenny would meet with Traynor and Gilligan on an almost daily basis. After his release Gilligan regularly visited Fergal Toal and the other INLA members in Portlaoise and lodged sums of money to their prison accounts to enable them to buy snacks, cigarettes and clothes. But "the Coach" reckoned that he was closer to the terror group than his partner. He once told his Garda handler that if it came to a row between himself and Gilligan then the INLA would back him. Whichever one of them was closer the result was the same – one of gangland's most unholy alliances had been formed.

Shortly after his release in 1993 Gilligan and Traynor had come into possession of a large number of stolen bank drafts and also stolen Garda pay cheques. The INLA, through John Bolger, a criminal from Crumlin, organised a system of laundering the valuable pieces of paper throughout the country. Bolger, the thirty-one-year-old father of three young children, was a hard drinking gambler who lived off the coat tails of bigger gangsters but he was well connected. He and his wife Jean were good friends with John and Geraldine Gilligan. He was also involved with the INLA, although he was not a member of the organisation. Bolger regularly took part in various fraud scams and robberies with the INLA and provided safe houses for their members who were on the run from the authorities. He socialised with Kenny's thugs and loved the respect and clout it brought him. The INLA's fearsome reputation ensured that the dangers of anyone informing to the police about the bank draft scam had greatly diminished. It proved to be a lucrative scam and everyone was earning from it. Bolger and his INLA pals also had another scam on the side. Bolger had come into possession of a key to open post boxes. The gang would simply open the boxes and steal envelopes containing cheques and bank drafts. Everyone was a winner.

While the INLA terrorists and Bolger were happily getting into bed with Gilligan and Traynor, their relationship with the General was not quite as amicable. Cahill disliked paramilitaries with whom he had a long and acrimonious relationship. The potentially bloody aftermath of the O'Connor's heist in 1983 was a typical example of Cahill's method of dealing with the terrorists. Whatever about his relationship with the Provos, Cahill's trouble with the INLA began in 1992 when a key member of Cahill's gang was charged with raping his own daughter. Despite the General's revulsion for his henchman's crime Cahill was determined that the matter would not be dealt with in the courts. In the General's warped logic the terrified teenager had committed a greater crime by co-operating with the police. Three weeks after the gangster was charged with rape, Cahill approached the girl as she walked along the street. He offered the child IR£20,000 in cash and a new home if she'd drop the charges. Her father, Cahill suggested, would be punished and would never go near her again. She refused the offer. Cahill decided to turn up the heat.

John Bolger, who was close to the incest victim and her family, decided to step in and protect her from the General. In the spring of 1993, Martin Cahill approached Bolger to discuss the problem. He invited Bolger to take a trip in a van along with the girl's father. Bolger, Cahill and the rapist had all known each other for a long time. Cahill and the rapist had been Bolger's friends and he had taken part in numerous 'strokes' (crimes) with them. The General calculated that Bolger's need for cash to back horses would help him to reconsider his position in relation to the victim, whom Cahill had labelled a "tout" (informant). He offered Bolger IR£10,000 in cash as an incentive if he would help to convince the girl to keep her mouth shut and drop the case. Uncharacteristically, Bolger told Cahill and the rapist to fuck off and got out of the van.

The General had another face-to-face meeting with Bolger a few weeks later. In the meantime Bolger had asked his pals in the INLA for help and they had agreed to give it. Unknown to Cahill, their meeting was being monitored by one of Kenny's henchmen who carried a nine-millimetre pistol under his jacket. Again Bolger refused to try to convince the child to drop her complaint. Cahill lost his cool and leaned into Bolger's face: "What are you goin' to do about the tout? That little bitch who is goin' to court with (criminal's name). You shouldn't have a tout like that in yer house," Cahill snarled at Bolger and stormed out.

In the weeks that followed Cahill's men intimidated Bolger and his family. Slogans were daubed on the walls outside his home. Finally the INLA's Dublin godfather Michael Kenny and his henchmen decided to visit Cahill at his home in Cowper Downs, in Rathmines, south Dublin. They told him that if the intimidation did not stop there would be "major problems". Following the INLA intervention Cahill ceased the intimidation, which surprised a lot of people none more so than Kenny and his mob. Cahill's apparent capitulation added to their growing sense of confidence and invincibility.

Traynor managed to stay out of the row and continued to carry stories from one side to the other. Gilligan had sided with Bolger in the ongoing row but he hadn't shared this information with the General. After all Cahill had agreed to invest over half a million pounds in Gilligan's new Crime Inc.

Bolger in particular was enjoying his new-found wealth and status in the underworld. Like Gilligan, he considered the INLA to be his own personal police force and if anyone wanted to fuck with him then they would be answerable to the thugs and thieves in the "movement". People in the organisation did not like the way Bolger seemed to have Kenny and the INLA working for him.

But then on the night of July 21, 1994, it all went tragically wrong for Bolger. He went drinking in the Glimmerman pub beside Harold's Cross Bridge in south Dublin. Included in the company were Michael Kenny and INLA hoods Richard "Ricky" Tobin and Robert "Bobby" Tohill. Tohill and Tobin were involved in the scams with Bolger and Kenny.

Tohill, a former member of the IRA from Belfast, who had switched sides to join the INLA was no stranger to trouble himself. A self-confessed killer he had served five years in a Northern prison for his role in the murder of a UDR soldier in 1981. After his release he took part in the 1987 feud during which he was shot and injured. Tohill then moved to live in Cashel Avenue in Crumlin in 1990. Forty-two-year old Ricky Tobin from County Down also lived in Crumlin. He was a fisherman and an infantry soldier in the Irish Army before he embarked on an inauspicious carer in terrorism.

Around 2am the following morning, as the gangsters were leaving the pub, a drunken row broke out about cash that was missing from the stolen bank drafts scam. Threats and accusations were exchanged as Bolger and Kenny got into a car and began to drive away from Tobin and Tohill. As they left the scene Tobin produced a semi-automatic rifle and shot at the car. Bolger and Kenny were both injured in the attack. John Bolger died from a gunshot wound to the chest. Kenny, who was not seriously wounded, was later released from hospital.

Detectives attached to Kevin Street Garda Station arrested Tohill and Tobin. While being questioned on July 24, Tobin told investigators: "It was him or me – I had to do it." He later retracted the comment and said: "All I'm saying now is that I was there and I had a gun." Tobin was subsequently charged with Bolger's murder but skipped bail and moved to England.

In an interview with the *Sunday World* in September 2003, Tohill admitted that the row that led to Bolger's death was about the misappropriation of money. Said Tohill: "I didn't know Gilligan at the time and I didn't know he was running the scam. It was a major money-making racket, only the money was going into people's pockets, not up North to the leadership. There was very little money going up North and I had a serious problem with that. I had a dispute with the Dublin CO [Kenny] and a man called John Bolger was shot dead because of it."

Following Bolger's murder there was consternation among the INLA in Dublin and Kenny ordered punishment for Tohill and Tobin. Gilligan also demanded action be taken over his friend's senseless murder. It was decided that Tobin would be executed for the murder and Tohill knee-capped as he'd had a lesser roll in the crime. Duffy wanted to kill both of them but he was overruled. In any event Tobin had disappeared.

On August 16, Bobby Tohill's comrades summoned him to a 'court martial'. If he didn't turn up he was a dead man. Duffy had ordered him to be outside Kiltalawn Shopping Centre in Jobstown, Tallaght at 12.30am. Agreeing to take his medicine Tohill went drinking for most of the day in the hope that the alcohol would lessen the pain of the bullets. When he arrived "Wacker" Duffy shot him once in the left knee and twice in the right. A few months later, in an interview with the *Sunday World*, Duffy actually bragged about the incident.

"If I had my way I would have shot him [Tohill] in the head. When we take a vote to shoot someone I always vote for the headshot for one simple reason – I couldn't bear the screaming. But I am often overruled. If I am doing a leg shot I make sure the man never walks again. It is not just the case of putting one bullet behind the knee. I always fire about nine, four into one leg and five into the other. It's hard for anybody to get over that," the thug boasted.

Bobby Tohill survived the attack. He has since claimed that he went looking for Duffy afterwards with the intention of 'executing' him. Tohill said that it was while he was hunting Duffy down that he was caught with a gun and jailed for five years. In reality Tohill had become an alcoholic.

Ricky Tobin was eventually tracked down by detectives and extradited from England in December 1999. In 2001, the Special Criminal Court jailed Tobin for five years after he pleaded guilty to the lesser charge of possessing a firearm for an unlawful purpose on the night of Bolger's murder.

By the time of John Bolger's death Martin Cahill had less than a month to live. The short-tempered, unpredictable gangster had made a lot of enemies over the years. The IRA suspected that Cahill had helped the Loyalists organise a bomb attack on a Sinn Féin fund-raising function in a Dublin pub in May 1994. At the same time the General also found himself in another conflict with the INLA. Their quarrel had nothing to do with bomb attacks. In July 1994, one of Cahill's relatives was evicted from a Dublin Corporation flat where she had been squatting for over a year. The flat had been assigned to "Wacker" Duffy's INLA associate Joseph Magee who intended moving in. The General was having none of it. Following a number of threats Cahill burned the flat down to ensure that no one could live in it. Kenny and his troops decided that it was time Cahill met his maker.

At the same time the INLA's de facto boss, John Gilligan, was thinking in the same way. Cahill had been putting the squeeze on him for repayment of his IR£600,000 loan and for a slice of the profits from Gilligan's growing drug trade. As the crisis deepened John Traynor managed to stay out of the row although, like Gilligan, Cahill's death would solve a lot of his problems too. Gilligan met with his pals in the INLA and discussed ending the General's life. The IRA had also had enough of Cahill's behaviour. Everyone was in agreement that he had to go.

On the afternoon of August 18, 1994, an IRA hit man, armed with a .357 Magnum revolver, shot Cahill as he stopped his car in Ranelagh, south Dublin. It was the most controversial and highly publicised murder of a gangster ever in the history of Irish crime. Unlike any other gangland execution there was an extraordinary rush to claim responsibility for the killing, as if it was a badge of honour. Within minutes of the fatal shots being fired the INLA called a local radio station. Using a recognised code word the caller said that the INLA had carried out the attack. Then, a few hours later, the Provos contacted a Dublin newsroom saying that one of their volunteers had dispatched Ireland's public enemy number one. Again using a recognised code word the Provos claimed that it was Cahill's " ...involvement with and assistance to pro-British death squads which forced us to act." An hour after that call was received the INLA were back on the phone again. This time, in a bizarre twist, they denied any involvement in the murder. Even stranger was their threat to murder "anyone who claims it was us". What was so perplexing about the INLA's denial was their effort to ensure that there was no doubt in anyone's mind that the Provos had done the evil deed.

On the evening after the Cahill hit, INLA's "Wacker" Duffy, also known in Dublin as "Northern Seanie", contacted the *Sunday World* reiterating the fact that his organisation had not been involved. It looked like the INLA were terrified of stealing the Provos' thunder. Two days after the murder the Provos again contacted the media, giving more details about the attack to dispel any lingering doubts about who had murdered Cahill.

In the months following the murder the Provos interviewed several terrified crime figures in Dublin. Many of them were hit for "contributions to the movement". In the end the Provos much-talked about 'investigations' came to absolutely nothing. Organised crime continued to prosper and thrive. John Gilligan, Traynor and the INLA probably did better than anyone else. By the end of 1994 they were part of the most powerful criminal organisation in the country. The future was beginning to look good for the INLA.

Gilligan and his mob had begun to import large amounts of high-powered weapons with their drug shipments, many of which they handed over to the INLA. The gang had been bringing in deadly handguns and Agram machine pistols that were particularly suitable for street assassinations. The gang's weapon shipments were more secure than the INLA's own supply lines, which were prone to capture thanks to the many informants working for the police. Gilligan and Traynor also supplied "Wacker" Duffy and his gang with cannabis at knockdown prices. They sold it in the Tallaght area of west Dublin which they had established as their exclusive turf. Another associate of the INLA was William Arthur Jordan from Tallaght, who was also a customer of the Gilligan gang. Jordan, with the help of the INLA, controlled one of the largest cocaine dealing gangs in the country. Jordan was also connected with the notorious Limerick crime gang headed by brothers Christy and Kieran Keane. (*See Chapter 9.*)

In Spring 1995, Duffy and his INLA cronies were called in to threaten members of the General's family after they tried to put pressure on John Traynor for money. The family believed that "the Coach" still had a large amount of the General's loot and they wanted it back. Faced with the prospect of a confrontation with the paramilitaries the Cahills backed down. As a compromise, however, Traynor bought a chip shop for Cahill's widow.

At the same time the INLA now had sufficient funds and the right contacts to purchase new firearms to resurrect their murder campaign in the North. In 1995, the Dublin Brigade initiated a plan to procure a haul consisting of two high-powered FN assault rifles, two Kalashnikov rifles, two US M-3 sub-machine guns, twenty Browning automatic pistols and 2,500 rounds of ammunition. On April 4, 1995, members of the Garda National Surveillance Unit (GNSU), backed up by the heavily armed Emergency Response Unit (ERU), watched the weapons being collected in Dublin by four INLA members. The INLA had been betrayed once again by a mole working for the Special Branch.

Anthony "Fanta" Gorman, the man who had beaten extradition to Britain, the 'self-appointed' INLA leader himself, Hugh "Cueball" Torney, Dessie McCleery from Lurgan and Sean Braniff from County Down collected the weapons in a van and a car. As the INLA men drove towards Balbriggan, North County Dublin, en route to the Border, the ERU moved in. The elite squad used stun grenades to disorientate the occupants as they swooped on the two vehicles. The terrorists found themselves handcuffed and lying face down on the roadway within seconds. They were later brought before the Special Criminal Court and charged with possession of firearms with intent to endanger life. The arrests were a spectacular victory for the police as they had netted the leader of the organisation and his closest henchmen.

At a subsequent remand hearing in the case "Cueball" Torney sent shock waves through the organisation when he declared an INLA ceasefire from the dock of the Special Criminal Court. This was in total violation of 'army regulations'. In his efforts to save his own skin and effect a plea bargain, "Cueball" Torney had humiliated the rabble he was supposed to be leading. The murderous psychopath, who had already presided over so many INLA feuds, had succeeded in setting the scene for another bloodbath.

It didn't take long for the trouble to start again. "Cueball" Torney's control began to slip after the Balbriggan arrest. He then spent nine months in custody in Portlaoise before being granted bail. While inside "Cueball" Torney's trusted lieutenant, Gino Gallagher, declared himself the new 'Chief of Staff' of the INLA. The Gallagher faction deposed Torney on the grounds that he had broken the organisation's 'regulations' with his declaration of a ceasefire. Most of the old GHQ faction remained loyal to "Cueball". Within days of his release from Portlaoise on bail Torney went on the run.

On January 30, 1996, the first shots in the new feud were fired when Gallagher was gunned down while waiting to sign for his unemployment benefit at the Falls Road Labour Exchange. The Gallagher faction retaliated with an attack on the home of one of "Cueball" Torney's associates. The conflict reached new depths when the intended target's nine-year-old sister, Barbara McAlorum, was shot dead as the reckless gunmen deliberately sprayed the front room of the house with automatic fire. That atrocity was followed with the murder in May 1996 of Dessie McCleery, who had also been charged with the Balbriggan arms seizure and had skipped bail with "Cueball" Torney. In the Special Criminal Court on June 14, Sean Braniff and "Fanta" Gorman pleaded guilty to having firearms and ammunition for an unlawful purpose at Balbriggan. Both men were acquitted of the more serious charge of possession of firearms with intent to endanger life. Braniff was sentenced to seven years and Gorman was jailed for five years.

Twelve days later John Gilligan's henchmen murdered journalist Veronica Guerin. The horrific murder led to an unprecedented wave of public outrage and revulsion. The crime also led to the most extensive criminal investigation ever seen in Ireland. As a consequence of that investigation the unholy alliance between the INLA and the Gilligan gang would finally be exposed. In the meantime instead of keeping their heads down the terrorists decided to exploit the palpable sense of public fear. "Wacker" Duffy and his pals staged an extraordinary publicity stunt that was supposedly directed against the drug gangs.

On August 1, 1996, just over a month after the atrocity, Duffy contacted *Sunday World* reporter Mike McNiffe and invited him and a photographer to a meeting that night at the Penny Black pub near Tymon Park in East Tallaght. Duffy told the reporter that a number of concerned residents had come together to take action against the drug dealers. When he met the *Sunday World* men Duffy stressed that the 'residents' they were about to meet had nothing to do with the INLA. They were simply a "group of concerned citizens" who had "taken enough" from the drug dealers plying their trade in the area.

"Wacker" Duffy brought the men through a darkened house and out across a six-foot garden wall. He led them through a warren of alleys and then told them to stop. "These people are with me now, are you ready?" Duffy whispered into a mobile phone. The three men then climbed another garden wall and went through a back door of another darkened house. Upstairs they were led into a brightly lit room where six men, wearing balaclavas, were waiting. Three of the men sat at a small table where two automatic handguns were laid out with ammunition clips. The scene had all been perfectly choreographed for maximum effect. It was a copy of similar press conferences orchestrated by Northern paramilitary groups through the years.

One of "Wacker" Duffy's men, who had a strong Dublin accent, read a prepared statement. It read: "East Tallaght Against Heroin, dated August 1, 1996. We are hereby serving notice on heroin dealers in this area. They must desist immediately from their activities. Failure to do so will be met with swift and direct action. Any attempt to intimidate or threaten residents against drugs in the east Tallaght area will be met with prompt and harsh action."

A man with a northern accent then answered questions from Mike McNiffe while the photographer took pictures. He told the reporter: "This is an ongoing matter. We stood back for so long that people were threatened by the dealers. We know who they are. They know who they are. If they want to come forward, they know the sources to go to. They have to stop their dealing, otherwise action will be taken against them. If they don't leave the area they will be dealt with. A lot of the kids here are on heroin. It has become so cheap. There is hash available and ecstasy is fairly big. The kids are using heroin to come down off the ecstasy. They smoke it and soon they end up injecting it." When asked did they intend to shoot the dealers the 'citizen' curtly replied: "We have the weapons and we will use them. We have their names. We will not get the wrong people. That's the end of our statement." Duffy led the *Sunday World* men back to the main street.

The following weekend the *Sunday World* ran the story. It sent a chill down the spine of every drug dealer in south Dublin except, of course, the INLA drug dealers posing in the photographs. It was an extraordinary publicity stunt designed to maximise the public's sense of fear after the Guerin murder. In reality "Wacker" Duffy and his pals were reaffirming John Gilligan's supremacy. Anyone involved in the drug trade in the west of the city knew exactly who was in the *Sunday World* pictures. If they didn't then the INLA thugs made sure they found out. Several scared drug dealers made 'contributions' to the INLA's 'cause' and no one dared venture into the areas controlled by the likes of Jordan's drug gang. The 'anti-drug' activists in the INLA were also involved in providing armed back up to both the Jordan and Keane gangs during various gangland feuds. In an even more cynical stunt the terrorists began collecting money from thousands of houses to help fund the 'anti drugs' campaign.

The publication of the story in the *Sunday World* was regrettable. On the surface it may have been seen as a worthy story but behind the scenes the INLA had blatantly manipulated the newspaper and pulled off a major publicity coup that only strengthened their position. The INLA then added insult to injury when an official circular from their political wing, the Irish Republican Socialist Party (IRSP), declared that Veronica Guerin had effectively got what she deserved. They also sent a direct threat to other crime journalists in the country, stating that they would receive the same treatment.

But within weeks, despite these scare tactics, the relationship between the INLA thugs and the Gilligan gang began to emerge. When this writer reported the story in the *Sunday World* "Wacker" Duffy's response was to issue threats. But by that stage the man heading the Guerin murder investigation, Assistant Commissioner Tony Hickey, had ordered a major operation to target the INLA in Dublin. It was the first time that the organisation and its links to organised crime had been placed under serious scrutiny. By late September 1996 the investigation team had compiled an extensive dossier on the organisation. In a series of dawn swoops over a dozen of the INLA thugs, including "Wacker" Duffy, Joeseph Magee, and Michael Kenny, the INLA Dublin 'Commander', were rounded up for questioning. Homes were searched and girlfriends and wives were also arrested. The dramatic swoop gleaned plenty of useful results. Practically everyone of those arrested gave valuable information.

In the meantime on September 3, 1996, Hugh "Cueball" Torney's reign of terror finally came to an end when a former comrade in Lurgan blasted him to death. One local Belfast wit remarked that the "Cueball" had finally been pocketed! Coincidentally Torney's death provided further evidence of the relationship between Gilligan and the terrorists. Police believed that the weapon, a lethal machine pistol, had been smuggled into the country with shipments of Gilligan's drugs and handed over to his paramilitary pals.

In the absence of their criminal benefactors – Gilligan was in custody in London from October 1996 and Traynor was in hiding in Spain – the INLA carried out armed robberies to boost their income. On June 4, 1997 four Tallaght based members of the gang Denis Thompson, Thomas Price, John Morris and Peter Maguire held up the Newspread newspaper distributor's warehouse in Inchicore, West Dublin. All four terrorists had been involved in the *Sunday World* publicity stunt and they had also been questioned about the Guerin murder. Armed Garda units were staking out the area after receiving information that the INLA was planning a robbery. Shortly after 11am seven officers attached to the National Bureau of Criminal Investigation (NBCI) challenged the robbers as they left the warehouse carrying a bag containing IR£880 in cash.

When the officers ordered the four men to drop their weapons John Morris pointed a .22 pistol at them and they opened fire. Three of the detectives fired a total of seven shots at the INLA man. He died instantly and the rest of the gang surrendered. It later transpired that Morris's pistol was not loaded but the officers had no way of knowing that. Morris was given a military style funeral during which mourners were told that he and his fellow gangsters had been on 'active service' when he was killed. They were told Morris had been engaged in " …a struggle against British imperialism and Irish capitalism". The IRSP made a statement claiming Morris had been executed and that his death would be avenged. As a result of the threats the officers involved in the shooting were allowed to testify from behind protective screens at Morris's Inquest. Their identities were also withheld. The Morris family claimed that there had been a cover-up and made an unsuccessful application in the High Court to have the officers identified. The rest of the gang subsequently pleaded guilty to robbery and possession of firearms. Peter Maguire was jailed for four years while Thompson and Price each received seven years with the last five suspended.

The organisation's run of bad luck was set to continue. On August 1, 1997, as part of their ongoing investigation into the INLA's involvement in crime, Michael Kenny and INLA member Christopher Magee were arrested in possession of two Walther PPK semi-automatic pistols, two silencers and thirty rounds of ammunition. It was suspected that the weapons had come from Traynor and Gilligan. Three years later Kenny and Magee were each jailed for five years by the Special Criminal Court after pleading guilty to the gun charges.

Old rivalries and feuds also continued to occupy the minds of the organisation's armed thugs. On the night of June 16, 1998, at 11.15pm, twenty-eight-year-old Belfast man Paul "Geek" Donnelly locked his small supermarket at Rathmines in south Dublin. Born in Belfast in 1960, Donnelly was known to the RUC as an active member of the IRA. At one stage he was an IRA training officer. In March 1979, he was convicted at Belfast Crown Court with possession of a firearm and explosives and jailed for three years. While in prison he changed sides and joined the ranks of the INLA and was closely associated with Hugh "Cueball" Torney. In August 1983, he was arrested after a bomb attack in Belfast and subsequently convicted on the word of "supergrass" Harry Kirkpatrick. He was released from prison with the other INLA members implicated in 1986 when the supergrass system was found to be unsafe. He then switched sides again and joined with Gerry "Dr Death" Steenson's so-called Army Council faction and was a central player in the ruthless 1987 feud. In March 1989, he was charged with murder, attempted murder and possession of firearms, following an incident on the Shankill Road in which five people were shot and injured. One person died. In September of the same year however the Crown Prosecution Service dropped the charges. In December 1991, he was again on the RUC's wanted list following the murder of a snooker hall manager. In early 1992 "Geek" moved to live in Dublin. He was closely associated with Tommy Savage and Michael Weldon and Garda intelligence were aware that he had regularly travelled to Amsterdam to meet his two former associates in relation to drug trafficking. He was also closely associated with several major criminals and drug dealers in Dublin.

"Geek" Donnelly walked to his luxury apartment at the Rathmines Town Centre. As he went under the archway into his apartment block he was confronted by two masked men, "Wacker" Duffy and Joe Magee. They had been lying in wait for him. Donnelly made a run for it when he saw Duffy pointing a sawn-off shotgun at him. Duffy fired a shot but it missed the shop owner. Donnelly ran through bushes in a garden beside the complex. As he did so a second shot was fired and this time hit Donnelly in the back, seriously injuring him. The INLA target managed to run around the apartment block. Duffy and Magee then made a run for it, escaping over a wall into an adjoining cricket ground. The two thugs went to a waiting stolen getaway car, which was later abandoned and set on fire at Belgrave Road, a few hundred yards away.

Donnelly had a hole in his back from the gunshot wound, which had punctured both of his lungs. As he was being brought by ambulance to hospital the injured man told Gardaí that, "Joe Magee and his friend from Tallaght" had shot him. Paul "Geek" Donnelly had become another victim of an INLA feud.

Donnelly later admitted to detectives that he had been a member of the INLA and IPLO and claimed he had left the organisation in 1992 but that he still had contacts there. Prior to the shooting incident Magee, who had been an associate of Donnelly, warned him that "bad people" were watching. Donnelly claimed that this was a veiled threat, and was an attempt by Magee to extort money from him.

Investigators later said that they were satisfied the attack had been the result of a row over money. After his release from hospital Donnelly positively identified Declan "Wacker" Duffy as the man who shot him and also Magee as his accomplice. A number of other witnesses also picked out Duffy from an identity parade. Donnelly later made a number of statements and said he was prepared to testify against his attackers in court. A file was prepared for the Director of Public Prosecutions recommending that the two INLA men be charged with possession of a firearm with intent to endanger life, causing serious harm to Donnelly and with membership of the INLA. The case, however, did not proceed and no charges were preferred after "Geek" Donnelly left Dublin in 1999. He is believed to have moved to live permanently in Amsterdam where he still associates with Weldon and Savage. Tommy Savage's own run of luck finally ran out a few years later, when Dutch police arrested him in January 2004, on foot of a Greek arrest warrant. It was in connection with a four tonne shipment of cannabis with a street value of €50 million that had been seized in Athens back in 1997. Savage was arrested at the sleazy De Harmonie hotel he ran on Prinsengracht in the heart of Amsterdam's red light district. He faces a potential twenty-year jail sentence. He was released on bail as he fought the extradition order. In a newspaper interview in May 2004, the Zombie claimed that he had been fleeced for two million Euro by other criminals and had been set up by the Gilligan gang. He ranted: "You never know what's going to fucking happen next. I've applied to see a psychiatrist because I'm being driven fucking mad. This is fucking torture. I'm being persecuted by people who want to get rid of me."

In any event Savage didn't hang around for long after he was released on bail. He opted to join his many old friends in Alicante in Spain where he was reportedly spotted in October 2004.

Magee and Duffy had had a close call with the "Geek" Donnelly attack. Detectives believed they had a strong case against the INLA men, based on Donnelly's testimony and independent witnesses.

In August 1998, less than two months after the gun attack, the IRSP announced an INLA ceasefire. The organisation's words were as hollow as their campaign against the drug scourge in Dublin. The declaration was intended to distance the INLA and IRSP from the worst outrage in the history of the Northern Ireland Troubles. The announcement came within days of the Omagh bomb atrocity in County Tyrone in which twenty-nine people died. The attack was the work of the Real IRA, a renegade Republican group opposed to the Good Friday Agreement and the cessation of violence. The INLA/IRSP wanted to refute speculation that they were supporting the Real IRA in the continuation of the war. Secretly of course, they did support them with INLA members joining with the Real IRA to take part in various crimes.

A year later, in August 1999, the INLA declared that their war was officially over. By 1999, several members of the organisation including Michael Kenny, "Wacker" Duffy and Joe Magee had either been charged with serious offences or were expecting to be charged. If their crimes were politicised then, in return for their new love for peace, the INLA hoods could look forward to lighter sentences and early releases. At the same time the INLA and IRSP in Dublin began campaigning for the release of Dessie O'Hare under the terms of the Good Friday Agreement. Gerry Burns, who had been released early from prison in 1995 as part of the peace process, spearheaded the campaign. Burns would later claim that he had not really benefited from the peace process: he was due for release three weeks later. For several months Burns protested outside Taoiseach Bertie Ahern's constituency office in Drumcondra. In his capacity as a representative of the IRSP he also attended a number of meetings with Mr Ahern and his advisors to discuss the INLA's involvement in the peace process and the release of O'Hare. The IRSP also negotiated and received a Government grant of IR£60,000 to set up a party office in Parnell Square in Dublin. But secretly Burns was now the commander of the INLA's Dublin Brigade and had begun a vigorous recruitment campaign. He even organised a recruitment video to show potential 'soldiers' how attractive and exciting life could be fighting for the illustrious 'cause'. At the same time the organisation's involvement in criminal scams continued unabated.

But the INLA's duplicity and lies were about to be exposed – in the night of the Ballymount Bloodbath.

Four

The Ballymount Bloodbath

By the late 1990s, the INLA's quest for personal gain had prompted their move into the lucrative private security sector. Providing 'security' became nothing more than an excuse for an elaborate protection racket. Soon the INLA were controlling the security on the doors of nightclubs and pubs in Dublin and counties around Ireland, including Louth, Limerick, Meath and Wicklow. Nicky O'Hare, an INLA member from Belfast, introduced his comrades to the racket.

Better known as "Mad Nicky", O'Hare had moved to live in Dundalk, County Louth in the 1980s while on the run from the RUC. He was considered to be an unpredictable psychopath who was even feared by his comrades in the INLA. Wherever he went "Mad Nicky" brought violence and intimidation with him. Following a series of armed robberies from businesses owned by nationalists along the border "Mad Nicky" was so out of control that the Provos threatened to murder him. Soon afterwards, in a bizarre twist of fate, he almost succeeded in doing the job himself. O'Hare's sawn-off shotgun accidentally went off during a car chase following a post office robbery in County Meath. The blast hit him in the side of the jaw – a centimetre to the right and it would have taken his head off.

O'Hare terrorised scores of business people for protection money. He then squandered the money gambling on horses. Whenever he ran out of cash he simply went to one of his 'clients' and demanded some more. If anyone refused to pay for his dubious 'protection services' "Mad Nicky" informed them that they would "get a bullet behind the ear". Gardaí who dealt with O'Hare have said that even by the INLA's standards of wanton violence "Mad

Nicky" O'Hare was one of the worst they had encountered since the Border Fox and "Mad Dog" McGlinchey. One night O'Hare gave two off-duty detectives such a severe beating that one of them was hospitalised. O'Hare got an eight-month sentence for the attack.

In 1989, O'Hare was jailed for four years by the Special Criminal Court for possession of guns and ammunition while working as a bouncer in a Dublin snooker club. Following his release O'Hare was again arrested, this time for attempting to extort IR£47,000 from, Dublin amusement arcade owner and property speculator, James Kennedy. O'Hare later attacked and seriously assaulted his own father from whom he had also tried to extort cash. He was jailed for both crimes.

Soon after he got out of jail "Mad Nicky" became a full-time extortionist. He employed Joe Magee, Declan "Wacker" Duffy and other INLA members in clubs throughout the region. By the time legitimate business people discovered who they had hired it was usually too late for them to do anything about it. O'Hare let it be known that sacking his people carried a serious health risk. Business was booming.

In 1999, Declan Duffy registered his own security company to work in conjunction with O'Hare. The terrorists also hired themselves out as heavies and debt collectors for a number of businessmen and drug dealers. In one case, Duffy and his gang were hired by a second-hand car dealer in Dublin to put the squeeze on a woman who owed him money for a motor. The dodgey car dealer, a convicted fraudster, was introduced to Duffy through John Traynor. He asked Duffy to pay the woman a visit to encourage her to pay up. He was horrified when Duffy called him to say they had kidnapped the woman at gunpoint. Duffy asked the fraudster what he wanted them to do with the 'bad debt'. The car dealer asked them to let the woman go. Associates of the car dealer say that he later "fell in love" with the woman concerned and moved in with her, possibly to prevent her reporting Duffy's heavy-handed tactics to the police. The INLA had unwittingly played cupid.

Duffy, O'Hare and company habitually took control of the drug business in the nightclubs where they worked. They beat, threatened and robbed dealers who were not paying them protection money. They made it clear that if other drug-dealers wanted to continue operating they had to pay-up. Meanwhile their 'friends' were ignored and allowed do as they pleased. Drugs seized from one gang were often sold to 'friendly' gangs. In one instance "Wacker" Duffy took a personal interest in one of the drug dealers plying his trade on the club scene.

Twenty-nine-year-old Brian O'Keefe, from Walkinstown in south Dublin, was one of the new wave of drug dealers to emerge following the break up of John Gilligan's criminal empire. He had previously been involved in smuggling illegal cigarettes from Spain. He made the move into narcotics by using the proceeds of a compensation claim to buy his first drug shipment. O'Keefe set up a courier company, Flash Couriers, as a front through which he could launder his money. A large group of young criminals from Crumlin and Drimnagh operated as his distributors. Very soon he was one of the largest suppliers of cannabis, cocaine and ecstasy in the south city.

O'Keefe came to Duffy's attention while operating a drug racket in a south Dublin night club where the INLA men worked as bouncers. The club had become a popular party venue for Dublin's new brat pack of young gangsters. Management at the club, who had unwittingly hired the INLA thugs, complained to the police but they could do nothing about it. They were finding it practically impossible to clean up the club. Word filtering back to the INLA mob was that O'Keefe was a very wealthy man. He had plenty of money, drugs and guns, and he even owned his own yacht. The INLA wanted a slice of the action. In the summer of 1999 a sequence of events began to unfold which would ultimately lead to the Ballymount Bloodbath.

On the night of July 25, Duffy and three cronies grabbed Brian O'Keefe shortly after he arrived at the club. O'Keefe was bundled down a side stairs and into a waiting van. They took him to a flat on Dominick Street in inner-city Dublin. O'Keefe was held for a number of hours, during which time he was stripped naked, beaten and questioned by the INLA. The drug dealer eventually managed to escape.

In the early hours of July 26, O'Keefe arrived at a petrol station on Bolton Street in Dublin's north inner-city. He was naked and it was obvious from his wounds that he had suffered a severe beating.

He told staff that he had been kidnapped. O'Keefe later refused to make a complaint about the incident to Gardaí. He claimed that he had been mugged. Members of his gang subsequently revealed that O'Keefe paid Duffy IR£30,000 in cash and handed over sixteen firearms for 'the cause'. One of his gang members told this writer: "O'Keefe was well pissed off that he had to fork out. He said Duffy and the INLA were nothing but a bunch of thieving rats themselves." But the pay-off wasn't enough – the war between O'Keefe and the INLA was far from over.

A few weeks later, three members of O'Keefe's gang, who were regular patrons in the same south Dublin night club, were pulled aside by Duffy's men and questioned about their activities in the club. Duffy released two of the young hoods but he held onto the third one, Danny Martin, who was O'Keefe's brother-in-law from Crumlin. Martin, a small time criminal, had also worked for O'Keefe. In a backroom Duffy stripped twenty-three-year-old Martin naked and questioned him about O'Keefe and his drug operation. In particular he wanted to know what guns and money O'Keefe had at his disposal. "Wacker" Duffy told Martin that O'Keefe was facing a bullet from the organisation.

In the meantime O'Keefe kept his head down and stayed out of the INLA men's sight. But then on the night of Sunday, October 3, a seemingly unrelated incident sparked off what was to become a spiral of increasing violence. In Tallaght a bitter row that had been simmering for some time between the younger members of two families, the Creeds and the Dalys, came to a head. On October 3, 1999, nineteen-year-old Wesley Creed and twenty-four-year-old Daniel "Half Ear" Daly had a row in a fast-food joint in Tallaght where Creed worked as a security man. During the row Creed produced a Stanley knife and slashed Daly's neck. "Half Ear" Daly was one of Brian O'Keefe's drivers in Flash Couriers. When he told O'Keefe what had happened the drug dealer organised a revenge attack.

The following night O'Keefe and a group of fifteen associates, employees and friends, met in "Half Ear" Daly's house. It was a short distance from the Creed's family home. The posse were armed with an assortment of sticks, pick axe handles and a sword. They went to Wesley Creed's mother's house, smashing their way inside.

Their intended target, Wesley Creed, managed to make it to safety in the attic as the O'Keefe/Daly mob stormed up the stairs in pursuit. A sword was driven through the ceiling several times in an attempt to stab Creed who was standing on the attic's trap door. The gang left when they failed to dislodge him.

Later that night, Brian O'Keefe approached Wesley Creed's older brother, John Creed, offering to settle the feud. Twenty-nine-year-old John Creed was the joint owner of a window company called Ballymount Windows, based at the Ballymount Road Industrial Estate in south Dublin. John Creed and O'Keefe agreed that four members of each group would meet the following day for a fair fight or for what is colloquially referred to as a "straightener". The fight, however, would not take place as planned.

On Tuesday night, October 5, Glen Creed, John Creed's fifteen-year-old younger brother, escalated the crisis. He set fire to curtains on the side of a courier truck that was parked outside Daly's house for which he was subsequently convicted. The truck, which was driven by Daniel Daly, belonged to Brian O'Keefe. The teenager was spotted running away and the next morning O'Keefe and his men went looking for the IR£600 it would cost to repair the damage. O'Keefe and "Half Ear" Daly met John Creed at his warehouse in the industrial estate. After a heated argument and threats from O'Keefe, John Creed agreed to pay the compensation but he said that he needed time to get the cash together. Later that day Creed sent word to Daniel Daly that the money would be ready for collection at his premises in Ballymount at 8pm that evening. The trap had been set.

Unknown to Brian O'Keefe and his mob, John Creed was well connected to the INLA. For several months twenty-two-year-old INLA member Patrick O'Toole from Jobstown in Tallaght had been working part-time for John Creed. In August 1999, Creed had also employed O'Toole's friend and fellow INLA member, Denis Thompson. Thompson had just been released from prison after serving eighteen months of his sentence for the Newspread robbery in Inchicore in 1997. John Creed called his employees and asked them to organise some protection. Thompson and O'Toole contacted Gerry Burns, who by now had the dubious title of 'commander' of the INLA rabble army, and he agreed to help.

Creed, Thompson and O'Toole met Declan "Wacker" Duffy at a pub in Smithfield Market in the north inner-city where Duffy ran the security for "Mad Nicky" O'Hare. John Creed related the various incidents that had taken place in the previous forty-eight hours. He explained that he was afraid that O'Keefe and his gang would attack his family again. Duffy took Thompson aside and asked if Creed could, "...throw a few quid in for the movement". Thompson assured him Creed was a supporter and would certainly cough up. In any event Duffy was easily convinced. Getting another chance to take on Brian O'Keefe was an added bonus. He began to plot the Ballymount Bloodbath.

Duffy instructed Patrick O'Toole to bring three sawn-off shotguns to John Creed's premises. He then contacted his trusted sidekick, twenty-two year old Patrick "Paddy Bo" Campbell. For the past year Campbell, who was from Belfast, had been living with Gerry Burns's daughter in Blanchardstown. Duffy also summoned his nephew, twenty-year-old Emmet Duffy, an INLA member from South Armagh, who was also working as a bouncer. Burns contacted Duffy during the afternoon to discuss the planned operation. He warned Duffy to be careful, pointing out that the meeting in Ballymount could be a police trap. Duffy said he would play it by ear.

At 6pm Patrick O'Toole drove "Wacker" Duffy, Emmet Duffy and Campbell to Ballymount. Denis Thompson and John Creed were already waiting for them. Duffy, Campbell and O'Toole armed themselves with the sawn-off shotguns. Everyone sat back and ate chicken and chips. Now all they had to do was wait.

Brian O'Keefe had asked Daniel "Half Ear" Daly to collect the money from Creed at 8pm. O'Keefe warned Daly to be careful and instructed him to bring back-up in case there was trouble from the Creeds. Daly recruited five friends, including his twin brother Gavin, to go with him to Ballymount. The others were nineteen-year-old Anthony Deegan, twenty-four-year-old David Hooper, twenty-five-year-old Johnaton Finnegan and twenty-five-year-old Sean Burke. Hooper, like Daly, worked as a courier for O'Keefe's company.

The following account of the events that occurred on the night of October 6 has been compiled from the testimony and personal statements of several of the individuals involved in the incident.

Around 8pm, O'Keefe's men rendezvoused across the road from the industrial estate. Some of them carried knives and knuckle-dusters in case there was trouble. When they reached the factory, Daniel Daly and Sean Burke decided to go in first. They told the others to wait at the door in case they were needed. John Creed was standing beside a machine at the rear of the factory. He appeared to be alone. Denis Thompson and Patrick O'Toole were hiding in the toilets on the ground floor just inside the main doors. Declan Duffy, Emmet Duffy and "Paddy Bo" Campbell were upstairs awaiting the signal to pounce. Creed spoke to Daly and Burke. Feeling reassured that there appeared to be no threat of trouble, the rest of Daly's men walked into the factory. When the six men were standing near him Creed switched on a loud saw. It was the prearranged signal for Duffy and his hoods to make their move. O'Keefe's men didn't have a chance.

Daly and his friends first knew that they were in trouble when they heard Duffy shouting at them to get down. By the time the six men swung around to see what was happening the armed and masked thugs were moving towards them. O'Toole and Thompson had pulled the shutters down on the main doors, blocking off any chance of escape. "Wacker" Duffy and his two cohorts were racing down the stairs, pointing their weapons and ordering O'Keefe's men to get down on the floor. "Right lads everybody get down. Get down on the fucking floor, get down, don't look up, don't fucking look up," Duffy roared.

When they spotted the guns O'Keefe's men dropped their weapons. The INLA men surrounded their victims, forcing them to lie face down on the floor. The six were then ordered to put their hands behind their backs and to keep their eyes shut. Each man was repeatedly kicked in the face, head and body, and bludgeoned with the shotguns. Cable ties were wrapped tightly around their hands and legs. Then they stripped each prisoner naked by slicing the clothing from their bodies. They were using knives and in the process were cutting the flesh on their victims' faces, legs and backs. The INLA men laughed and danced up and down on the naked bodies. "You lot are only fuckin eejits… we normally fight soldiers," one of them bragged. Each man was asked for his name and address. Meanwhile Duffy began shouting questions at his prisoners:

"Where's the money? Where's the guns? Where has O'Keefe hidden his money and guns?"

Over the next two hours the prisoners were continuously beaten as they lay trussed-up on the floor. Ice-cold water was thrown over them and they were told they would be drowned. In between the buckets of freezing water, boiling tea was poured over their bleeding wounds. The screams of pain and pleas for mercy echoed around the factory walls.

Duffy and his torturers then decided to single out Daniel "Half Ear" Daly. "Where's the ringleader, where's Daly?" Duffy asked out loud. The terrorists dragged Daly away to the rear of the factory. "Danny you work for O'Keefe. What are you doing extorting money from my people? Who do you think you are going into other people's houses? Where is O'Keefe's money and guns?" Duffy demanded.

Daly said he didn't know what they were talking about. He screamed for mercy as the boots and guns came down hard all over his body. He was tortured like this for several minutes. The torture ceased when Daly stopped screaming and his battered body suddenly went limp. One of the prisoners later recalled how Daly seemed to stop breathing. There was a momentary silence. Then the INLA men began laughing. "This one's dead. Does anyone know anything about resuscitation?" asked Duffy. "This one's gone. Someone bring him back." One of the INLA gangsters turned Daly on his side and he could be heard wheezing again. "Grand he's back with us. Now who's next?" asked one of the torturers.

Then it was David Hooper's turn. Scared out of his wits Hooper had initially given the INLA a false name because he was terrified that they would murder him. "Wacker" Duffy and Joe Magee had previously threatened Hooper. They'd told him that he would be shot if he continued selling ecstasy in the south Dublin nightclub where they worked. Later to Gardaí, Hooper conceded that he had been dealing in E but stopped following the INLA threats. When the INLA men discovered Hooper's real identity Duffy walked over to him and, just as if he was booting a football, kicked Hooper in the head. "Mr Hooper you are a dead man because you are a drug dealer for Brian O'Keefe," Duffy screamed. "You are going to die a young man, we're going to kill you. We're goin' to bring you up to the border where the real torturing is done… scumbags, trying to extort money from my friend."

According to the recollections of those present that night, Hooper was severely beaten by two or three of the INLA gangsters for about twenty minutes. He lapsed in and out of consciousness. In between blackouts he could be heard screaming his heart out and begging them to stop the torture.

Each of the four remaining prisoners was individually hauled up the stairs to John Creed's office where the beating and interrogation continued. In the office Anthony Deegan's head was slammed repeatedly into a filing cabinet and he was ordered to face the wall. He already had a large, gaping wound on the side of his head from the initial assault. A hood was placed over his head and a voice asked him: "What the fuck are you doing here son? Why'd you come up here?" Deegan replied that he was there as back up for his mates. "We're going to release you, you are a lucky man because there's one person here not going home tonight. If you go to the guards you will be shot," the voice continued behind him.

Deegan was dragged down the stairs and dumped beside his friends as another one was taken away. The factory reverberated to the sound of beatings, screams and shouted questions and threats. After almost two hours the six bodies on the cold concrete floor had become a mess of blood, bruises and swollen wounds. They shivered uncontrollably from a combination of the cold, shock and fear. Their teeth chattered and they whimpered and groaned. Later one of the victims said that at that point he would have preferred death rather than enduring any further torture. "Wacker" Duffy and "Paddy Bo" Campbell were enjoying the episode. Both of them wanted to shoot Hooper or Daly.

In the meantime Gerry Burns had arrived in the factory to oversee his INLA unit's latest brave 'act of war' on behalf of the working-class people of Ireland. He was annoyed that the torture had gone on so long because someone could have alerted the police. He told Duffy to begin wrapping things up. Burns overruled shooting anyone at that stage. He wanted the prisoners taken away and dumped on the side of a road. During interrogation one of the prisoners gave Burns a list of the names of people who knew more about O'Keefe's drug operation. It would merit further investigation. John Creed was instructed to empty the back of his van and reverse it into the factory to take O'Keefe's men away.

One of the INLA thugs then started a hand drill that he playfully held to the back of each prisoner's knees. "Ah Jesus no, no," each man pleaded, believing that he was about to be kneecapped. The barrel of a shotgun was then pressed into the heads of Deegan, Burke, Finnegan and Gavin Daly. A voice shouted: "The one's I have pointed to have twenty-four hours to leave the country or I'm going to kill you and your families. Remember what I said, Yis have 'till tomorrow to get your bits and pieces and go."

None of them knew what was planned for David Hooper or Daniel Daly. One by one each prisoner's bounds were tightened further and they were thrown into the back of Creed's van in a heap. "Paddy Bo" Campbell and Emmet Duffy had already climbed into the front of the van, as they got ready to leave with their bruised and bloodied cargo. Two other INLA men jumped into the back of the van and stood on the prisoners. The guns were packed into a bag to be returned to their hiding place. Duffy shut the van door and was getting into the driver's seat when he saw the headlights of another van speeding towards them. He shouted at his mates to run for it, that the cops were coming. A few minutes later he would be wishing it was the cops.

* * * *

The torture session had been going on for almost an hour when Brian O'Keefe first became concerned about his friends. He had expected a call from Daniel "Half Ear" Daly as soon as he had collected the IR£600. He tried to call Daly's mobile phone but it was switched off. He tried it several more times and couldn't get through. O'Keefe also tried David Hooper's phone again without success. At the time of the Ballymount ambush he had been out making a number of deliveries with his wife Margaret Butler. They arrived at their home in Walkinstown shortly before 9.30pm. A friend of the family, Ernie Draper from Tallaght, had called to the house. A few minutes later, Draper and O'Keefe drove to Ballymount to find out what was happening. When they arrived in the estate O'Keefe went to the closed door of John Creed's premises and heard screams coming from inside. He looked in through a window and saw the horrifying torture chamber. O'Keefe raced back to Draper and they immediately began to summon help on their mobile phones.

Within minutes O'Keefe's underworld mobilisation had begun. Reinforcements began arriving at his house. Among them were his brother-in-laws Danny and Eric Martin, Draper's son Ronnie and pub bouncer Pat Neville. Others arrived from Ballyfermot and Tallaght. O'Keefe told his pals that a gang of travellers was torturing the six men sent to collect the money from John Creed. The gang armed themselves with a variety of weapons – hurleys, hammers, bars, knives, brush handles, a hatchet and a sword. One member of O'Keefe's rescue team even ripped off one of the spindles in the stairway banister. A total of twelve men piled into one of O'Keefe's courier vans and a car as they headed for Ballymount.

At the same moment that Declan Duffy was shouting about the cops and trying to get away, O'Keefe and his mob were blocking the INLA's escape route. His gang spilled from the van and charged towards the factory doors. Some of the INLA men made a run for it. The windows of Creed's van were smashed in with hammers and bars. O'Keefe, Neville and two others went to the passenger door and trapped "Paddy Bo" Campbell inside before he could get out. On the other side of the van, three other members of O'Keefe's gang attacked Duffy, beating him with bars and planks of wood. They tried to drag Duffy into the back of O'Keefe's van but he managed to run off. In the factory the rest of the gang laid into the retreating INLA men. At this stage there were a total of twenty-four men involved in what was to become known as the Ballymount Bloodbath. In a frenzied attack, O'Keefe and Neville hacked at "Paddy Bo" Campbell with a long knife and a hatchet. The INLA man was struck in the head and his legs were sliced almost through to the bone.

Then O'Keefe ran to the back of the van and shouted: "Where's me mates." The six men in the back of the van began screaming for help. O'Keefe opened the door and began pulling them out. Danny Martin grabbed one of the naked men, throwing him over his shoulder, and ran towards a waiting car. One of the INLA men fired a shot hitting the door of O'Keefe's van. The shot also hit one of the rescuers, Ian Dowdall, in the eye and he fell into the van screaming. A second shot was fired but no one was hit. Rescuers and prisoners were piled in on top of each other as O'Keefe's gang sped from the factory complex.

In the aftermath of the attack "Paddy Bo" Campbell lay lifeless on the ground, beside Creed's van. Blood poured in dark crimson streams from his two legs and his head. Gerry Burns and another member of Duffy's gang ran to an industrial unit nearby. The rest of the INLA mob, including Duffy, had run off to save their own necks. Two men had been working late and had been alerted to the mayhem outside by the sound of shouts, revving engines, smashing glass and gunshots.

A few minutes later Gerry Burns and his cohort burst into the premises in a state of panic. Burns demanded that one of the men drive him and "Paddy Bo" Campbell to Tallaght hospital. At the accident and emergency unit Burns ran in and shouted at nurses that he had a dying man in a car outside. Medical staff rushed out to help. Burns got a lift back to Walkinstown where he collected a van he had been driving before all the mayhem started and returned to Tallaght hospital.

Meanwhile the car and van, now carrying O'Keefe's gang of eighteen men, drove the short distance to his house at speed. The blood-soaked victims were carried into the house and the restraints were cut from their feet and hands. In the kitchen and bathroom the injured men hurriedly tried to clean-up some of their worst wounds. They had started going into shock. Blood was spattered everywhere and one witness would later recall that it resembled a scene of sheer chaos. Dowdall, the only rescuer injured in the fight, was crying out with the pain of his injury. He was taken away in a car to a house in Tallaght. Cans of beer were drunk to ease the shock and the pain. O'Keefe's wife gave the injured men children's clothes to wear.

Shortly after returning to the house O'Keefe's mobile phone rang and his wife answered. It was "Wacker" Duffy on the other end, asking for O'Keefe. She replied that he wasn't there. "Those were our lads that were up in that place tonight. O'Keefe has stepped on the wrong toes and he's dealing with us now. We're going to blow everyone of youse out of it tonight," Duffy shouted as the phone went dead. O'Keefe began to panic and ordered everyone out of the house. His wife and kids were taken away in a taxi. The injured and the rescuers piled back into O'Keefe's van and they drove to a safe house in Ballyfermot. O'Keefe instructed another gang member to take his van away and have it burnt out to destroy any forensics, including the gunshot holes and the blood. Everyone was terrified of what would happen next. None of them had expected to be facing down the fearsome INLA. O'Keefe's gang knew the identities of three of the INLA members, Declan "Wacker" Duffy, O'Toole and Thompson. Despite their appalling injuries the injured men were too scared to attend hospital for treatment.

Meanwhile Gardaí arrived at Tallaght hospital, after receiving a call that a man had been admitted with critical injuries obtained in a violent attack. Armed protection was placed at "Paddy Bo" Campbell's bedside after reports from colleagues in Ballymount that there had been a serious incident involving a shoot out. When Gerry Burns returned to the hospital a short time later he identified Campbell for them. Burns claimed that he had received a phone call telling him where the injured man had been left. When he found Campbell, Burns said he stopped a car and had him brought to the hospital. Burns was agitated and confused. His clothes were heavily blood-stained. At the same time a cursory check showed that Burns was known to the Garda Special Branch as the current Commander of the INLA in Dublin. The injured man was also known as an INLA associate. At 12.27am Gerry Burns was arrested under the Offences Against the State Act.

Two hours later, at about 2.30am on October 7, John Creed knocked on the door of a house in Clondalkin. He was wearing only underpants and asked the owner could he use the phone to call the police. Creed claimed that he had been abducted and stripped by a number of men who had called to his factory demanding protection money. Gardaí arrived and found Creed in a shocked state. Officers who had begun investigating the incident at Ballymount wanted to visit John Creed. He agreed to meet them to clarify what had happened.

Back at the hospital "Paddy Bo"Campbell was barely hanging onto life. He had not regained consciousness since the attack. When doctors first saw him he was saturated in his own blood. He was resuscitated in the emergency unit and he later underwent nine hours of surgery. A brain scan found that the INLA man had suffered severe brain damage and also kidney and liver failure. He was placed on a life support machine.

Patrick Campbell was pronounced dead at 12.25am on the morning of Sunday, October 10. The following day the INLA's political wing, the Irish Republican Socialist Party (IRSP), issued a statement claiming that Campbell had been a member of the INLA and had been murdered "...in defence of his community and the Irish working-class in the ongoing struggle against drugs and drug traffickers.". Campbell was buried three days later in Milltown cemetery in Belfast with full paramilitary honours.

In the days following the Ballymount Bloodbath Brian O'Keefe and several of those involved in the incident fled into hiding. At least ten of the people involved in the rescue travelled to England. The young gangsters were terrified of the INLA. Three days after the incident, two of O'Keefe's men spoke to this writer. They gave a further interview in London a week later. After "Paddy Bo" died on October 10, they were terrified that they, and their families, would be murdered in revenge for his death and for the INLA's humiliating defeat at the hands of a group of, mainly, non-descript, petty criminals.

In an interview with the *Sunday World* one of them explained: "When we went up to Ballymount we went there to save our friends who were surely going to be murdered. This was over a row about a damaged truck and had nothing to do with drugs. When we went to save our mates we thought we were going up against a gang of travellers not the fucking INLA. But what if we did know, we couldn't just leave the lads there anyway. There could have been six fellahs dead instead of one and no one intended killing anyone. The INLA would have killed us too. They were the ones with the guns. Not one of the lads involved is in any way heavy except for maybe O'Keefe and he was quick to fuck off and leave everyone else in the shit. This fucking INLA crowd say they are an army and they claim to be entitled to the same rights as any soldier under the Geneva Convention, well torturing people is not allowed by the Geneva Convention."

In the first days after the Ballymount Bloodbath it was suspected, according to members of O'Keefe's gang, that Declan "Wacker" Duffy had been seriously injured with a hatchet blow to the head.

This later turned out to be incorrect. Duffy and the rest of his mob had also gone into hiding.

The INLA leadership in Belfast launched its own enquiries into the incident. The organisation was concerned generally about the Dublin 'Brigade's' activities and particularly its blatant involvement in criminality. In Dublin the word was sent out that teams of INLA hit men were being sent down from the North to take revenge for "Paddy Bo" Campbell's murder. The Provos were also conducting their own enquiries. "Paddy Bo's" father was a prominent Provo with a lot of influence in Republican circles. The problem was further complicated by the fact that a member of the O'Keefe gang, who had been targeted for revenge, was a close relative of a senior IRA figure. A relatively minor dispute over IR£600 had turned the underworld of criminals and terrorists upside down. Gangland had become a tinderbox.

* * * *

The Garda G district, which polices the Ballymount area, had never seen anything like it before. This is quite a distinction considering that the G district includes the working-class suburbs of Crumlin and Drimnagh. For over three decades Ireland's most infamous gangsters and organised crime gangs have originated in Crumlin and Drimnagh. The areas once housed criminals such as the General' gang, the notorious Dunne drug family and most of John Gilligan's crime gang. The country's wealthiest international drug trafficker, George "the Penguin" Mitchell was also from the area. It also had a large transient population of terrorists and quasi-terrorists from the INLA and IRA. Cops who learned their trade while attached to the district's two stations, at Sundrive Road and Crumlin Village, were considered to be among the best crime investigators in the country. But, even to them, the Ballymount Bloodbath presented a new challenge.

As Gardaí arrived at the scene in Ballymount it was clear that this would be a complex investigation. Eye-witnesses told the first officers to arrive, Detectives Denis Nagle and Sean O'Mahoney, of hearing shouts and breaking glass, followed by gun shots. Three or four naked men with their hands tied behind their backs were seen hopping between the factory and a waiting van. One witness said that at first he thought it was some kind of mad stag party until he saw people being beaten-up. Another man had been brought off to hospital seriously injured. John Creed's van and factory had been abandoned. The windows in the van had been smashed in and its doors left open. On the ground beside the passenger side was a mass of congealed blood. There were large bloodstains in the back of the van and around the factory floor. Various blood-stained weapons were scattered around the factory. This was no ordinary crime scene.

With reports coming in of Patrick Campbell's admission to hospital in Tallaght, a major investigation was immediately set-up. Within an hour of the initial calls to the Gardaí, senior officers arrived at Ballymount. Detective Inspector Tom Mulligan and Detective Superintendent Denis Donegan were experienced serious crime investigators who had been involved in investigating many of the city's serious crime gangs and murders. They ordered that the scene be preserved for forensic examination and they ordered an investigation centre to be set up at Crumlin station. Detective Inspector Mulligan instructed his officers at Tallaght hospital to detain Burns for questioning. An hour later he dispatched officers from Crumlin to look for Duffy, Burns's sidekick. As they were searching Duffy's flat in Fatima Mansions the terrorist rang the officers asking them what they were doing there. He hung up when Detective Sergeant Peter O'Boyle asked Duffy where he was.

The following morning, October 7, the investigation team gathered in Crumlin station. Other specialist units were called in over night to assist the detective units attached to G District. The Head of the National Bureau of Criminal Investigation, Detective Chief Superintendent Sean Camon and a squad of his officers arrived. Members of the Special Detective Unit (SDU), or Special Branch, had also been mobilised to assist in the investigation because of the INLA's involvement. Over seventy officers had been assigned to the case by 8am.

The first investigation conference had a packed agenda. Officers were assigned to interviewing witnesses and doing house-to-house enquiries. Landline and mobile telephone traffic would be analysed and a list of suspects drawn up. The Gardaí in Tallaght provided intelligence of an ongoing row from the previous weekend, between the O'Keefes and the Creeds. It tied in with the appearance of John Creed that morning in Clondalkin. Then the arrest of Burns, the SDU's identification of Campbell as an active member of the INLA and the disappearance of Declan Duffy, clearly connected the terror group with the bloodshed at Ballymount. The underworld was already humming with stories about the events of the previous night. By mid-day the investigation team began to compile a rough picture of what had transpired. Officers were amazed at the sheer scale of the incident and the numbers involved.

To unravel the complex case the investigation divided the suspects into three groups: the first group were the people who had been abducted; the INLA gang were the second group; and the third group were the men who had arrived to rescue the first group. There were also a number of serious crime charges involved: possession of firearms with intent to endanger life; possession of offensive weapons; false imprisonment; assault; and membership of an illegal organisation – the INLA. Three days later, on October 10, the charge of murder was added when Patrick Campbell died.

The Gardaí knew that in order to gather evidence they would have to identify and locate the people in each group. But the threats of retaliation and the disappearance of several suspects meant the investigation team would have to move fast to avert all out gang warfare. The level of fear meant that the chances of bringing criminal cases before the courts were extremely slim.

On October 7, John Creed turned up for his interview as agreed. In a statement given to detectives he claimed that he had hired a man called "Joe" to provide him with security against a criminal gang who were demanding protection money. He claimed he had no idea who Joe was or the identities of the men he sent. Creed said the group he hired had abducted the six men when they arrived in his premises. Shots had been fired and he had "legged it out of the factory". He said he had walked to Clondalkin where he'd hid his clothes and then pretended to have been abducted.

Detectives felt that Creed's explanation of what had happened on October 6 just didn't add up. Enquiries and analysis of telephone traffic began to provide a clearer picture of what really occurred. On October 12, Creed was arrested and questioned. During interrogation he finally told the truth about what had actually happened before and during the Ballymount Bloodbath. Two days later Detective Inspector Tom Mulligan formally charged Creed with false imprisonment, assault and possession of firearms at Ballymount.

Over the following weeks a total of forty people were arrested for questioning, including most of those involved in the incident. The majority of the O'Keefe gang were located and identified. They provided detailed information about what had happened but were unlikely to testify in court out of fear for their lives. Some of O'Keefe's men began nominating other members of the gang as likely suspects for Patrick Campbell's murder. The INLA members who had been arrested, Gerry Burns, Patrick O'Toole and Denis Thompson, denied any involvement in the incident and were released without charge. Searches were still ongoing for other members of the gangs, particularly Declan "Wacker" Duffy and Brian O'Keefe. O'Keefe and his wife Margaret Butler had gone into hiding in England. The couple held a number of informal meetings with officers attached to the investigation team in Manchester but refused to return to Dublin. In the absence of any hard evidence with which to charge O'Keefe, there was little the police could do about it.

By the beginning of November Gardaí knew the full story of the Ballymount Bloodbath, including the identities of everyone who had participated in the incident. But the officers were not optimistic about their chances of successfully prosecuting the main players. Nevertheless, cases were being compiled with a view to preferring murder charges against one or maybe two members of O'Keefe's gang, including O'Keefe himself. But the INLA appeared to be getting off the hook. The investigation team needed a major break. It was about to come from the most unexpected source.

Over the previous weeks Declan Duffy's face had become well-known to the public. On Sunday, October 17, the *Sunday World* ran a front-page investigation piece in which Duffy and O'Keefe were named as the men responsible for the Ballymount Bloodbath. The articles included detailed interviews with members of the gang who had taken part in the mêlée. The interviews also ran alongside pictures of O'Keefe and Duffy.

On November 4, the Garda hunt for Duffy finally got their break.

The Special Detective Unit received a tip-off that Duffy would be around the Smithfield Market area of the north inner-city. Detective Gardaí Frank O'Sullivan and Declan O'Byrne were waiting as Duffy parked a car not far from the pub where he worked as a bouncer. Duffy was about to meet representatives of the INLA from Belfast to explain the events of the past few weeks. The officers got out of their car and walked over to the terrorist. As they did so, Detective Garda O'Sullivan spotted Duffy taking a document from his pocket and stuffing it under his seat. When the terrorist saw the cops he got out of the car. The officers identified themselves to Duffy and asked how he was. He replied: "Well I have no hatchet marks if that's what you're looking for." O'Byrne arrested Duffy on suspicion that he had been in possession of firearms with intent to endanger life at Ballymount on October 6. He was taken by squad car to Crumlin station for questioning.

Detective Garda O'Sullivan then searched Duffy's car. He found a three page folded document which Duffy had concealed earlier. When he opened and read it he could hardly believe his eyes. There, in Duffy's own handwriting, was a complete account of the events leading up to and during the incident in Ballymount. The document was written for his INLA bosses in Belfast. It reported in damning detail Duffy's role and the actions of John Creed and his INLA comrades on the night of October 6, 1999. Duffy had stated that he wanted to shoot someone and had instructed O'Toole to bring firearms to the warehouse. The man, who would later be immortalised in a *Sunday World* front-page headline as 'Ireland's Dumbest Terrorist', had even signed the statement. When Detective Garda O'Sullivan brought the statement back to Crumlin the investigation team were astonished. Never before had a hardened terrorist, or criminal, actually written and signed his own confession without police involvement or encouragement. Duffy had handed himself, and his INLA mob, to them on a plate.

The following is the entire content of Duffy's statement to the leadership of the INLA:

'I started work 7am ... at Smithfield market. At about 3pm I got

a phone call to the pub from Denis Thompson saying that himself and Paddy O'Toole had a problem. He told me it was to do with his boss so I told him to come down to the pub. When he came down Denis Thompson was also with Paddy O'Toole and they also had John Creed their boss with them. John Creed explained to me a man, Brian O'Keefe, had wrecked his mother's house and he was afraid he would repeat this. I then called Denis Thompson aside and asked him would John Creed be able to throw the movement a few pound. Denis Thompson told me he was a supporter of the Movement and he employed both himself and Paddy O'Toole. So I left it at that. I asked Denis Thompson did Gerry Burns know and he said he did.

I then told Paddy O'Toole to bring some guns to Ballymount as John Creed had arranged to meet O'Keefe at 8pm at the warehouse. I had Emmet with me … so I rang Paddy Bo (Patrick Campbell) and told him to come and meet me. I had told Paddy O'Toole to come back to the pub at 6pm to collect us. At about 5.30pm I got a phone call from Gerry Burns who told me it might not be best to go ahead with anything on that night as he said it did not sound right and it could be a set-up with the cops. I said I would play it by ear and that he should phone me when he gets out of work and I would get him picked up. I thought when we went up to Ballymount it would be our only chance of catching O'Keefe.

When we were in Ballymount we had three sawn-off shotguns. I had one and Paddy Bo [Campbell] and Paddy O'Toole had one each. I told John Creed that when O'Keefe and his mates came for him to bring them in down the back of the factory so that we could get the front shutters pulled down and they would have no escape. As Paddy O'Toole and Denis Thompson saw them pass the toilets and heard the saw machine at the back go on that was their cue to pull the shutters. When we heard all the talking myself and Paddy Bo loaded the shotguns. Then we heard the saw being turned on so we started to run down the stairs to where they were. When we got down there were six of them so we started to beat them on the ground. When we had them on the ground we tied their hands and feet and stripped them naked. Then we started to question them about O'Keefe's money and guns. I then got a phone call from Gerry Burns who said he was at Walkinstown Roundabout so I sent Paddy O'Toole to pick him up.

When Gerry Burns came he said we had been there too long and we started to wrap things up. Me and Paddy Bo were looking to shoot one of them but Gerry said that we couldn't. Gerry had got a list of names from one of them and then we started to load them into the back of a Hiace van. I then closed the back door of the van with John inside. Paddy Bo and Emmet were in the front just as I was getting into the van. I looked over my right shoulder I saw headlights of a van coming into the factories. As the van came speeding up I shouted for everyone to run that it was the cops. I ran towards the direction and up the side of the van and towards the front gates. When I got up a bit a car tried to knock me down. I ran down the road and jumped over a wall into a garden and hid in a hedge. I then heard a shotgun blast go off. So I got onto a roof of a bungalow to see what was going on.'

Duffy signed the statement.

The document was forensically examined, put in a protective cover and placed in a locked safe. Documents bearing Duffy's signature, including driving licence applications, were quickly obtained. During his initial interrogation that evening Duffy lied through his teeth. He denied being involved in the INLA but bragged about his anti-drug activity in a south Dublin night club. When the officers put it to Duffy that named members of the two groups involved in Ballymount had identified him as the ringleader, he smirked and replied: "Can't say that I know them. I'm definitely not a member of the INLA. I definitely wasn't there." He knew no one would stand up in court against him. Duffy was asked did he know Brian O'Keefe. He replied: "Only what I heard about him and read in the *Sunday World*. I don't know him, never met him."

When his interrogation resumed the next morning Duffy was still in a confident mood. He was well accustomed to these sessions with the police, having been arrested and quizzed on several occasions in the past. It was only a matter of putting in the forty-eight hours and then the police had to release him. It would be no sweat to a hardened 'soldier'. Shortly before 2pm on the following afternoon it was again put to Duffy that a number of O'Keefe's gang members had identified him as being responsible for the torture in Ballymount. He replied: "They're all fucking druggies and they're telling lies about me because of the hassle I gave them in [the night club]. I was bad for their business."

Detective Sergeant Dominic Hayes of the NBCI then showed Duffy a copy of his passport and his driving licence application. Detective Sergeant Hayes asked Duffy to confirm that the signatures on both documents were his. Duffy agreed they were his signatures. Having patiently waited for the right moment, the experienced investigator then placed a copy of Duffy's statement on the table in front of him.

Duffy leaned forward and looked at it for a moment. He sat back and laughed. "I was wondering if you found it," he replied. When asked about the document he told the officers: "I wrote it yesterday before I was arrested. I was going to meet somebody when I was arrested, can't say who. I was told to write it by people from above."

When asked was it for an INLA internal enquiry he said: "Yeah there had to be one after 'Paddy Bo'." The detectives then read Duffy's statement over to him. When they finished Duffy remarked: "I have done all the work for ye. I wasn't going to shoot anybody. I only said that. We were only teaching them a lesson, nobody was going to be killed."

The detectives asked Duffy what he had intended doing with the hostages and if he stood over what was in his statement. "We were only going to dump them, definitely none of them were to be killed. I've done all the work for ye. Everything is right except where I said I wanted to shoot one of them, that's a spoof," Duffy explained. The officers asked him why it was a spoof. Duffy replied: "It's just to make me look good."

The officers then suggested that Duffy was in trouble with the INLA for losing a volunteer in what appeared to be a personal vendetta. "I have nothing to worry about from them [INLA]," he replied.

But Duffy now had plenty to worry about from the Gardaí. In addition to the signed confession they also had telephone records which corroborated much of Duffy's own statement. On November 6, Detective Inspector Tom Mulligan formally charged Declan Duffy with the unlawful possession of a firearm and false imprisonment at Ballymount exactly one month earlier. He was brought before the Dublin District Court and remanded in custody. Armed with this dramatic new evidence it was decided to re-arrest the INLA gang. Five days later Denis Thompson was arrested and questioned again. Faced with Duffy's statement he admitted his involvement in the incident and was also charged.

On November 19, the investigation team had another breakthrough. Twenty-two-year-old Mark McGann from Fairview in north Dublin was arrested at Bus Arus (Central Bus Station) in Dublin. He was carrying a bag, containing a sawn-off shotgun, a sword and ammunition, which he had been hiding for Patrick O'Toole since the Ballymount incident.

Five days later Detective Sergeant Joe O'Hara arrested O'Toole for the second time. O'Toole took responsibility for the weapons found on Mark McGann but denied that he had fired any shots on the night of the Ballymount incident. When Detective Sergeant O'Hara read out Declan Duffy's INLA statement O'Toole broke down and began to cry. "I'm embarrassed over all this dragging my name over the paper. I know I'll have to go to court over what I did, but I don't want to talk about it for the time being," said O'Toole.

Later the officers put it to O'Toole that according to Duffy's statement he had played a major role in the events of October 6. O'Toole was incensed: "He [Duffy] is a thick, he's a fucking eejit. I didn't bring any guns to that place, I didn't. I was at the shutters when they went in." The following day, November 25, Det. Sgt. O'Hara charged O'Toole with five counts of possessing firearms and ammunition at Bus Arus and the Ballymount Road Industrial Estate. He was also charged with false imprisonment and remanded in custody.

The INLA had suffered most as a result of their involvement in Ballymount. One of their men was dead, three of their members were facing serious charges and they had been exposed as criminals. They were determined to even up the odds somewhat. Pat Neville, the pub bouncer, who had been one of O'Keefe's gang at Ballymount, had remained the prime suspect for the murder of Patrick Campbell but had not yet been charged. His terrified companions had let it be known that it was Neville who had caused Campbell's fatal injuries. The INLA believed them. As Dublin 'commander', Burns was determined to find Paddy Bo's murderer and the unwanted attention the incident had generated in IRA circles was another incentive.

For several months after the Ballymount bloodbath Pat Neville had been living in fear of his life. He constantly changed his daily routine and was very vigilant, keeping a low profile. In April 2000, however, he told a friend that the problem with the INLA had been "sorted" and he was no longer under threat. He dropped his guard and returned to his normal routine.

Shortly before 7.30am, on Saturday April 29, 2000, Neville left his flat at Saint Michael's Estate in Inchicore where he lived with his wife and four young children. He was going to work the morning shift as a bouncer at an early opening pub in the city centre. As he reached the bottom of the stairs in the block of Corporation flats, a gunman was waiting for him. Neville was shot five times at point blank range. He was hit twice in the head and twice in the chest. The assassin finished him off with a bullet through the back of the neck. Neville slumped in a pool of blood and died instantly. The hit man stuffed the gun into the front of his trousers and ran off.

Less than twenty-four hours later a shotgun blast was fired through the front window of the Crumlin home of Danny and Eric Martin, O'Keefe's former brothers-in-law. Detectives believed that the INLA had been involved in both incidents. "Mad Nicky" O'Hare had used his contacts in Dundalk, County Louth, to help recruit the hit man used to kill Neville. Investigators also knew the identity of the man who organised the murder itself.

Detective Superintendent PJ Browne headed the investigation into the Neville murder and suspected that it had been the work of the INLA in revenge for Ballymount. Browne's team made a vital breakthrough when they traced Belfast-born Kevin McLaughlin. The officers had discovered that, according to intelligence sources, the thirty-four-year-old doorman had asked a number of people to identify Neville before the murder. McLaughlin had grown up in New Barnsley Crescent in Belfast, a short distance away from Patrick Campbell's childhood home. McLaughlin had reportedly been approached by a senior figure in the INLA and asked to keep Neville under surveillance.

On July 27, 2000, McLaughlin was arrested under the provisions of the Offences Against the State Act and questioned about the Neville murder. In the last hour of his forty-eight hour detention period the INLA sympathiser finally admitted his role in the crime. "I was asked to do surveillance on Pat Neville. I decided to do this because not only did I know Paddy Bo but I was afraid to refuse this man 'cos I knew he was in the INLA and high up in it," McLaughlin told investigators. He described approaching another security man who identified Neville for him. "I then arranged to meet this INLA man in Slatterys' pub [where Neville worked] and I identified Neville to this man." McLaughlin refused to identify the mystery hit man and was charged under the Offences Against the State Act legislation with gathering information for an unlawful organisation so that they could "commit serious harm".

In 2001, McLaughlin became the first man in the Republic to be convicted of this crime. He pleaded guilty in the Special Criminal Court in Dublin and was jailed for four years.

As part of the follow-up investigation detectives also arrested a number of INLA figures for questioning, including Gerry Burns and Joe Magee. In a search of Magee's Corporation flat off Charlemont Street in July officers found four sawn-off shotguns. Magee later admitted that he had been holding the weapons for another man and he was charged with possession of firearms. That same July, Magee's fellow INLA member, "Mad Nicky" O'Hare was also heading for disaster.

For several months "Mad Nicky" had been threatening to murder a twenty-six year-old Dundalk publican Stephen Connolly unless he paid O'Hare 'protection money'. Connolly had refused to hand over IR£12,000 'back money' which O'Hare claimed he owed. The publican simply could not pay the money and was forced to close the pub. On July 28, "Mad Nicky's" assassin pumped several bullets into Connolly as he tried to make a run for it. Less than three weeks later two killers then pumped nine rounds into "Mad Nicky" O'Hare's body. They finished the INLA terrorist off with a single shot through each eye which was chillingly similar to the IRA 'cross of bullets' murder of Mary McGlinchy thirteen years earlier. A detective investigating the case would later comment: "There was real hate in that killing." No one has ever been charged with the murder although detectives pursued two possible theories: he was either shot in revenge for the Connolly murder or his INLA godfathers decided that he could no longer be controlled. Following O'Hare's funeral in Belfast the IRSP claimed that "Mad Nicky" had been kicked out of the INLA several years earlier. A rather tongue-in-cheek IRSP statement read: "Mr O'Hare had been dismissed for nefarious activities on the grounds that they brought the movement into disrepute. The IRSP view the shooting of Mr O'Hare as further evidence of the decline in public standards and the rise of organised crime." It was hypocrisy at its breathtaking best.

On January 15, 2001 Declan Duffy and Patrick O'Toole were both jailed by the Special Criminal Court for their part in the Ballymount Bloodbath. Both men pleaded guilty to charges of false imprisonment and the unlawful possession of a shotgun. The victims of the Ballymount incident had refused to attend the court to give evidence. They were too scared. But Duffy's extraordinary written confession had, as he said himself, done the job for the police and the witnesses weren't required. The INLA men had no choice but to put their hands up. Duffy smirked as the court sentenced him to nine years and O'Toole to seven years. Mr Justice Diarmuid O'Donovan said that Duffy was in charge of the operation and that it was clear that he had wanted to shoot one of the victims but was prevented by a colleague. As the two men were being led away O'Toole's father called Duffy a "scumbag" for leading his son into so much trouble. O'Toole's dad also lashed out at Duffy's supporters in the public gallery, calling them cowards. From the time of his arrest Patrick O'Toole had distanced himself from the INLA. In prison he opted to serve his time away from the paramilitaries. John Creed had already been convicted in November 2000 after pleading guilty to the charge of false imprisonment. He was sentenced to five years with the final two years suspended.

In May 2001, Denis Thompson was jailed for six years when he pleaded guilty to the false imprisonment of Hooper, Deegan, Finnegan and Daly at Ballymount. In passing sentence Mr Justice Freddie Morris said the incident was "an extremely serious case of gang warfare which had the eventual result of the death of one of the people partaking in it."

Eleven days after Duffy and O'Toole were jailed the INLA struck another blow for their dead comrade, "Paddy Bo" Campbell.

On January 26, 2001, a bomb was attached to a car driven by Ronnie Draper, one of the men who had taken part in the Ballymount incident. As Draper drove from the Kingswood Shopping Centre in Tallaght, where he worked as a security man, he heard a loud bang. He immediately jumped out of the car. Luckily for him the device had failed to fully explode. An Army Bomb squad later found that the bomb had enough explosive in it to kill the driver if it had gone off. The attack caused panic among all those who had been involved in the bloodbath. Despite a Garda investigation no one was charged although Gerry Burns was arrested and questioned about the bombing. Officers were convinced that the attack was in retaliation for October 6, 1999.

The only man charged with the murder of Patrick Campbell was twenty-year-old Daniel Finnegan from Crumlin in Dublin. Finnegan had pleaded not guilty to the charge. At the opening of his trial in July 2001, prosecution counsel said that Finnegan had played a central role in the Ballymount incident. "Although there were a number of people involved in the mêlée it is the State's case that the accused took a full and active part in the very serious assault, which led to the death of Mr Campbell," Mr. George Birmingham SC told the Central Criminal Court. However, after lengthy legal argument, the murder charge was dropped. The State Pathologist, Dr John Harbison, had confirmed that knife wounds to the legs of the deceased had significantly contributed to the cause of death. It was found that Finnegan could not have caused those specific injuries and the prosecution decided not to proceed with the case. Finnegan later pleaded guilty to a lesser charge of causing an affray and was subsequently convicted and received a suspended jail sentence.

In October 2001, the INLA were in trouble again. Joe Magee was jailed for three years, by the Special Criminal Court after pleading guilty to the charge of possession of firearms. He was sent to Portlaoise to join the rest of his old team.

* * * *

Despite their ongoing run of bad luck, the remaining Dublin INLA

members didn't seem able to stop themselves from becoming
involved in thuggery and violence. The organisation continued to
recruit members in Dublin's working-class suburbs, confirming that
the 'ceasefire' was a sham. Twenty-eight-year-old Derek Lenihan
was typical of the new members. Lenihan lived near Blanchardstown
and was close to Gerry Burns, the INLA Dublin 'commander'. A
general machine operative, he was known to anti-terrorist detectives
but had no criminal record. Lenihan enjoyed the dubious status that
came with membership of the INLA. In January 2001, detectives
from Blanchardstown Garda Station searched Lenihan's home and
found a sawn-off shotgun and ammunition. He was subsequently
charged with the offence and released on bail.

Lenihan's older brother John, a qualified panel beater, was
working in a garage on the city's north side in May 2001. He had a
minor argument with a more senior member of the garage staff.
Following the incident John Lenihan became paranoid, believing
that the man was "bad mouthing" him behind his back. John Lenihan
decided that he wasn't going to stand for it and called his INLA
brother for help. Derek Lenihan agreed to give the innocent worker
"a shock". John Lenihan had told his brother: "No one is going to
fuck with me and get away with it." Derek Lenihan decided to
terrorise the workman with a firearm. Gerry Burns the INLA leader
agreed to 'the action' and gave Lenihan a handgun. The worker
lived in north-west Dublin with his wife and their four children,
ranging in age between eleven years and six months. They were
respectable, decent people living ordinary lives. The husband
worked hard to provide for his family while his wife cared for their
children. They were the last people in the world who should suffer
intimidation and terror.

On the night of June 7, 2001, the worker watched a movie with
his wife and then went to his local pub for a drink, as he usually did
three nights a week. Shortly before midnight his wife had just
checked her sleeping children when she heard a knock on the door.
She asked who was there. A man's voice requested her husband by
name. She opened the door slightly to talk to the man who suddenly
forced his way into the hallway. A second man stood outside. Derek
Lenihan began shouting in an angry voice, demanding to know the
whereabouts of her husband. He pinned the terrified woman against

the wall. Lenihan lifted up a pistol and pushed it into the side of her forehead.

The woman later told detectives what happened next: "I could feel the cold end of the gun against my skin. I felt like I couldn't breathe. I was so terrified I could see that this man was getting more aggressive. He was pushing the gun against my head. I thought that it would definitely go off. He was saying my husband's name and the place where he worked. He kept saying to tell my husband not to mess with …[other workers] that they have friends."

By this stage the woman was crying, terrified that one of the children would hear the commotion and come down the stairs. Lenihan kept repeating the message he wanted her to give to the husband. He repeatedly demanded to know did she understand. She said she did. Before the two thugs left the INLA man told the woman that she and her husband would be shot dead if they called the police. He said her children would then have no parents. He put the gun into his jacket and left the house. She recalled later: "I ran into the kitchen and I thought that I was going to be sick but I couldn't get sick. I phoned my husband and told him to come home. I was crying and shaking. I was feeling sick; I was terrified. I never thought that anything like this could ever happen to us. I thought I could have been shot dead. I was in fear of my children's lives. When I was being threatened by this man I was terrified my daughter would come down and be hurt."

Shortly before the attack, as the worker was having his customary pint in his local, John Lenihan and two friends arrived into the pub. Lenihan actually used the same local as his intended target. The worker spotted John Lenihan and said hello but Lenihan ignored him. The worker might have wondered what was up with Lenihan but it wasn't long before he had other things on his mind. His quiet drink was interrupted by the frantic phone call from his wife. He rushed home and immediately phoned the police.

In the meantime staff in the pub became suspicious of Lenihan and his friends. They feared that the men were planning to rob the premises. The police were called. As Gardaí arrived, Lenihan and his companions moved to the pub car park where they were apprehended. When Gardaí searched the car being driven by Lenihan they found shotgun cartridges. The officers also discovered that the car was officially stolen. The three men were arrested and brought to Whitehall Garda Station for questioning. At the same time other units were arriving to answer the call from the worker's house up the road.

Detectives believed that there was a connection between John Lenihan and the incident at the worker's house. Initially officers suspected that the panel beater and his companions were responsible for the attack. When he was quizzed about the incident Lenihan admitted that he was having a problem with the work colleague. He also admitted approaching a number of people who offered to give the man "a shock". In further interviews Lenihan revealed that he had gone to his brother Derek and his friends. He finally admitted that he knew his brother was going to "get" his work colleague.

Officers attached to Fitzgibbon Street and Mountjoy Garda Stations launched a major investigation. On a personal level many of the investigators were sickened by the attack on an innocent family. It was resolved that the culprits would be found and prosecuted. The investigation team were determined to locate the weapon used in the attack. They focused on the connection with the INLA. Intelligence obtained by Detective Sergeant Walter O'Sullivan revealed that the weapon used in the attack was in the control of Gerry Burns. On June 15, 2001, teams of officers swooped on the homes of Derek Lenihan and Gerry Burns and arrested them for questioning in relation to the incident at the house. During a search of a wardrobe in the main bedroom of Burns's house they found what they were looking for. Hidden in three plastic bags were two semi-automatic sawn-off shotguns, a .38 revolver and over 100 rounds of ammunition. The officers were surprised that Burns had not made a better attempt to conceal the weapons. After all, since the Ballymount Bloodbath, he had already been arrested on a number of occasions. While the detectives were searching upstairs Burns talked freely to their colleagues downstairs about the ongoing ceasefire and the INLA's commitment to peace. When the officers showed him the weapons he took responsibility for them. Burns was charged with possession of firearms and ammunition and remanded in custody. Derek Lenihan was later released without charge. There was not enough evidence to charge him for the attack on the worker's wife.

The arrest of Burns and the arms seizure were another bitter blow to the INLA and provided more proof of their involvement in crime. Again they had been caught red-handed indulging in brutal thuggery. It showed that the INLA's commitment to peace was a farce. There was nothing political about their deeds. They would have been a complete joke was it not for the fact that the fools were actually armed and dangerous. It was also highly embarrassing to the IRSP. Burns had been the IRSP's front man in negotiations with the government to secure the release of Dessie O'Hare under the Good Friday Agreement. Burns had even met with Taoiseach Bertie Ahern and his advisors.

The INLA began to investigate this latest embarrassing episode. In November 2001, Derek Lenihan and another associate from Blanchardstown, west Dublin, were summoned to a meeting in Dundalk. From there they were brought to South Armagh. After being questioned about the incident on June 7 and the subsequent arrest of Gerry Burns, Derek Lenihan and his companion were gagged and shot in the legs. Both men were dumped along the side of an unapproved road between Forkhill and Dundalk. Derek Lenihan bled to death as a result of his injuries. His companion, who was also seriously injured, survived the attack but refused to co-operate with police. John Lenihan was subsequently convicted of unlawful possession of the ammunition that was found in the car. Lenihan suffered from depression as a result of his brother's death.

A week later Gerry Burns pleaded guilty to the firearms offences in the Special Criminal Court and was jailed for five years. Officers who dealt with the case were surprised that he had received a relatively short sentence considering his activities and his violation of the conditions of his release in 1995 under the terms of the Good Friday Agreement.

Two months later in January 2002 the INLA hit the headlines again when one of their members Colm Peake walked into Fitzgibbon Street Garda Station and shot himself in the head. Originally from the Divis Flats in Belfast, Peake had been living in Dublin's north inner-city since 1995. He had been involved in armed robbery and other INLA rackets. Two days after the shooting he died from his injuries. What many saw as the curse of the INLA had struck again.

In less than three years the INLA had suffered a string of serious setbacks. At least ten of their henchmen, including their so-called commanders Burns and Duffy, had been convicted and jailed and four of their members were dead. However members of the INLA, along with other dissident Republican groups and the IRA are still heavily involved in controlling security for the sleazy lapdance club scene and in prostitution. The jailed INLA men have since begun enjoying temporary release from prison to the extreme annoyance of the police who worked so hard to put them there in the first place. It appears astonishing that the Irish Government continues to release these men considering the INLA's blatant violation of their own cease-fire. Police intelligence on both sides of the Border also points to the involvement of the INLA with other dissident groups who are trying to wreck the peace process.

INLA members are also mixed up in drug and protection rackets. In January 2003, this led to the organisation's heavy involvement in a bitter gangland war that blew up in Limerick, following the execution of notorious crime lord Kieran Keane. Arthur Jordan, the terrorist drug dealer who was still running a huge cocaine dealing racket in Tallaght, and the INLA had been closely associated with Keane's drug and gun running operations. Back in July 2002, Jordan had found himself facing eviction from his apartment at Moynihan Court in Tallaght and had decided to fight off the eviction attempt with the help of three associates, armed with three sawn-off shotguns. But the Gardaí had been tipped off and Detective Superintendent Diarmuid O' Sullivan of the Special Detective Unit deployed members of the Emergency Response Unit around the apartment block. The incident had ended peacefully when the Superintendent had convinced Jordan to open the door. Jordan and his INLA associates were later charged with possession of firearms for an unlawful purpose. While still facing that charge they continued to be actively involved in trying to move arms, explosives and hit men to Limerick for an all-out war.

Following the murder of Kieran Keane, Jordan's gang helped procure guns and a number of car bombs for use in the Limerick feud. Luckily detectives intercepted the arms before they could be used. Jordan's luck ran out in early May 2003 when the motorbike he was driving crashed into a tree in dense fog in County Kildare. He died instantly. Three weeks later, on May 23, 2003, Jordan's INLA associate Stephen O'Shaughnessy was sentenced to five years when he pleaded guilty in the Special Criminal Court to the unlawful possession of a sawn-off shotgun at Jordan's apartment in July 2002. The court suspended the final two years of the sentence when it heard that he had not been the prime mover in the crime. Detective Superintendent O'Sullivan commented that Jordan was a member of the INLA and had been involved with serious criminals in Dublin.

In March 2003, Declan Duffy and Patrick O'Toole appealed the severity of their sentences for the Ballymount Bloodbath. The Appeal Court upheld Duffy's nine-year sentence while O'Toole's seven-year sentence was reduced by two years. Duffy told an officer who attended the hearing that he was now a political prisoner. Despite the court's ruling and the fact that he is not eligible for release until 2007, on several occasions Duffy has been granted temporary release from prison. The Gardaí's job has been made all the more impossible as the Department of Justice continues to release Duffy as part of the peace process. Police intelligence suspect that the INLA 'commander' is again involved in plotting crime with his cronies and he is known to have met with individuals involved in the Limerick feud.

Shortly after Duffy's failed Appeal, the Ballymount Bloodbath had another horrendous sequel. On June 14, 2003, twenty-five-year-old Ronnie Draper was shot dead as he stood at the door of a pub on Eden Quay in Dublin. A masked gunman stepped off the back of a motorbike and shot Draper three times in the head before making his escape. Police believe that the murder was directly linked to the Ballymount incident. It was a chilling reminder from the INLA that they have not gone away.

Gangland had never experienced an event quite like the Ballymount Bloodbath. In a little less than two hours on that fateful night in October 1999, one man was dead, several were seriously injured and the INLA organisation was publicly exposed for what it really was – an organised crime gang. It led directly to two other murders and a number of assassination attempts. The Ballymount Bloodbath also sparked one of the largest and most complex police investigations ever, resulting in the imprisonment of several INLA members. In the end the INLA's utter corruption and thuggish attitude proved to be its fatal flaw.

A year before the Ballymount incident a member of Sinn Féin in Belfast summed up that organisation's attitude to the INLA/IRSP's role in mainstream Republicanism when he described them thus: "These people [INLA/IRSP] are just gangsters, interested in their own opinion. In reality the nationalist community do not endorse the INLA's actions, or heed the IRSP's rhetoric; for they perceive the INLA/IRSP as opportunists using the banner of Republican socialism as a convenience to cloak their true intentions, that is, to provide for their own personal gain."

Five

"A Good Catholic"

"I am an honest man, a good father and a good Catholic. I love animals so I wouldn't hurt another human being. I had nothing to do with that hideous crime."

It was April 1999 and the tall, dark-haired man sitting in the witness box of the Central Criminal Court looked at the jury, his eyes exhorting them to believe him. At first glance, he could certainly justify the description he had just given of himself. Aged in his early fifties and wearing a smart business suit, he used reading glasses, perched on the end of his long nose, to consult a legal document in his lap. In the next breath this "respectable" gentleman proceeded to accept that he was also a cocaine-snorting drug dealer and an alcoholic. The man in the witness box was Joseph Delaney, otherwise known by his underworld cronies as "Cotton Eye" Joe – a drug dealer, a pimp, a torturer, a murderer and an all-round psychotic monster. Delaney was in every respect a truly evil man, who had even threatened to murder his own sons. The "hideous crime" he was referring to was the abduction, gruesome torture and execution of one Mark Carolan Dwyer, a twenty-three-year old drug dealer and killer, who had once been a member of "Cotton Eye's" gang. It was the first time a gangland murder case had actually been brought before the Irish courts. The case would give a chilling insight into the underworld and the mindset of its ruthless inhabitants. A judge would later describe the crime as one of "the most vile and sadistic acts of savagery" to come before the courts. The plot for this story was almost unbelievable in its horror.

Joseph Delaney was born in Ballyfermot, West Dublin, on February 20, 1945. He had one brother and two sisters, none of whom were ever involved in crime. Their brother, however, was involved in crime and violence for over thirty years. "Cotton Eye", as he was nicknamed as a result of a weepy eye, had always been regarded by associates as someone with a very short fuse. He notched up a number of convictions for serious assaults and was involved on the fringes of a number of criminal gangs. Although he was listed by Garda intelligence as an associate of several criminals, Delaney largely went unnoticed, and unknown, by the police.

In 1970, he married Stella Kane and the couple moved to live in Swords, north County Dublin. They had three children, a daughter and two sons. Delaney was employed as a production manager for twenty-three years with the Cadbury's chocolate company in Coolock. "Cotton Eye's" heavy drinking and uncontrollable temper made life in the family home a living hell. He regularly beat his wife and children. Stella Delaney later described him as an alcoholic psychopath. She said he had a "split personality" and was "...a dangerous man capable of doing anything."

After twenty-three years of brutality, drunkenness and infidelity, Stella could take no more. She obtained a barring order to keep him out of the family home. "Cotton Eye" had begun a relationship with one of his wife's former friends and moved in to live with her. In 1993, Stella formally ended the marriage with a legal separation. But Delaney continued to harass his wife. In 1995, she was forced to seek another barring order. Some years later she told detectives that during a court hearing objecting to the order, Delaney told her that he was going to, "...give it to you good and proper." Then, while giving evidence at the Family Court, he had told the judge that his wife's sister was "a nosy bitch" and vowed that he was going to "sort her out". The judge was horrified by the remark and had ordered Delaney off the witness stand, saying he had heard quite enough. The judge had barred the gangster from ever going near Stella or their eighteen-year-old daughter again. People who knew Delaney commented that the extraordinary outburst was characteristic of the man.

By the time "Cotton Eye's" marriage first foundered in 1993, he had been let go from his factory job and had used his redundancy money to buy three taxi licences. He got involved in prostitution rackets in the city and was running a successful brothel in Stephen Street in south inner-city Dublin. When police raided the premises they found four working girls. Delaney's mistress, who was the brothel Madam, had been interviewing prospective "employees" when the raid took place. Later that evening the officers arrested Delaney as he arrived to collect the day's takings. In October 1995, he was convicted in the Dublin District Court on a charge of living off immoral earnings and given a £500 fine. His mistress was also convicted.

At that stage, however, the £500 fine meant very little to "Cotton Eye" Joe Delaney. He had discovered a new way of making a dishonest buck – drugs. He had started dealing in small amounts of hashish, cocaine and ecstasy, using his two sons, Robert and Scott, and a group of other young men, to distribute his drugs. Those who knew Delaney, described him as a "wannabe gang boss". Despite this ambition other criminals, and even members of his own gang, regularly ripped him off. Later he would claim that he had suffered from depression and alcoholism. He blamed Robert, his oldest child who had been born in 1970, for introducing him to narcotics as a way of making a living. "He [Robert] had contacts, I didn't. The part I was to play was to just collect the money. He [Robert] was well-known – a big mover, I think they call it. One of the top people," Delaney would later claim in court.

One of Joe Delaney's associates was PJ Judge, the feared crime lord, aptly nicknamed the Psycho. Delaney bought a lot of his drugs from Judge and the pair were as friendly as psychopaths can be. Judge, from Finglas in north-west Dublin, had one of the most fearsome reputations for violence and murder in gangland. The Psycho controlled a huge drug distribution empire, supplying all kinds of drugs, across west and north Dublin. He had established his territory following his release from prison in the early 1990s. To maintain control of his turf he made no secret of the immense pleasure it gave him to inflict pain on anyone who crossed him. Judge was responsible for a string of gun attacks and he tortured and murdered at least two of his associates. Mark Dwyer was Judge's right-hand man.

Dwyer was considered to be the Psycho's protégé, with a similar fondness for violent crime. Born in 1973, Dwyer had been involved in crime from an early age and had a reputation for extreme violence. He was a small man who had been bald since his late teens. Although born Mark Carolan, he was named Dwyer after his stepfather, Christy "Bud" Dwyer, who married his mother Hilda when Mark was eighteen months old. "Bud" Dwyer was also well-known in criminal circles. He had been convicted for the murder of two men on a Dublin street in the late 1960s. Dwyer and his brother John ran a roofing business from a yard in the inner-city. The yard was also a base for criminal enterprises. The only legal work Mark Dwyer ever did was to occasionally work for his stepfather on roofing jobs.

In January 1996, a small-time criminal and drug courier, called William "Jock" Corbally, flew to Amsterdam to pick up a kilo of heroin for associates of Judge and Mark Dwyer. Corbally had grown up in the Psycho's neighbourhood and for several years Judge had harboured a pathological hatred for "Jock". This was despite the fact that "Jock" was nothing more than a "chancer" and a conman, way down the criminal scale, Judge had been waiting for a chance to murder him for some time.

Corbally returned from Holland with the heroin – and a life-threatening plan for his best scam ever. He tipped off a Garda contact and told him where he could recover a stash of heroin. "Jock" arranged for it to be found near Sutton Dart station, in north Dublin. His plan was to take over a quarter of the heroin consignment from the haul to sell for himself before leaving the rest to be found by the cops.

On January 19, "Jock" arranged to meet a known heroin addict near the Dart station. Corbally told the junkie that he was going to deliver the kilo of smack to Judge's gang. At the same time a Garda unit arrived to search for the drugs and Corbally ran off. The conman intended to tell Judge and his associates that he had been forced to abandon the heroin when he spotted the police. Unfortunately, when "Jock" first thought of his hair-brained scam, he had not counted on the police giving details of the quantity of heroin they had found to the media. Information about the heroin haul was splashed all over the morning newspapers.

On February 28, 1996, Mark Dwyer contacted another gang member and Garda informant, Declan "Decie" Griffin. "Decie", a twenty-five-year-old convicted armed robber from Coolock in north Dublin, had been arrested in the airport two months earlier with IR£1 million worth of heroin. At the time, he claimed that he was working as an informant for a Garda detective and was helping to set up the owner of the drugs. Griffin was an extremely devious and duplicitous hood. Dwyer told Griffin to arrange to meet Corbally and take him to a field near Baldonnell, off the Naas Motorway in South County Dublin.

Griffin drove Corbally to the field on the pretence that they were going to collect drugs. When they got there Dwyer, Judge and a third gangster were waiting to pounce. They beat Corbally with iron bars as he screamed for mercy. Corbally was kicked and stabbed several times all over the body. Judge made sure that none of the wounds would kill his victim too soon – he was enjoying himself too much. The three men gave "Jock" Corbally a horrifying death. It was one of the most gruesome and depraved murders ever perpetrated in gangland. At one stage, Judge turned Corbally on his back and smashed in his pearly white teeth with an iron bar. "Jock", a handsome, fit man, had prided himself on his teeth. The beating and torture continued. Corbally, however, could not take the ferocity of the attack and after some time he stopped screaming and fell silent.

Dwyer and Griffin, happy with their night's work, drove back to Dublin on Judge's instructions. Meanwhile Judge and the other remaining criminal dumped Corbally's body into the boot of a car and drove him to an unknown location somewhere in County Kildare. Later they buried the small-time criminal in an unmarked grave. It is unknown whether "Jock" was still alive when he was put in the ground. Both Judge and Dwyer told associates that Corbally's throat was sliced before he was dumped in the hole. At the time of writing that grave has not been located.

Later that night the Psycho phoned Dwyer. "Is the baby asleep?" Dwyer asked. "The baby has been tucked in and is sound asleep," Judge is said to have replied. The Corbally murder sent a shiver through gangland and sent out a clear message to the criminal fraternity – it was unwise to mess with the men responsible. Ironically ten months later, Dwyer and Delaney would replicate this horrific episode. To the superstitious the events that followed were viewed as "Jock" Corbally's curse from the grave.

In the meantime Dwyer also began "working" with Delaney's gang – selling ecstasy, hashish and cocaine. Compared to other operations, Delaney's gang was a small, as yet insignificant, outfit consisting of a core of six people. They sold wholesale quantities of ecstasy and cocaine to dealers, plying their trade in several of the city's rave clubs. "Cotton Eye" was the boss and the wholesale distribution and money collection was left to his henchmen. They included his two sons, Robert and Scott, a drug dealer from Coolock nicknamed "Killer" and Mark Dwyer, all of whom were in their early twenties. Delaney liked having Dwyer on board and saw him as his own personal hit man. An equally fearsome member of the gang was Chris Curry from Leopardstown, in fashionable South Dublin. Curry was an unlikely gangster. He had been adopted and reared by a respectable family and was educated at prestigious Blackrock College. The former bouncer was a body builder and known as a hard man. Curry had served time for an armed robbery in which an elderly man had died as the result of a heart attack. Curry had originally been charged with manslaughter but the charge was later dropped. Delaney and his mob began dealing in larger quantities of drugs and business began to pick up. "Cotton Eye" reckoned that he was on his way to achieving his main ambition in life – to become a big time drug baron.

In September 1996, he negotiated a deal to buy 40,000 ecstasy tablets from a source in Amsterdam who was also supplying PJ Judge and other Irish criminals. Delaney agreed to pay less than IR£20,000 for the shipment. He then planned to sell the ecstasy wholesale for an estimated profit of IR£160,000. By the time they had been sold at street level the consignment would have turned over up to IR£500,000, depending on the price per tablet at the time which is dictated by supply and demand. Delaney plotted to re-invest the money in larger quantities, thus driving up profits, and ensuring that he made the major league. He met his son Scott in the Gresham Hotel, in Dublin's O'Connell Street and told him to get someone to move the drugs from Amsterdam to Cherbourg. A courier, working for "Killer", would then pick up the drugs and bring them into Ireland. Scott asked his best friend Mark Dwyer to do the job.

A few days later "Cotton Eye Joe" met Dwyer and agreed to pay him IR£4,000 for doing the run. Dwyer had made a number of other drug runs to Amsterdam with Scott Delaney and PJ Judge and he knew the ropes. Mark Dwyer's younger brother, nineteen-year-old Christopher, accompanied him on the trip.

The run from Amsterdam went smoothly and Dwyer handed the package, containing the E, to one of the gang's couriers, an associate of "Killer", also from Coolock. The Dwyers escorted the courier on a train to Paris and then he went onto Cherbourg from where the consignment was brought to Ireland by ferry. The Dwyer brothers, however, had run out of cash in Paris and they had no way of getting home.

"Cotton Eye" told Scott to organise a courier to bring money over to Dwyer in Paris. Scott in turn asked Adrienne McGuinness to bring cash over to Mark Dwyer. The twenty-six-year-old, unmarried mother-of-one, was a close friend of Scott Delaney and Mark Dwyer. She had met them while hanging around with the same group of young drug dealers. From the East Wall area of north-inner-city Dublin, McGuinness had also dabbled in the drug business and had acted as a courier. By her own admission she was a "gangster's moll" who enjoyed the excitement and the buzz she got from hanging out with dangerous criminals. She had only met "Cotton Eye" a few weeks before Scott contacted her. She later recalled: "I remember meeting "Cotton Eye" with Mark and Scott. He used to come around to a friend's house looking for Scott. He always wore dark glasses and gave off the image that he was a big time gangster. Scott was terrified of his Da and told me that he couldn't handle him. Scott asked me in October if I had a passport. He said his father wanted money brought over to Mark Dwyer. Scott gave me an envelope with over IR£2,000 in it which I took to Paris and paid for my air ticket out of it." McGuinness met the Dwyers in a train station in Paris and they spent two days there partying before returning to Dublin on October 15, 1996. They were arrested in Dublin airport on suspicion of importing drugs but the three friends were released after a few hours.

In the meantime the consignment of E had arrived safely in Dublin. "Cotton Eye" instructed Scott to arrange for the shipment to be collected. The ecstasy tablets were to be split into two batches of 20,000 tablets each. Mark Dwyer was to collect one batch and sell it in conjunction with Scott Delaney: the other batch was to be picked up by Chris Curry and his associate "Japo" Merrigan and Curry would distribute it. They organised to meet the courier in the car park of The Goblet pub in Artane, North Dublin, where the handover was to take place. But the plan did not go as smoothly as they had hoped.

Dwyer and "Japo" Merrigan arrived at The Goblet pub without any problems and met the courier. However, as the handover was just about to take place, an armed man emerged from the shadows and identified himself as a Garda. He ordered the criminals to lie down on the ground. The 'Garda' then grabbed the E and ran off. As soon as the 'Garda' had gone the drug dealers did a runner, thinking they were going to be arrested. But no police turned up. They had been ripped off.

When "Cotton Eye" was told what had happened he was apoplectic with rage. Later that night he met the Dwyer brothers, Curry and Scott Delaney, in a pub in Grangegorman to discuss what had happened. It didn't take long to confirm that the Gardaí had not seized the drugs. "Cotton Eye" was not going to take this lying down. Delaney was determined to find the culprit and recover his 40,000 ecstasy tablets. He couldn't bear to contemplate the loss of so much money. Just like his friend the Psycho, "Cotton Eye" wanted it made clear that no one was going to mess with him. The person responsible would pay with his life.

The next evening, "Cotton Eye" called a meeting at his home in the countryside at Newhall, near Naas, County Kildare. Chris Curry collected Mark Dwyer, Christopher Dwyer and Scott Delaney from a pub in Grangegorman. Two weeks before the Dutch ecstasy deal, "Cotton Eye's" eldest son, Robert Delaney, had emigrated to live in San Francisco, so he was out of the picture. On the way to Kildare the four gangsters discussed what had happened. They were all nervous of how "Cotton Eye" was going to react, none more so than his own son. They all agreed that the most likely suspect was "Killer".

They arrived at Delaney's house just after 7pm. As they drove up to the door "Cotton Eye" turned off the lights. He was standing outside with his beloved dog, Beethoven. The 'gang boss' told them that he was afraid that whoever had ripped off the drugs would come to shoot him. The young thugs went inside and Delaney made them coffee. As he was preparing the coffee, the drug dealer told his henchmen that he had smashed the sink in his bedroom in a fit of rage over his stolen ecstasy. He said he couldn't sleep all night thinking about it and had downed a bottle of whiskey to ease the trauma. As they sat around the table "Cotton Eye" and his son agreed that "Killer" was the definite suspect. Curry, however, was keeping an open mind and said that they had to be sure of the culprit before they started "killing people". No one had mentioned killing anyone until then. They had all simply assumed it would be the natural course of action. "Cotton Eye" walked around the kitchen, swinging a baseball bat between his hands. He showed the bat to Christopher Dwyer and asked him: "What do ya think of that?" Dwyer replied: "That's the business." "Well whoever did the rip will get plenty of this," Delaney said. It was decided that "Killer" would be abducted and taken away for questioning. Mark Dwyer, who already had a track record in this kind of crime, suggested tying the suspect's arms and legs to make sure there were no problems during the abduction. Gang members would later recall how Dwyer had often bragged about the Corbally murder. He said "Jock" had deserved his horrific fate because he was an informant. Mark Dwyer claimed that he had helped the Psycho 'slice' Corbally's throat and the protégé had made no secret of how much he had enjoyed it.

The plotters moved from the kitchen to the sitting room to discuss their plan further. Joe Delaney sat in an armchair still playing with his baseball bat. After more talk, it was decided that "Killer" hadn't done "the rip" himself but that he had got someone else to do it instead. Then the gang boss suggested kidnapping "Killer's" girlfriend and keeping her as long as it took to get the ecstasy back. Curry and Mark Dwyer disagreed. Dwyer suggested taking "Killer" out into a field and torturing him. "Cotton Eye" then declared that he would personally take charge of dealing with the suspect. "Killer" would be brought back to Delaney's house where he would have a room specially prepared for the purpose. It would be covered in plastic sheeting with a chair standing in the middle. "Cotton Eye" jumped out of his seat and began swinging the baseball bat, acting out what he would do: "I'll take him into the room and tie him to the chair and then beat him for a few hours. Then I'll have a drink and leave him for a while and relax. Then I'll start on him again. I won't kill him until I find out where my Es are. I won't hit his head too much because he might die too quick. After a few hours I'll find where the Es are."

Delaney said he planned to dig a grave in a field, bring "Killer" to it and shoot him. He said he would do it by himself so no one would know where the grave was located. The plan was a chilling replica of the Corbally murder. The gang members would later describe how the boss was frothing at the mouth, like a demented lunatic, as he ranted on about his diabolical plan. Scott told his mad father to take it easy and calm down but he was told to, "shut to fuck up". Chris Curry also told his boss to calm down – his size and sheer strength meant Delaney was a little less abusive. "We'd be better questioning a few people before we rush into this to be sure to get the Es back. I'll talk to a few people myself," said Curry. It was eventually agreed that everyone would make their own enquiries about the missing drugs. "Before anything else I want a piece up here now," Delaney said, meaning a gun. He said he was afraid that someone might try to shoot him. Mark Dwyer volunteered to pick up a pistol from an associate in Tallaght and bring it back to him. The meeting broke up after an hour. Dwyer picked up a Luger pistol from a man in a car park just off the Greenhills Road. When Dwyer brought it back to "Cotton Eye" he showed 'the gang boss' how to use it. "Thanks Mark," said Delaney, as his young lieutenant headed back to Dublin.

The following day, "Cotton Eye" Delaney and Chris Curry had a meeting with "Killer" in the Black Sheep pub in Coolock. After a long interrogation session, during which "Killer" was often reduced to tears, Delaney was convinced that he was not responsible for "the rip". But the elimination of the prime suspect had done nothing to assuage Delaney. He had become obsessed with finding the person who stole his 'gear' and dealing with him. He had also asked Mark Dwyer if he had ripped him off. "I resent the accusation but I know that you have to ask… I had nothing to do with it," Dwyer had replied. Delaney said that Curry and his associate, who had been in the pub car park at the time of "the rip", had seen the thief put the drugs in the back of Dwyer's car. The following day Delaney told Dwyer that he now suspected Curry and his own son Robert of ripping him off even though Robert was in the US. Dwyer thought he was out of harm's way.

As the days went by Delaney grew more and more obsessed with finding his drugs and seeking vengeance – his obsession was exacerbated by his cocaine-induced paranoia. By this stage he was snorting up to two grammes of the drug daily. He phoned Chris Curry and other members of the gang several times each day to discuss theories about who had done "the rip". Soon everyone in the gang felt that he was a suspect and everyone of them tried to insinuate it had been the other who had stolen the E. They were all terrified of "Cotton Eye Joe". Chris Curry would later recall how the gang boss was "turning on his own" and how he now suspected his son Scott. Scott Delaney expressed his fears to his friends and said that his father would murder him if he thought he had stolen the drugs. There was no such thing as honour among this bunch of thieves.

But as the days passed the man who kept re-emerging at the top of Delaney's list was Mark Dwyer. His fate was sealed when "Cotton Eye" had a meeting with PJ Judge to discuss the theft of the E and their ongoing problems with Dwyer. Judge by this stage had plans to murder Dwyer himself. He suspected that Dwyer had been talking about the "Jock" Corbally murder to the police and to the *Sunday World* newspaper. Judge told Delaney that Dwyer had offered him a large amount of E for a good price. The Psycho said he turned down the offer because he didn't trust Dwyer. Judge promised to help Delaney investigate the disappearance of the E while Delaney said he would help Judge locate five kilos of his missing heroin.

After that meeting "Cotton Eye" was under no illusions about who had ripped him off. By the beginning of November 1996, Delaney had made his mind up. It was Mark Dwyer and he was going to pay for the crime. At a meeting with Scott Delaney and Carl "Yorkie" Dunne, one of the gang's street dealers, "Cotton Eye" told them that it had been Mark all along who had ripped him off. Delaney was grinding his teeth and seething with anger. "I'll get the little bastard… I'll fucking kill him," he declared. Delaney told his son to set Dwyer up for abduction. Scott warned his friend to "get off side" and gave his father false information about Dwyer's cars and about his whereabouts.

On Thursday, December 5, "Cotton Eye" again demanded that his son help him find Mark Dwyer. He said that there were now three gangs looking to whack Dwyer and he wanted to get his drugs back before that happened. Delaney even claimed that he would only "give Dwyer a few slaps" and then give him IR£5,000 to go to Malta to get away from his other pursuers.

A few days later, however, the number of people out to kill Dwyer was reduced by one. On the night of December 7, 1996, PJ Judge went for drinks with his girlfriend in the Royal Oak pub in Finglas. Later that night as he was about to drive away from the pub, at around 12.30am, a gunman ran from the shadows and shot Judge twice in the back of the head. The Psycho died instantly. There were a number of suspects for the murder, including the IRA. Another potential suspect who had the motive – and the ability – to murder Judge was Mark Dwyer. He could have decided to kill Judge before Judge killed him. In any event no one has ever revealed the identity of the killer. The only thing that is certain about the Psycho's demise is that there were plenty of potential suspects with a multitude of motives. Within a week Mark Dwyer would be following his former boss to the grave.

Dwyer, who had gone to ground since being tipped off by Scott Delaney, was conspicuous by his absence at Judge's funeral. "Cotton Eye" had sent people to the funeral to look out for the wanted gangster who was now a dead man walking. In the meantime Dwyer had moved to a first floor flat at 55 Foster Terrace in Ballybough with his sixteen-year-old girlfriend Jennifer Byrne. Dwyer only told close family members his new address, which he intended keeping a secret. Jennifer Byrne later recalled that Mark had been behaving differently since Judge's murder. He told her that there was a possibility he could also be shot.

The day after the Psycho murder "Cotton Eye" again met his son and told him that he wanted Dwyer lifted in the coming week. He screamed abuse at Scott and threatened to kill him if he didn't do it. "If I see you on the street, I'll mow you down," he snarled at his son. He was in a paranoid aggressive state. He said that Dwyer had already killed Judge and would do the same to him – it was now a matter of kill or be killed. "Cotton Eye" reckoned the timing would be ideal as the real motive for Dwyer's murder would be covered up.

Whoever had murdered The Psycho would also be blamed for killing Dwyer. The police would think it had something to do with the Corbally murder and go in the wrong direction. Scott Delaney went to work.

On Wednesday, December 11, the same day as the Psycho's funeral, "Cotton Eye" was appearing in Naas District Court on a common assault charge. The previous September a man driving to see his elderly mother in hospital had accidentally hit Delaney's dog, Beethoven. Later that day, while on his way home, the man had called into "Cotton Eye's" house to apologise to Delaney for the incident and to explain that it had been an accident. But that wasn't good enough for "Cotton Eye" and he had punched the man in the jaw. In court Delaney was fined IR£50. While his father was in court, Scott was contacting Michael Ryan from Clondalkin in west Dublin. The twenty-three-year-old thug was a customer of the Delaney gang, buying cocaine and ecstasy which he sold in pubs and clubs in Clondalkin, Ballyfermot and Tallaght. Ryan was a member of the then notorious M50 gang, a group of young criminals mainly from Ballyfermot and Clondalkin, who specialised in stealing high-powered cars for use in ram-raids on business premises around the country. The gang got their name from the Dublin outer ring motorway where they regularly jousted with the police in high-speed chases. The M50 gang had also been involved in a string of armed robberies around the country and in one incident, gang members had shot and seriously injured an unarmed Garda in an attempted armed robbery. They were also heavily involved in the drug trade and several of them had been part of PJ Judge's rackets.

Later that day, Ryan met Scott Delaney in the car park of the Silver Granite pub in Palmerstown, near Ballyfermot. Scott Delaney told the M50 gangster that "Cotton Eye" had been ripped off by Mark Dwyer and that his father wanted to "have a word" with Dwyer about his missing ecstasy. Scott Delaney asked Ryan to steal a car and to recruit a good driver for the job. They would be paid IR£5,000 for their time and effort. Ryan agreed and told Delaney to call him when he knew Dwyer's exact whereabouts.

The following night Ryan and another thug robbed a BMW 525i outside a house in Knocklyon. They had no problem getting around the car's sophisticated security systems and had stolen the car in minutes. This was their stock and trade. Later they stashed the BMW in the car park of Donnybrook Manor, an upmarket block of private apartments in south Dublin, where every second car was a BMW.

In the meantime, Ryan recruited two other members of the M50 mob for the job: the driver, twenty-three-year-old Anthony "Gammy" Adams from Clondalkin and twenty-seven-year-old Jeremy Cooper from the North Strand in the inner-city. Both men, like Ryan, were violent thugs with a string of convictions for car crime, robbery and drug offences. Cooper in particular had an extensive record for violence and drug crimes with over twenty previous convictions. He had spent most of his life behind bars. The bisexual body builder had been part of a gang led by Tommy Freeman from Clondalkin – a man described in court as one of the "most ruthless and violent" criminals in the country. Freeman's mob specialised in terrorising their victims by holding them hostage during robberies.

Scott Delaney found out where Mark Dwyer was living and it was decided that the abduction would take place on Friday night into early Saturday morning. On Friday, December 13 Delaney phoned Chris Curry to tell him that he had "got a unit together" and asked him if he would take part in the abduction. Curry said he was busy.

Later that night Scott Delaney phoned Ryan and arranged to meet him, with Cooper and Adams, in O'Connell Street. When they met up Delaney showed them a photograph of Dwyer and then pointed out his new flat. Delaney said he would ring Ryan when he wanted them to move in. Scott spent the rest of the night drinking in city-centre pubs with his friend Carl "Yorkie" Dunne. He was agitated and nervous.

Around 1.30am, on Saturday December 14, they went to visit Mark Dwyer at his flat. Earlier in the night Scott Delaney had phoned Dwyer and said he would call over later. Dwyer was unsettled by the proposed visit. When they arrived at the flat shortly before 2am, Dwyer was there with his girlfriend and her friend listening to music and drinking cans of lager. An hour earlier the three M50 gang members had picked up their stolen BMW in Donnybrook. They killed time driving around the city waiting for the call to move in. "Gammy" Adams was driving. It was a freezing cold night. Back in the flat Scott Delaney, Dunne and Dwyer began snorting lines of cocaine. They talked about the Judge murder and speculated that it had been the work of the IRA. They talked in almost melancholic tones about how the underworld was changing for the worse with so many gangland murders. At one stage a neighbour knocked on the apartment door looking for sugar. Scott Delaney jumped up and became very agitated. Dwyer told him to calm down.

At 2am Ryan and the team in the stolen car rang Delaney to find out if Dwyer was there. Delaney took the call out in the corridor. He said Dwyer was there and he had left the downstairs door open for them. Some time around 2.30am the raiders burst into the apartment and ordered everyone onto the floor. A fourth man, who had joined the rest of the abduction mob and was never properly identified, had produced a shotgun and stood by the door while Ryan and Cooper grabbed Dwyer and put a pillowcase over his head. He was pushed face down on the floor and kicked repeatedly. "We want to talk to you, you little bastard. You were a silly boy… you fucked up," the man with the gun said to Dwyer. "What's all this about lads?" Dwyer asked. The kidnappers grabbed cable wires from behind the TV and video system and used them to tie up Dwyer's hands and legs "like a chicken". They also tied a piece of cable wire around his neck. Then Dwyer was bundled out to the waiting car.

The gang also took Scott Delaney with them and warned the others that if they called the police the abductors would hear the calls on a scanner and kill Delaney and Dwyer. "Calm down we will have him back in the morning," said Adams as the gang left. Dwyer and Delaney were shoved into the back of the waiting BMW. Dwyer asked them: "Is it death for me this time lads?" No one answered. Ironically the gang were following the plan Dwyer himself had suggested to "Cotton Eye" six weeks earlier when "the rip" first occurred. The car drove at speed out of the city and headed to "Cotton Eye's" home in County Kildare.

"Cotton Eye" Joe Delaney paced around his house as he waited for news from his son in Dublin. He sat down every now and then to snort a line of cocaine and gulp a shot of whiskey. He had been waiting for this moment for weeks. Delaney had phoned Adrienne McGuinness earlier in the evening and asked her to collect some cocaine for him from one of Chris Curry's runners. Around 2am she arrived at the house to deliver the drugs. "Cotton Eye" made

McGuinness tea and she helped herself to cocaine and then smoked a few joints.

After about ten minutes Delaney's mobile phone rang. He walked out into the hall to take the call and when he came back he announced: "Scott is on his way down." About twenty minutes later the BMW arrived outside. McGuinness, who was still in the sitting room, heard a commotion in the hall. Scott Delaney barged into the room and said to his father: "There, Mark's down the hall, now are you satisfied." Masked men were carrying Dwyer down the hall. He still had a hood over his head. They took him to a bedroom and put him lying face down on the bed with his knees on the floor. Scott Delaney then noticed McGuinness was in the sitting room. "What's she doing here?" he asked his father. "She is all right – she can be sorted," Delaney replied. He already had a plan to cover all eventualities and McGuinness was going to play a crucial role in executing it. The father and son left the room and went to inspect their victim. From that moment on Adrienne McGuinness was terrified: "I had no idea what I had just walked myself into here. I really thought that I was going to be next. Joe Delaney looked angry, agitated and evil."

Scott Delaney returned to the sitting room without his father and asked McGuinness for cocaine. He was holding his head in his hands. His father walked in behind him and told her to give him some coke. She took out the stash, which was hidden under a couch, and gave it to Scott. While he was snorting the lines of coke laid out on the table he told McGuinness that they were going to question Dwyer about the missing E. He left the room and closed the door. "Cotton Eye" then walked in, snorted a line and left. And then the screaming started. "Cotton Eye" Delaney had armed himself with an array of weaponry. He had a jemmy nail bar, an iron bar, a pickaxe handle and a number of knives. One of the men still carried a sawn-off shotgun. "Cotton Eye" began smashing the bar across Dwyer's back. "Where are they you little bastard? Who did you give them to? You little cunt your gone now," Delaney shouted. One of the other men told the victim: "Make it easy on yourself tell us where the Es are."

Everything that "Cotton Eye" had planned at the meeting with Dwyer and the other gang members back in October was now happening to Dwyer himself. Mark Dwyer's screams and cries of pain filled the house. As the torture continued the nail bar and the other weapons flailed his chest, back and legs. When the torturers kept demanding to know where the Es were he shouted: "The Delaneys, the Delaneys they live in Naas take me down and I'll show you the house." "Cotton Eye" was in a frenzy and Dwyer's answers were followed by more beating. He continued to smash Dwyer to a pulp on the ground in front of him. Adrienne McGuinness heard what happened next: "I heard Mark plead with them that he hadn't taken the drugs. 'If this is death for me then you are killing the wrong man... I had nothing to do with the rip.' Delaney came back into the sitting room. He was ranting and roaring: 'He'll tell us where they are if it's the last thing he does.' He had his shirt-sleeves rolled up and he was sweating like mad. I was afraid to open my mouth. I thought that I would be tortured next. I felt so helpless I couldn't help Mark. He [Delaney] snorted another line of coke and sat down and drank some more whiskey like he was on a break."

After a while Cooper and Adams walked into the sitting room while "Cotton Eye" was having a break. They also helped themselves to some cocaine. One of them said to Delaney: "This fellow isn't going to open his mouth, what are we going to do with him?" Delaney jumped up from his seat grabbed his iron bar and stormed off to the bedroom. "I'll make the little bastard talk," he snarled. The spine chilling screams began again moments later as Delaney laid into his former associate. During the ordeal Dwyer was also repeatedly stabbed with a knife in the arms. At one point the shotgun was pressed so hard into his chest that the track of the barrels could clearly be seen in his skin. Joe Delaney put on a CD by *M people* and turned up the volume to drown out the screams of pain. The other men went back to the room and joined in the madness. Adrienne McGuinness couldn't take it any longer and she cowered down beside the speakers to drown out the nightmare of a dying man's screams. Ironically one of the tracks thumping through the speakers was called 'Search for the hero'. She recalled: "The screams were unbearable. No human being could stand this. I kept looking at my car keys and contemplated making a run for it but I knew that I would have been dead before I got to the car."

The torture lasted for between two and three hours more before "Cotton Eye" and his sadists finally gave up. Two of the kidnappers talked to Delaney in the sitting room. "What are you going to do with him?" one of them asked. "Fuck him he'll have to be killed now," Delaney replied. Scott Delaney called his father into the kitchen and argued that Dwyer should not be killed. "What are you doing, you are after doing too much," he told his father. "Fuck him, he'll have to be killed now," Cotton replied. Then he punched his son in the face and told him to shut up. "Look son, there is nothing left of him. You have to kill a person after leaving him that bad," said one of the thugs. "If someone battered you like that what would you do to them afterwards? If he gets out of this he'll kill us all," he said. Scott Delaney drank more whiskey and snorted more cocaine. Everything was going out of control.

In the kitchen "Cotton Eye" negotiated a further IR£5,000 payment for the gang to finish Dwyer off. The men took the bloodied bundle that was Mark Dwyer out of the house through the back door. As they were leaving Scott Delaney turned to his father and pointed to McGuinness who was now a quivering wreck in the corner: "What about her Da, you know birds talk." His father smacked him in the face and pushed him out the door in front of him. Delaney drove behind the stolen BMW as the masked thugs took Mark Dwyer to a field off Scribblestown Lane between Finglas and Castleknock in west Dublin. He was dumped onto his knees and sat there hunched over, still tied and bound. PJ Judge had used the same field a few years earlier to murder another "rip off" suspect, Michael Godfrey. A sawn-off shotgun was placed against the back of Mark Dwyer's skull and a single shot ended his agony. "Cotton Eye" presided over the execution, ensuring that it was done properly. Scott Delaney, who was now in a ragged state from the booze and drugs, was left lying semi-conscious on the frosted ground beside his former best friend. "Cotton Eye" wanted it to look like outraged vigilantes were responsible for the murder. He reckoned it would put the police off the scent.

At 6.45am, a male caller made a 999 emergency call that was received at the Garda command and control centre in Dublin. An unidentified voice said: "River Lane, Finglas, near some factories, about 30 yards inside some white gates, there are two dead bodies, drug pushers, let this be a message to all drug pushers." The phone went dead. Minutes later a squad car was sent to Scribblestown and they discovered Mark Dwyer's body. Scott Delaney was barely conscious and suffering from hypothermia.

When "Cotton Eye" returned home he took the blood-soaked bedroom carpet off the floor and put it in into Adrienne's car. He also put his clothes and the bed covers in plastic bags. He told her to drive him to a back road near his house where he dumped the carpet in a ditch. Delaney then directed McGuinness to drive towards Dublin. On a roundabout off the M50 motorway he told her to pull in. He handed a bag containing Dwyer's jacket and other items to a man who was waiting along the road. They then drove back towards Naas and on the way had breakfast in McDonalds. "Cotton Eye" was hungry after a night of murder: McGuinness couldn't eat.

After a few hours sleep back at the house Delaney woke McGuinness and sent her to a chip shop for food. Later he got her to drive him to Dublin. On the way he phoned Chris Curry. Delaney said: "I suppose you've heard the news? It's all over." Curry said he had heard the news. "It was the hardest thing I ever had to do to leave Scott lying in the field. It's to throw the scent off myself and throw it onto the Corballys for "Jock's" murder. The little bastard didn't even talk," he told Curry. "Cotton Eye" was furious that his drugs were still missing despite his best efforts but he knew he now needed to cover his hide. He was planning to use McGuinness as his alibi. He asked her to stay at the house for a few days. At that stage local vigilantes in the East Wall area where McGuinness lived had made threats over her involvement in drugs. Despite her fear of Delaney she decided that she would stay in his house. She also agreed to be "Cotton Eye's" alibi by pretending to be his lover. The "gangster's moll" found herself in the middle of a mess that she was too terrified to do anything about. The cover story she agreed to tell the police was that on the night of the murder she and "Cotton Eye" had "been messing around on the couch" before going to bed. They had spent most of the night having sex. The next morning Delaney told her to say that she woke him and told him she was hungry and that they both went for breakfast to McDonalds on the Kylemore Road in Dublin. After breakfast they "went back to Naas and went back to bed for more sex".

"Cotton Eye" was also anxious to know what his son had told the police. Later on the evening of December 14, McGuinness dropped him off at the James Connolly Memorial Hospital in Blanchardstown where Scott was being treated. When he arrived at the ward he met three detectives who were guarding his son. They told him that his estranged wife had already been to the hospital and left strict instructions that he was not to see his son. Scott Delaney had told his mother he did not want to see "Cotton Eye". When Delaney got back to the car he was crazy with rage.

At around 1am McGuinness drove him to his wife's home in Palmerstown. He began banging on the door and shouting at his wife. "If I don't get in to see Scott in the hospital I'll be back here tomorrow night to blow your fucking brains out with a gun," he screamed. Stella Delaney and her daughter hid in an upstairs bathroom and rang the police. "He was shouting abuse and obscenities at myself and my daughter. He was calling us whores, scumbags, and prostitutes. He went on like a complete lunatic. He seemed totally deranged. We were absolutely terrified that he would break down the door and kill the two of us," Stella later told police. "Cotton Eye" had left by the time the local Gardaí arrived, forty minutes later.

On the following Wednesday, Delaney and McGuinness booked into the Jurys Custom House Inn on the North Wall Quay, under an assumed name. While staying there he talked to his associates and a solicitor. He heard that the police were looking for him and started making arrangements to get a false passport and money in order to leave the country. But in the meantime undercover officers from the National Surveillance Unit (NSU) were watching McGuinnes. The Garda search for Delaney paid off when the undercover officers followed McGuinness back to the hotel after she had called home for a brief visit with her child. Delaney was on his way to meet his 'banker' when detectives arrested him in Coolock. He was taken in for questioning to Fitzgibbon Street Garda Station, the headquarters of the Mark Dwyer murder hunt. A short time later Adrienne McGuinness was also arrested and taken to Store Street Garda Station.

* * * *

In the twenty years of organised crime, from the mid-seventies to the mid-nineties, scores of gangland murders had been notoriously hard to solve. It was the only area of serious crime investigation in which the police had zero success. While in most cases the Gardaí knew the motive and identity of the killers, none of the cases had been strong enough to bring before the courts. In underworld executions the hit man tends to disappear behind the largest wall this side of China – the great wall of silence. Fear and coercion had ensured the death of many Garda investigations. Two gangland killings, within a week of each other, were the last thing the Garda Chiefs in the Dublin Metropolitan Area wanted. Resources were already stretched to the limit because of the ongoing, and massive, inquiry into the murder of Veronica Guerin six months earlier. That investigation was progressing at an incredible pace and, in order to maintain the momentum, would require a large team of officers for many months to come. The establishment of the new Criminal Assets Bureau and the re-organisation and enlargement of several specialist units, like the Garda National Drug Unit and the Special Detective Unit, had also drained large numbers of officers from districts across the city as the new posts were filled. Set against this was the public disquiet over the apparent omnipotence of organised crime gangs, a feeling that was already exacerbated as a result of the Guerin murder. The Gardaí desperately needed to crack a gangland case.

It didn't take detectives long to informally identify Mark Dwyer. Luckily his face was still intact despite the shotgun being held to the back of his head when it was fired. Automatically investigators suspected Dwyer's murder was linked to that of PJ Judge, a week earlier. If that was the case then this could be the first round in an all-out bloody gang war. By 9am on December 14, Dwyer's identity was confirmed when Jennifer Byrne contacted the Gardaí to report his abduction. In the hours immediately after the incident at Foster Terrace she was too terrified to call the police because the kidnappers had said that they would be listening to the Garda radio frequencies. She had made contact with Christy "Bud" Dwyer who had agreed that she should not call the police in case the kidnappers intercepted the call.

The murder investigation then became the responsibility of the detective unit attached to Fitzgibbon Street Garda Station, the headquarters of the Garda 'U' district where the abduction had occurred. The overall Commander of the investigation was Chief Superintendent Dick Kelly who controlled the North Central Division. Detective Superintendent Cormac Gordon and Detective Inspector Hubert Collins were the officers in immediate charge of the enquiry on the ground and who, because of the prevailing shortage of resources, would have to rely largely on their own detective and uniformed units. Following an initial emergency conference, it was decided to maintain an open mind as to motive. Although they suspected a link between the Judge and Dwyer murders, Gordon and Collins did not want to put all the investigation's eggs in one basket, so to speak. The presence of Scott Delaney at the murder scene was the first major break. Information began to trickle through the gangland grapevine, from informants like Declan "Decie" Griffin, that "Cotton Eye" had been "going wild" looking for his missing ecstasy tablets.

As the investigation progressed the murder emerged as a particularly gruesome case. A preliminary report from State Pathologist Dr John Harbison showed that Dwyer had been horrifically tortured. In fact the renowned pathologist would later state that the Dwyer case was one of the worst he had encountered in a career spanning over fifty years. Officers believed that Dwyer had been brought directly to Scribblestown Lane after his abduction. There was no evidence or information to suggest another murder scene. As a result the Gardaí would miss vital forensic evidence. The investigation team began to compile detailed statements from all those who had witnessed the abduction.

On Sunday afternoon, December 15, the Gardaí interviewed "Cotton Eye's" estranged wife. Stella Delaney. She told Detective Sergeant Gerry McDonnell that her son had told her that he did not want his father to visit him in hospital. Their colleagues who were on duty at the hospital had already informed them of this. Stella then told them about "Cotton Eye's" terrifying 'visit' the previous night and about his extremely violent tendencies. It also appeared from the initial statements taken the morning after the abduction from Jennifer Byrne and her friend, that Scott Delaney had been suspiciously "jumpy" in the period just before the abduction. One of the girls said that it looked like he was expecting something to happen. In the hour after the abduction Scott's friend, Carl "Yorkie" Dunne, who was left behind in the flat, had slipped away at the first opportunity and was keeping his head down. A picture was beginning to emerge.

On Tuesday, December 17, Scott Delaney was discharged from hospital. He agreed to accompany Detective Sergeants Gerry McDonnell and Eamon O'Grady to Fitzgibbon Street Garda Station to make a statement about his ordeal. Scott Delaney claimed he had been visiting Mark Dwyer when the masked men broke into the flat. He briefly described what had happened after they were taken away from the flat. He remembered being put into a car and claimed he then passed out. The next thing he "recalled" was hearing a shot and passing out again. Then he saw the squad car lights.

The investigation team held a meeting to discuss Scott Delaney's statement. Everyone present believed he was lying. Det. Sgt. McDonnell pointed out that Scott Delaney claimed he never received a phone call from his father on the night of the abduction. Scott had said the call came from " ...the supplier of the coke asking was it OK.". But according to the witnesses in Dwyer's flat Scott had clearly stated that his "auld fellah" had just been on the phone. Scott also had not furnished any details relating to the gun, the raiders or the type of car used. He had even refused to give information about anyone he had phoned that night.

At this stage, the investigation team had already begun to collate the records of calls made to and from the mobile phones of those they knew had been involved, including Scott Delaney, "Cotton Eye" and the victim. Cell net analysis, first used in the Guerin murder hunt, gave officers an invaluable tool with which to roughly locate the position of the phone users at the time they made the calls. The pattern of calls included the time and duration of each and the numbers called. It also provided corroboration. The officers suspected that, at best, Scott Delaney was covering up for those responsible for the kidnapping and murder. He had moved from being an innocent victim to being a suspect in the case.

Gordon and Collins agreed that he should be arrested under Section 30 of the Offences Against the State Act for being in possession of information relating to the commission of a scheduled offence and the unlawful possession of a firearm on December 14,

1996. Delaney could be held for up to forty-eight hours. Det. Sgt. McDonnell arrested Delaney at 11.17pm, as he was about to leave Fitzgibbon Street station. At the same time the investigators began looking for "Cotton Eye" Joe Delaney. As a result of the assault case a week earlier they were able to locate his County Kildare bolthole. When they got there he had already gone into hiding.

The following morning Detective Sergeants Gerry McDonnell and Fran Sweeney began interviewing Scott Delaney. Both officers would play crucial roles in the investigation. Scott refused to answer any questions put to him about the kidnapping. When asked if he was scared, he said he was but he would not elaborate. That evening, the officers got an unexpected break when Delaney's mother visited him at the station. Detective Sergeant McDonnell and Detective Garda Terry McHugh brought Delaney to a room so that he could talk to his mother. The officers present informed Scott that anything he said during the visit could be taken down by them and given in evidence if required.

Stella Delaney asked her son why he was being detained.

"It's about me auld fellow, he shot yer man," he replied. His mother became distressed and emotional when she heard this. One of the detectives gave her a drink of water.

Then Scott told her: "That's why I have been so depressed all the time."

"Oh my God, did he kill that young fellow and is that why he tried to kill you?" his mother asked, as tears welled up in her eyes.

"That's right, he got me to set it up," said Scott. Stella Delaney asked the officers did they know where her ex-husband was and would her address be in the newspapers. She was obviously scared that "Cotton Eye" was on the loose and posed a threat to her safety. "We don't know where he is," said McDonnell. "Oh God is that why he came up to me the other night. What will I do?" she exclaimed. Det. Sgt. McDonnell offered to get her police protection.

Then Scott told his mother: "He [Mark] ripped me auld fellow off."

"And then your father dumped you in a field," his mother remarked, as she tried to comprehend the enormity of what her estranged husband had done to their son.

After the visit Scott Delaney's interrogation resumed. He started to tell part of the truth relating to the murder of Mark Dwyer. He admitted that he and Dwyer had worked for his father for two years selling drugs. He said of Dwyer: "He is a mad bastard. Things were getting out of hand. He was too heavy for me." He confirmed the story of the stolen ecstasy and how "Cotton Eye" had blamed him and Dwyer because they had been supposed to collect the E. On the day of the murder he said "Cotton Eye" had called him on his mobile phone, to confirm that a meeting had been arranged with Dwyer. Scott said that, as far as he was concerned, Dwyer was only to be questioned about the missing drugs. "Cotton Eye's" son said he "bottled it" at first and did not want to do it. "I wanted to tell Dwyer to leg it but I was afraid he ["Cotton Eye"] would kill me," he said.

The detectives had been given enough information with which to charge Scott Delaney with false imprisonment. They were also now convinced that their prime suspect was the elusive "Cotton Eye" Joe.

On Friday, December 20, Det. Sgt. McDonnell brought Scott Delaney before the Dublin District Court where he was formally charged with falsely imprisoning Mark Dwyer. Delaney was remanded in custody. As Det. Sgt. McDonnell was leading him to the cells Scott Delaney shook his hand and thanked the officer. The quick decision by the Director of Public Prosecutions to prefer charges paid off for the investigation team. "A lot of people started coming forward with information because they assumed that we knew the whole story because we had charged Delaney. Things started to fall into place," recalled one detective.

While Scott Delaney was being questioned in Fitzgibbon Street the Gardaí also caught up with Carl "Yorkie" Dunne. The young drug dealer confirmed the story about the drug theft and what "Cotton Eye" had planned to do about it. He also told the investigators about "Cotton Eye's" threats to murder his son. Dunne identified the voice of the caller to the 999 emergency services as "Cotton Eye" Joe himself. Detectives would later say that they were satisfied that the caller had in fact been Jeremy Cooper. Christopher Dwyer was also questioned. He told the police about the meeting he had attended in October and subsequently made a full statement.

By now the detectives had a much clearer picture of what had happened. As a result of "Yorkie" Dunne's comments and

Christopher Dwyer's information they now suspected that Chris Curry and a number of his henchmen had probably carried out the abduction on "Cotton Eye's" orders. On December 21, the same morning that "Cotton Eye" was finally nabbed, a team of detectives under the command of Det. Sgt. McDonnell and Det. Sgt. Sweeney raided Curry's home and arrested the drug dealer for questioning. They also arrested his wife.

After a night in the cells, Chris Curry decided to come clean and tell the Gardaí what he knew. Curry had resolved that he was not taking the rap for a crime he had nothing to do with. Later, in an interview with detectives, he said: "I want to see Joe hang. He is a psycho and I'm prepared to wear a [surveillance] wire." Curry had also witnessed how dangerously unbalanced Delaney had become. He realised that if "Cotton Eye" got away with Dwyer's murder then he could be the next target for torture and execution. Curry gave a detailed statement about what he knew of "the rip". In particular he talked about the meeting in Delaney' s house and told Gardaí about the phone call he had received the evening after Dwyer's murder. He also told them that "Cotton Eye" had asked him to help with the abduction. Curry told the officers that he was quite prepared to stand up in court and "set up Joe". The net was closing in on "Cotton Eye" Delaney.

While Curry was spilling the beans Joe Delaney was being questioned in another interview room, down the corridor. During his interrogation Delaney spun his pre-prepared alibi. He denied all knowledge of the crime and said he knew nothing about his son's abduction until the following evening. He had been in bed having sex with his 'girlfriend', Adrienne McGuinness. The officers told him they believed he was responsible for the abduction and murder of Mark Dwyer. In one interview with Det. Sgt. Fran Sweeney and Det. Garda Terry McHugh he was asked about Mark Dwyer and his 'relationship' with McGuinness. The interrogation went as follows:

Q. How long do you know Mark Dwyer?

A. I met him through Scott. I met him five or six times.

Q. What did you think of him?

A. He is an evil little bastard.

Q. Why do you say that?

    A. He was bad news. I often told Scott that. I often told him not to be hanging around with Mark.

On the night of the murder he claimed that McGuinness had called to his home at 1.45am.

    Q. Was this not a strange time for a girl to call on her own to your house?

    A. She said that she had been trying to contact me on my mobile and she was concerned that she couldn't contact me.

    Q. What happened after she arrived?

    A. We had a bottle of wine and played a few CDs and were just talking. I could see something was happening between us. I told Adrienne that she was only a young girl and that I was involved in another relationship. She made some reference to younger fellows that she had lived with and they had beaten her. I know how to treat women, you don't push yourself on them, you let them make all the moves, then you have them for life. It was like that with Adrienne. She made all the moves and we ended up in bed together.

Then Detective Sergeants McDonnell and Sweeney asked him about the incident at the home of his estranged wife.

    Q. What happened at Stella's house?

    A. I shouted through the letterbox. She wouldn't let me in. I told her that I didn't mind her taking IR£150,000 off me but she couldn't stop me seeing my son.

    Q. Did you threaten her?

    A Yes I told the cunt I'd get her.

    Q. Were you shouting abuse at your wife?

    A. I told her a few things.

Later "Cotton Eye" was asked about his relationship with his son Scott and with Chris Curry.

    A. I love Scott.

    Q. Is Scott very loyal to you?

    A. Yes he is very loyal and honest.

    Q. Would he ever tell a lie on you?

    A. No, never absolutely not.

    Q. Is Chris Curry a friend of yours?

    A. Yes he is, he is like a son to me.

Q. Would he tell lies about you?

A. No way, absolutely not, he is a good friend of mine.

Q. If Chris said you took him to a restaurant in Naas would that be true?

A. It sure is if Chris says it.

Q. Did you ever call Chris to a meeting in your house?

A. A meeting, what kind of meeting? I know nothing about a meeting.

Q. So if Chris said this would he be telling lies?

A. Chris doesn't tell lies.

The interviews progressed and "Cotton Eye" confirmed that he had regular telephone contact with Curry. Delaney was adamant that Curry was his friend and he was a man incapable of telling lies. After a while the detectives brought the subject back to a specific point as they prepared to spring the trap.

Q. So if Chris Curry says that you rang him and asked him did he hear the news of Mark Dwyer and that you went on to say that Scott was OK, would that be correct?

A. Yeah, Chris asked about Scott.

Q. So if Chris Curry goes on to say that you then told him that it was the hardest thing that you ever had to do leaving Scott in that field with the body, what would you say?

A. That's a load of bollix. Chris would never say that.

Q. So you don't believe that he said such a thing?

A. No I don't.

Q. Chris is here in the Station, do you want to hear what he has to say?

A. Yes, I'd like to hear what he's saying.

At 10.40pm, Chris Curry's interview was interrupted and he was invited down to the room where Delaney was being questioned. Curry sat down on a chair opposite "Cotton Eye". Detective Sergeant Jerry Healy, who had been interviewing Curry, asked Delaney: "Christopher Curry wants to say something to you, do you want to hear what he has to say?"

"Let him go ahead," Delaney replied, nonchalantly.

Curry looked his former partner-in-crime in the eye: "You rang me at 4.30pm on Saturday after the murder. You said: 'I suppose you heard the news about Mark Dwyer. It's all over.' You said Scott is OK but that it was the hardest thing you ever had to do leaving him behind with the body in the field. You said you left Scott behind to throw the scent off yourself and blame the Corballys. You killed Mark Dwyer and left your son behind with the body. You have destroyed my family; my wife has also been arrested all over you. Face up to it and tell the fucking truth. Tell the fucking truth." Curry became emotional as he pointed his finger across the table at Delaney in front of four detectives. Then he tried to jump across the table to beat Delaney and had to be restrained.

When he had left Det. Sgt. McDonnell sat down again across the table from Delaney.

Q. You have heard Chris Curry, what have you got to say to that?

Delaney did not answer. He had turned white and started swallowing hard. He appeared visibly shaken and couldn't speak. After a few minutes he asked for a cigarette. McDonnell lit it for him. Delaney sat back and drew hard on the cigarette, sucking in the smoke as he tried to think on his feet.

Q. Have you anything at all to say about what Curry said about you?

A. What can I say? [He shrugged his shoulders.]

Q. Well is Chris Curry still your friend?

A. Not after all that, he's fucking deranged.

Q. Is Chris Curry telling the truth?

A. No, he is fucking deranged.

The detectives began to tell him everything Scott had said about his father's problems with Mark Dwyer.

Q. Why did you want to see your son in Blanchardstown Hospital on December 14?

A. Because he is my son and I love him.

Q. If you love him why did you leave him in the field in Scribblestown beside the body of Mark Dwyer?

A. I had nothing to do with that.

Q. You know that Scott is spending his first Christmas in prison?

No reply.

Q. Are you happy to see your son shoulder all the blame for this?

"Cotton Eye" Delaney didn't reply.

The above are short extracts from a large volume of interview notes compiled by the various detectives during Delaney's detention. By the end of the detention period the investigators had to decide whether Delaney should be charged or released. The evidence they had so far compiled clearly implicated him in the crime. If he was released it was likely he would either intimidate witnesses or disappear. Following consultations with the DPP, Chief Supt. Dick Kelly gave the order to charge him with the same charge as his son – the false imprisonment of Mark Dwyer. In the meantime the murder investigation would continue with a view to preferring murder charges. On Christmas Eve, Det. Sgt. Gerry McDonnell formally charged Joe Delaney with the false imprisonment of Mark Dwyer and brought him before the Dublin District Court.

Joe and Scott Delaney applied for bail on Tuesday, January 7, 1997, in the High Court in Dublin. Objecting to bail for both men Det. Sgt. Gerry McDonnell said that Scott Delaney had made statements incriminating himself, by outlining his involvement in the abduction and murder of Mark Dwyer. The officer said he believed the prisoner would abscond and not stand trial. Scott Delaney said he would be pleading not guilty to the charges and would be contesting the validity of the statements he made while in custody. "When I went into the police station I was on anti-depressants. I can't even remember the statement I made," he said. Det. Sgt. McDonnell said that witnesses had made statements implicating both men in the crime. He said he believed that "Cotton Eye" would also fail to appear to face trial and that he had been hiding from the Gardaí following the Dwyer murder. Delaney had lived at six different addresses over the previous five years. The officer stated that he believed that "Cotton Eye" would try to intimidate witnesses if he was released on bail. The investigator also told the court that Stella Delaney was living in "considerable fear" after her estranged husband had threatened to kill her.

Mr Justice Smyth refused both applications remarking that he did not want the police running around the country "like fools at a fair" trying to find the Delaneys. The Judge said that he did not take death threats as empty threats.

Following the hearing Det. Sgt. McDonnell and Det. Gda. Tony

Lane escorted "Cotton Eye" back to the holding cells under the court building. Delaney said to them: "You fuckers are stitching me up on this case because you haven't been able to catch me for the last thirty years. I know who did this but I'm not telling you fuckers nothing."

Two months later the father and son were both charged with the murder of Mark Dwyer and on May 21, 1997, they were sent for trial to the Central Criminal Court. The investigation files went into several volumes including hundreds of statements.

In March and April the detectives had made two more crucial arrests when they'd lifted Anthony "Gammy" Adams and Michael Ryan. Declan "Decie" Griffin had passed on information, through his Garda handler, that they should be taking a closer look at the M50 gang with whom Delaney had been closely associated. During interrogation both men had admitted to varying degrees of involvement in the abduction but they did not tell the full truth about the incident because they were afraid of being charged with murder. Ryan had confirmed the initial meeting he had with Scott Delaney. He had also named "Gammy" Adams and Jeremy Cooper as two of the gang members he recruited for the job. In their statements both men claimed that Dwyer had been taken directly from Fosters Terrace and then murdered in Scribblestown Lane. The statements had provided valuable information. There was also enough evidence with which to charge both men. Then the investigators went looking for Jeremy Cooper.

The Dwyer investigation team's interest in Cooper coincided with another major operation involving the National Bureau of Criminal Investigation (NBCI). The NBCI had targeted a robbery gang which included Cooper and was led by Tommy Freeman. On May 10, 1997, Freeman, Cooper and another man had burst into the home of cigarette vendor Frank Britton in Clonmel and held him and his family hostage at gunpoint. The terrified family were bound and gagged and dumped into a small storeroom with no ventilation. They were discovered seventeen hours later by neighbours. The robbers took IR£40,000 worth of cigarettes and IR£9,000 in cash. Following the robbery Freeman's gang were identified as the prime suspects and members of the NBCI arrested Cooper, Freeman and other gang members. They were taken to

Clonmel for questioning.

Detective Sergeant Fran Sweeney and Detective Garda Tony Murphy travelled to Clonmel to interview Cooper in relation to the Dwyer murder. Armed with the information they already had in their possession Cooper admitted his involvement in the abduction of Mark Dwyer. He later also admitted his role in the Britton robbery to the same officers. Cooper was initially charged with the murder and false imprisonment of Mark Dwyer and then subsequently charged with the Britton robbery.

The investigation team had also continued to try to convince Adrienne McGuinness to tell the truth about what happened that night. They knew that she knew a lot more than she was saying. In the summer of 1997, she made a number of statements to Detective Sergeant McDonnell, in which she revealed that she had agreed to give Delaney a false alibi on the night of the murder. She told them that, in order to keep up the alibi story, Delaney had instructed her to visit both him and Scott in prison, which she did on ten occasions after their remand. But, the pressure was getting to McGuinness and when she told Delaney she "wanted out" he offered her IR£10,000 in cash and a car. He gave McGuinness the number of a well-known criminal based in Tallaght who also dabbled in cars. She didn't meet him because she feared for her life. The investigators knew that McGuinness was still holding back crucial parts of the story.

* * * *

On Wednesday, October 22, 1997, Scott Delaney's trial opened in the Central Criminal Court. He pleaded not guilty to the charges of murder and the false imprisonment of the victim. Opening his case prosecution counsel, Patrick Gageby SC, said that the State would not contend that the accused man had actually killed the victim. He told the jury, of seven men and five women: "Most importantly we say that Scott Delaney was involved up to his neck and for that reason is as guilty of murder as if he himself pulled the trigger. The facts of the case are going to be somewhat gruesome and somewhat distressing."

He said that a number of the witnesses in the case came from the criminal underworld and that the deceased was a person who "apparently had been involved in quite serious crime". The prosecution pointed out that there was also a very strong suggestion, which was probably true, that Scott Delaney assisted in the distribution of drugs in this country and did so "...as part of the gang of the man who actually pulled the trigger".

Referring to "Cotton Eye" Joe Delaney, Mr Gageby said he was "...quite a large figure apparently in the Dublin underworld and had employed Mark Dwyer, who would appear to have crossed him in some way.". The prosecutor explained the motive for the crime: the disappearance of 40,000 ecstasy tablets for which Dwyer had been blamed. On the surface, he said, Scott Delaney and Mark Dwyer appeared to be good friends. He said it would be the State's case that Scott Delaney agreed to set-up his friend by making sure that he would be in a place from where he could be easily abducted. Mr Gageby said that Mark Dwyer had been shot in the back of the head in what appeared to be a "gangland execution". And he asserted that not only did the defendant know Dwyer was to be abducted but that there was also clear evidence that Scott Delaney knew Dwyer was going to be killed or seriously injured. The State Pathologist Dr John Harbison gave evidence that Mark Dwyer died from a laceration to the brain due to a single shotgun wound in the back of the head which had been discharged at contact range. The dead man had received a "...severe punishment beating before his death.".

Both Chris Curry and Christopher Dwyer gave evidence of attending the meeting in "Cotton Eye's" home in October 1996, with Mark Dwyer and Scott Delaney, in which the gang boss described what he planned doing with the person who had ripped him off. The prosecution also read the series of statements made by Scott Delaney while in custody. Delaney did not testify in his own defence but his counsel, Brendan Grogan SC, said his client claimed that while he knew Dwyer was to be abducted and questioned he was not aware he would be shot.

Evidence in the case concluded on the fifth day of the trial. In his summing up to the jury the prosecutor, Patrick Gageby, said that they had been given a glimpse of the criminal underworld. It was a world he said, in which there seemed to be quite a lot of money earned for very little effort and in the criminal world people did not solve their problems by calling the police or sending a solicitor's letter. Delaney's defence counsel, Brendan Grogan, told the jury that there was nothing to suggest that his client would be a willing party to the murder of someone he knew on a regular basis. Neither was there anything to suggest that he was capable of being a party to that murder.

The jury retired to consider its verdict on Thursday, October 30, 1997, a year after the "rip off" had taken place. At 4pm the following day the jury found Scott Delaney guilty of murder by a majority of ten to two and an unanimous verdict found him guilty of the charge of false imprisonment. Scott Delaney stood in silence, his face pale and drawn, as Mr Justice Fredrick Morris sentenced him to life imprisonment on the murder charge and a second ten-year sentence for the abduction charge. The Judge said the circumstances of the case were "quite horrific".

At that moment, Scott Delaney began shouting angrily at the judge. "I was fucking set up for those drugs and I'm to spend the rest of my life in prison?" he shouted, as prison officers tried to restrain him. "Why don't you give me ten life sentences? I was set up. I want the death penalty." Scott Delaney was in tears as he was led away in handcuffs to a waiting prison van.

The Fitzgibbon Street investigation team had won their first victory but they knew the real fight would come in the trial of "Cotton Eye" Joe Delaney. The officers could see that Scott Delaney had finally realised that his father had got him into this mess. As the team left the court for a well-deserved drink in a local pub one thing dominated the conversation – how long would it take before Scott Delaney was prepared to come clean and tell the truth about his father's crime? Scott Delaney's evidence could help them catch the real bad guy here – "Cotton Eye" Joe Delaney himself.

In February 1998, the breakthrough the investigation team had been waiting for finally happened. Scott Delaney was serving his life sentence in Arbour Hill Prison when he handed his solicitor, Michael Hanahoe, a ninety-one-page document, outlining everything that had happened before, during and after the murder of Mark Dwyer. The document was handed to the Gardaí in accordance with Delaney's instructions. Then, over a two-day period from April 20, 1998, Scott Delaney dictated a fifteen-page statement to Detective

Inspector Hubert Collins and Detective Sergeant O'Grady. Scott Delaney finally agreed to testify at his father's trial which was due to commence the following week. It was a significant breakthrough that dramatically strengthened the State's case against "Cotton Eye". Scott Delaney was serving life for murder and had no motive to lie. He had nothing to lose and even less to gain. For the first time the officers found out that the actual crime scene had been in Joe Delaney's house in County Kildare. Although it was extensively examined, immediately after the revelation, any credible forensic evidence had long since faded. There was one important detail however, which corroborated Scott's statement: the carpet from "Cotton Eye's" bedroom floor was missing.

Armed with Scott Delaney's statement the investigators went back to see Adrienne McGuinness. She now had no choice but to tell the truth. The information given by Scott Delaney clearly showed that she was lying and was therefore, a potential accessory to the crime. Adrienne McGuinness finally told the full truth in two statements she gave to Detective Sergeant McDonnell and Detective Inspector Collins on April 20 and April 23. It was the first time that the tough "gangster's moll" had broken down in several interviews with Gardaí. McGuinness said she was glad she had come clean and agreed to take the witness stand and testify. The investigation squad's hard work over the past eighteen months had finally paid off – with only days to spare before Delaney's trial.

* * * *

"This case will give you an unparalleled view of the Dublin criminal underworld," Patrick Gageby SC promised the jury. He was making his opening address in "Cotton Eye" Joe Delaney's trial as it commenced in Court 3 of the Central Criminal Court on Wednesday, April 28, 1998. The State prosecutor was certainly not exaggerating. This was the first major gangland murder case ever to come before a jury in Ireland. The underworld, the police and the media had all eagerly anticipated the trial. The Scott Delaney trial had effectively been a sideshow and this would be the main event. Each day of the five-week hearing would produce lurid and disturbing insights into the raw realities of life in gangland. The murder of Veronica Guerin, less than two years earlier, had already shocked and terrified the entire nation. It had woken everyone up to the fact that organised crime was alive and thriving in modern Ireland. This was the first time that an Irish jury would be confronted with anything like the evidence that would be presented before them – a harrowing tale of violence, drug trafficking and murder. The eight men and four women of the jury would be brought into a sordid world that they had only ever read about or seen in fictional gangster movies. In the cold, clinical environment of the courtroom, a succession of self-confessed drug dealers and criminals would sit in the witness box and talk in the gangland vernacular about torture, murder and madness. With names like "Limpy", "Gammy", "Killer", "Yorkie". "Psycho" and "Jappo", the murder of Mark Dwyer would be summed up as a "loose end that had to be tied up after the rip off". Patrick Gageby, the State prosecutor, encapsulated what the drug culture was all about. He said that the case would show that behind what people considered innocuous drugs, there lay a "sordid world based on criminality and violence". The trial would hear that "Cotton Eye" Joe Delaney was an alcoholic and a drug abuser, who had been a pimp and a drug dealer. His victim was a violent thug who had been involved in at least one gruesome murder, that of "Jock" Corbally.

All eyes in the packed courtroom focused on Delaney as if he was the fascinating star attraction in some kind of freak show. Every day, as more horrific evidence emerged, members of the public came to the court just to get a glimpse of this gangland monster. They would listen to the horrifying evidence while staring at the man in the dock. Several well-known members of the criminal fraternity also came to listen and watch, including "Cotton Eye's" henchmen, adding to the sense of menace that hung over the court. The members of the investigation team mingled with the crowd in the court making eye contact with the hoods.

"Cotton Eye" Joe Delaney sat in the dock, with glasses perched on the edge of his long nose, reading through legal documents. Despite the evidence of an out-of-control violent drug addict, he looked every bit the part of the polished godfather. With his long black hair slicked across his head, he wore a variety of smart suits with a full-length black leather coat draped across his shoulders.

He regularly scanned the courtroom to pick out familiar eyes. In particular, he made a habit of trying to catch the eyes of individual jurors. Each time he did make contact with a juror, their eyes were nervously averted and Delaney moved to another face on the jury bench. It was like he was playing some kind of mind game. It was an awesome burden for an average, law-abiding citizen – to be asked to adjudicate on the guilt or the innocence of the accused in an atmosphere of such fear and intimidation.

The prosecution case was that in the early hours of December 14, 1996, "Cotton Eye" had falsely imprisoned Mark Dwyer, who was "tied up like a chicken and bundled out of his flat". Mr. Gageby told the jury: "A couple of hours later, having been beaten soundly, a shotgun was put to his head, its trigger pulled, and he died instantly. Joe Delaney either administered the shot that terminated Mark Dwyer's existence or ordered it to be done. In any event he was present for it."

The events, which took place between the disappearance of the ecstasy in October 1996 and the murder, were explained to the jury. Carl "Yorkie" Dunne told how he and his friend Scott Delaney made their living selling drugs for "Cotton Eye". He said that he had been present at a meeting where the accused said Dwyer had ripped off his drugs. "Joe was bulling about the drugs and he said: 'I'll get the little bastard,'" said Dunne, in his flat Dublin accent. On the night of the abduction "Yorkie" Dunne said that Scott had told him that "Someone was going to go up to Mark to talk to him about the missing drugs.".

Christopher Dwyer told the court about his trip to Amsterdam and Paris with his brother and about attending the meeting in Kildare where Delaney planned his revenge for "the rip". Christopher Dwyer told the court: "He was adamant that he would do it himself. He said that he would shoot him. He would have a hole dug in a field and shoot him in the head."

Delaney's defence team, led by Mr Blaise O'Carroll SC, contested the Garda notes of interviews with Delaney. They alleged that he had been beaten, punched and otherwise ill-treated while in custody. At one stage, early in the proceedings, there were six days of legal argument over the legality of Delaney's detention, his treatment and the notes of what he had said to investigators.

Detective Sergeant Fran Sweeney rejected claims that they had tortured Delaney by bending his thumbs back, pushing him up against a hot radiator, hitting him in the face or punching or dragging him, with the intention of making him sign a "pre-prepared statement".

Detective Sergeant Sweeney told Delaney's defence counsel: "At no stage did we enter the interview room with a prepared statement. I never laid a finger on Mr Delaney during any period of his detention." The experienced detective then told the court that Delaney had been photographed during his detention and there were no marks on him. The accused could also have availed of a doctor to examine him.

The court then heard that during a High Court adjournment hearing in June 1997, Delaney had stood up and alleged detectives had broken his teeth. The following morning, in the presence of his solicitor, Delaney had withdrawn the allegations and apologised.

On Monday May 14, 1998, Scott Delaney took the stand to testify against his father. Escorted into court in handcuffs by several prison officers and armed police, he was put sitting a safe distance from "Cotton Eye". Scott Delaney said that he had not given evidence or told the truth during his own trial because "my father had told me not to". Scott Delaney told the court how, on his father's orders, he had organised Dwyer's abduction. He said he appealed to his father and the three men who had abducted Dwyer not to kill him. "They were saying to me we have to kill him, and I kept saying don't kill him," he said. Scott said that after the torture he had travelled with his father, the three masked men and Mark Dwyer to Scribblestown. As he'd had so much alcohol and drugs in his system the events thereafter were a blur: "I remember hearing a gunshot and the next thing I saw the lights of a squad car were shining in my eyes. I was slipping in and out of consciousness."

The following day Chris Curry gave his evidence. He admitted to prosecution counsel that he had worked with Joe Delaney, distributing cocaine and ecstasy and collecting money for him. He recalled the events leading up to the Dwyer murder. "Joe was freaked over the ecstasy robbery. He'd been taken to the cleaners. He said he didn't care if he had to nut those responsible," said Curry. The drug dealer spoke about the meeting in County Kildare that had been attended by Mark Dwyer, his brother Christopher, and the two Delaneys. Curry said that "Cotton Eye" had wanted "to get himself tooled up". Otherwise Delaney believed that whoever had stolen the drugs would come after him and "finish him off". Curry claimed that "Cotton Eye" believed that he was being stalked by the thief and that the gang boss thought that Mark Dwyer was going to kill him before he could "get Mark".

Curry recalled Delaney's phone call the day after the murder and how he had said it was "the hardest thing he ever had to do", leaving his son in the field with the dead body. Curry denied a suggestion from Delaney's defence counsel that he was a "double-agent" who worked for another named Clondalkin-based drug dealer, Derek "Dee Dee" O'Driscoll, who was also a member of the M50 gang. Curry denied another suggestion that he had told Scott Delaney to wait until Hallowe'en because he was going to "…dress up as the grim reaper to do Mark" and that "Mark would be dead". Experienced observers attending the trial would later note that the questions Delaney had instructed his legal counsel to ask his former associates were also aimed at finding out who stole his ecstasy.

The intense drama continued when Adrienne McGuinness took the stand. She told the court how a man had been sent to "get rid" of her so she would not turn up for the trial. She said: "I fear for myself and my daughter, even though he is behind bars. I know what he is capable of." Often breaking down during her evidence, she revealed that she had feared Delaney enough to want to take her own life after the Dwyer murder. "I tried to slit my wrists because of the pressure… I'd rather kill myself than have any of them kill me," she told the court. She said that in eighteen months she had never told anyone what she had been through and now she wanted to clear her conscience. She said she had refused Delaney's offer of IR£10,000 and a car in return for giving him an alibi because it would have meant "digging a deeper hole for myself" and she was glad to be telling the truth. Adrienne McGuinness told the hushed courtroom everything she had witnessed in Delaney's house while Mark Dwyer was being tortured: "I heard Mark screaming in pain on and off for three hours, horrifying screams. I hear him when I close my eyes lying down in bed. Joe was the one in control, he was grinding his teeth saying: 'I'll find out where they [the drugs] are.'

He grabbed a steel bar and he was looking mental." Later she said that when it was all over Delaney had said: "The little bastard is dead."

As part of the bid to corroborate "Cotton Eye's" story that McGuinness had been his lover, Delaney instructed his lawyers to embark on an extraordinary line of questioning about their sex life together. Defence barrister Blaise O'Carroll put it to McGuinness that she had been involved in various sordid sex practices with "Cotton Eye". He accused her of enjoying anal sex and using a lubricator called KY-gel. Mr O'Carroll told her his client seemed to prefer shaved vaginas. McGuinness denied the allegations and replied: "It would be easy for him to conjure up stories like that to try to discredit me. He does run brothels."

At the height of that particular section of cross-examination a class of female teenagers, on an educational trip to the Four Courts, were brought in to listen to a 'typical' criminal case. One of the teachers accompanying the students went pale, as she heard the sexually graphic questioning. One of the youngsters turned to her friend and asked: "What's KY-gel?" The visit had certainly been an education.

"Cotton Eye" Delaney's testimony was equally dramatic. He admitted that he was "absolutely desperate" to get his stolen drugs back and claimed that he only "fronted" the ecstasy part of an extensive drug empire run by his son Robert. A number of anonymous investors, he said, owned the drugs and he claimed four attempts had been made on his life since "the rip".

He told his counsel: "On the night that Mark Dwyer was killed I was fifty-one, grossly overweight, alcoholic and on medication. How was I to attack a much younger man?"

He claimed that it was his son Robert who had introduced him to " ...the criminal underworld where a person would pay for his mistakes with his life.". He claimed that he had once attempted to commit suicide with pills and alcohol and had started using cocaine to "ease the depression". Implicating his son in drug dealing he said Robert was a "rip off merchant" who had fled to the US "fearful of the people who had invested in deals and lost it". He claimed that his son had been involved when a consignment of drugs went missing before and that Robert had asked him to "operate" this shipment in return for a commission. "Robert was calling the shots and not me," Joe Delaney said.

When quizzed about his comments to the police that Mark Dwyer was "an evil little bastard", Delaney replied that the dead man was "an absolute gentleman" and they got on extremely well. "I was not involved in his killing, that sort of thing would not suit me," he said.

On a number of occasions during his testimony Delaney looked across the courtroom and addressed Mark Dwyer's mother, Hilda. "I tell you Mrs Dwyer I never touched your son. I look directly into your eyes. I never set it up. I never killed your son. That's the truth to God."

Delaney claimed that he never believed that Mark Dwyer had taken the drugs and said that Scott and three masked men had turned up at his house at short notice with Mark Dwyer "tied up like a chicken". "I was drunk and coked out of me head and I told them this wasn't fucking on," said Delaney. He denied that any beating had taken place in his house but he agreed that the men had questioned Dwyer. He said he had no idea what the questioning was about and that after a short while they all left.

The gangster claimed: "I asked the men to leave Scott and Mark with me in the house but when they left I was happy that they [Scott and Mark] were happy. The three men told me they'd drop Scott near his mother's house and leave Mark off at Fairview so he could walk home."

"Cotton Eye" denied that he was the ringleader of a drugs' gang. "I wasn't any leader and Mark never worked for me directly. He worked for my son Scott," he said. Robert, his eldest son, had "sucked" him into the drugs business and he said it was most likely that Robert and Chris Curry had ripped him off.

Delaney's most extraordinary evidence centred on his alleged relationship with Adrienne McGuinness and he went to sordid lengths to substantiate his claim that they were lovers. When asked at one stage in cross-examination could he explain how a towel found in his house had been covered in blood, he claimed McGuinness had menstruated in his bedroom. In an even more ludicrous revelation he told the court that the couple had to use a lubricant for "sexual intercourse" because of the sheer size of his manhood. Under cross-examination he also revealed his preference for shaved vaginas. When asked why he liked this practise Delaney replied: "I don't like spitting out hairs." Patrick Gageby SC remarked that the tell tale signs that Delaney was feeling "amorous" would be when he turned up with "a philishave in one hand and a tube of KY-gel in the other."

Summing up in the case began on Wednesday, May 27. In his final address to the jury Patrick Gageby compared Delaney to the Nazi Minister for Propaganda, Josef Goebbels. "Like Goebbels, Mr Delaney believed it was useless to tell small lies. When Joseph Delaney tells lies, he tells whoppers," the lawyer declared. At the core of the case, Patrick Gageby said, was the conversation between Delaney and Curry on a mobile phone on the morning of the murder. During the call Delaney had said: "the little bastard is dead" and "it was the hardest thing I ever had to do to leave Scott in that field." Gageby commented: "Only the guilty could say that and only a father would say it had been the hardest thing to leave a son lying in a field with a man beaten and shot." He asked the jury to consider whether or not they believed Delaney's version of events that he was the " ...George Mitchell of the Kildare conference, an accounts clerk and a good family man."

In his summing up for the defence, Blaise O'Carroll SC said that Adrienne McGuinness had told "blatant lies with twists and turns". O'Carroll said that the idea that Delaney had masterminded the abduction and murder was absurd and that if he got marks out of ten for his efforts he would have been awarded a "one".

O'Carroll commented: "To organise something as stupid as abducting Mark Dwyer at a time when Adrienne McGuinness was in the house beggars belief. Ms McGuinness has a vivid imagination and is a fearless, venomous creature using her power to put pressure on Joseph Delaney." It was, he continued, Scott Delaney who was responsible for "orchestrating people" to bring Mark Dwyer to the house and out again.

After Mr Justice Patrick Barr gave instructions to the jury on points of law and how to assess the evidence, the jury finally retired to reach a verdict. It was 4.06pm on Thursday, May 28, 1999. By 7.57pm that evening they still had not reached a verdict and the jurors were sent to a hotel for the night under armed Garda protection. The following morning they resumed their deliberations at 10.30am.

The investigation team were getting anxious about the length of time it was taking the jury to reach their verdict. On the surface it had been a pretty straightforward case and the evidence seemed overwhelming. Everyone in the court building expected a unanimous verdict. But the detectives would later comment that they felt certain jurors seemed very nervous. "You wouldn't blame them. Imagine being an ordinary housewife and then being called for jury duty and finding yourself in the middle of a huge criminal case with torture and murder and drugs. It was an intimidating atmosphere for even hardened observers," one of the investigators later told this writer.

As the time wore on the tension was palpable. Hilda Dwyer sat in the round hall of the Four Courts building surrounded by friends and family. She told them: "The jury is not going to find him guilty. I know it. There's something not right with this. I don't believe he is going down. If he goes for a re-trial he won't be convicted."

Adrienne McGuinness nervously paced around the Round Hall with two friends, talking on her mobile phone. At 1pm the jury returned and legal counsel, police, witnesses, and the press, rushed back into the courtroom. The forewoman of the jury's tone told everyone that there was a problem reaching a verdict. "Cotton Eye" stared at them. She said the jury couldn't reach an unanimous verdict on one of the charges. The judge asked whether a decision had been made on the second charge and she asked for more time.

At 2.28pm that afternoon the jury returned. They looked exhausted and worn out. They told Mr Justice Barr that they could not reach a verdict. The forewoman said that members of the jury had "fixed views" and did not believe they could reach an unanimous verdict. Mr Justice Barr thanked the jury for their time and effort and discharged them.

"Cotton Eye" Joe Delaney heaved a sigh of relief as the judge remanded him in custody for the fixing of a new trial date. Everyone in the court was stunned. "Cotton Eye" immediately started talking to his counsel to discover what the verdict actually meant. He was smiling and congratulating his legal team on a job well done, before being led away in handcuffs. As far as he was concerned it would be highly unlikely that a second trial would even get off the ground. Even if it did there was now a very real chance that he would walk. Things were looking good for "Cotton Eye" Joe.

Adrienne McGuinness broke down in tears and headed for the door. "I'm dead. Jesus I'm fucking dead. I thought he was going down... I just can't believe it. What am I going to do... I'm dead... I'm not going to see the next trial...I'm dead," she exclaimed. Detective Sergeant McDonnell, who had put so much work into the case, went after McGuinness to reassure her that she would be protected.

The other members of the investigation team stood around shaking their heads in utter disbelief. "Jesus Christ, if after all that evidence the jury couldn't convict that evil bastard we might all as well fucking resign and never bother catching a 'gouger' again. In all my years I have never seen so much damning and corroborated evidence," one of the detectives told me later, over a pint. He took a drink and shook his head. "I can't fucking believe it."

The fact that the case was re-scheduled and did go ahead was a tribute to the exceptional hard work and determination of the investigation team. But they had all gone too far to give up now. Collins sent his men to meet each of the witnesses in the case to re-assure them and, more importantly, to keep them on side for the next showdown. If any of the witnesses pulled out before a new trial then it was likely that the case would fall apart and this monster would be back on the streets again. Although none of the witnesses were in the Witness Protection Programme it was left to Collins's men and the officers attached to the Garda 'U' District stations in Mountjoy and Fitzgibbon Street to offer them as much protection as possible. At the same time the Gardaí involved still had to work their normal heavy workload, investigating everything from sex crimes to ordinary burglaries.

* * * *

"Cotton Eye" Joe Delaney's second trial was scheduled to begin on Monday, March 1, 1999. But before lunch on the first day of the trial it was already in jeopardy. After lunch Mr Justice Quirke informed the court that one of the jurors had "very properly" told him that he knew one of the witnesses. The Judge said this was "clearly undesirable" and that " …justice needs to be done and be seen to be done.". The jury of eight women and four men had just heard the opening address from the prosecution counsel, Mr Denis Vaughan Buckley SC. The juror had recognised one of the names in the prosecution's address. The jury was discharged.

The third attempt to try "Cotton Eye" Joe Delaney began before a new jury panel a week later on Monday, March 8, 1999. In his opening address Denis Vaughan Buckley said the witnesses would give "overwhelming" evidence to support the contention that Mr Delaney had " …orchestrated and executed Mr Dwyer's murder or that it had been done at his behest.".

Over the next twenty-three days the evidence was again painstakingly examined before the jury. This time the witnesses were even more forthright in their evidence than they had been the previous year. Chris Curry again told his side of the story but this time he explained why he had turned on his former partner-in-crime:

"I had been embroiled with Joe right up to the neck in his drug selling business to make money. From when I got out of prison to Mark's murder I was heavily involved in drugs, selling drugs, taking drugs. Mark's murder made me change. I made a statement to the Gardaí because it was safer. What if six months down the road Joe got it in his head I did something and he killed me? Either way I was on a loser. If I did make a statement I'd be murdered. If I didn't make a statement and Joe walked I could be murdered."

He admitted that he was "highly involved" in the drugs business and that he had "…no qualms about it, but when it comes to murdering someone in the criminal underworld everyone knows about it.".

Then on the following day, as Curry was about to resume giving evidence, there was another dramatic development. The foreman of the jury said that there was "unease and apprehension" in the jury, due to the presence of certain people in the courtroom. "I don't want to go into details but ultimately after this trial people have to go on living in Dublin," he told Mr Justice Quirke. "We are all here to do our duty but there are people here with families. Over the past three days we have heard about some very serious crimes, people being shot and whacked, as Mr Curry said. For or against, members of the jury have to go back to living in the greater Dublin area," said the jury foreman, adding that jurors were concerned about "retribution".

After requesting a Garda Superintendent to come before the court to discuss security arrangements the judge told the jury that he had gone to "considerable lengths" to ensure that they were protected. Security around the court was also dramatically stepped up and armed officers were brought in to escort individual jurors to and from the court in the morning, evening and during lunch. Mr Justice Quirke said he would ensure that the jurors would be free from intimidation or oppression

At the same time, one of the jurors in the third trial had expressed concern that he or she knew a witness due to give evidence – this was the second time this had happened in one week. The juror was dismissed, without being identified. Judge Quirke had to then consider an application by the Director of Public Prosecutions not to proceed with eleven jury members.

On the following morning the judge ruled that the trial would go ahead. Blaise O'Carroll SC, Delaney's defence counsel, resumed his cross-examination of Curry. "At the end of the day Joe murdered Mark Dwyer. He asked me to help him kidnap and kill him," said Curry. But that afternoon Curry's evidence was again adjourned amid a major security alert when there was a bomb scare. The court had to be evacuated. Joe Delaney had good reason to feel that things were going his way.

When cross-examination again resumed Chris Curry revealed how Mark Dwyer had bragged about murdering "Jock" Corbally, saying that "Jock" deserved what he got. "He [Dwyer] got great joy out of slitting his [Corbally] throat and pulling his teeth," claimed Curry, adding that Dwyer "possibly had two or three bodies under his belt.". Curry added: "Mark was the best thing that ever happened to Joe, according to Joe. Now he had his own hit man and people would take him seriously."

Blaise O'Carroll put it to Curry that he had himself been directly implicated in the abduction and murder of Dwyer and had told Joe Delaney this. The counsel also accused Curry of concocting a story with the help of statements from the case that he'd had access to for a long time.

Curry replied: "Joe was down to the value of £160,000 and he murdered Mark and he murdered Mark in the wrong. Joe lost a huge parcel. He blamed Mark in the wrong, God love him. It could've been a flip of a coin. Mark could be here and I could've been in a hole. I was in the drug business to make a few quid, not go around killing people. If Mark had taken the drugs he would have come clean after twenty minutes of torture. I'm sure he was begging him to stop. I'm sure Mark would've said Novenas to get him to stop."

The same witnesses from the underworld and the Gardaí proceeded to again testify before the court. In her evidence Adrienne McGuinness said that she had not come forward with the truth because she was more afraid of Delaney than of the police. She took the opportunity to make it clear that she never had a relationship with Delaney and she had only said so out of fear.

There were more dramatic moments when Scott Delaney was called to give evidence against his father. He again told the court of his involvement in the abduction and of his father's actions. Defence counsel then began to read out a letter, written by Scott to his father, in which he said, "prison doesn't bother me", that his state of mind had changed. According to the letter, he was advising his father to "keep the faith" and that he was doing "excellent".

At that moment Scott Delaney suddenly leapt from the witness box and lunged at his father in the dock, screaming: "You poxy bleeding scumbag, you fucking killed me mate. He [Cotton Eye] told me he'd look after me. It's hard to do a life sentence for murder. He knows the truth as well." Prison officers and Gardaí rushed to restrain Scott from attacking his father.

Later when the situation had calmed down, Scott Delaney claimed that he had warned Mark Dwyer to "watch every move he made" because his father was out to get him. He again gave evidence of his role in the abduction of Mark Dwyer. Scott said that while he and his father were on remand in prison together his father had threatened him and told him not to open his mouth to the police. "He said if I opened my mouth the next time he sees him, he'd kill Robert, my brother. He said he'd kill Robert when he got out, when he gets his hands on him," said Scott Delaney. In reference to the people hired to do the job he told the court: "One of them was OK, he was only a young fellow, but the other two of them were savages. They were head cases just as mad as what my old fellow was." He said that he had since named the other men involved in the incident to the police because the "joke is over" and he did not want to serve a life sentence for a murder he did not commit.

In his own evidence "Cotton Eye" repeated his claims about his role in the drug business and the events on the night of the murder. He claimed at one stage that he had never used a weapon on another human being in his life and was innocent. He declared: "I want to make it abundantly clear I can look anyone in the eye. At no time did I have Mark Dwyer taken out of his home or beaten or shot. I wasn't party to it at all. I had absolutely nothing to do with Mark Dwyer's death." He then made the extraordinary claim that he was: "An honest man, a good father and a good catholic." When asked if several prosecution witnesses were lying Delaney said that their testimony was "…not all lies but some if it was exaggerated… ". Then he told the court that "certain people" who had left the court for refreshment breaks while giving evidence were drug users and they "weren't actually going to the toilet". He said: "It was a strong possibility they were taking coke so they could answer questions."

In the summing up of the case Junior Counsel for the prosecution, Shane Murphy BL, told the jury there was clear evidence of a common design in the case that "could be described as a gangland murder". The accused was "trying to shift the blame onto younger people" but he was "not a mule, a carrier or inferior – he was the boss". The State counsel pointed out that the prosecution case was corroborated by telephone evidence, witness statements and a clear motive.

In his summing up Defence Counsel Blaise O'Carroll told the jury if the State's case was to be believed "Cotton Eye" had been one of the most "inept criminal minds of all time". And he warned them not to reply on witnesses who were Scott Delaney's accomplices. He asked the jury if Scott Delaney was the "sort of person who would inspire confidence" that he was telling the truth.

On Tuesday, April 27, 1999, the jury retired to consider its verdict. One hour and forty-seven minutes later they were back in court and this time there was no confusion, no disagreement, no doubt. They unanimously found Joseph Delaney guilty on the two counts, of murder and false imprisonment. As the foreman of the jury read out the verdict, there was a collective sigh of relief throughout the court. Extra units of armed Gardaí had been brought into the court building to ensure that there were no incidents. The cops, who had so doggedly pursued the man in the dock, maintained their poise. Members of the dead man's family patted them on the back and others shook their hands. Hilda Dwyer wept. "Cotton Eye" Joe Delaney remained impassive and showed no emotion when he stood up in the dock.

Addressing Delaney directly Mr Justice Quirke commented: "You are guilty of a particularly foul and evil crime. You recruited others, including your son, to abduct Mr Dwyer before subjecting him to unspeakable savagery before paying others to kill him." The Judge told "Cotton Eye" that he had "destroyed the lives of countless young people" directing his business from "the sewers of our society". He said Delaney had shown: "No mercy and no remorse and was entitled therefore to no mercy." He sentenced "Cotton Eye" to life imprisonment on the count of murder. On the second count the Judge stated that Delaney had " …recruited armed and dangerous criminals to abduct Mr Dwyer from his home" and had him taken to "Cotton Eye's" own home where Dwyer had "paid for his death". Sentencing Delaney to fifteen years on the charge of false imprisonment, the Judge said it was, " …one of the gravest cases of false imprisonment that has come before the courts.".

Mr Justice Quirke then turned his attention to Detective Inspector Hubert Collins and his men. "I would like to personally thank the courageous Gardaí for their tremendous assistance throughout this trial," he said. He also thanked the jury " …on behalf of the community for the great care and attention… " they had given to the case.

"Delaney is going to know what real fear is all about now. He is going to count the studs on the back of the door for a long time," said Hilda Dwyer, as she left the court. Later Adrienne McGuinness told the *Sunday World*: "It is like a huge weight has been lifted off my shoulders. I know that my life will never be the same again and I will never be able to get Mark's screams out of my mind. I sometimes pray to Mark, asking him to forgive me for not doing anything to save him. Telling the truth and going through the ordeal in court was the only way I could make it up to him. I will always be looking over my shoulder and I don't think the dreams will ever go away."

In November 1999, Jeremy Cooper was jailed for twelve years after pleading guilty to a charge of false imprisonment. In November 1998 Scott Delaney had given Detective Inspector Hubert Collins an additional statement in which he named Cooper, "Gammy" Adams and Michael Ryan as three of the accomplices. Nevertheless the State had dropped the murder charge. Mr Justice Kinlen told Cooper: "You have been involved in some violence and in this particular case you were involved in the abduction and false imprisonment of a person who was tortured and ultimately died." Cooper who had just turned thirty was already serving another twelve-year stretch after pleading guilty to the Clonmel robbery.

On July 22, 2003, Anthony "Gammy" Adams was also jailed, for a total of six years after he pleaded guilty to the false imprisonment of Dwyer. Detective Inspector Fran Sweeney (who had since been promoted) told the court that the Gardaí were satisfied Adams had not taken an actual part in the torture or murder of Dwyer. "Gammy" Adams was the fourth person jailed in relation to the Mark Dwyer abduction and murder. It was an impressive result.

Despite his life sentence "Cotton Eye" just could not forget about his missing drugs. He brought his obsession behind bars with him. In August 2002, Delaney attacked his former associate and the self-confessed police informant Declan "Decie" Griffin in Mountjoy prison. Griffin, who had been involved with PJ Judge, Mark Dwyer and Delaney's gang, was on remand in prison after attempting to intimidate a juror in the controversial IR£1,000,000 heroin-seizure case against him. "Cotton Eye" had decided that the spineless crook had stolen his 40,000, precious, ecstasy tablets. Delaney crept into Griffin's cell, armed with a toothbrush that had been fitted with razor blades, and savagely slashed "Decie" several times. Griffin suffered wounds to the inside and outside of his mouth, his wrist was cut to the bone and he had cuts on his cheeks, forehead and neck. Griffin needed over one hundred stitches to repair his appalling wounds.

Delaney was moved to Cork prison and later to Castlerea prison in County Roscommon. During that time Delaney spent several months walking around his cell naked as he refused to wear any clothes. Then in March 2003, Delaney again hit the headlines when his sexual harassment of a female prison officer in Castlerea led to the first work stoppage in the prison system in fifteen years. Delaney was moved to Portlaoise Prison but managed to send an uncensored letter to the female prison officer in Castlerea.

In another incident in May 2003, prison inmate Thomas Connors escaped from a Dublin hospital after undergoing surgery for a clot on his brain. In the escape he jumped thirty-five feet. Later he told the media that he was running in fear of his life from "Cotton Eye" Delaney, who had already tried to murder him inside. "You don't realise how dangerous Delaney is. He'll get me in any prison that they put me in. He has friends everywhere and he has plenty of money," said Connors, shortly before he was recaptured and moved to a different prison. In the meantime "Cotton Eye" has vowed to have his son Scott murdered. Today Joe Delaney is categorised by the prison service as " ...a highly dangerous and problematic prisoner who must be treated with extreme caution.".

In June 2002, the Court of Criminal Appeal quashed Scott Delaney's conviction for murder and a new trial was ordered. The Appeal was allowed after the court held that there was new evidence that might lead a jury to decide that Delaney had tried to withdraw from any common enterprise and that he had taken steps that might not make him responsible for the Dwyer murder. Describing the crime as one of "the most vile and sadistic", the court ruled that there was new evidence that had not been available at the first trial. That evidence was from Scott Delaney himself and from Adrienne McGuinness.

In October 2002, Scott Delaney pleaded guilty to a lesser charge of being an accessory to the murder of Mark Dwyer. In December of the same year, he received a five-year sentence on the accessory charge. Mr Justice Paul Carney said the language of accessory to murder was to give "comfort, assist and maintain" the perpetrator. This he said translated into "not shopping your Dad" but in this case Delaney's father had threatened his son's life and was a particularly dangerous individual.

The conviction of "Cotton Eye" Joe Delaney made Irish criminal justice history. He was the first gang boss convicted of masterminding and carrying out a gangland execution in twenty years of organised crime. What was most impressive about the case was the fact that a relatively small group of detectives had managed, against all the odds, to convince several self-confessed criminals to stand up in open court and testify against their former boss. No-one had availed of a Witness Protection Programme and there had been no deals. The "Cotton Eye" Joe Delaney case was one of the finest hours in the battle with organised crime in Ireland.

As a postscript to this extraordinary story it is interesting to reflect on the murder of William "Jock" Corbally: three of the men who took part in that outrage went on to suffer similarly brutal deaths; PJ Judge and Declan "Decie" Griffin were gunned down – Griffin was murdered in March 2003 in an unrelated feud – and Mark Dwyer was himself tortured and murdered in the same way Corbally had been dispatched. Continuing the violent cycle "Cotton Eye" Joe Delaney will spend the rest of his life behind bars and his son will have also served a significant sentence. Two other men involved in the Dwyer case have also died. Carl "Yorkie" Dunne – whose role in the incident was the least of those involved – and Michael Ryan both died from drug overdoses. As a further consequence of the Mark Dwyer murder two more men would also lose their lives. (*See Chapter 6.*) A chain of events were connected through circumstance and personalities and "Jock" Corbally was the first link in the chain. The cycle of death ended when the eighth criminal involved also died. It would be difficult for even the most hardened cynic not to be a little superstitious.

Scott Delaney was released from custody early in 2004 and immediately went into hiding. "Cotton Eye" Delaney's associates on the outside had vowed to pay Scott back for his decision to testify against his father. No doubt "Cotton Eye" would like to see that happen to his son.

Six

Murder and Suicide

Anthony "Chester" Beatty was an associate and customer of "Cotton Eye" Joe Delaney and his gang. Beatty bought quantities of ecstasy and cocaine from Mark Dwyer and Scott Delaney. "Chester" then sold them on in the nightclubs and bars where he worked as a bouncer. Delaney could also call on "Chester" as extra muscle, whenever the need arose. As a result of this association Beatty was one of those arrested and questioned in relation to Mark Dwyer's murder. Although he was subsequently cleared of actually taking part in the crime, "Chester" Beatty remained a suspect in the eyes of some members of Mark Dwyer's family. That suspicion would fester like poison and ultimately lead to two more gruesome gangland deaths. Anthony "Chester" Beatty had become a dead man walking.

Born in Dublin, in 1959, "Chester" Beatty was literally a monster of a man. Standing at over six feet three inches in height and weighing seventeen stone he had a formidable reputation as a street fighter. Beatty was the quintessential underworld hard man who was available for hire as an enforcer and bullyboy. No one messed with "Chester", simply because there were very few who could physically match his strength. He was loud, vulgar and brutal. His friends called him "Chester" after the Chester Beatty Library in Dublin which, ironically, had once been robbed by his criminal associates. Like so many other villains he nurtured the image of himself as a gangland equaliser and he admired criminals like the notorious London gangster twins, Ron and Reggie Kray. He often told friends that his favourite movie was *The Krays*. "Chester" was a devotee of the doctrine that a good smack in the mouth sorted out most of life's misunderstandings.

Beatty was involved in crime for most of his adult life and had a string of convictions to prove it. However, he was no big time crime boss. His convictions were for assault, theft and possession of drugs. He did associate with many of the country's best-known godfathers and one of his closest friends was Martin Cahill, the General, with whom he shared a keen interest in pigeons. He was well-liked and popular among those whom he was not throttling or intimidating. He was particularly popular with women and had a string of young lovers. He could be having affairs with two or three women at any one time. Beatty even wore what is known as a Prince Charles' ring on his penis – to enhance his sexual performance!

In 1993, "Chester" left his wife, Theresa, and their four children and moved in to live with a sixteen-year-old girl from Lucan. While that relationship was going on he met Jennifer Melia, his girlfriend's best friend, who was also sixteen. Jennifer would later tell this writer: "I first set eyes on him in a nightclub where he was celebrating his thirty-seventh birthday. I met him through his girlfriend who was my best friend. I moved in to live with both of them and later "Chester" and I moved out to a place of our own. "Chester" was a hard man on the outside but he was a softie underneath. I loved him so much that I had his name tattooed on my chest." In June 1997 the couple had a baby boy together. They called the child Chester Jordan.

* * * *

Forty-eight-year-old John Dwyer and his younger brother, forty-seven-year-old Christy "Bud" Dwyer, were well-known among the city's criminal fraternity. For over twenty years the Dwyer brothers had run a roofing business from a yard at Beresford Street in the north inner-city. They operated various scams from the yard. John Dwyer had a handful of convictions for relatively minor offences, including larceny and breach of the peace. He was also involved in the sale of smuggled cigarettes and fireworks. "Bud" Dwyer, however, who was a year younger, had a more 'impressive' record for violent crime. It included a conviction in 1969 for the murder of two men he had been fighting on the street. In 1973, the Court of Criminal Appeal reduced the two counts to manslaughter and gave him two four year suspended sentences. He also had convictions for possession of a knife, larceny, burglary and fraud.

By the early 1990s, the Dwyer brothers were involved in a lucrative compensation racket, masterminded by gang boss Stephen "Rossi" Walsh. The widespread scam involved up to fifteen people who took turns being either victims or culprits in dozens of accidents. Most of the claims were aimed at the Gas Board and Dublin Corporation who had dug up hundreds of holes around the city in the early 1990s to replace ageing gas and water mains. Fraud Squad detectives estimated that the racket turned over millions of pounds. Coincidently, in the early 1990s, "Bud" Dwyer also sold his former home in Ashbourne, County Meath to Chief Superintendent Pat Byrne who was later promoted to Assistant Commissioner and then Garda Commissioner, a post that he held between 1996 and 2003.

"Rossi" Walsh did not continue to benefit from the fraud scam. In November 1993, he was jailed for fifteen years for blowing up a North Dublin city pub. The former soccer international had been found in the rubble of what had once been Collins Pub in Ballybough after he was caught in the blast. He had a miraculous escape.

The Dwyer brothers, however, did continue to reap the rewards from the scam, throughout the nineties. In 1997, John Dwyer received IR£25,000 in compensation for a "whip lash" injury he received when a vehicle driven by Mark Carolan, who was better known as Mark Dwyer, hit his car. The payment was made because the person responsible for the accident had since died and could not give evidence. In any event, as part of the scam, Mark 'Carolan' had accepted responsibility, leaving the insurance company with no option but to pay out.

Working together in the insurance scams was only one aspect of "Bud" Dwyer's complex relationship with Mark. "Bud" Dwyer had married Hilda, Mark Dwyer's mother, when Mark was a baby and reared him as his own son. However, in 1989, he had thrown Mark out of the family home when he discovered that his son had been smoking cannabis. Around the same time, Mark Dwyer had discovered that "Bud" was not his real father. Despite the rows "Bud" Dwyer continued to employ Mark on a part-time basis in the roofing business until 1995 when Mark became a full-time drug dealer. In 1996, "Bud" Dwyer and his wife Hilda went through an acrimonious separation.

The murder of Mark Dwyer deeply affected "Bud", who also

had to formally identify his son's body. Mark's stepfather had been appalled at the extent of his son's injuries and the manner of his death. At the time of the murder "Bud" was aware of Mark's involvement in the Delaney and PJ Judge gangs and of his role in the murder of "Jock" Corbally. Initially "Bud" believed that the same people responsible for the hit on the Psycho, a week earlier, had also murdered his son. Declan "Decie" Griffin had been abducted by the IRA and questioned about the Corbally case. While he was being interrogated the informant had told the IRA that Mark was Judge's right-hand man. "I believe that Mark was abducted and shot because of his involvement with PJ Judge or the Corbally affair and of Judge's involvement in the distribution of drugs," Dwyer told detectives, in a statement the day after Mark's murder.

However, within a week of the murder, the Garda investigation had begun to unravel the truth and "Bud" naturally took a keen interest. At the time of Mark Dwyer's death "Chester" Beatty was still closely associated with the Delaney mob. He had been helping "Cotton Eye" investigate the disappearance of the infamous stolen ecstasy tablets. At his father's trial, Scott Delaney later revealed that "Chester Beatty's crew" were also after Mark Dwyer. The Dwyer brothers' suspicions were also influenced by the fact that there was already little love lost between Beatty and the dead man's family by the time Mark Dwyer was murdered. The problems stemmed from an incident on September 15, 1996, when Beatty fired three shots at John Dwyer as he parked his car near a pub on Cork Street in the south inner-city. John Dwyer had an incredible escape from death or serious injury in the attack. The shooting was the result of a pub row during which John Dwyer had hit another man whose daughter was Brian "The Tosser" Meehan's girlfriend. Meehan was a member of the Gilligan gang and Beatty was alleged to have carried out the attack on Meehan's behalf. John Dwyer later armed himself with a Smith and Wesson .22 revolver for his own protection. With all this in mind "Bud" and John Dwyer began to focus their attention on Beatty.

To make matters worse around the same time, "Chester", the loudmouthed thug, began "bragging and blowing" about his role in Mark Dwyer's murder in pubs that were also frequented by the Dwyer brothers. As a result of his sheer size and formidable reputation no one challenged Beatty. "He had been boasting about breaking Mark's back with a baseball bat. This was going on for nine months and it was having an awful affect on the whole family. Something had to be done," John Dwyer later admitted. "Bud" Dwyer would also confirm that Beatty's comments tormented him and his family. "It was wrecking my head and driving me mad," he claimed. The Dwyer brothers began plotting their revenge.

In February 1997, detectives heard a whisper through the gangland grapevine that "Chester" Beatty was to be shot dead in retaliation for the attempt on John Dwyer's life the previous September. They contacted Beatty and warned him to watch his back. In the meantime, Beatty had changed "for the worse", according to former friends and family. He had become a heavy drinker and a cocaine addict. The cost of his addiction could barely keep pace with the money he made from selling drugs. By the time his son was born in June 1997, "Chester" was flat broke. Jennifer Melia recalled just how bad things had become: "Chester couldn't even afford to buy a pair of shoes for our little baby for his baptism. On the way to the church he had to get super glue from my mother to fix his own shoes because the soles were falling off."

Later on in the summer of 1997, Beatty had an altercation with another bouncer in Dublin who allegedly had links to the IRA or the INLA. On August 11, Gardaí attached to Store Street station arrested a drunken Beatty after they discovered he was carrying a knife.

In October 1997, Gardaí went looking for "Chester" in relation to another crime but they couldn't find him at any of his known addresses or drinking haunts. Beatty finally called one of the detectives looking for him and told him he was hiding in Limerick from a "club bouncer with Sinn Féin connections" and that if he returned to Dublin he would be shot. It was obvious that Beatty was in fear of his life.

Throughout the years, the underworld heavy had maintained contact with his estranged wife, Theresa, and the pair remained friends. He had already told her that he was in "big debt" to a number of drug dealers and she had lent him IR£5,000 towards paying it off. She recalled that he was very badly dressed and appeared depressed. Beatty told her that he was afraid he was going to be shot. He didn't say who wanted to kill him or why. However, despite his money troubles and fears of assassination, Beatty resumed drinking in his old haunts around the city centre. The Dwyer brothers soon heard that their sworn enemy was back in the area.

The Dwyers contacted an old criminal friend from Crumlin, who had been suspected of carrying out a number of gangland murders in the past. The gangster, who was in his late forties, was considered to be extremely violent. He had eighteen convictions for serious crime, including two for possession of firearms, larceny, assault and wounding. The hit man had been given sentences totalling over eight years. He was a long-time friend of the Dwyer brothers and knew all about their problems with Beatty. They also contacted Martin Comerford, a thirty-six-year-old criminal from the Corporation flats at Tom Kelly Road in Dublin 2. Comerford worked as a motorbike courier and was married with three children. He was "Rossi" Walsh's closest associate and had plenty of criminal form, including convictions for possession of firearms, burglary and assault. Comerford had helped Walsh blow up Collins Pub in 1992 but he had escaped when the place exploded. Comerford had suffered serious burns but he did not attend a hospital. While in hiding, over a two-month period, his burns were treated by family members. Although arrested and questioned about the explosion there had been insufficient evidence with which to charge Comerford.

From early November 1997 the Dwyers and the hit man had been discussing how best to "teach Beatty a lesson". The matter was foremost in their minds since Scott Delaney had been convicted of Mark's murder a month earlier. "Bud" Dwyer had asked associates to watch out for "Chester" and to report back on his whereabouts. When Beatty resurfaced it didn't take the Dwyers long to track him down.

On the evening of Sunday, November 30, "Bud" Dwyer rang John Dwyer at his home at Church Street and told him he had spotted Beatty. "Chester" was drinking in the Wild Heather pub on Mary Street in Central Dublin. John Dwyer and the hit man drove over to Comerford's house in Dwyer's van. John told Comerford that "your man is over in a pub in Mary Street" and asked him to follow him to the roofing yard on his motor bike. Comerford had been expecting a call because he knew the Dwyers were actively looking for Beatty. When they got back to the yard on Beresford Street John Dwyer told Comerford that his brother had spotted Beatty in the pub. John then went to a vacant building in the yard and took a Smith and Wesson pistol from a bag. It was the same pistol Dwyer had armed himself with after Beatty's gun attack in September 1996. John Dwyer loaded six bullets into the weapon and the three gangsters went for a cup of tea.

At 6pm, Dwyer asked Comerford to scout the area of the pub to see if there were any police in the vicinity. When he got to Capel Street, Comerford spotted a uniformed Garda directing traffic. He returned to the yard and John Dwyer decided that they should wait a little longer before moving. In the next hour Comerford made two more patrols around the Wild Heather pub. When he again returned to the yard John Dwyer instructed him to go into the pub. "Bud" Dwyer wanted to leave and he would point out Beatty to Comerford. "Bud" Dwyer did not want to be in the pub at the time of the hit and Comerford was to finger Beatty for the hit man. John Dwyer gave the courier a mobile phone and told him that "Bud" would ring Comerford as they didn't know each other by sight. Comerford went into the pub and ordered a pint. Shortly afterwards "Bud" Dwyer rang Comerford's phone but they found it difficult to talk to each other because the reception was so bad. The two hoods literally bumped into each other when they went outside the pub door to get better reception. "Bud" Dwyer told Comerford where Beatty was sitting in the lounge upstairs and described him. Comerford went to the toilet to make eye contact with the target. When he came back down he confirmed he had spotted Beatty and "Bud" Dwyer left the Wild Heather. However, he returned a short time later and told Comerford to follow him back to the yard where they met John Dwyer and the hit man. "Bud" Dwyer told the hit man to do the shooting but John Dwyer appeared to be reluctant to go ahead. "Bud" said that Beatty "had to be done" because he had broken Mark Dwyer's back with a pickaxe handle. Comerford later described "Bud" as "all fired-up". The hit man never spoke. After a half-hour of debate between the brothers, John Dwyer changed his mind. "Right, let's get it over with," he said.

Comerford was asked to bring the gun to the pub but he refused.

The police knew his motor bike and he could easily be stopped for a routine search. Comerford agreed to scout the area again for the police while John Dwyer drove the hit man, in his wife's car, to the side of the Wild Heather pub. As the final plan was put in place the hit man made a balaclava out of the sleeve of a jumper. "Bud" Dwyer said he would also drive around the area in his own car to keep a look out for cops. Comerford patrolled the area and then met John Dwyer and the hit man in a laneway at the side of the pub. The courier told the hit man where Beatty was sitting and described what he was wearing. The hit man was standing in the lane with the pistol pointing to the ground and the balaclava over his head. Comerford drove away and went home. He brought his wife Karen out to the pub for the night. It was now a few minutes before 8.40pm.

"Chester" Beatty had been on a marathon booze binge that had started on Friday night. At 7am on Saturday morning, November 29, he had arrived in The Fusion pub in Townsend Street in Central Dublin. The pub was an "early house". Beatty had spent the entire day in the bar drinking with various friends. Jennifer Melia had joined him that afternoon but later in the night the couple had a row and she'd left the pub in a taxi. Beatty had followed her, saying that he would throw himself into the river if she left. She'd refused to stay and the taxi drove off. Melia never saw Beatty again.

After midnight Beatty and his cronies went to a snooker hall at Henry Place in the city centre where they stayed until 9.30am on Sunday morning. They'd gone to a Sinn Féin drinking club and then on to Slatterys Bar on Capel Street. He'd arrived in the Wild Heather around 4.15pm. Beatty had previously been barred from the Wild Heather by the owner but he wasn't on the premises and Beatty was served because the staff didn't know him. As the marked man walked into the pub he hadn't noticed Christy "Bud" Dwyer sitting drinking at a table on the ground floor. "Bud" Dwyer had called his brother and Beatty was sentenced to death.

At 8.40pm the Wild Heather was quiet. Two women were sitting drinking in the ground floor section and there were twelve customers upstairs where Beatty was holding court. The hit man came through the front door and ran upstairs. He headed straight for "Chester" who was sitting on a high stool at the bar. The hit man pulled Beatty from his stool and fired a shot at him. The underworld hard man lifted his arm to defend himself as the hit man fired another two shots: one of the bullets hit Beatty in the chest; the second bullet travelled through his left upper arm and also lodged in his chest; a third shot grazed his right ear. Despite the fact that he had been severely injured and had been boozing and taking drugs for over two days, Beatty pursued the hit man down the stairs as the assassin made his escape. The killer turned and fired another three shots at his target but missed. One of the bullets lodged in the stairs while two others hit the wall beside where a number of people were sitting drinking. One of Beatty's drinking companions, Gerry Brown, threw a stool down the stairs at the hit man knocking the gun from his hand. Amazingly Beatty picked up the gun and continued after the killer. They disappeared through the front door. When bar staff and customers got to the door they found Beatty's body lying on the pavement. His lifeless eyes stared into space and blood oozed from his nose, mouth and ear. The murder weapon was lying on the pavement under his body. Anthony "Chester" Beatty was dead.

A Garda murder investigation was set up at Store Street Garda Station just after the first 999 calls were received at command and control. Within hours the detectives attached to the case had uncovered a significant lead. Closed circuit cameras connected to the Garda office on O'Connell Street cover practically every street and laneway in the city centre. Several business premises in the area also use high quality security camera systems. The cameras would prove to be of invaluable assistance. Martin Comerford's motorbike was identified as it scouted the area around the Wild Heather pub, minutes before the murder. The same bike had also been spotted by a Garda patrol a short distance from the city centre as Comerford made his way home. The bike was registered in Comerford's name. In addition the officers had retrieved the pint glass Comerford had used when he went into the pub to meet "Bud" Dwyer.

At 4.14pm the following afternoon detectives located the motor bike. When Martin Comerford arrived to take the bike away the waiting detectives arrested him. His home at Tom Kelly Road was also searched. In the meantime video footage taken at the Wild Heather pub clearly showed Comerford meeting with "Bud" Dwyer and talking on his mobile phone. Analysis of phone records would also corroborate the connection between the two men. At first Martin Comerford claimed that the previous night he had been cruising the area while trying to buy drugs. He said that he went to the Wild Heather to meet a man who "sold drugs for Bud Dwyer". He claimed that neither man had any drugs. Then he said he went to Baggot Street and had sex with a prostitute, to whom he paid IR£20. Comerford had had plenty of experience of being interrogated by the police.

However, after several hours of questions, the truth began to emerge. In an interview with Detective Inspector John O'Mahoney and Detective Garda Bernie Hanly, on the night of December 2, Comerford finally told his side of the story. When asked if he would make a statement he said: "I will get shot, I will think about it tonight and tell you in the morning."

The following morning Comerford gave the two detectives a detailed statement of his involvement in the murder. At an investigation conference in the murder incident room it was agreed that the video footage from the area corroborated significant portions of Comerford's statement. The man in overall charge of the case, Detective Superintendent Cormac Gordon, consulted with the Director of Public Prosecutions and it was decided to charge Comerford with the murder of Chester Beatty. Under Irish criminal law an accessory to murder is just as culpable as the person who actually commits the murder. Gordan had also been the officer in charge of the Mark Dwyer murder case. On December 3, 1997, Comerford was formally charged at a sitting of the Dublin District Court and he was remanded in custody.

It the meantime it had been decided to arrest the Dwyer brothers and the hit man. On the same day Comerford was being brought to court, the homes of the three remaining suspects were searched and the hit man and John Dwyer were arrested. During a search of "Bud" Dwyer's house officers found two passports and four birth certificates none of which belonged to any of Dwyer's relations or friends. They also found two rather bizarre hand-written notes addressed to the police. One of the notes read: " If you are looking at this you are here to arrest me so here I am pig. PS You won't find anything you are looking for, only me, so let's go for another 48 hours you insignificant people." The second note was less graphic

– it read: "You again pig!"

In John Dwyer's house the investigators found an official Garda stamp which had been stolen from Ashbourne Garda station earlier in the year.

During John Dwyer's early interviews he was hostile and aggressive. At first Dwyer denied all knowledge of the murder or of "Chester" Beatty. The investigators asked Dwyer about the gun attack in September 1996 and about the subsequent attack on Beatty. John Dwyer claimed he had never been near the Wild Heather pub in his life. He denied knowing Martin Comerford and told the officers to fuck off when they asked if he "hated" "Chester" Beatty. However, when they told the suspect that Comerford had made a detailed statement about the murder, John Dwyer began to change his story. He told the detectives that he had very little to do with the murder and that he had not been near the pub. He said: "This is a fucking disaster, my life is ruined since I was shot last year…" When the investigators asked him to tell his side of the story he replied: "Comerford is putting himself a lot more out of it than he was." Then he told them that Beatty had been "bumming and blowing" about his involvement in Mark Dwyer's murder. John Dwyer then asked to speak with a detective he knew, Detective Sergeant Dominic Hayes, from the Bridewell Station. When Hayes arrived Dwyer told him the full story. He admitted that the gun was the one he had got to protect himself after Beatty attacked him the year before. Dwyer claimed that the intention was to "put the frighteners" on Beatty and not to kill him. He refused to name the hit man to whom he had given the murder weapon.

Later in the interrogation John Dwyer changed his stance and claimed that Martin Comerford's statement was "trumped up". He asked to see if Comerford's signature was on the statement. When he saw that the statement was indeed authentic he gasped: "I'm fucked, why did he have to make a statement, my life is ruined." When the Gardaí asked him if he wanted to tell the truth, Dwyer then replied: "What can I say? I'm fucked."

The suspected hit man, however, refused to talk to the investigators and gave an alibi for the day and night of the murder. Members of his family, who had also been arrested, corroborated his alibi. He denied knowing Beatty or Comerford. In his statement

Comerford had said that he'd known the hit man for over ten years.
The suspect killer was released without charge.

On December 5, John Dwyer was formally charged with
possession of a firearm and six rounds of ammunition in
circumstances that would infer that he did not have it for a lawful
purpose. When asked had he anything to say, Dwyer replied: "The
man was not supposed to die. I'm full of remorse, it was only
supposed to be a frightener, I'm very sorry to see this man dying."
John Dwyer was also remanded in custody.

Meanwhile "Bud" Dwyer was keeping his head down. He'd
gone to Waterford the day after the murder with his twenty-seven-
year-old girlfriend. On the morning of December 5, detectives from
Store Street located "Bud" Dwyer in the Bridge Hotel in Waterford
City. He was arrested and brought back to Dublin. During his
interrogation "Bud" claimed he wasn't sure of his movements on
the night of the murder because he had been on " …a bender for the
past two weeks.". He also denied any involvement in the murder. "I
know I was in the pub before it but I had nothing to do with it [the
murder]," he said. When officers put it to him that both Comerford
and his brother had made statements, which implicated him, "Bud"
at first denied the claims. But faced with an impossible situation
"Bud" Dwyer also began to tell the truth. He admitted to the
detectives that when he heard Beatty bragging about Mark's murder
in the pub it " …was wrecking my head." He then claimed he made
a call to "somebody" and he knew that "someone" would come to
the pub and put the "frighteners" on Beatty. When Dwyer was asked
if he had set up Beatty's murder and had he paid for the hit, "Bud"
replied: "No way, it was only supposed to be a frightener and only
meant to put the shits up him. I don't know if any money was
promised to frighten Beatty. I believe it would have been a small
amount hypothetically."

On December 6, 1997, "Bud" Dwyer was charged with the
same offence as his brother. In answer to the charge he said: "Just
briefly that this unfortunate situation was not meant to happen, I
feel remorse that the man lost his life." "Bud" Dwyer was also
remanded in custody. After the successful result of Mark Dwyer's
murder investigation the Gardaí had now effectively solved a second
gangland murder. Comerford and the Dwyer brothers were

subsequently released on bail, pending their trials.

In February 1998, "Bud" Dwyer went on the run to Malta where he stayed for a number of months. From there he began an extraordinary whispering campaign. He contacted the media in Dublin informing them that he had sold his Ashbourne home to Garda Commissioner Pat Byrne. Dwyer was attempting to embarrass the top cop in a bid to have the charges against him dropped. In a *Sunday World* interview with this writer, conducted over the telephone in May, Dwyer actually admitted that he was trying to "bargain" his way out of trouble. "Don't get me wrong I have nothing against Pat Byrne. He is a nice man who is doing a great job of fighting the drug situation. But why would he buy a house from me: Bud Dwyer not a very nice person who was convicted of two murders? I am using this to bargain with." Dwyer made a number of spurious allegations about the house purchase for which he could offer no evidence. He was anxious to have the story appear in the *Sunday World*.

"I don't want to talk about the Beatty situation, a jury will decide my guilt if I decide to come home. But I will tell you the whole story about gangland if you run the story about Pat Byrne buying my house. I have enough knowledge and stories about all the big gangsters, the General, John Gilligan and George Mitchell, to fill your paper for four weeks. I even had breakfast with the Monk. He is a good friend of mine. I am not trying to blackmail the Commissioner. I am looking for bargaining power here. If you are not prepared to go to press about Pat Byrne buying my house then I will find it very difficult to talk to you about anything else. I will have to talk to other newspapers," said Dwyer. "Bud" claimed that he was even prepared to "come home" to Ireland with the *Sunday World*. Dwyer was eventually re-arrested when detectives caught him while he was staying in a hotel, under an assumed name, in Donabate, County Dublin.

* * * *

In the meantime Martin Comerford's trial was scheduled to begin in the Dublin Central Criminal Court on April 26, 1999. As a result of the weight of evidence against him, and his own admissions,

Comerford knew that he had no choice but to plead guilty. If he denied the charge he was still likely to be convicted. Either way he was on a loser and on a one-way trip to prison for a long time. As the trial approached, Comerford decided to take a tragic course of action to beat the rap. He decided to end his life but it would be no ordinary suicide. Comerford approached his best friend since childhood, Paul McCarthy, with a heart-breaking request – the father-of-three, wanted his closest pal to shoot him.

"If I asked you to do something would you do it?" Martin Comerford asked Paul McCarthy over a pint one evening, about three months before his trial. When McCarthy asked his friend what the "something" was, Comerford refused to say. Some time later Comerford brought the subject up again. This time he came to the point. "Will you shoot me?" he asked. McCarthy thought he was joking.

At first Comerford claimed that he only wanted his friend to wound him so that his trial could not go ahead. But after several conversations McCarthy realised what his friend really intended. Then Comerford revealed that on February 22, he had taken out a life insurance policy on himself with Norwich Union worth IR£100,000. He said he wanted to ensure that his wife and children were financially secure. Comerford confided that if he was shot and it looked like murder then no one would guess it was effectively a suicide.

Over the following two weeks Comerford repeatedly discussed the shooting with his friend. Then early on the evening of Sunday, April 25, the day before the trial was due to begin, Comerford and McCarthy went drinking. At one stage during the evening the two friends were sitting with Comerford's wife and other friends drinking in the Mountpleasant Inn in Rathmines. The pair moved out of earshot of the rest of the company. "Are you doing that thing for me, is it on tonight?" Comerford asked. McCarthy told him to fuck off. Comerford said he had got a sawn-off shotgun. Nothing more was said and the group later went on to another pub.

McCarthy left the pub with Martin and Karen Comerford after 12.30am and went back to the flat at Tom Kelly Road. When Karen had gone up to bed the two friends discussed the shooting again. The old pals were now drunk but Comerford had not swayed from his decision. He said that he didn't want to do it in the flat or outside in the flat complex in case the children would find his body. He went upstairs and looked in on his sleeping wife and children for one last time. It is hard to imagine what he must have been thinking.

Comerford and McCarthy collected the sawn-off shotgun that he had hidden in a storeroom in the flats. It was around 1.30am when the two friends walked out of the complex and onto South Richmond Street. They walked by the Portobello Pub and over the Portobello Bridge down Canal Road. From there they turned onto Mountpleasant Avenue and then into the darkened laneway at the rear of Ontario Terrace in Rathmines. They had probably taken a similar route on many occasions during their childhood. But those trips had been full of fun, adventure and villainy. This was the last time they would ever walk this route together.

In the laneway, Comerford handed McCarthy a pair of gloves and told him to put them on before handling the gun. Comerford kept telling his friend: "Don't bottle it." He loaded the weapon and told McCarthy how to hold it so that it fired properly. McCarthy aimed the shotgun at his friend's legs but Comerford caught the barrel and pulled it into his chest saying: "There, there." McCarthy closed his eyes and squeezed the trigger. His friend took the full brunt of the blast and slumped to the ground, groaning in pain. McCarthy turned Comerford over on his back. "Go, go now," Comerford told his friend. McCarthy was in shock but he did what he was told. Martin Comerford died within minutes.

McCarthy put the gun into a holdall bag and ran out of the laneway and back to the flats where he again hid the weapon in the storeroom. When he went back to his own flat he was crying and shaking. His girlfriend, Eva Fitzpatrick, would later recall: "He was just pacing the room, up and down, shaking. He told me that he shot Martin and I didn't believe him. He was very upset and shaking. I don't think he could believe what happened."

The body was found shortly after 8am that morning, prompting yet another gangland murder investigation. Detective Superintendent Denis Donegan and Detective Inspector Tony Brislane headed the investigation team. Donegan had also headed the Ballymount Bloodbath case. Later that morning when Comerford failed to show up in court a bench warrant was issued for his arrest. Coincidentally, at the same time, just across the Round Hall of the Four Courts, counsel was summing up the evidence in the second trial of "Cotton Eye" Joe Delaney, whose murderous attack on Mark Dwyer had indirectly led to Comerford's absence from court. Mark Dwyer's murder had caused the destruction of at least a dozen lives, including the dead and those left to mourn their passing.

Detective Inspector John McMahon, one of the officers in charge of the "Chester" Beatty murder case, identified the body of the man he had charged with murder the year before. From the start the investigation team felt that there was an obvious motive for the crime. Comerford had given Gardaí a detailed statement about the Beatty murder and it was possible that the criminal had been killed to prevent him from giving evidence against his co-conspirators. But again CCTV proved to be an invaluable asset in the murder investigation. Security tapes taken from a number of business premises in the area clearly showed the two men, as they walked across Portobello Bridge. This was around the same time that residents had heard a loud shotgun blast from the back of Ontario Terrace. Then, minutes later, the tapes showed McCarthy returning across the bridge, alone, and carrying the bag that Comerford had originally been holding. The police now had a suspect.

On Tuesday, May 11, Paul McCarthy was arrested in relation to the murder of Martin Comerford. He was taken to the investigation headquarters at Terenure Garda Station for questioning. Over the next two days the heart-broken shooter told the detectives his extraordinary story. Officers would later reveal how they had "felt pity" for McCarthy. It was a genuinely tragic case and McCarthy had been left to face the consequences of his friend's death wish. McCarthy was in no way a hardened or violent criminal. He had not enjoyed much luck in his life and was a bit of a waster. He had a seven-month-old baby with twenty-one-year-old Eva Fitzpatrick, and another six children from three different relationships. His only criminal convictions were two minor burglaries during the early 1980s. He was about to pay a heavy price for his loyalty to a friend. On Thursday, May 13, Detective Inspector Tony Brislane formally charged Paul McCarthy with murder and he was brought before the Dublin District Court where he was remanded in custody. He was later released on bail.

In December 1999, John and "Bud" Dwyer pleaded guilty to charges of possession of a firearm for an unlawful purpose. John Dwyer, who had been the victim of death threats following his initial arrest, was given a suspended sentence. "Bud" Dwyer was remanded on bail for sentencing the following May. There was considerable surprise at the court's decision to release "Bud" Dwyer on bail because he had already skipped bail in February 1999.

In May 2000, "Bud" Dwyer appeared before the court for sentencing. In evidence, Detective Sergeant Dolan said that "Bud" Dwyer had been traumatised after the death of his stepson and that on the night of the murder he and his brother had intended to "frighten" Beatty. Dwyer's counsel said that his client had not been in trouble for twenty-six-years and that he had "gone to the dogs" following Mark Dwyer's murder. Judge O'Donnell, however, said that Dwyer had been the main instigator in the plot and had expected to get away with it. "Bud" was jailed for three years on the firearms' charge. This was seen as a relatively mild sentence for what was a serious crime. At the time of writing Christy "Bud" Dwyer is a free man again.

The final chapter in this story took place in July 2001 when Paul McCarthy went on trial for the murder of Martin Comerford. Now aged thirty-seven, McCarthy admitted shooting his friend but he denied an intent to kill or to cause serious injury. The prosecution case was that under law this was still murder. Mr Justice Paul Carney had earlier told the jury that it was "irrelevant" to their deliberations whether or not Martin Comerford had requested to be shot.

After a six-day trial the jury unanimously found McCarthy guilty of murder. Passing sentence Mr Justice Carney said: "The sentence is mandatory. I sentence the accused to imprisonment for life." McCarthy smiled to relatives as the verdict was passed. One of his sons stood crying and his partner Eva Fitzpatrick sobbed uncontrollably. There were immediate cries from the back of the court from both the Comerford and McCarthy families. They both fully supported McCarthy's claim that he had not intended to kill his best friend.

The cycle of death had finally ended.

Seven

The Colonel and the Dutch Connection

November 1999: a car park on the outskirts of Amsterdam on a bitterly cold afternoon. Gangland money launderer Peter Lingg parks his car in a discreet corner and waits. Minutes later a second car drives in and pulls alongside. A hidden police surveillance camera zooms in, as Lingg gets into the passenger seat beside the driver, a tall, thin man with dark receding hair. The meeting lasts for a few minutes and then the two men drive off in separate directions. The squad of undercover police officers monitoring Lingg's every move, do not recognise the man in the second car. There is nothing in their intelligence database to match the face with a name. They have no idea at this stage just how important the mystery man would prove to be.

Amsterdam, the hub of Western Europe's sex and drugs industries, is a city full of anonymous, mystery men. From all over the world these mystery men arrive, in their thousands, to organise drug deals, party and keep their heads down. The undercover cops were anxious to identify Lingg's acquaintance. There was no point wasting time and resources monitoring a criminal who was of no consequence to their investigation. As a result of a tap on Lingg's phone they had heard the mystery man organising the meeting with the money launderer. Their only clue was that the man was Irish.

The Dutch serious crime squad requested assistance from their colleagues in the Garda National Drug Unit (GNDU) in Dublin. When GNDU officers were shown the pictures they immediately recognised the mystery man. Their Dutch colleagues had indeed stumbled across a major player. The face in the picture belonged to one John Cunningham. The forty-eight-year-old Dublin crime lord, otherwise known as the Colonel, was an armed robber, kidnapper and fugitive. The Colonel was the mastermind behind a huge drug and gun trafficking operation worth over €200 million.

Cunningham, who, for over three years, had successfully hidden from the Irish authorities in Holland, had, quite literally, driven into the net when he arrived in that car park. Senior officers at the GNDU could not believe the lucky break. Following a conference between the Irish and Dutch police Cunningham was elevated to the last place he wanted to be in any investigation – the number one target. This was the beginning of one of the largest international organised crime investigations ever undertaken by the Gardaí.

The Irish police had last set eyes on John Cunningham in September 1996 when the colourful gangland figure had absconded from Shelton Abbey open prison, near Arklow, in County Wicklow. The Colonel had been serving out the last two years of a seventeen-year sentence he'd received for masterminding the 1986 kidnapp of Jennifer Guinness, the wife of John Guinness, the wealthy Chairman of the Guinness Mahon Bank in Dublin. The infamous crime had earned Cunningham and his older brother Michael notoriety overnight. Needless to say, when the pair plotted the kidnapping the last thing they had been seeking was renown. They had been pursuing their life-long dream of pulling off the ubiquitous 'big one' – the one big crime that would set them up for a life of luxury, where the only bars were of the cocktail variety. By the time John Cunningham drove into the Dutch car park in 1999 he had finally achieved his goal.

****

John Cunningham was born in the slums of Blessington Street in Dublin's north inner-city on October 10, 1951. He was one of seven children born to Frank, a soldier from County Clare and his wife Lily, from County Mayo. Shortly after his birth the Cunninghams moved to one of the new sprawling estates being built on the edge of the city to alleviate the appalling living conditions in the slums. The Cunninghams moved to a house on Le Fanu Road in Ballyfermot, West Dublin. While the new working-class suburbs provided families with vastly improved standards of accommodation and sanitation, they were also plagued by unemployment and a lack of infrastructure and facilities. The suburbs soon became notorious breeding grounds for a new generation of criminals who would introduce Ireland to organised crime.

John and two of his brothers, Michael and Fran, were typical of the young criminal class emerging at the time. From their early teens they were in trouble with the law. John Cunningham received his first custodial sentence in 1966 when he was fourteen, for house breaking and larceny. He was given a stiff two-year sentence and sent to Daingean Industrial School. Daingean, was a notorious institution run by religious brothers where, it later emerged, sexual and physical abuse were part of a horrendous daily regime. Over the next twenty years Cunningham would accumulate another twenty-seven criminal convictions for larceny, receiving stolen goods, assault and malicious damage. His only legitimate employment was when he spent a short period of time working as a metal worker.

By the early 1970s, armed robbery had become the stock and trade of the new generation of criminals. The Cunninghams had forged links with all the major players. They were close friends and associates of another young Ballyfermot thug John Gilligan, who would go on to earn infamy as Ireland's most reviled godfather. While in Daingean, John Cunningham had also befriended Martin Cahill, another troublesome teenager, who would grow up to become the criminal mastermind known as the General. Cunningham and his brothers also associated with members of the Dunne family.

By the end of the seventies the Cunninghams, both independently and as members of Martin Cahill's notorious gang, were considered to be amongst the top crime figures operating in the country. At the same time Cunningham had started a relationship with Mary McCormack an attractive, separated mother-of-one who was a sister of Michael Cunningham's girlfriend. Mary was the love of John Cunningham's life and, despite his long absences from home at the pleasure of the Irish prison system, she remained loyal and faithful to her man. Cunningham treated Mary's then twelve-year-old girl Caroline like she was his own daughter.

In 1981 he bought a house for his new family in Tallaght, West Dublin, using cash he had robbed from various banks. John Cunningham loved the high life. He liked expensive clothes, flash

cars and exotic holidays – and he spared no expense on his new
family. But the high life cost a lot of money and it took a lot of
armed robberies, and considerable risk of being caught, to keep the
money coming in.

In 1982 he was questioned about the murder of a security guard
during a raid at Clerys' department store in central Dublin. He was
also questioned about an armed hold up at the Carlton Cinema in
the city centre. In the same year he took part in an IR£120,000 post
office heist in Mallow, County Cork, with Martin Cahill.

In July 1983, John Cunningham played a central role in the
robbery that was to establish the General as a major league criminal
mastermind – the O'Connor's jewellery heist. It netted the gang
two million Irish pounds in gold and diamonds. The meticulous
planning that went into the robbery earned Cahill the nickname the
General and Cunningham, the pseudonym the Colonel. The night
following the spectacular robbery – the largest at the time in the
history of the State – Cunningham was badly burned. With his
partners-in-crime, Cahill and John Traynor, the Colonel was trying
to set fire to the van used on the 'job'. As Cunningham was about
to throw a petrol bomb into the van, it prematurely ignited and the
rubber glove he was wearing melted into his hand.

The O'Connor's robbery, however, was one of the last jobs
Cunningham did with the General. Cunningham preferred smaller
teams so that the loot would not have to be split up so many times.
John and Michael Cunningham began operating with another armed
robber from Tallaght called Anthony Kelly. Kelly, who was
originally from Dublin, had spent much of his life living in Leeds
in the north of England. Kelly and the two Cunningham brothers
began doing armed robberies in Leeds. In a three year period up to
1984 they were estimated to have stolen in the region of one million
pounds Sterling from banks and security vans across the north of
England. The gang would often fly from Dublin to carry out a
robbery and then catch a return flight home on the same day. In
October 1984, however, the lucrative day trips came to an end when
the three hoods were suspected of being involved in the murder of
police Sergeant John Speed, who was shot dead during a chase in
Leeds.

The investigation into Sergeant Speed's death proceeded and

in early 1986, the West Yorkshire police informed the Gardaí in Dublin that, among others, they wanted to extradite the Cunninghams and Kelly to face charges. But the three hoods were tipped off and went into hiding before they were lifted.

At that stage the Colonel had already begun plotting a major kidnap as a means of pulling off the 'big job' that would solve all his problems. They needed cash, lots of cash, to set themselves and their families up with a new life somewhere in the sun out of reach of the long arm of the law. Faced with the prospect of a long spell behind bars in the UK, Cunningham decided to bring their kidnap plans forward.

On the afternoon of April 8, 1986, the three hoods kidnapped forty-eight-year-old Jennifer Guinness from her home in Howth, North County Dublin. The gang demanded a ransom of two million Irish pounds for her safe return.

The high-profile kidnapping drama ended eight days later when armed police surrounded a house on Waterloo Road in south Dublin where the gang were hiding with their hostage. After a ten-hour stand-off, during which John Cunningham threatened to blow himself up with a hand grenade, the gang finally gave themselves up. Jennifer Guinness was released unharmed. As he was being brought away by police, detectives asked the Colonel if he had really believed he could succeed in pulling off the crime. "We wouldn't have done it if we didn't think that we were going to get the money. Two million was only a starting figure... it was going to be the big one but it all went wrong," John Cunningham ruefully replied. Instead of the large ransom John Cunningham received a large seventeen-year prison sentence for the kidnapping. His brother Michael and Anthony Kelly were each jailed for fourteen years.

* * * *

After serving nearly ten years of his sentence John Cunningham was transferred from Limerick high security prison to the much more relaxed open prison at Shelton Abbey, County Wicklow, in January 1996. He was due for full early release on March 2, 1999. He had been granted special temporary release to attend the wedding of his adopted daughter Caroline in September 1996. The Colonel was planning to lead her up the aisle in front of ninety invited guests. Cunningham was looking forward to the big day – the biggest day in his life after a decade behind bars. He had even been measured for his wedding suit. He was particularly excited about spending time with his ten-year-old daughter Hazel, who was born four days after the end of the Guinness kidnap. It would be the first time he would see her as a free man. Up to a year earlier Hazel had thought her dad was a policeman because every time she saw him there were uniformed men present.

Then two weeks before the wedding everything went horribly wrong. An off-duty prison Governor spotted Cunningham and another former member of the General's gang, Eamon Daly, drinking in a pub not far from the prison. This was in contravention of the open prison rules. The two prisoners were accompanied by a prison officer, who was later suspended from duty pending an investigation into the incident. Daly was serving the remainder of a twelve-year sentence for armed robbery. As a punishment for the abuse of their privileges the two criminals were to be returned to an enclosed prison and Cunningham's temporary release for the wedding was cancelled. It was too much for Cunningham to take. On September 16, just hours before he was due to be returned to Limerick prison, he absconded. His old friend John Gilligan aided his escape. The fugitive stayed in the home of one of Gilligan's bagmen, Russell Warren, for a number of days. He was then smuggled out of the country in a truck travelling to the continent. In the end his brother Michael led Caroline up the aisle, watched from a discreet distance by a small army of detectives.

Cunningham travelled to Holland and was warmly welcomed by his gangland pals. Many of them, including Gilligan, had become wealthy men while the Colonel was inside. Gangland had undergone dramatic changes during the ten years between 1986 and 1996. A big party was thrown in his honour at one of the city's plush restaurants. Cunningham was regaled with stories of how easy it was to make money in the drug business. Gilligan had plenty of good contacts in the 'Dam, as the ex-patriot gangsters called their new home, and his business was booming despite the heat created in the aftermath of the Veronica Guerin murder a few months earlier. Cunningham was stunned by the amounts of money being made by

Gilligan. He was also impressed with the fine-tuned distribution and laundering operation the godfather had set-up between Ireland and Holland. Cunningham was given money and a nice place to live. If he wanted to get involved in the rackets then there was plenty of 'work' available for him. The Colonel had arrived in the land of milk and honey.

But then, just one month later, John Gilligan and Michael Cunningham were arrested in Heathrow Airport in London by HM Customs. Gardaí investigating the Guerin murder in Dublin had tipped off Customs officers that Cunningham was delivering drug money to the mob boss. Gilligan was charged with money laundering and at the same time his entire distribution network was discovered and smashed. Former members of the gang had agreed to become the state's first "supergrasses" and had turned over their evil boss. Overnight John Gilligan's multi-million Euro empire was shut down. Michael Cunningham was found carrying a false Irish passport containing John Cunningham's picture. He had been about to catch a flight to Holland with Gilligan when the customs officers moved in. Cunningham was later questioned about the robberies in the Leeds area in the early 1980s but was released without charge and he returned to Ireland.

Shortly before Gilligan's arrest Mary Cunningham had revealed in an interview with the *Sunday World* that her husband John had no intention of ever returning to Ireland again: "I'm standing by Johnny, I've always stood by him. He was a great husband and a good father. I just hope myself and the girls get to see him again. I don't know when that will be. I'm sure we'll all meet up together sometime. It's a terrible strain on us all right now. John has left Ireland and he won't be returning. I'm not sure where he is but he is moving all the time. I don't know what advice to give him. I just hope he makes the right decision in the end."

Mary Cunningham did not have to worry about her husband for very long. Following Gilligan's arrest Cunningham began to do business with another ex-patriot Dublin hoodlum called Christy Kinahan. Born in inner-city Dublin in 1957, Kinahan was considered to be an extremely clever and ruthless criminal. Handsome and suave he was described as something of a gangland sophisticate who used various stretches in prison to obtain university degrees and to learn several languages. In fact Kinahan could just as easily have been a successful businessman in the legitimate world but he opted instead for a life in the drug trafficking business. In 1986, officers from the Garda Drug Squad had caught Kinahan in possession of seven ounces of high quality heroin which at the time had a street value of IR£100,000 and in March 1987 he had been convicted on the possession charge and jailed for six years. After his release Kinahan had gone back to crime, specialising in the importation of drugs, funding his import business by organising armed robberies and fencing stolen goods. It wasn't long before he was in trouble again. In June 1993, a twenty-five-year-old armed robber called Thomas "Bomber" Clarke had carried out an armed robbery on the First National Building Society in Drumcondra on Dublin's north side. (Clarke would later make a name for himself by breaking out of an English prison and for escaping again when he was subsequently re-arrested in Ireland for a string of robberies when members of John Gilligan's gang ambushed a prison van taking him to court in 1996.) Gardaí had received information that Christy Kinahan was planning to fence IR£16,000 worth of travellers cheques which had been taken in the Clarke heist. Following a surveillance operation Kinahan had been arrested a week later and charged with handling the proceeds of the robbery. While being questioned by detectives Kinahan had not been particularly talkative but he had shared a rather strange ditty with his interrogators. It went something like this: "Out in the garden beside the stone wall there was an old man who said nothing at all. He sat in the garden and said nothing at all." When the puzzled cops had asked him what he meant, Kinahan replied: "Nothing at all."

While out on bail Kinahan had then fled to Holland where he'd continued his involvement in the drugs business. He had again found himself in trouble with the law. He had been arrested by Dutch police in possession of ecstasy, cocaine and firearms and was jailed for four years and sent to Amsterdam's Bijlmeerbajef prison. While inside Kinahan had studied several languages and also made valuable contacts with drug traffickers from Holland and Britain.

By the time John Cunningham arrived on the scene in 1996, Kinahan and one of his prison cronies, Dutch drug dealer and gun-runner, Johannes "Joopie" Altepost, were back in business.

Shaven-headed Altepost, who had a reputation for serious violence, had extensive contacts with gun dealing gangs in the former Yugoslavia. Criminal gangs in the old Eastern Block countries specialised in the sale of deadly automatic weapons which were copies of the American equivalents. Altepost and his colleagues in crime were also supplying weapons to John Gilligan and George "the Penguin" Mitchell and had supplied the weapon used by members of Gilligan's gang in their attempt to murder Martin "the Viper" Foley in February 1996.

By the end of 1996, John Cunningham had become a full partner-in-crime with Kinahan and Altepost. Business was soon booming. The new criminal enterprise effectively replaced the Gilligan operation. They began to ship huge quantities of cocaine, ecstasy, hashish and high-powered firearms to gangs throughout Ireland and Britain. Their operation soon completely dwarfed the Gilligan racket. During a three year period, from 1996 – 1999, it was conservatively estimated that Cunningham's syndicate smuggled drugs with a street value in excess of €120 million and an unknown quantity of arms and ammunition. They were supplying gangs in Dublin, Limerick, Belfast, London, Manchester and Liverpool. Back in Ireland, Cunningham's old pals from the General's gang also became partners. Eamon Daly, who was released from prison in 1997, became one of Cunningham's biggest customers in Dublin. Martin "The Viper" Foley, his sidekick Clive Bolger and Seamus "Shavo" Hogan also became the Colonel's clients.

To smuggle the merchandise the gang used corrupt long distance truck drivers and a transport company owned by haulier Kieran Smyth from Dundalk, County Louth. Smyth came from a respectable family background and had worked as a fireman for eleven years before getting into the haulage business. At first Smyth's company, Westlodge Freight Limited, with an address at Ravensdale, Dundalk, County Louth, operated a small business working mainly for the Heinz factory in Dundalk. But within a short time Smyth became a central cog in the narcotics and smuggling trade, North and South of the border. One senior Garda would later describe Smyth: "He was involved in serious and highly organised international crime syndicates. He was a very powerful bagman who was vital to the operations of several major criminal organisations." Westlodge Freight's main sources of income came from smuggling drugs, cigarettes, oil and guns, for criminal and paramilitary gangs. Smyth used drivers to courier money to Europe and then to bring back multi-shipments of contraband on the return trips. In addition Smyth acted as a money launderer for the various terrorist groups and criminal gangs. He used an illegal bank that masqueraded as a Bureau de Change at Dromad, County Louth on the border with Northern Ireland. A Criminal Assets Bureau (CAB) investigation would later uncover evidence that Smyth personally made an estimated IR£12 million which he laundered through the illegal bank in less than two years. With no criminal convictions of any note and a thriving business front Smyth was soon indispensable. He would help make John Cunningham a very wealthy man.

As business prospered beyond his wildest expectations Cunningham believed that he had finally achieved his dream of the big time. Within a few months of his arrival in Holland, after the dust and fuss settled on his prison escape, Cunningham set up a new home and organised for his wife and their daughter Hazel to come over. They were soon living an opulent new life of luxury in Holland. He paid a man named later in a Dutch court as Henk Scharrighuizen, an Amsterdam estate agent, to 'employ' Mary Cunningham as his assistant, paying her a registered wage of €1,200 per month for working a fifteen hour week. Mary couldn't speak a word of Dutch and never set foot in the estate agent's offices. The ruse enabled her to qualify for Dutch residency and therefore ensured that the family did not attract the unwanted attentions of the authorities. Scharrighuizen also fixed Cunningham up with 'offices' – two rented apartments in Amsterdam – where he stored drugs, guns and money. The apartments were carefully chosen. They were anonymous, were not over looked and had easy, discreet access. Cunningham rented a luxury residence in the countryside beside the village of Weteringbrug. It was a few convenient miles from Schipol Airport, and a few minutes from the motorway that serves as one of the main transport arteries along Europe's western coast. The converted farmhouse seemed modest and unremarkable on the outside, but inside it had been extensively renovated and luxuriously fitted with every convenience. Behind a high garden fence was an indoor heated swimming pool. He sent his daughter Hazel to one of Amsterdam's most expensive private schools, attended by the children of wealthy foreign business people living in the region. Cunningham was an ideal father and husband and ensured his wife and child wanted for nothing. Mary soon forgot the worries she had expressed in her *Sunday World* interview a few months earlier. She spent her time out shopping and, as one Dutch detective later recalled, "spent money like it was water". Cunningham himself did not officially exist in the Netherlands. He used two false British passports and forged driving licences. He owned nothing in his own name, had no bank accounts and only ever used cash.

The thriving new business arrangement hit a glitch in October 1997. Kinahan was arrested in Dublin on foot of a warrant relating to receiving the stolen travellers cheques from "Bomber" Clarke in 1993. Kinahan, who was then operating between England, Spain and Holland, had slipped back into Ireland to attend his father's funeral. At the same time the newly organised Garda National Drug Unit (GNDU) had busted a Tallaght-based gang as they took delivery of a shipment of hashish with a street value of IR£3.5million. Kinahan and Cunningham had organised delivery of the drugs for the west Dublin gang, concealing the merchandise in the base of potted plants. Ironically Kinahan's arrest coincided with the seizure, but detectives did not have enough evidence to link him directly to the shipment. Kinahan was jailed for four years in March 1998 after he pleaded guilty to the handling charge. With Kinahan behind bars in Portlaoise Prison, Cunningham took full control of the drug distribution business. Despite his incarceration, Kinahan continued to oversee a drug distribution ring he had organised through a group of young criminals in Dublin. John Cunningham organised their supplies.

It was around this time that Cunningham was introduced to forty-one-year-old Peter Lingg, the owner of a smokey café called the Spanish Arch on Singel Straat. The café was frequented by shadowy underworld characters and most particularly by Irish criminals. The Spanish Arch was a convenient meeting place as it was across the street from the Ibis hotel tower, beside Centraal Station in Amsterdam. In the years before the advent of the Euro currency this area was littered with scores of Bureau de Change outlets. These outlets were popular with various criminal organisations who used them to launder drug money. John Gilligan and his mob, for example, had used a Bureau de Change across the street from Lingg's place to launder millions of pounds in Irish and English currency by exchanging them into Dutch guilders. A predisposition to corruption and financial difficulties encouraged Lingg to offer his services to his underworld customers as a Mr Fixit. Soon he became the lynch pin in Cunningham's operation, laundering money and organising cover loads of legitimate goods, to conceal drug and gun shipments. This new relationship would prove to be a fatal mistake for Cunningham.

In December 1998, the pair organised a huge shipment of drugs and guns to Ireland that would have serious long-term consequences for the Colonel. On the morning of December 21, 1998, eight pallets of pitta bread, which had been shipped from Holland, arrived at the premises of a company called Castlecoole Cold Storage, at Moraghy, Castleblayney in County Monaghan. Castlecoole provided cold storage facilities for customers who rented space in their warehouse. The storage company handled up to forty containers of perishable goods every day. Gardaí at Castleblayney Station were called in when a member of Castlecoole's staff discovered something more than just pitta bread. One of the pallets had accidentally opened while it was being unloaded and inside there were several kilos of cannabis. Gardaí decided not to open the pallets and a surveillance operation was put in place to monitor the collection of the load.

That afternoon, at 4.50pm, a truck owned by Kieran Smyth's company, Westlodge Freight, collected the pitta bread containers. It was stopped by Gardaí as it left Castlecoole. When detectives began searching the entire load they were astonished by what they found. Inside the pallets were a total of 780 kilos of cannabis resin and herb with a street value of IR£8 million. Beside the dope they also found an even more disturbing cargo. Carefully wrapped and concealed in the middle of the load were fifteen lethal Intratec, or "Tec 9", 9mm automatic machine pistols capable of firing hundreds of rounds per minute. There were also ten Smith and Wesson 9mm automatic pistols. The haul included silencers for each of the "Tec 9s", with spare magazines and ammunition for all the weapons. It was the largest cache of illegal weapons ever intercepted by the

Irish police in the midst of a drug haul. Technical experts later found that all the weapons had been manufactured in Eastern Europe. The discovery was about to spark one of the most complex international investigations into the trafficking of guns and drugs in Irish history.

The large haul of arms found with the Castleblayney seizure caused grave concern to both crime ordinary and anti-terrorist police units North and South of the Irish border. It was reasonable to suspect that many more such weapons had already been successfully delivered into criminal and terrorist hands. There had been no intelligence about this smuggling route and it appeared to be elaborate and well-organised. The connections between crime gangs, the IRA and dissident Republicans, were already an established fact. For a number of years intelligence sources had been aware that the IRA had been re-equipping themselves with guns supplied by drug gangs while at the same time making peace 'gestures' by decommissioning other weapons. The guns, and large amounts of protection money, were 'donated' to the Republicans, who then seemed to 'turn a blind eye' to the criminals' activities. It was also known that a number of corrupt hauliers and individual truck drivers who operated in the border region were involved in smuggling rackets. There was also evidence that criminal gangs were arming themselves with much more lethal firepower, as had been discovered during the investigation into the Gilligan gang in 1996. The main concern of the Castleblayney investigation was to discover the destination of the lethal cache. On the ground the divisional Detective Superintendent, Noel White, was in charge of the investigation and he worked closely with the Garda National Drug Unit (GNDU). The investigation to unravel the complex international conspiracy would have to involve several Garda and RUC units. In time the investigation would also involve police and customs units in The Netherlands, Belgium, France and the UK.

From the beginning, the investigation team were satisfied that Castlecoole Storage and their staff were innocent of involvement in anything of an illegal nature. However, thanks to the accident with the pitta pallet, the team were left with one major clue– the link between Smyth's transport company and the shipment. On December 9, Castlecoole Storage had been contacted about the pitta bread load, by a man who claimed he was a small frozen goods distributor from Newry, County Armagh. The investigation established that there was no such frozen goods distributor. The caller had told staff at Castlecoole Storage that he needed their facilities because his own refrigerated unit was out of commission. He had asked for the phone numbers of freight companies who could handle shipment of his goods. He had then, rather pointedly, asked if there was a company called Westlodge Freight who could transport his goods from Castlecoole Storage. The following day, another transport company in Dundalk, which again was totally unconnected to any criminal conspiracy, had been contacted by the same "frozen goods distributor". He had claimed that he was given their number by Westlodge Freight. He had instructed the company to pick up six pallets of pitta bread from a cold storage facility at Barreich in Holland. The legitimate company had then arranged for the collection of the pallets in Holland and delivered them to Castecoole Storage in County Monaghan, on December 21, 1998.

The investigation team homed in on Westlodge Freight. An international trawl showed that the company had already been involved in several suspicious criminal incidents. In August 1997, Customs and Excise officers at Dun Laoghaire Port in Dublin found Stg£73,000 in cash that was being carried on a Westlodge Freight truck. The money was seized and a forensic examination revealed that it was heavily contaminated with traces of illegal drugs. The money was held under a receivership order. As recently as November 26, 1998, HM Customs at Dover in England had uncovered over 1.4 million smuggled cigarettes on board another Westlodge Freight lorry. Then on December 3, 1998, over Stg£172,000 was seized from a Westlodge Freight lorry at Holyhead Port in the UK by HM Customs. The second lot of money was also contaminated by traces of illegal drugs and it was confiscated by order of an English court under drug trafficking legislation. The day before the Castlecoole Storage seizure, Kieran Smyth was himself arrested in the process of loading 21.1 million cigarettes onto one of his trucks in a secret warehouse at Hasselt in Belgium. Smyth was arrested and later released pending further enquiries. The Belgian police subsequently issued an International Arrest Warrant for his arrest. An investigation into the mobile phone number that had been left with Castlecoole

Storage by the bogus frozen foods distributor was later traced back to an associate of Kieran Smyth. The plot was beginning to unravel.

Meanwhile Detective Superintendent Noel White forwarded a request for assistance to the Dutch police. They needed help to trace the source of the pitta bread shipment and to thereby identify the source of the drugs and the guns. Chief Inspector Thomas Wievel of the Special Business Investigations Service, of the Central Information Service, in Zoetermeer, established that the pitta bread delivered to Castlecoole Storage had been bought in Jaffa bakeries in Amsterdam. Two men had contacted the bakery on December 10, 1998. One of them, a Dutch man called Peter, with a company called De Spaanse Gevel, registered at Singel Straat in Amsterdam, paid for the pallets of pitta bread. A check of the mobile phone number given by the bakery customer came back to one Peter Lingg, the owner of the Spanish Arch café. The De Spaanse Gevel company was registered as the owner of the café. Further enquiries established that the same two men had collected the pallets of bread on December 15. Two days later a truck, registered to Westlodge Freight, had delivered the pallets of pitta bread to a cold storage facility outside Amsterdam. The following afternoon the legitimate Irish haulage firm, which had been hired to pick up the bread, collected the load and travelled back to Ireland. After a number of months of investigation the Irish and Dutch now had a suspect – Peter Lingg. An operation, codenamed Plover, was set up. Peter Lingg had become a target and time was slowly running out for the Colonel.

* * * *

The Dutch police authorities receive more requests for assistance in international criminal investigations than any other police force in the world. Amsterdam is the hub of organised crime in Western Europe – the underworld's equivalent of a major business centre where criminal organisations negotiate billions of Euro worth of drug deals every year. With so many criminals, doing so many deals, on their territory the Dutch authorities never have to worry about a lack of action. But with so many requests for assistance police forces around the world literally have to queue before the Dutch can get around to helping them. Investigations are undertaken based on their size and level of priority. The first thing the Irish investigation team had to do was convince the Dutch that the Castleblayney operation was important enough to justify and sustain several months of full-scale investigation.

In June 1999, Detective Superintendent White and Detective Chief Superintendent Ted Murphy, the head of the GNDU, flew to the Netherlands for a secret conference with the Amsterdam police and the State prosecutor's office. At the meeting the Dutch agreed to commence an undercover investigation into Peter Lingg. The Dutch authorities were particularly concerned that such a large cache of deadly weaponry had been sourced in Amsterdam. They were now as anxious as the Irish to find the source of the firepower. Inspector Bob de Vries, the officer in charge of Unit Four of the Amsterdam Serious Crime Squad, was assigned to work on the Irish case. The unit was one of a number of such specialist teams which could be assigned specific cases to investigate. Unit Four had fifteen officers who were trained in financial investigation and surveillance. The team was self-sufficient and capable of conducting electronic surveillance, such as tapping phones and tracing calls.

The first stage of the Dutch investigation took the form of an in-depth financial inquiry into Lingg's activities. In such operations the preferred *modus operandi* is to do a financial investigation before moving onto physical surveillance. During a surveillance operation an entire team watches the target's every move and taps every phone he or she uses, be it landline or mobile. Then, as other targets are identified, the operation is broadened to include them. As an investigation proceeds, transcripts of the phone taps are compiled with surveillance reports and photographs. A case analyst, who is also a member of the investigation team, then assesses all the material. The analyst decides which information is of evidential importance and then passes it on for scrutiny by a prosecuting magistrate, who supervises the operation.

Peter Lingg's sheer laziness was to make the first part of the investigation, the financial inquiry, relatively easy for Inspector Bob de Vries and his team. At the time Lingg was exchanging millions of pounds into Dutch guilders for Cunningham. But instead of spreading the cash around several Bureau de Changes Lingg decided to save himself the hassle – he used just one, Pott Exchange on Damark Street. Under Dutch law all currency exchange banks in The Netherlands face immediate closure unless they inform the police when sums equivalent to IR£10,000 or higher are changed into Guilders. Lingg had left a money trail that a blind man could follow. Cunningham handed Lingg large holdall bags full of Irish and English currency. The corrupt café owner then brought the bags to Potts Exchange. On average Lingg was changing sums of IR£30,000 or more at any one time, with the money invariably coming in small denominations. The cash bags would often have to be left for hours so that staff at the exchange could count and sort the money. It never seemed to dawn on Lingg that he was attracting a lot of attention to himself. It would later emerge that in a two-year period, from the beginning of 1998, Lingg exchanged sums worth almost twenty million Guilders. The investigation also discovered that in 1999 seventy per cent of all the Irish currency exchanged in Amsterdam had come from Lingg. In an interview, during research for this book, Inspector de Vries explained: "Lingg was a very arrogant and stupid individual. It was incredibly dumb for him to think that he could get away with laundering on that scale, but it also showed us that this was a huge operation because of the enormous sums of cash he was handling. By the beginning of September [1999] we had established a clear money trail involving Lingg but we still did not know who he was dealing with or where he was getting his supplies. It was time to begin our surveillance operation."

In September 1999, the Garda National Drugs Unit hosted a special international police conference in Dublin castle, under the EU funded Oisin programme. Senior officers from Spain, Portugal, Germany, Belgium, the UK and the Netherlands attended the conference. Detective Superintendent Noel White was one of the Irish representatives. At this stage he had transferred from Monaghan and was now second-in-command of the GNDU and was in charge of the Irish end of Operation Plover. During a day of secret briefings, Detective Chief Superintendent Murphy and Detective Superintendent White gave their European counterparts a wish list. It detailed five major Irish drug traffickers who were operating from bases in the various jurisdictions covered by the officers present.

One of the names on the short list was John Cunningham. The GNDU knew that the Colonel had become involved in drug trafficking but as yet they did not have anything concrete with which to commence an investigation. In the meantime the Dutch police decided to begin full-time surveillance on Peter Lingg.

In October 1999, Unit 4 went into action. Lingg was followed everywhere he went. All the phones he had access to were identified, tapped and continuously monitored. Inspector de Vries recalled: "We had already established a direct link between Lingg and the Castleblayney seizure. And we had found the money trail and its obvious connection to Ireland. When we began tapping Lingg's phones we heard a lot of conversations between him and a man with an Irish accent. We had no idea who he was. We also had difficulty with understanding some of the words this man was using and later on our Irish colleagues came to listen to the tapes and translate for us."

Then one evening, early in November 1999, over a month into the investigation, the undercover squad tailed Lingg to his meeting with the unknown Irishman in a car park on the edge of Amsterdam. It was during this brief meeting that the man was photographed. Inspector de Vries contacted the GNDU and informed White and Murphy of the development. Det. Supt. White and a number of his officers immediately flew to Amsterdam to view the picture of the man meeting Lingg and also to listen to the phone taps. When White was shown the picture of the mystery man he couldn't believe his eyes. The mystery man was Cunningham himself. A big fish had just dropped into the net. The Dutch and the Irish had hit what could only be described as the undercover cop's equivalent of the jackpot. Operation Plover was about to take a dramatic change in direction. John Cunningham was placed under full-time surveillance. He was about to become target number one.

The discovery of Cunningham's central involvement in the Castlecoole Storage plot caused a flurry of activity back in Dublin. The GNDU's boss, Det. Chief Supt. Ted Murphy, wanted to cover all eventualities just in case the Dutch police were unsuccessful in their attempt to catch Cunningham. From preliminary enquiries in The Netherlands the police had already discovered that Cunningham did not officially exist there. The Colonel was obviously living under a false name with documents to match. Inspector Bob de Vries could not put a tail on the Colonel until he next met with Lingg. From the next meeting they would be able to find out where Cunningham lived. In the meantime, Det. Chief Supt. Murphy ensured that the Garda Extradition Section were ready with a warrant to seek Cunningham's immediate return to Ireland if Operation Plover failed. As the Colonel was living under a false name and was unlawfully at large from an Irish prison his extradition was a formality. The international drug lord would be back in Ireland within twenty-four hours of his arrest.

Within a few weeks the Dutch had found Cunningham and identified the phones he was using. Two GNDU detectives made weekly trips to Amsterdam to listen to the tapes from Cunningham's phones. A phone kiosk in the village near Cunningham's home, that he often used, was also bugged. The undercover team soon established how Cunningham ran his operation. Cunningham arranged deals over the phones and in person. He organised the supply of the firearms through Johanne "Joopie" Altepost's Eastern European contacts. For his ecstasy operation he bought powder from a gang in the south of Holland, which he then used to manufacture thousands of tablets. He brought the powder to a number of flats equipped with sophisticated tablet-making machines. They were then vacuum packed and placed in foil-lined boxes. The average cost of a single tablet to the Colonel was about IR£1. By the time he sold it to his Irish contacts he had at least quadrupled his initial investment. The Colonel's cannabis and cocaine operations were also sourced from a number of gangs in Amsterdam.

In a typical transaction Cunningham would collect cash from truck drivers coming from Ireland and England. He would then deliver the cash to Lingg and put together the various orders and arrange for their delivery to Ireland in a similar fashion to the Castleblayney haul, or he would hand the merchandise to the truck drivers in holdall bags. Dutch military intelligence were brought in to decode the Colonel's elaborate code system which he used for telephone numbers, times, amounts of money and quantities of drugs. Cocaine was described as "computers", "leaves" and "wallpaper" were bank notes, guns were "toys" and "taximen" described couriers and money on their way to Holland. From the amount of telephone traffic it was obvious that business was booming. Inspector de Vries recalled: "Cunningham was an extremely busy man. He was constantly driving around meeting people in bars, hotels and car parks. We followed him as he met with truck drivers at points along the motorways. Whenever he arranged an appointment he always turned up on time. He was a very good family man and looked after his wife and child very well."

Operation Plover soon entered a crucial phase when the taps produced top grade intelligence that enabled the GNDU to identify most of Cunningham's Irish associates. Eamon Daly and Clive Bolger, the Viper's sidekick, were in regular contact with Cunningham. Bolger and the Viper were also working closely with another important client of Cunningham's, thirty-five-year-old Chris Casserly, from Beaumont Crescent in north Dublin. Casserly had been a target of the GNDU as far back as 1995. He had cut his teeth as a member of a notorious brat pack of young heroin dealers from North Dublin. The main players in that operation had been Thomas "The Boxer" Mullen and Robbie "The Technician" Murphy. "The Boxer" was put out of business in 1997 when Scotland Yard charged him with conspiracy to smuggle heroin into the UK. He was subsequently convicted and jailed for eighteen years. In the meantime, "the Technician" had fled the country to avoid the attentions of anti-drug activists and the Criminal Assets Bureau. Casserly had taken over the business his pals left behind. By 1999, he had become one of Cunningham's main customers in Dublin. In March 1999, the GNDU had arrested "Shavo" Hogan and Dean McCarney from Artane, North Dublin, after they had picked up 28 kilos of hash that Casserly had organised through Cunningham.

Soon the information from Holland was paying dividends in Dublin and the GNDU mounted surveillance operations on a number of the gangsters identified through Operation Plover. On December 13, Keith Hastings, a member of Martin Foley's gang, collected a shipment of 30,000 ecstasy tablets. Chris Casserly had organised the delivery with Cunningham. Hastings picked up the drugs from a truck driver in Northern Ireland and headed for Dublin. However, in County Meath, Hastings was stopped by Detective Sergeant Pat Walsh of the GNDU. Hastings was subsequently convicted of drug trafficking and jailed for seven years. It was only a few days later that Dutch police heard Bolger calling Cunningham. He was trying to arrange a replacement load for the lost ecstasy. Around the same time the Dutch undercover team monitored Cunningham delivering two firearms to two men working for Eamon Daly. Thirty-two-year old, Daniel "Irish Dan" Kelleher, a truck driver from Sallins in County Kildare and a criminal from Cabra, West Dublin, picked up a 9mm automatic pistol and a micro-Uzi machine gun, equipped with a silencer. "We were following Kelleher as he got to the Belgian border and he got suspicious and decided to dump the weapons in water at the side of the road. He phoned Daly in Ireland and told him what he had done. Daly laughed at him and told him he was just being paranoid. Kelleher went back and collected the guns and continued on his way to Ireland," recalled Bob De Vries. When the pair arrived in Ireland on December 18, 1999, the GNDU gave Kelleher good reason for feeling paranoid. The two men were arrested and the guns were seized. Kelleher was subsequently convicted when he pleaded guilty to the firearms offences. In court evidence was given that Kelleher was working for "a major criminal godfather".

Immediately after the bust Daly was on the phone to his old prison friend and partner-in-crime, John Cunningham. Neither man could understand how the GNDU had rumbled them. They both agreed to change their mobile phones. As soon as Cunningham bought a new ready-to-go phone, however, Inspector Bob de Vries and his people had it tapped before he even switched it on. By now it was obvious that Cunningham was the prime mover in a huge drug operation and Lingg was his lieutenant. By the beginning of the New Year in 2000, the Dutch had reassessed their investigation and changed Cunningham's priority to their main target.

Operation Plover struck another blow against Dublin drug-dealer Casserly, on January 27, 2000. The Irish and Dutch police tipped off their colleagues in Northern Ireland that another shipment from Cunningham was being brought through the North, on its way to Dublin. It is a regular feature of such large-scale international operations that police in other jurisdictions are tipped off to intercept drug shipments. This is intended to cover-up the real source of the information and to keep the traffickers guessing about how they are being caught. On this occasion Campbell Lunn was arrested in possession of 200,000 ecstasy tablets and a firearm when he was stopped in Hillsborough, County Down. The haul was to be another joint venture between Foley, Bolger and Casserly. Despite the setback Casserly arranged for yet another consignment from Cunningham. As the Colonel was always paid before he organised any drug shipments the seizures weren't actually costing him any money. He agreed to organise the delivery of another 200,000 ecstasy tablets but as per usual he wanted payment up-front. Casserly instructed two of his associates, Philip Whelan and Colin Grinell, to hire truck driver Gary McNulty to bring IR£100,000 in cash to Holland.

When McNulty arrived in Holland in February 2000 he had been given a Dutch mobile phone number to ring and was told to ask for Jack. Cunningham, 'Jack', arranged to meet McNulty at a truck stop near Breda, in Southern Holland. When Cunningham turned up McNulty gave him the money. Two days later, on February 9, the pair met again at the same location just before McNulty's return trip to Ireland. This time Cunningham handed the trucker a bag. Inspector Bob de Vries and his squad were watching and listening to everything. He contacted his Belgian counterparts. Within minutes of crossing the Belgian border the local police were waiting to pull McNulty over. When they searched his truck they found the 200,000 ecstasy tablets.

As a result of the joint operations in Belfast, Holland and Belgium, Campbell Lunn pleaded guilty and was jailed for six years by a Belfast court while McNulty received a two year suspended jail term from a Belgian court. In Dublin the GNDU's follow-up investigation resulted in the convictions of Colin Grinell and Philip Whelan. Both men were given two years on charges of conspiracy to commit crime. In another offshoot of the operation a man from Tallaght was convicted on a charge of money-laundering and given a fifteen month sentence after being stopped in Dublin with IR£100,000 of Casserly's money. While being questioned by GNDU officers Grinell identified Casserly as the man who had organised the Belgian operation.

The ongoing Operation Plover was having a devastating effect on the drug dealers. In a matter of months over 400,000 ecstasy tablets had been seized. On the night before McNulty's arrest in

Belgium, Casserly had met with Foley and Bolger in the Leinster Pub on Harold's Cross Road, where they regularly held meetings. It was to be one of the last meetings between the three thugs. The Lunn and McNulty arrests led to serious recriminations and Casserly had a bitter falling out with Bolger and Foley. The two hoods decided to dissolve their partnership with Casserly. (See Chapter 2)

Operation Plover had uncovered even more fascinating information, on the Irish side, in early February. The GNDU officers, listening to the Dutch phone taps, were amazed when they heard Christy Kinahan phoning Cunningham from his cell in Portlaoise maximum security prison. They were astonished to hear the jailbird, who had another year to serve of his four-year sentence, actually organising the purchase of 5 kilos of cocaine from Cunningham. Kinahan was using a mobile phone that had somehow been smuggled into what is regarded as one of the most secure prisons in Europe. At the same time in between drug deals and walks in the exercise yard, Kinahan was continuing to study for a degree in Environmental Science through the Open University. In fact he turned down a chance for early release in order to finish his studies! Back at the GNDU headquarters Ted Murphy and Noel White considered it prudent to allow Kinahan to continue using his phone.

On February 6 and 7, Kinahan made two phone calls to Cunningham. Two days later "Joopie" Altepost arrived in Dublin on a flight from Holland. He was collected from the airport by one of Kinahan's sons, Daniel, and driven to Portlaoise Prison. Altepost then had a two hour meeting with his former cell mate. That night the Dutch drug dealer and gun runner checked into the Kileshin Hotel in Portlaoise and the next day, February 10, he had another two hour meeting with Kinahan in the prison. On the following day they had yet another two hour meeting before "Joopie" returned to Dublin and flew back to Amsterdam.

* * * *

In sensitive investigations such as Operation Plover in the end timing is everything. By the beginning of March 2000, the investigation teams in The Netherlands and Ireland prepared for the final swoop. Inspector Bob de Vries and his unit were aware that Cunningham had gathered a large amount of weapons and drugs which he was preparing to send to England and Ireland. Cunningham had been doing a lot of business with one Clifford Millar, the owner of Millar Trailers, a transport company in Blackpool in England. Millar had been taped organising drug shipments for Cunningham into England and on to Ireland. Kieran Smyth and Westlodge Freight were no longer being used by the syndicate because of the amount of attention they were attracting from law enforcement agencies. In October 1999, Kieran Smyth had found himself at the centre of a huge money laundering and smuggling investigation when the Criminal Assets Bureau raided the Bureau de Change he was using in Dromad, County Louth. On November 4, 1999, in a separate operation, French customs and police working with the GNDU had seized 156 kilos of amphetamines, with a street value of IR£1.5 million, from a Westlodge Freight truck, as it had boarded a ferry at Calais. The drugs had also come from Cunningham.

A final meeting took place between the Dutch and Irish teams to decide when to move on Cunningham. In Dublin, surveillance was placed on a distribution gang associated with Casserly and Cunningham. The operation had to be carefully co-ordinated between both countries to ensure maximum success.

On Friday, March 10, 2000, the Dutch made their move. At 8am, Cunningham drove to the south of Holland to meet with "Joopie" Altepost and to collect a consignment of ecstasy. For a brief period the surveillance team lost sight of Cunningham but they picked him up again on his way back to Amsterdam. The Colonel drove to one of his safe apartments at Meander 191, Amstelveen, on the outskirts of the city. He emerged a short time later with a shopping bag, containing two handguns and drove to his home at Weteringbrug. He left his home at 11.15am and drove to a hotel in Amsterdam to meet with two Englishmen who were working for Clifford Millar. The previous day they had given Cunningham Stg£56,000 for a consignment of guns and drugs. One of the men got into Cunningham's car and they drove around for a short time. Then Cunningham dropped the man off.

The Colonel was on his way home again when the undercover team swooped. John Cunningham was surrounded and ordered at gunpoint to get out of the car and lie on the road. When he was searched he was found to be carrying an automatic pistol in his belt. He also had a false UK passport and a driving licence in the same name. At the same time other police teams arrested Peter Lingg, the two Englishmen and the driver of a van that had been used by Cunningham. In the van the police found four handguns, 1,000 kilos of cannabis and 100 bags of ecstasy, each containing 300 grammes of the drugs. In a search of Cunningham's home the cops found 50 kilos of amphetamine powder, 100,000 ecstasy tablets and two handguns and ammunition. Mary Cunningham was also arrested and brought in for questioning.

In a search of one of Cunningham's safe houses they seized an awesome arsenal of weapons. Among the cache were two Intratec machine pistols, identical to those found in Castleblayney in December 1998; one sub machine gun; one Steyr military assault rifle; nine handguns and magazines along with silencers; and hundreds of thousands of rounds of ammunition. In another of the Colonel's hideouts they found an industrial machine for vacuum-packing ecstasy pills. By international standards Operation Plover was an outstanding success. In total the entire operation had led to the seizure of over €11.4 million worth of drugs and an arsenal of twenty-three high-powered weapons.

Over the weekend the arrests were kept secret from the media while Detective Chief Superintendent Ted Murphy's squad prepared for the next phase of Operation Plover. In the early hours of March 13, the GNDU, backed up by officers from the National Bureau of Criminal Investigation, the Fraud Bureau, the Criminal Assets Bureau, and several local drug units, searched thirteen addresses across Dublin and arrested seven people. All those caught in the swoop had worked for Casserly: five of those arrested were subsequently charged with drug trafficking and money laundering offences. Mark Hall (26), Dermot Wearen (36), Brendan Davis (25), Helen Lynch (25) and Stephen Martin (33), from addresses in North Dublin and County Meath, were subsequently convicted and jailed for terms ranging from eighteen months to six years.

Brendan Davis from Ashbourne, County Meath, was found to have kept ledgers, keeping a track of the drug racket. His records made for astonishing reading. Between November 1999, at the start of the Dutch operation, and March 2000, the gang had moved over

2,400 kilos of hashish and 80,000 ecstasy tablets through a flat they used as a distribution centre in Harold's Cross. The total street value of the drugs involved was over €31 million. Davis admitted that, for the previous fourteen months, he had run the operation for Casserly. During that time he estimated that they had sold drugs with a street value in excess of €100 million. Davis and the others had not been known to the police before the investigation into Cunningham and were not considered to be hardened criminals. Using compensation money he had received from a traffic accident, Davis had invested over €50,000 in the operation. Chris Casserly and another accomplice, named later in High Court documents as Sam O'Sullivan from south County Dublin, fled the country before they could be arrested. Casserly continues to do business in Ireland and, at the time of writing, is believed to be operating with Christy Kinahan from a hideout in Spain. Kinahan has taken control of Cunningham's operation. In July 2003 the Criminal Assets Bureau sold off the only asset they could find belonging to Casserly, his BMW motor car. The State made €20,000 from the sale.

When the Criminal Assets Bureau had raided the illegal bank Kieran Smyth had been using at Dromad in County Louth in October 1999, a lot of major criminals and terrorists had feared that Smyth was about to blow the whistle on them. If he did Smyth could cost them millions in lost revenue. On February 5, 2001, Smyth was abducted from his home and vanished. His body was found four days later, dumped near Ashbourne, County Meath. Smyth had been severely beaten and tortured. He had been bound, gagged and blindfolded. Then he was shot twice in the back of the head at close range with a sawn-off shotgun. The timing of the murder could not have been more coincidental. In the same week, in early February 2001, John Cunningham went on trial in an Amsterdam court on charges of trafficking in drugs and guns. He was jailed for nine years, but the following December the Court of Appeal reduced the Colonel's sentence to seven years. Peter Lingg meanwhile was jailed for five years and "Joopie" Altepost got four years. Two Englishmen and another Dutch national were also convicted on charges relating to drug trafficking. An arrest warrant was issued for the owner of Millar Trailers. Mary Cunningham was never charged.

John Cunningham was due for release in 2004 when he will be

extradited to Ireland to serve the rest of his sentence for the Guinness kidnap. The Colonel, armed robber, kidnapper, drug dealer and gun runner, will probably be sixty years old the next time he is free to try for that illusive 'big job'.

On Tuesday, November 2, 2004, John Cunningham was extradited to Ireland after completing his sentence in Holland. Cunningham was escorted back to Dublin on a scheduled flight. On arrival he was immediately returned to Shelton Abbey, the open prison from which he absconded in September 1996. The authorities then returned him to a "more secure" prison facility to complete the remainder of his sentence for the Guinness kidnapping. He will be a free man early in 2006. Then it will probably be business as usual for The Colonel.

Eight

The Blagger

Older criminals reminisce about the 1970s as if that era encapsulated the halcyon days of gangland history. The seventies were the first decade of serious crime in Ireland when the country was plunged into a state of virtual lawlessness. The outbreak of the Troubles in Northern Ireland led directly to a huge increase in armed robbery in the Republic, as the IRA robbed banks and pay rolls to raise funds for their 'war'. It didn't take the young petty criminals in Dublin, Cork and Limerick long to get in on the act. By the mid-seventies, armed heists had jumped from a mere handful to over one hundred and fifty a year. The Gardaí, who were suddenly confronted by a whole new type of terrorism and a generation of organised criminals, could only play catch-up. It was the era of the blagger.

The armed robbers represented the first generation of serious criminals in Ireland. The blaggers' generation produced many gangsters who in years to come would progress to becoming multi-millionaire drug barons and godfathers. Among the criminal fraternity the blaggers were seen as celebrities. To the police they were dangerous hoodlums, desperadoes, who always came out shooting. From their ranks star characters emerged and stood out as more ruthless and violent than the rest. One of the worst blaggers in the history of Irish crime was a man called Frank Ward.

By 2003, as far as the public and most of the country's younger police officers were concerned, Frank Ward was an anonymous criminal. To many his release meant nothing and Ward is an unknown quantity but to a generation of blaggers and seasoned serious crime squad officers Ward will always be known as one of the country's most professional and dedicated armed robbers. To the criminal he was a serious player with "great bottle" and a flair for planning. To the experienced cop he was a lethal weapon who thought nothing about blowing them out of his way. Frank Ward lived up to both reputations when he took on the law in two of the most dramatic 'cops and robbers' confrontations in gangland history.

* * * *

Born in Sligo on June 6, 1953, Ward was destined for a life on the wrong side of the tracks. He had a dreadful childhood from birth, spending a number of years in orphanages and in the notorious industrial schools, where sexual and physical abuse were a reality of daily life. Like many of his criminal peers at the time, Ward emerged from the system as an extremely damaged and angry young man. Henry Dunne, a member of the Dunne crime family and a one-time professional armed robber, once explained the Industrial Schools' damaging influence and the catastrophic effect they had on youngsters who later turned to crime: "They beat and sexually abused us so much they made animals of us. When we came out of there all we wanted to do was hit back at society. We were angry and warped with no loyalty to anyone except our own. They savaged us even when we played by the rules. After that we felt 'what's the fucking point?' The brothers made us the way we became and crime was the obvious choice." Frank Ward was no different and wasted no time 'hitting back'.

By the early 1970s, Ward was a young reckless hood who was up for anything. He spent time living in Manchester and Belfast before marrying Marie Lynch at the age of seventeen. The couple lived in Tallaght, west Dublin, and had three children together. From the beginning of his criminal career Ward stood out for his meticulous planning and his sheer ruthlessness. He had no compunction about using firearms in a heist. One former associate interviewed for this book recalled: "Everyone went on jobs well tooled up but Frank always brought a fucking arsenal with him – machine guns, automatic pistols, rifles and grenades. He planned everything, down to the smallest detail and had mad bottle. Frank had no problem killing a guard if one got in the way and he nearly always fired shots during a job. He was fucking mad." An example of Ward's violent nature was an incident that occurred outside a Dublin nightclub in the late seventies. Ward arrived at the club wearing an odd-looking, Stetson cowboy hat and dark glasses. When one of the bouncers saw him he laughed and asked the blagger: "Jaysus are you in disguise tonight Frank Ward?" The armed robber didn't like the rub. He produced a handgun and shot the bouncer in the stomach. Although the Gardaí knew he had done it the bouncer would not co-operate in the investigation and Ward was never charged. After that, no one dared to jeer at his dress sense again.

Ward's first recorded conviction as an adult was in 1978 when he was given a suspended sentence for car theft. By the time of his first offence, however, Ward was already a dedicated armed robber who was well-known to the Gardaí. His painstaking planning and organised approach to each job, which included not leaving forensic evidence behind, meant that he was very hard to catch. The police did not have the resources to mount long-term surveillance operations on criminals such as Ward. The policy at the time was based on the idea of catching the gangsters in the act. This meant that, in effect, the blaggers had a free hand. Ward was part of a closely-knit gang of robbers who were based in Dublin. The mob was a collection of Republican renegades and criminals from Dublin, Cork and Northern Ireland. They did scores of heists throughout the country, hitting factory pay rolls, banks and post offices. According to Garda intelligence at the time Ward 'trained' criminals, teaching them how to organise heists.

In one daring raid on May 28, 1979, Ward and his crew simultaneously robbed two banks in the village of Kilcock, County Kildare. During the heist, shots were fired from several firearms, including a machine gun, terrifying the occupants and forcing the police to put their hands up. The Kilcock 'jobs' were typical of several such crimes around the country in the seventies and early eighties. The 'jobs' invariably involved a large gang of heavily armed raiders hitting a country town or village with military precision. In some cases desperadoes held the unarmed Gardaí at gunpoint in their stations, as their colleagues wreaked havoc nearby. The police rarely knew if the heists were the work of paramilitaries or of criminal gangs. Ward's name was way down on a very long alphabetical list of suspects. Nevertheless, in October 1979, he was taken away from the action for a brief period when he was convicted for possession of an offensive weapon. The offence had nothing to do with the robberies. Ward was found carrying a knife inside his jacket. He served one month of a three-month sentence.

The year 1980 became infamous as one of the worst ever years in the history of armed crime in Ireland. Practically everyday the IRA, INLA and criminal gangs were carrying out heists throughout the country. It was a time of apparent anarchy for which the Garda Siochana paid dearly. In July, two officers, John Morley and Henry Byrne, were shot dead by an INLA gang, following a robbery in Ballaghaderreen, County Roscommon. In October, Garda James McQuaid, who was investigating a double-armed robbery, was murdered by a suspected Provo in County Wexford. Before 1980 was over Frank Ward and his gang attempted to add the names of two more officers to the roll of the fallen.

At the time, Ward led a five-man gang which he had organised along the lines of a terrorist cell. He picked the targets and planned each job himself. The rest of the gang were not informed about the location or the identity of the target until just before a job. It ensured total secrecy surrounded each heist and prevented tip-offs to the Gardaí. The gang included Johnny Doran from Ballyfermot. In Garda files Doran, who was a year older than Ward, was also described as a ruthless armed robber with a long record for burglary before he moved onto more dangerous crimes. Another member of the team was thirty-two-year old Anthony "Tonto" O'Brien from the Oliver Bond House flats in Dublin's inner-city. O'Brien had a string of convictions, including one for manslaughter in 1969, for which he served four years in prison. Ward's second-in-command was twenty-six-year-old James Daly from the north inner-city. He was classified as "very vicious" in Garda intelligence reports. In November 1980, Ward decided he had found the perfect target – the Bank of Ireland branch at Stillorgan Shopping Centre in south County Dublin. It was to be one of the worst decisions of his life.

On November 28, Ward bought a green Volkswagen van from a used car lot owned by John "The Coach" Traynor, the man who would become the trusted lieutenant of both the General and John Gilligan. The salesman had the impression that the buyer was a member of the travelling community. Ward gave a fictitious name and signed the order form with an 'X', claiming he could not read or write. The van was then hidden off side, in preparation for the Stillorgan robbery. In keeping with his flair for meticulous planning

Drug dealer and murderer Joseph "Cotton Eye" Delaney.

Murdered drug dealer Mark Dwyer.

Mark Dwyer in happier times.

©Sunday World

William "Jock" Corbally, murdered in February 1996 and buried in an unmarked grave.

Murdered drug dealer and police informer Declan "Decie" Griffin.

Adrienne McGuinness, who gave crucial testimony in the trial of "Cotton Eye" Joe Delaney.

Christopher "Bud" Dwyer, Mark Dwyer's step-father.

Martin Comerford, who took part in the Chester Beatty murder and later organised his own death.

Murdered gangland figure Anthony "Chester" Beatty with Frances Cahill, the General's widow, at Martin Cahill's funeral.

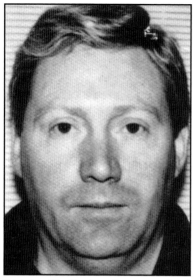

PJ Judge, The Psycho, who was murdered in December 1996.

Eamon Daly, a close friend of John Cunningham, who became a major drug trafficker on his release from prison.

Convicted kidnapper and international drugs and gun dealer John Cunningham.

Cunningham's wife, Mary, pictured shortly after he escaped from an Irish prison and fled to Holland.

©Sunday World

John Cunningham's brother Michael, who was also convicted of kidnapping, pictured standing in for his missing brother at the marriage of John's daughter Caroline in September 1996.

Dermot Wearen

Gary McNulty

Brendan Davis

Mark Hall

Members of Casserly's gang who were convicted as part of the international swoop on John Cunningham's operation.

Drug trafficker Christy Kinahan.

Murdered haulier and international smuggler Kieran Smyth who was executed in January 2001.

Det. Chief Supt. Ted Murphy (now retired) who, as head of the Garda National Drug Unit, led the international investigation into John Cunningham's Dutch crime empire.

Det. Supt. Noel White (now Chief Superintendent) who co-ordinated Operation Plover.

©**Sunday World**

Liam Keane gives his infamous two-fingered salute to photographers as he leaves the Central Criminal Court.

© **Maxwell's Photo Agency**

Owen Treacy, Kieran Keane's nephew who survived a horrific attack in Drumbanna, County Limerick, in January 2003.

John McGrail, one of George "The Penguin" Mitchell's main organisers.

Shane Coates and his partner-in-crime, Stephen Sugg.

Stephen Sugg at the funeral of his murdered brother, Bernard "Verb" Sugg in August 2003.

Herman "The Vermin" White who was convicted of a brutal attack on drug addict Derek "Smiley" McGuinness.

Drug addict Neil Hanlon who was murdered in 2001 and whose body was later found in Crumlin.

Dave McCreevey, an associate of heroin dealer Jeffrey Mitchell, pictured after he was arrested with Mitchell's drugs in 2001.

Crumlin drug dealer and Westies' associate Jeffrey Mitchell.

Bernard "Verb" Sugg who was shot dead in August 2003.

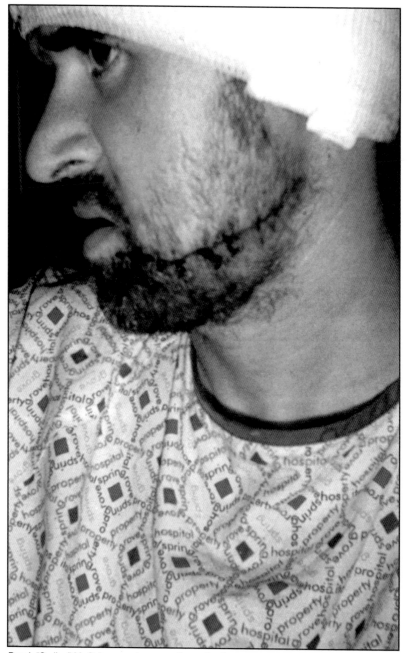

Derek "Smiley" McGuinness who narrowly survived a savage beating in October 1999.

The Westies: Dylan O'Sullivan, Shane Coates and Stephen Sugg, on holiday in Spain.

Detective Superintendent Tony Sourke who led the investigation into the Westies.

Detective Inspectors Todd O'Loughlin and John Mulligan who investigated the Westies' reign of terror.

One of Ireland's most infamous crime bosses, George "The Penguin" Mitchell.

Mickey Boyle, a member of the Penguin's gang.

Frank Ward.

Limerick crime boss Christy Keane.

Murdered Keane henchman Eddie Ryan.

Kieran Keane, the younger brother of Christy Keane, who was executed in January 2003.

ERU and Gardaí forces on the streets of Limerick in 2003.

Ward had picked the Volkswagen for two very good reasons. The van could comfortably carry a group of armed men and the rear mounted engine provided protection in the event that the gang came under fire.

Ward's plan was that the robbery would take place on December 30, 1980. Banks throughout the country would be bulging with cash as a result of the pre-Christmas spending spree and the Stillorgan bank would be no different. At the time most business, including pay rolls, were done using cash which meant easy pickings for the blaggers.

At 2.30pm on the afternoon of December 30, Doran and another member of the gang took a taxi from the city centre and travelled to Rathfarnham. They joined Ward and the two other gang members who were waiting in the van. As per usual Ward did not travel lightly. The gang were equipped with a total of eight firearms – a machine gun, an automatic pistol, a revolver, two .22 rifles and three shotguns. Each weapon was loaded and had plenty of extra ammunition. At 3.30pm Ward's gang arrived at their target. The bank had closed at 3pm and there were still fifteen staff members inside.

Johnny Doran stayed with the van on the Old Stillorgan Road while the other four, who were all wearing balaclavas and carrying firearms, ran through the shopping centre heading for the bank. The sight of the armed men caused panic among shoppers and people began running in all directions to get away. The raiders ran up to the plate glass window at the side of the bank and used a sledgehammer to smash it in. Ward and two others jumped through the broken window and into the bank while the fourth man kept watch on the car park from just inside the window. The gang threatened staff with guns. A bayonet was held to the throat of one employee. They snatched over IR£102,000 which they stuffed in two sacks before making their getaway. The raid had taken less than three minutes.

The four robbers ran back through the car park, racing towards the Old Stillorgan Road and the van. As they ran, Ward's men turned around several times, pointing their weapons at onlookers to scare off any have-a-go heroes. Sean Keeley, an off-duty detective attached to the Special Detective Unit (SDU), who was in the shopping centre heard about the audacious raid and went to investigate. Keeley spotted the raiders rushing out of the bank and running to the van. As they got inside the officer stepped into view and pulled his .38 revolver. Ward and his men smashed out the rear window of the van and aimed their rifles at the detective. Keeley fired a shot at the van and the gang promptly retaliated with a volley of shots, forcing the detective to duck down behind a parked car. The gang were still firing shots as the van sped off, narrowly avoiding the cop.

By now Garda units across south Dublin had been alerted that an armed robbery had just taken place at Stillorgan. Detective Gardaí William Daly and Richard Curran were patrolling near Cabinteely Village when they heard the alert. Both men were veteran officers. Daly, who was forty-three-years-old, had been in the force since 1959 and his fifty-five-year-old partner had been a police officer since 1947. Detective Garda Daly drove his unmarked squad car, codenamed "Whiskey 8", towards Foxrock Village in order to intercept the getaway van.

In the village they met the green Volkswagen and gave chase. The Garda car was more powerful than the getaway van and it soon began to close in on the blaggers. Ward and his men then fired a number of shots at the squad car, forcing it to drop back. The detectives continued to follow the van from a safer distance. They lost sight of it as Doran turned right at Carrickmines Cross into Glenamuck Road. As they approached the junction Detective Daly was anticipating that the van would drive down the old Glenamuck Road, travelling on the winding road past Carrickmines Lawn Tennis Club. He thought this would slow them down. (It is important to remember that this area of south Dublin has undergone dramatic building development and new road construction since 1980.) But Frank Ward had other ideas.

He had ordered Doran to suddenly stop the van, fifteen yards into the Kilternan side of the Carrickmines Cross junction. Ward had a deadly plan. The van was now hidden from view. Ward's intention was to ambush and shoot the pursuing detectives, before the gang resumed their getaway. Seconds later the squad car drove into the middle of the junction, chasing the van. By the time the detectives spotted the waiting Volkswagen it was too late. Ward and his gangsters opened fire with everything they had got, peppering the squad car in a merciless hail of buckshot and bullets.

The gang used a machine gun, a rifle and a pistol and hit the two officers several times. Richard Curran was shot in the hand and fingers while two more machine gun rounds grazed the right side of his head. A bullet ripped through William Daly's right forearm, causing extensive bone damage. Other rounds hit him in both legs. As the firing continued, Curran opened his passenger door and rolled onto the road, followed by Daly. The officers lay on the ground for cover and waited for the firing to stop. When the van sped off Detective Garda Curran staggered to the side of the road and fell down. Daly, who was bleeding heavily, radioed in his position and the direction in which the van was travelling. Then Daly crawled over to the grass margin and said a prayer. Technical examination of the squad car later found that the two detectives had a miraculous escape from death.

As Ward's gang headed into the Dublin Mountains, more Garda units were converging on the area. About two miles up the mountain the gang abandoned the van on Glencullen Road and hi-jacked a Fiat 132, forcing the occupants out of the car at gunpoint. As the gang drove a few miles further along the Glencullen Road they crashed the Fiat. They then hi-jacked a second car as it slowed down to pass the crashed Fiat. One of the raiders wanted to hold the driver hostage but there was no space for him in the car. As this catalogue of disasters was occurring Detective Garda Martin Doyle, of the Special Detective Unit, arrived at the scene of the crash in his car. He recognised James Daly, who had taken off his balaclava. One of the gunmen raised his rifle into an aiming position to shoot at the detective and another armed raider walked towards his car, brandishing a gun. The raider with the rifle had to adjust the weapon and as he was doing so the officer seized his opportunity and reversed the car out of the line of fire. As he reversed down the road the gang members crowded into the second car. Doran's shotgun accidentally went off as they were getting into the car. "I got a fright, I nearly shot meself," he later recalled.

As Detective Garda Doyle sped down the road he met Detective Gardaí Martin Donnellan and Kieran Brennan, who had arrived from Donnybrook Garda station. The officers blocked the narrow mountain road with their cars. Seconds later Ward and his gang appeared round a corner, driving at speed in the hi-jacked car. The car ground to a halt about twenty yards from the officers. Doyle, the only one of the three detectives who was armed, took cover behind a tree and drew his automatic pistol. Donnellan and Brennan crouched behind their car. Brennan aimed his walkie-talkie at the gang while Donnellan pointed his hands at the robbers to give the impression that they were both armed. There was panic in the getaway car and it reversed at speed back up the road before sliding into a drain. Detectives Brennan and Donnellan then ran towards the five raiders who were getting out of the car. The officers were still aiming their 'weapons' at Ward and his mob while Doyle covered them. The gang turned and made a run for it, up the side of the mountain. Doyle fired a warning shot over the robbers' heads while his colleagues continued their pursuit. Doyle fired a second warning shot as one of the gang members turned and pointed a gun at him. The detective then fired another three shots directly at the gangsters, hitting "Tonto" O'Brien twice in the knee. Two of the gang members, O'Brien and Doran, dropped to the ground while Ward, Daly and the fifth robber continued to run up the mountainside. A few yards further up Ward also stopped but the other two raiders kept sprinting away.

The three raiders were ordered to put their hands up as Donnellan and Brennan continued to pretend that they were armed. Doyle moved up to cover them as more units began to arrive. Brennan and Donnellan first arrested Doran and passed him back to another officer. The two detectives then ran a few yards further up and arrested O'Brien who was sitting with his hands in the air. O'Brien was put lying on the ground beside Doran. Donnellan then made for Ward who was also sitting. The blagger was breathing heavily and in a distressed state. "Shoot me now, I want you to shoot me now," he shouted, as Donnellan grabbed him and put him lying on the ground. The officers found a loaded pistol in his pocket. Ward refused to walk back down the mountain with detectives and had to be literally dragged down. Ward kept repeating his request for the officers to shoot him. A short distance away, Martin Donnellan found the Thompson machine gun Ward had been carrying on the job. Forensic examination later found that the machine gun was the same weapon used in the double bank raid in Kilcock in May 1979. By now several detectives had arrived in the area and an extensive search continued for the two missing raiders but they had got away.

Later that day, while in custody in the Bridewell Garda Station in Dublin, Doran made a statement admitting his part in the robbery to Detective Garda Donnellan. During the interview he said: "Sure I am well caught. I will be pleading guilty." A detective then said to him: "Ye did a lot of shooting out there today." Doran admitted: "We went mad shooting. We all lost our heads and started shooting. The gun I had blew up and I thought I was after shooting meself. I know I've been caught red-handed." Doran said he regretted that two officers had been shot.

At 9pm on New Year's Eve, 1980, Johnny Doran and Frank Ward were brought before the Special Criminal Court and charged with the attempted murder of Detectives Daly and Curran and also with robbery or the Bank of Ireland, Stillorgan branch. On January 16, 1981, "Tonto" O'Brien was also brought before the same court and charged with attempted murder and robbery. He had been released from hospital the previous day.

On July 21, 1981, the trial of Ward, Doran and O'Brien opened in the Special Criminal Court. All three pleaded not guilty. On July 28, the court convicted them on the charges of attempted murder and the aggravated burglary of over IR£102,000. They received a total of twelve years each on the two charges. The Court of Criminal Appeal subsequently rejected an Appeal by all three men. James Daly had been lucky enough to get away. He later fled to the UK where his luck eventually ran out. He was subsequently jailed for sixteen years when British police caught him during a post office robbery. The fifth man was never located.

The Gardaí were extremely lucky on December 30,1980, that their officers did not die in Frank Ward's ambush. Even years later the incident is still talked about by senior officers who had held their breaths that day as Ward's mob went "mad". Detective Garda Curran was released from hospital two weeks later and recovered from his injuries. Detective Garda Daly suffered serious damage to his arm and was hospitalised for almost a month.

The following year the six detectives involved in the pursuit and arrest of Frank Ward and his gang were awarded Scott Medals for valour in the course of their duty. Detectives Curran and Daly were awarded gold Scott Medals, while Detectives Donnellan and Brennan were awarded silver medals. Detectives Keeley and Doyle were presented with bronze medals.

The award ceremony in 1981 was one of the most poignant moments in the history of the Garda Síochána. In all fourteen officers were honoured at the event, three of them posthumously. The widows of the three murdered officers sat beside their husbands' colleagues. "It was the most heart-breaking day in my career when I saw a little child of no more than four holding his daddy's medal. People in this country do not appreciate the sacrifices people have made in the line of the duty for their country," recalled one officer who attended that ceremony. All the bravery medals awarded in 1981 were given as a result of confrontations between the Gardaí and armed robbers.

* * * *

Frank Ward did not like prison life and he decided to do something about it. On December 12, 1983, Ward and an INLA member attempted to escape from Mountjoy Prison, armed with an imitation firearm. Ward and his companion managed to get to the perimeter wall but were recaptured in a violent struggle. Frank Ward was injured in the escape bid and he also lost remission on his sentence.

On December 6, 1990, the blagger was released from prison, after serving almost ten years behind bars. During his absence the underworld had undergone a major transformation. Former associates, who had been relatively minor-criminals ten years earlier, were now powerful godfathers with multi-million pound drug empires. Ward, with the help of his contacts, quickly re-established himself as a major armed robber.

Timing, they say, is everything in life and when Ward came out of prison the timing could not have been better for a hood determined to get back into the action. Johnny Doran had been free for over a year and was back in the thick of things. He had become the right-hand man of his long-term friend, the criminal mastermind George "the Penguin" Mitchell. Born in Drimnagh, south Dublin, in 1951, Mitchell had been involved with the General and John Gilligan for several years. Originally a truck driver for the Jacobs biscuit factory, he was involved in armed robbery, hi-jacking and the burglary of warehouses around the country. In 1987, an internal Garda survey of organised crime gangs described the Penguin as an "arch criminal" and categorised him as one of the top five gang bosses in Dublin. In 1988, Mitchell was jailed for five years with another associate, twenty-eight-year-old Gerry Hopkins, for the armed robbery of over IR£100,000 worth of cattle drench. On his release Mitchell established a large gang, which included some of the country's most hardened criminals, and moved into drug trafficking, gun running and robberies. Mitchell became the ultimate godfather – the Penguin had had his fill of directly taking part in the action and he concentrated on organising deals and masterminding the crimes that members of his gang then carried out. Frank Ward became a major player in the new gang.

Frank Ward's name was soon back in the Serious Crime Squad's files. On December 16, 1992, as a result of ongoing enquiries into a number of large robberies and kidnappings, detectives raided an apartment that was being used by Ward at Morehampton Road in Dublin 4. During the search they found a number of disguises, including false wigs and beards. Also found were detailed notes of surveillance carried out on a bank official in County Meath and notes on the movements and transport used by the distinguished Senior Counsel Adrian Hardiman, now a Supreme Court Judge. Gardaí suspected that Ward and a number of other gangsters were planning a major crime against the two men they had under surveillance. There was insufficient evidence with which to prefer charges but the police made sure that Ward and company knew that they were onto them. Whatever they were plotting was immediately aborted.

In early 1994, Mitchell rented a yard and large lock-up building in Mount Brown in Kilmainham, west Dublin. The premises were perfect for what the Penguin had in mind. The lock-up was situated on a small lane, off the main street behind other businesses. A high wall and substantial steel gate surrounded the yard. From there he ran an efficient and highly successful criminal operation. The gang included criminals and members of the INLA. Convicted-armed robber, thirty-year-old John McGrail from Saint Theresa's Gardens, was one of the gang's main organisers. The mob also included

Armagh INLA man Danny Hamill, who also had convictions for armed robbery and assault. Another key member in the organisation was one Mickey Boyle from Bray in County Wicklow. Boyle was one of the Penguin's hit men and had spent several years inside for armed robbery and kidnapping. On the Penguin's behalf, Johnny Doran co-ordinated drug shipments, arms supplies, armed robberies and hi-jacking from the yard. The lock-up was used to store stolen goods and vehicles. Cash and valuables, stolen in various heists were then handed over to Mitchell who invested the loot in cannabis, ecstasy and firearms. The Penguin spent most of his time travelling between Dublin and Amsterdam organising deals. Using a Kildare-based haulier, he arranged the delivery of weapons and drugs from Amsterdam to Dublin. The mob soon had access to an awesome arsenal of firepower, including at least one Russian-made AK47 assault rifle. The Penguin was building an international crime empire. "It was a very efficient operation and the yard in Mount Brown was run like a central depot for a large legitimate business. There were about fifteen in the gang and they were up to everything," recalled one Serious Crime Squad officer. Ward fitted right in.

The existence of the Penguin's crime depot first came to police attention during a routine investigation by the then Garda Drug Squad. The Drug Squad later became the Garda National Drug Unit or GNDU. The Drug Squad had tailed a suspected drug dealer back to the lock-up. They decided to mount a basic surveillance operation on the yard, to see what was going on there. This simply involved an officer keeping a discreet watch on the yard on an irregular basis. It quickly became apparent that this was no dodgy little back street lock-up. At the time the Drug Squad was one of a number of specialist investigation units working under the umbrella of the Central Detective Unit (CDU). The CDU also included the Fraud Squad and the Serious Crime Squad. (The CDU was later re-organised and re-constituted as the National Bureau of Criminal Investigation or NBCI and the Fraud Squad became the Garda Bureau of Fraud Investigation or GBFI.)

The discovery of the yard coincided with the appointment of Detective Chief Superintendent Kevin Carty as the new head of the CDU. Carty, who had spent most of his earlier career as a secretive Special Branch officer, was one of the force's most talented officers with an impressive reputation as a tough and resourceful investigator. On one occasion he was awarded a Scott Medal for bravery after he disarmed and arrested a wanted IRA man despite the fact that Carty was unarmed and off-duty. Carty was an astute strategist who believed in taking a proactive approach to criminal investigations. At the time, there was a distinct reluctance to mount long-term, costly investigations without a guarantee of success. The new CDU boss disagreed with the current policing policy which was driven purely by the financial bottom line. Carty's belief was that in order to catch a criminal you had to invest time and resources to get the job done. The Gardaí would never get the upper-hand by merely reacting to the crimes perpetrated by professional villains. There was no point trying to close the stable door after the horse had bolted. Implementing his theories, Carty had a dynamic policy of recruiting informants and using the latest sophisticated surveillance techniques to fight the criminals.

Within days of his arrival in the late summer of 1994, Carty and his new second-in-command, Detective Superintendent, Austin McNally, convened a conference in CDU headquarters in Dublin. Assessing the preliminary surveillance on the yard was on the agenda. It was obvious that this was a meeting place for the hierarchy of serious crime: George Mitchell, Johnny Doran, Frank Ward, John McGrail, Mickey Boyle, Danny Hamill and several other major league villains had already been spotted visiting the yard on a regular basis. Carty got sanction for a special surveillance operation on the Penguin's gang from the then Deputy Commissioner in charge of operations, Pat Byrne. Carty and McNally went to work. Members of the Drug Squad, Serious Crime Squad, National Surveillance Unit (NSU) and the Emergency Response Unit (ERU) were mobilised to take on the Penguin's mob. There was only one way to find out what the villains were up to and then to catch them in the act – using surveillance technology to get inside the yard. Carty decided to bug the yard and lock-up with microphones and hidden cameras.

Late one night a team of surveillance experts secretly gained access to the yard. They were led by Carty's most trusted sidekick, an undercover officer known in the force simply as 'Feisty'. A Detective Sergeant, "Feisty" was an unconventional and extraordinary cop who was considered a bit of a maverick among his peers: he was not a nine to five cop. "He could disappear for a month and you wouldn't know where he was. Then he'd suddenly appear with information that would result in a major arrest or seizure of drugs or guns or anything. He was the only Detective of that rank who was allowed to work that way because he always got results," a colleague revealed.

Within days the surveillance was producing remarkable results. Members of the investigation team were astonished at how much was going on behind the locked gates of the little yard. One Serious Crime Squad member recalled: "It was amazing. Not a day would go by without some crime being planned there. It was like taking fish out of a barrel. They were talking about all kinds of criminal activity. It was clear that they considered the yard a completely safe haven." Carty's first victim would be Frank Ward.

Frank Ward had brought his twenty-six-year-old nephew-in-law David Lynch into the gang. Lynch, who was also from Sligo, was every bit as violent as his uncle and he had convictions for burglary, assault and robbery. He and his uncle had become close friends while serving time together in prison. Lynch was jailed for five years in 1988 for possession of firearms and attempted robbery in Sligo. His accomplice on the botched job later agreed to testify against him. During a preliminary hearing to take depositions in the case in Coloorey District Court, Lynch's accomplice was called to give evidence. While the accomplice was in the witness box Lynch suddenly lunged forward and kicked him several times in the head, knocking him unconscious in the process. In the spring of 1994 Lynch was granted temporary release from a separate jail sentence for assault and immediately went back to work.

On April 8, 1994, Ward and Lynch had hit the Bank of Ireland branch in Nenagh, County Tipperary. They made off with over IR£7,000 in cash – the robbery took just fifty-six seconds. They had later crashed their getaway car and then hi-jacked a Telecom Eireann van at gunpoint. Over the following months Ward and his nephew had done at least four similar jobs together. But then Carty's "midnight callers" dropped into the yard.

As the surveillance operation continued into September 1994 the Serious Crime Squad were gleaning an awesome amount of top-grade intelligence from the yard. The main problem the investigation squad now had was how to deal with each crime without making it obvious to the gangsters that their safe haven had been compromised. If the gang abandoned the yard then the investigation would be over. The squad had to be careful to make arrests in a way that didn't make the mobsters suspicious that the yard was bugged. The investigators were also very conscious of the personal risks involved. One chilling piece of information overheard through the hidden microphones was that the gang members were prepared to shoot their way out of trouble if things "came on top" and they ran into the police on a 'job'.

In the middle of September the investigators had their first major surveillance breakthrough when Mitchell imported a cache of deadly machine guns and automatic pistols for his associates in the IRA. The weapons, lethal 9mm Heckler and Koch MP5 machine guns and Glock pistols, were smuggled into the country with a load of drugs in the back of a container truck. The MP5 and Glock are the weapons preferred by specialist military and police units throughout the world, including the SAS and the Irish Army Ranger Wing. As a direct result of the operation, Carty's men found two MP5 machine guns and five Glock pistols when they searched bogland, near Clane in County Kildare. They also recovered a large amount of ammunition and drugs. In another search two Armalite military assault rifles were found.

In the meantime, Frank Ward and David Lynch began planning another robbery. The two robbers planned to use a Proton car that had been stolen from the North Circular Road in Dublin earlier that year. The car had been re-plated, using the registration of a legitimate Proton, and hidden in the yard for use in a heist. Carty's team were aware that Ward was involved in organising a robbery but they knew nothing more. One investigator explained: "When they discussed robberies they [gang members] would not go into great detail about what they were planning. At the end of the day they were all rogues and no one trusted each other completely." During the nocturnal visits "Feisty's" surveillance team had also planted tracking devices on a number of stolen cars in the lock-up, including the Proton. Ward had decided to use the car because it was not a typical high-powered getaway vehicle and therefore should not attract as much attention.

On the afternoon of October 23 the investigation team were alerted that something was about to happen. The Proton was moved from the yard to a car park in the grounds of the Children's Hospital in Crumlin, south Dublin. As soon as it moved, the tracking device was activated. Surveillance teams were dispatched to watch the car overnight. The cops had no idea where the robbery was going to take place or who would be taking part. They could only sit and wait for the action to start. And they took every precaution to ensure they stayed on the robber's tail. On the ground two undercover squad cars had been fitted with equipment to pick up the signal from the Proton's hidden tracker. At the same time an Air Corps Cessna spotter plane, electronically equipped to track the car from the air, was put on standby. The military aircraft would provide back-up in case hills or mountains interrupted the tracker signal's transmission to the squad cars. A large team of officers from the Serious Crime Squad and the ERU were also mobilised.

At 10am the next morning a man wearing a beard drove the Proton out of the hospital car park and headed in the direction of Naas. The officers following the car could not positively identify the driver although they suspected it was Ward who was behind the wheel. The surveillance teams shadowed the car through Kildare, carefully staying out of eye contact and relying on the tracking device because Ward was always on the lookout for spooks. At the same time the Army Cessna was scrambled. The situation was now "live".

The operation was fraught with difficulties. They didn't know where or what Ward was going to hit and they could do nothing until he made his move. At the same time, they couldn't get too close to him or else they risked being rumbled. There was also the chilling realisation that the blagger and his gang were usually armed and prepared to shoot their way out of trouble. The squad could not risk a confrontation with the gang in the middle of a busy town where innocent people could get hurt. A similar situation had happened four years earlier in Athy, County Kildare, when the ERU trapped a gang in a local bank. During that operation the police shot and killed a bank robber but also injured a number of bystanders when bullets and buckshot ricocheted everywhere. As Ward got close to each town Carty's men braced themselves to move.

After driving through Naas, Ward turned onto secondary roads and headed up through the Midlands. Meanwhile, unknown to the cops, Lynch took the 1.25pm train from Dublin to Longford. He was carrying a holdall bag containing two firearms, a sawn-off shotgun and a .357 magnum revolver. On the ground the officer in charge of the surveillance team, Detective Sergeant John Mulligan, was still tracking Ward who appeared to be in no hurry to get wherever it was he was going. He was a careful driver and never exceeded forty-five miles per hour. As Ward drove into Mullingar town the various teams got ready for action. The bustling Midland town was a perfect target. But Ward drove on – in the direction of Longford.

Ward drove into Longford and went to the railway station where Lynch was waiting. They entered Longford's one-way system, down through Ballymahon Street and onto Main Street, where the town's banks were located. The surveillance teams were just driving into the town but had they still not made visual contact with Ward.

At exactly 3.53pm, Ward and Lynch burst into the Ulster Bank on Main Street, brandishing their weapons and ordering everyone to get down on the ground. Lynch vaulted the counter, swinging a sawn-off shotgun. Both men wore bullet-proof vests and Lynch had his weapon attached to his neck with a strap. He carried a pillowcase that was also strapped around his neck. Clothes hanger wire was inserted to keep the pillowcase open so that he could use both hands. Lynch ran behind the counter pulling open drawers and shouting: "Give me the fucking money. Where is the fucking money?" He raced up to bank official Mary O'Beirne and screamed: "Get the fucking money, get the fucking money or I'll blow the head off you." At the same time Ward was standing outside the counter covering the front door and the occupants of the bank. He shouted at his nephew to hurry up. "Get to fuck out of here, you are too long in there," said Ward.

The robbers left the bank with IR£10,000 in cash. They had been there for around one minute. They ran out to the getaway car and drove out of town, towards Mullingar, using the one-way system on Dublin Street. At the same time the local Garda station was alerted about the raid and within minutes officers arrived at the bank. The surveillance and Serious Crime Squad teams heard the call on their radios and headed in the direction of the tracker signal.

On the outskirts of Longford, Ward left the main Dublin Road and took a secondary road heading for the villages of Ardagh and then Ballinacargy. The backroads would eventually take him to Mullingar where he planned to drop Lynch off with the guns and money. Then Lynch planned to take the train back to Dublin while Ward got rid of the hot car. Again Ward drove at a modest speed along the quiet country roads. Carty's teams were travelling in the same direction as the robbers, driving from Longford to Mullingar, as the Army plane overhead relayed the car's movements. Detective Sergeant Mulligan and his partner Mary Fallon had followed the Proton but lost eye contact with it. They urgently needed to know where they could intercept it so that they could co-ordinate the chase with the other units. The aircraft dropped below the cloud cover and the pilot directed the units into position. From the air he could see that the squad cars were driving along another country road, directly parallel to Ward's car. The pilot instructed the units on the ground to take the next three right turns which would bring them to a T-junction known as Strand Cross at Walshetown, Mullingar.

On the ground Detective Sergeant Andrew McDonough and two Emergency Response Unit colleagues arrived at the junction and blocked it with their car. It was now shortly before 4.30pm. Minutes later Serious Crime Squad officers, Detective Sergeant Jerry Healy and Detectives Maurice Downey, Tony Howard and John Clancy also arrived and took up positions. The armed officers stopped a local school bus that was coming down the road. They took the children off the bus and brought them to safety behind a high wall while an ERU man parked the bus across the road, completely blocking any escape route. The aircraft overhead warned the team that the raiders were just minutes away. The officers pulled their handguns and got ready. Danger was literally around the corner.

The stolen Proton drove around the corner from the direction of Ballinacargy. Detective Sergeant McDonough stood in the middle of the road with his gun drawn. The getaway car halted seventy yards away from McDonough. As he signalled to the occupants of the car to approach the roadblock Ward reversed at speed in the opposite direction. As he did so McDonough and three detectives jumped into a squad car and sped after the Proton which crashed into a ditch fifty yards further down the road. The ERU officers jumped out of their car and threw a stun grenade under the Proton. The officers then rushed the car. At the last moment they spotted Lynch who had been hiding on the back seat. The stun grenade had disorientated both him and Ward. "Armed Gardaí put your hands up…put your hands up now," McDonough shouted into the car. There was a violent struggle as the cops dragged the blaggers from the car and handcuffed them. Jerry Healy cut the sawn-off shotgun from around Lynch's neck. It was later discovered that the shotgun had been stolen in a burglary in Sligo two years previously. When the two men were searched the detectives found Elastoplast on their fingers and palms, so that they would avoid leaving prints behind them. They also wore wigs, false moustaches and even make-up to obscure the chances of anyone identifying them from a security video.

Lynch and Ward were formally arrested by Detectives Maurice Downey and Tony Howard and brought to Mullingar station where they were detained under the Offences Against the State Act. As Ward was being processed at the front desk he said to the station orderly: "You know that I have been arrested for being in possession of a firearm. I had it, there is no suspicion about it, I want to go to court now and get this over with." After that Ward refused to answer any questions and Lynch claimed he had been kidnapped.

On October 26, Ward and Lynch were brought before Kilbeggan District Court and charged with robbery and possession of firearms and remanded in custody. For a second time in his life Frank Ward had run out of road. Carty's squad also identified both men from the security tapes recorded during the Nenagh raid in April and they were subsequently charged with that robbery too. Within an hour of Ward's arrest the Serious Crime Squad searched a flat in Ranelagh, south Dublin, where the blagger had been living. What they found there said a lot about the character of the man. Everything in the flat was immaculate and precisely organised. Ward had lists for everything including a reminder list for the day of the heist. It read: "Shower. Shave. Breakfast. Maps. Wigs. Vests. Bags. Car. Train."

Ward successfully obtained bail while awaiting trial. The conditions were that he presented himself each day at Tallaght Garda

Station and surrendered his passport. But Ward had other ideas. Unfortunately for the blagger, however, someone talked about his plan to leave the country with the Penguin's help and to go into hiding on the continent. It was clear from the information received that Ward had somehow obtained a legitimate passport in a different name. One Friday night Carty sent three members of the Serious Crime Squad involved in the Ward operation, Detective Sergeant Healy and Detectives Howard and Downey, to the passport office to sift through thousands of passport applications made since the blagger's arrest. The officers spent all night looking at passports. It wasn't until the following morning that they found what they were looking for, Ward's picture on an application form. It was later discovered that the application had been endorsed with an official Garda stamp, stolen some time earlier from Ballyfermot Garda Station. When Ward turned up the next day to sign on in Tallaght the three officers were waiting for him. Ward was re-arrested and brought to the High Court where his bail was revoked.

In the meantime the secret investigation at the yard continued. This time Johnny Doran was the man in the spotlight. Carty's team heard Doran planning to pick up a shipment of 50 kilos of cannabis. On the night of November 28, 1994, Doran and a twenty-four-year-old gangster from Baldoyle, north Dublin, who was considered to be the Penguin's protégé, picked up the hashish from a courier in Naas. As they drove back to Dublin along the M50 motorway the Serious Crime Squad tried to pull them over. Doran drove off at speed and the police gave chase. In his bid to get away Doran rammed one of the squad cars but lost control and veered off the motorway. A second squad car collided with the rear of Doran's car and sent him spinning into a fence. The same team who had nabbed Ward the previous month arrested the two criminals. Doran and the young hood were charged with drug trafficking offences.

Other members of the gang were to have better luck than Doran and Ward although they didn't know it at the time. The surveillance team heard John McGrail and a gang of four planning a post office robbery in Shankill, south Dublin. All the preparations for the job were made in the yard. Guns were oiled and loaded and the getaway vehicles were stored there, all under the watchful eyes of the cops. On the day of the planned heist a surveillance team, again backed up by the Serious Crime Squad and the Emergency Response Unit, were mobilised to catch McGrail and his gang in action. The robbery outfit went in one stolen car while another gang member from Crumlin brought the guns to be used in a second car. But at the last minute McGrail aborted the job and sent the gang member back with the firearms. As the man made his way back into the city from Shankill he was stopped at a "routine check point" and the guns were seized. Just like Ward and Lynch, McGrail's gang had no idea that the cops were onto them.

Buoyed up by the arms seizure and the successful arrests of Ward and Doran the undercover operation continued. The Serious Crime Squad continued to monitor the yard, knowing that it wouldn't be long before McGrail organised another big job. This time he planned to ambush a security van and rob over IR£500,000. A flat bed truck was stolen and brought back to the lock-up where the gangsters spent a number of days welding a large metal girder onto the body of the truck. The end of the girder was sharp and pointed and they intended to use it to smash open the doors of a security van in Blackrock. The security van had been kept under surveillance for several weeks and McGrail had planned the best place to hit it while it went along its route.

On the morning of the job five members of the gang set off with the truck and a number of getaway cars. They were heavily armed. As the convoy of robbers set off so too did a large force of armed police. Carty's plan was to catch them in the act. But fate stepped in the way of a spectacular arrest.

As the gang were driving towards Blackrock a friend of the owner of the stolen truck happened to be on the road at the same time. Despite the alterations to the vehicle – a tarpaulin covered the battering ram – the friend instantly recognised the truck as he had previously done some work on it. He began following it in his own van. The undercover teams spotted the van and thought at first that it belonged to the gang. But then the van driver drove ahead of the truck and pulled in to make a call from a coin box. As the undercover cops tried to work out what was going on the van driver was calling the police. Then the van driver went after the truck. He blocked it in while waiting for the uniformed Gardaí to arrive. To the absolute horror of the watching cops McGrail and his hoods immediately jumped out of the truck and ran away. There was nothing the police could do. The operation was aborted. The gang abandoned their cosy yard and lock-up shortly after that incident. There was a chance that the recovery of the truck could lead straight back to the yard. However, by that stage, the investigators had already gained a lot of valuable intelligence. As an indirect result of the surveillance operation in 1994 the newly organised GNDU busted an ecstasy factory Mitchell's gang had set up in a farmyard in north County Dublin. Four people, including a chemist, who had been involved in manufacturing the ecstasy mix and making the tablets, were arrested and subsequently convicted of running the operation. If the farmyard factory had gone into production it would have been capable of churning out one million pounds worth of ecstasy per week.

In May 1996, Frank Ward pleaded guilty to the armed robberies in Nenagh and Longford. Lynch had been jailed the previous December after he too pleaded guilty to the same charges. Judge Cyril Kelly imposed an eleven-year sentence on Ward with the final three years suspended. He said that Ward was the more culpable of the two, was more senior and had a more serious record. However the Judge said that he was suspending part of the sentence so that Ward could "see the light at the end of the tunnel". A month after Ward's conviction his old partner-in-crime, Johnny Doran, was jailed for twelve years when he pleaded guilty to the drug charges. The forty-four-year-old villain had been "encouraged" to take the blame so that his young companion, the Penguin's favourite hoodlum, could be spared. According to reliable underworld sources it was claimed that the Provos and the Penguin forced Doran to take the rap. Since then the young hood has become a major drug trafficker.

Four months later, in October 1996, Frank Ward was back in court seeking the return of belongings seized from him, under a Police Property Application, at the time of his arrest. Ward represented himself in the application and was brought to court amid tight security. Judge Desmond Windle heard the case in the Dublin District Court. When Ward's application was called Judge Windle reminded him that he had not itemised the property he wished to have returned by the Serious Crime Squad. So Ward began listing off the property for the Judge, who wrote each item down. The blagger wanted a number of books, pictures and dole money that had been seized in the raid on his flat returned. He went on: "And Judge I want my .357 magnum revolver which the Gardaí took off me back as well." Judge Windle stopped writing and looked down at the blagger. "This is highly irregular," he remarked. "If it pleases the court I don't mind the magnum being returned in a decommissioned state Judge," Ward replied, to hoots of laughter around the court chamber. "This is highly irregular and in any event you should have the property itemised. The Gardaí should have given you a list of the property they took at the time of your arrest," the judge informed him. Ward replied: "Believe me judge when these men swoop they don't issue fuckin' receipts." The blagger eventually got most of his property returned including his IR£80 dole money and his books. He never saw his precious .357 magnum again.

Nine

The Limerick Feud

A dimly-lit city street on a freezing cold Winter's night. Uniformed police officers stop and scrutinise each car as it drives up to the checkpoint. Behind them two men in dark paramilitary combat uniforms stand in the middle of the road. Each one holds a powerful Uzi machine gun at the ready and an automatic pistol strapped to his hip as a back-up weapon. A jeep parks nearby on the pavement. It contains more men equipped with machine guns, pump action shotguns and automatic pistols. No one is taking any chances. Overhead a police helicopter hovers somewhere in the dark, the chopping of its rotor blades shattering the eerie silence. Intermittently a powerful light glows from the belly of the invisible aircraft, illuminating entire streets below, where heavily armed police units are patrolling in cars and jeeps. Then the light vanishes and reappears again a few blocks away. The sense of nervous tension is palpable as both civilian and cop watch and wait for the shooting to start.

This scene was not in Bogotá or Belfast. This was Limerick in January 2003 as gangland violence threatened to literally engulf Ireland's third city. The image just described was unprecedented in the history of the Irish underworld. Never before had the authorities felt the need to display such high profile firepower and force against criminal gangs. The Emergency Response Unit (ERU), the Garda's elite specialist weapons and tactics unit, would never usually be deployed to patrol a city's streets. Never had so many armed detectives been mobilised on the streets for one purpose – to take on what amounted to gangland death squads.

But then there was nowhere quite like Limerick, a city of 80,000 people, that had first earned the dubious title of "Stab City" and was now known as Ireland's murder capital. There is a dynamic to serious crime in Limerick that makes it different. There is a level of violence and hatred there that is spine-chilling. Killers make no secret of the fact that they have hit a rival or an old enemy. The socio-economic divide is stark – the city is spilt in two between 'the haves and the have-nots'. There is no middle ground. A recent survey conducted by Limerick Regional Hospital's casualty department found that a person was nine times more likely to be stabbed there than in Cardiff. In a two-year period between 2001 and 2003 there were twenty-five murders in the city. Gardaí in Limerick are acknowledged as having the toughest and busiest beat in the country where it is not unusual for the criminal gangs to openly threaten the lives of the officers and their families.

The extraordinary situation, which blew up in January 2003, was the result of the fallout from a bitter feud between two criminal families. Two groups of heavily-armed, savage thugs, had embarked on a mindless cycle of murder and absolute mayhem which even attracted international headlines. A group, numbering no more than fifty had declared war on each other in a small pocket of Limerick. In the process they threatened to drag the whole place down with them. They had done irreparable damage to the good name of what is otherwise a progressive, cosmopolitan city. The warring clans had helped to prompt the cringe-inducing description in a prestigious international travel guide that commented "Limerick is best seen through the rear view mirror.". The feud had also cost the taxpayer millions of Euro in policing and prison bills alone. The two groups have been responsible for a mind-boggling catalogue of attacks and counter-attacks – there were drive-by shootings, kidnappings, executions, bombings and stabbings. Limerick is the only place in the country, apart from Loyalist enclaves of Belfast, where the protagonists strut around in bullet-proof vests, intimidating and threatening each other in front of the police. In Limerick teenagers, some as young as fifteen, use machine guns and even an AK47 assault rifle to settle scores. The feud is driven by blind, murderous hate that has passed, like a family heirloom, from generation to generation. It is not unusual in Limerick for a schoolyard row between children to escalate into shootings and murder. The local Garda boss, Chief Superintendent Gerry Kelly has described the situation as "madness". This madness has become synonymous with two names: Ryan and Keane.

On January 29 and 30, 2003, the simmering feud, which had

already caused one murder, forty gun attacks, petrol and booby trap bomb incidents and countless stabbings, exploded like a powder keg. Over the previous week the situation had escalated dramatically. The city had held its breath as hundreds of soldiers and police searched woodlands in County Clare. They were looking for the bodies of teenage brothers, Eddie and Kieran Ryan who had supposedly been kidnapped by ruthless crime lord, Kieran Keane. Seasoned observers and experienced local Garda chiefs, who knew the opposing sides best, were sure the brothers had been murdered. But the plot suddenly took a bizarre and unexpected twist when Kieran Keane was abducted and murdered with a bullet in the back of the head on a country road. His sidekick and nephew, Owen Treacy, was stabbed several times and left for dead by his side. Then six hours later the Ryans turned up at a Midland Garda station, unscathed and in a celebratory mood. This mysterious development posed more questions than answers. And only one thing was certain – the bloodshed was far from over. But how did it all begin? What started Ireland's most dangerous feud?

* * * *

For over a decade Christy Keane was the undisputed godfather of crime in Limerick. This is quite a distinction considering the city has more hard men per capita than anywhere else in the country. Described by Gardaí as "ruthless, extremely violent and highly strung" Christy Keane ruled his empire with an iron fist. Born in 1960, he was the third youngest of a family of ten, six boys and four girls, born to Theresa and Richard Keane. The family grew up in Saint Mary's Park, a run-down corporation estate in the shadow of King John's Castle just north of the city centre. The area is also known as the Island Field where many centuries ago the British Army kept their animals. The Island would become the Keane family's personal fiefdom. Christy Keane and his mob controlled anything that went on there. There was only one way in and out of the Island and strangers were quickly spotted. From a police perspective it was an extremely difficult area to keep under surveillance. From a crime lord's point of view it was a perfect base for establishing an organised crime network.

Keane's father Richard, a casual worker at Limerick docks, married his mother Theresa in 1948 when she was sixteen years old. A short time later she gave birth to her first child. Richard Keane was a heavy drinker and it was left to Theresa to provide for her young family. She was known as a hard worker and a dedicated mother. According to local people, Theresa passed on her hard work ethic to her sons who started a successful coal business in the Island. It is often said in the area that Christy Keane could have been a hugely successful businessman in the legitimate world of commerce. Instead Christy Keane decided to operate on both sides of the fence, working hard and robbing at the same time. By the time he was twenty years old Keane had a string of convictions, mostly for larceny and burglary.

In the early 1990s, together with his younger brother Kieran, he moved into the more lucrative criminal drug rackets. Within a few years the Keanes controlled the largest drug distribution network in the mid-west region, supplying cocaine, ecstasy and cannabis. The gang was also involved in money laundering, trading in illegal firearms, counterfeit money and documents, protection rackets, prostitution, smuggled goods and stolen vehicles. Christy Keane had extensive links with other gangs around the country, particularly with a Dublin-based cocaine-dealing mob made up of members of the INLA and led by a man called Arthur Jordan. Other INLA associates included Anthony "Fanta" Gorman, Joe McGee and Declan Duffy. *(See Chapter 3.)* He had close ties with the John Gilligan gang and the Flynn crime family in Cork as well as the renegade Real and Continuity IRA. In addition he had connections with gangs in Northern Ireland and the UK. Based on his contacts alone Christy Keane was a major criminal godfather.

Every major crime network has one or more enforcers, feared violent men who do the gang's dirty work. Outside the family Eddie Ryan was Keane's most trusted lieutenant. A year older than Keane, Ryan had a long criminal record for theft and violence, dating back to his first offences as a twelve-year-old. Eddie Ryan grew up in Hogan Avenue in Kileely just across the River Shannon from Keane's territory. He was the quintessential thug, a violent dangerous criminal who took pleasure in inflicting pain. Ryan was a close friend of another notoriously violent Limerick criminal, Michael

"Mikey" Kelly from Southhill, with whom he did several armed robberies. In 1977, Ryan stabbed another man, Christy Jackson, to death in a row outside a city centre cinema. Eddie Ryan was seventeen years of age at the time. On February 27, 1978 he was convicted of manslaughter and jailed for five years. The following June he was also convicted of five counts of breaking and entering for which he got another three years. On his release from prison Ryan was soon up to his old tricks again. In November 1984 he was jailed for a total of six years for three counts of receiving the proceeds of an armed robbery.

By the time Ryan got out of prison again his old friend Christy Keane was beginning to move into the drug scene. Keane started building a criminal empire with Eddie Ryan by his side as his full-time enforcer. Ryan was feared by some of Limerick's toughest criminals. He conducted heavy-handed investigations into suspected police informants and collected unpaid bills.

"When Eddie Ryan called to your door looking for something you gave it to him or else he'd give you something you didn't want. He was a ferociously violent man and everyone was scared of him," one former associate recalled.

Gardaí suspected that the Kileely killer was also available as a hired hit man for gangland shootings around the country. Ryan made no secret of his Republican leanings and was a regular visitor to convicted IRA cop killers Noel and Marie Murray and to Eddie Gallagher, the kidnapper of Dutch Industrialist Tiede Heremma. The Murrays and Gallagher were serving long jail sentences for crimes they committed during the 1970s.

The relationship between Ryan and the Keanes was forged in blood at the end of 1993. Two murders and an attempted massacre on New Year's Eve firmly established the gang's brutal reputation. The episode began on February 1, 1993, as thirty-year-old Kathleen O'Shea was walking in St Mary's Park with her common law husband Patrick "Pa" McCarthy. McCarthy, who was also aged thirty, was a member of the travelling community. The couple lived with their four young children in a caravan at the Canal Bank, Clare Street in Limerick City. McCarthy was one of eleven children from a dysfunctional family background. His parents were chronic alcoholics and as a result "Pa" and his siblings were neglected growing up. None of the children got a good education and most of them turned to drink and petty crime when they reached their teenage years. From the age of thirteen "Pa" McCarthy had twenty-six convictions recorded against him, for burglary, larceny, assault, indecent assault and car theft. Those convictions related to a total of one hundred individual offences. Gardaí who knew "Pa" described him and his brothers as "fifth division" street fighters.

As the couple were walking down Senan Street in the Island, Kathleen O'Shea stumbled out in front of a van which struck and killed her. Daniel Treacy, Christy Keane' nephew was driving the van. A Garda investigation later found that the incident was a tragic accident and Daniel Treacy was exonerated of any wrongdoing. "Pa" McCarthy, however, was heartbroken by Kathleen's death and threatened to kill Treacy. In an attempt to compensate McCarthy, the Keanes and the Treacys paid for Kathleen's funeral. After that "Pa" McCarthy began putting the squeeze on the Keanes, demanding more money. For a while they paid him but finally they refused to pay any more. McCarthy moved to Cork with his children.

He returned to Limerick for Christmas 1993 and went on a non-stop drinking binge. On the night of December 28, McCarthy drove to St Mary's Park with his brothers, Willie and Joe, and a friend David Ryan. All four were drunk and McCarthy was in an aggressive mood. After calling to a friend's house McCarthy drove to Christy Keane's home at St Ita's Street. At the front door McCarthy met Keane's nephew Owen Treacy who was Daniel Treacy's brother. McCarthy began making threats and demanding money. Christy Keane joined Owen Treacy at the door and a scuffle ensued, during which McCarthy was stabbed in the chest. His brother Joe quickly set-off for the hospital but "Pa" died a short time later in the back of his van.

Joe and Willie McCarthy and David Ryan later told detectives that they had witnessed Christy Keane stabbing "Pa". A few hours later Gardaí arrested Christy Keane and Owen Treacy for questioning about the murder. The two men were later released and a file was forwarded to the Director of Public Prosecutions recommending that Keane be charged with murder.

Patrick "Pa" McCarthy was buried on December 31, 1993. Later that night his family held a wake in his brother Martin's caravan. A group of ten adults, most of them members of the family, crowded into the caravan drinking beer and cider. Martin McCarthy's two children, aged five and three, were asleep. The mourners huddled around a small fire and the only light was from a candle.

At 10.30pm two of the guests, Roger Ryan and Jacqueline Casey, left the caravan to get more alcohol at a local off-licence. As they walked out of the campsite two armed and masked men stepped from the shadows. The couple were told not to make any noise and to go away while they still could. A minute later the two gunmen stepped into the door of the caravan and began blasting into the cramped space with a sawn-off shotgun and a .32 automatic pistol. A total of seven shots were fired: six from the handgun and one from the shotgun. One of the shooters was Eddie Ryan.

Investigating Gardaí were in no doubt about the motive for the appalling attack. It was clearly intended to wipe out the entire McCarthy family. As police and ambulances arrived at the scene Michael McCarthy was found lying on the caravan floor. He was bleeding heavily from two neck wounds, caused by the entry and exit of a bullet. His brother Joe had been hit in the back and leg by the shotgun and his sister Nora was shot in the hip. Their cousin Noreen also suffered gunshot wounds to her leg. Michael McCarthy was pronounced dead on arrival at hospital. The appalling attack shattered the festive peace and provided the first shocking news story of 1994. Later that day Gardaí arrested six people for questioning about the attempted massacre. Among those lifted were Christy and Kieran Keane, Eddie Ryan and his wife Mary.

On January 4, 1994, Christy Keane was formally charged with the murder of "Pa" McCarthy. The following morning Michael McCarthy was buried beside his brother in Mount Saint Laurence Cemetery. At his funeral Mass Canon William Fitzmaurice said the dead man had been the victim of "senseless and mindless" violence. "Violence begets violence, leading inevitably to more suffering and more grief and more loss of lives," he told mourners. His comment could have been a paradigm for life in Limerick's seedy underworld.

At a subsequent High Court bail hearing on January 10, Superintendent Liam Quinn asked the court to keep Keane in custody. Quinn told the court he believed that Keane would "interfere with witnesses" if he was released. The court however granted Keane bail. The McCarthy family later left Limerick but returned to testify in the trial of Christy Keane. However, they proved to be unreliable witnesses and a jury acquitted Keane in the Central Criminal Court.

It was only during the investigation of the McCarthy murders that Gardaí began to discover the full extent of the Keane gang's criminal rackets. They knew that their efforts to smash the operation would be fraught with difficulties. The gang's Island Field base was almost impossible to keep under surveillance, let alone penetrate. The murder of the McCarthys had also illustrated how the Keane gang would deal with potential witnesses and informers. Eddie Ryan let it be known that there would be no protection for anyone suspected of "touting" to the cops. The McCarthy incident had built a wall of silence around the gang.

In the meantime the Keane gang's drug business grew bigger and spread to new areas. Each year Christy Keane was supplying millions of Euro worth of drugs to gangs throughout Munster and the mid-west. They laundered money by buying houses throughout the Island. The money was coming in so fast that they set-up a number of counting centres in safe houses in the area. At one time Keane had to resort to using a wheelie bin to store his cash. Over the following years local detective units made several major drug seizures and convicted a number of gang members. But they couldn't get to the Keanes or the Ryans themselves. However, as the Gardaí were soon to find out, all was not well in Limerick's most dangerous gang.

* * * *

Inter-family feuds are not a new phenomenon in Limerick. In fact feuds have been a part of everyday life in the working-class ghettos of Limerick for as long as people can remember. Vendettas are passed like a baton from generation to generation, resulting in dozens of needless murders throughout the decades. To the outsider these tribal feuds are labyrinthine. One such row had been going on for several years and involved Eddie Ryan's brother, John.

John Ryan was married to Christina McCarthy. Her two brothers Samuel and Thomas, had been stabbed to death in 1982 in a pub row with another notorious criminal, Anthony Kelly, the younger brother of Eddie Ryan's friend Mikey Kelly. The row began when one of Ryan's brothers-in-law had a fight with another local family, the Collopys, over damage to a car. The families all lived around St Mary's Park. The McCarthys blamed one of Jack Collopy's children for the damage but Collopy denied the charge. The row led to an incident in The Moose Bar at Cathedral Place when one of the McCarthys attacked and injured Jack Collopy's wife and she had to receive five stitches. Later, that same night, John Ryan and one of his in-laws attacked Jack Collopy at his home. John Ryan stabbed Collopy in the gut with a knife and beat him around the head, causing serious injury. Jack Collopy spent two weeks on a life support machine and later had to learn how to walk again. To further complicate an already explosive situation the Collopys were close friends with the Keanes. Gardaí investigated the case but the Director of Public Prosecutions decided not to proceed with charges against Ryan or his brother-in-law.

In October 1997, Ryan's brother-in-law Pa McCarthy (no relation of the McCarthys murdered in 1993) was attacked in his car, near the Collopy's house. A number of shots were fired into McCarthy's car, hitting him in the back and narrowly missing three young children who were sitting behind him. McCarthy later identified three members of the Collopy family as the attackers. They were subsequently charged in relation to the incident but were found not guilty following a trial at Limerick Circuit Criminal Court in 1999. In another incident one of the Collopy's children was in a schoolyard fight with John Ryan's daughter. Following that incident John Ryan fired shots at the Collopy's home. His brother, Eddie Ryan, and the Keanes had agreed to remain neutral in the ongoing row between John Ryan and the Collopys. But Eddie was with John during the attack on Collopy's house. Eddie Ryan was gradually moving away from the Keanes and had started to set-up his own drug distribution network. There were also allegations that Ryan owed Christy and Kieran Keane money for drugs. It was the beginning of the end of the relationship between the Ryans and the Keanes.

By Summer 2000 the bitterness had reached boiling point. Eddie Ryan had found himself getting more deeply involved in the ongoing feud. The Keanes had also formed up behind the Collopys. Rumours and gossip further fuelled the growing enmity between the two sides. Then a row broke out between Samantha Ryan, John Ryan's daughter, and Natalie Keane, Christy Keane's daughter. Both fathers agreed that the only way to resolve the dispute was for an arranged fight to take place between the two girls. After a half-hour of fighting Natalie Keane gave up. The nineteen-year-old had a piece of her ear bitten off and the victory went to the Ryan family.

On October 25, there was another row this time between John Ryan's daughter and a niece of Christy and Kieran Keane at St Mary's Secondary School, Corbally. The following day the girl's mother, Anne Keane, the wife of Christy's brother Anthony, called to Bishop Street Primary School to collect her daughter. She met two of John Ryan's daughters and another row broke out. Anne Keane was knocked to the ground and punched and kicked and then she was slashed in the face with a Stanley blade. Samantha Ryan was subsequently charged with assault and making death threats. She was later given a court reprimand in the form of the probation of offenders act and the charge of threatening Anne Keane was withdrawn.

Later that evening, a number of shots were fired through the front window of John Ryan's home at the Lee Estate which was situated in the heart of the Keane territory. He called his brother Eddie who immediately went to the house to find out what had happened. Eddie Ryan said he would sort out the problem by visiting Christy Keane and his sidekick Owen Treacy. Ryan told his brother he wanted "to give Christy a box". The Ryans drove up to Treacy's house on Colmcille Street. Eddie Ryan was armed with a sawn-off shotgun. As they approached the house two shots were fired at the Ryans, hitting their car. Eddie Ryan fired back as they sped away. The car was hit by more shots, which shattered the rear window. What had started as a relatively innocuous row had suddenly escalated into a shooting war. Eddie Ryan was determined to spill Keane blood. There was no longer any chance of reconciliation. Full-scale war was about to begin.

On the afternoon of Friday, November 10, 2000 there was another serious escalation in hostilities. Christy Keane was waiting to collect his son outside the Ignatious Rice College on Shelbourne Avenue. Eddie Ryan was also waiting – for Christy – with a 9mm automatic pistol under his jacket. When Keane spotted Ryan walking towards him he opened his window to talk to his former partner. But Ryan was not in a talkative mood and immediately pointed his gun at Christy Keane's head. Ryan tried to shoot the weapon but it jammed as he squeezed the trigger. He tried again but Keane drove off at speed down the pavement, sending children and parents scrambling out of the way.

Later that evening Ryan travelled to Newcastle, County Down in Northern Ireland to visit his girlfriend. Over the last number of months he had been spending a lot of time in the North. Ryan remained there until the following Sunday afternoon when he returned to Limerick for the funeral of his brother-in-law. Ryan's decision to pay his respects to the dead would turn out to be a big mistake.

That evening Ryan arrived at the removal ceremony in St John's Cathedral. As a mark of respect on the sad occasion he had decided not to wear his bullet-proof vest. After the ceremony he spoke with his pregnant wife Mary before going to The Moose Bar at Cathedral Place with his son Kieran. It was the first time Ryan had visited The Moose in two years. The feared gangster arrived in the packed bar just before 9pm. He sat down at a table, on the right, just inside the front door. He ordered drinks for himself and his son. Ryan was sitting beside Mary Reddan and her daughters Deirdre and Majella and he had a friendly chat with them. Ironically Mary Reddan was Jack Collopy's sister-in-law but she was not involved in the feud between the Collopys and the Ryans and McCarthys.

Following the incident with his brother Christy, Kieran Keane had vowed to kill his former partner. He had sent spies out to locate Eddie Ryan and had been waiting for news all weekend. As Ryan entered the pub, Kieran Keane got a call on his mobile phone informing him that his target was in The Moose Bar having a drink. Keane was with his accomplice, a nineteen-year-old member of another St Mary's Park crime family, when he got the tip off. The previous night his minions had stolen a Vauxhall Cavalier from a pub at Murroe, County Limerick to be used in the hit. Keane told his accomplice to get a driver for the getaway car. Eddie Ryan was running out of time.

At 9.30pm, Keane's accomplice stopped another gang member,

twenty-three-year-old Paul Coffey, as he was driving down the Island Field with his girlfriend and their two-year-old son. Coffey, who was a close friend of the Collopy family, was serving a sentence for assault in Limerick prison and had been unlawfully at large for over a week. The accomplice asked Coffey to "drive a car" for him and Keane. Coffey immediately went off to meet Kieran Keane at the coal yard at St Munchin's Street where the crime boss was waiting with ten gang members. The engine of the stolen car was running as Coffey slid in behind the wheel. A gang member placed a gallon of petrol in a plastic container in the back seat so that the car could be destroyed after the attack. "If (name of a Ryan associate) is there he is getting it too," said Keane, as he sat into the back seat holding a .357 magnum revolver. His henchman, who was sitting in the front passenger seat, carried an automatic 9mm pistol. The same .357 magnum had been used in the gun attack on John Ryan's house on October 27.

Keane instructed Coffey to drive to The Moose Bar. When they arrived the killers parked in a yard across from the pub and Keane got out to make a phone call. He then got back into the car and told Coffey to pull across in front of the pub for "a few minutes". As the car stopped, Keane and his accomplice pulled balaclavas down over their faces and got out of the car.

At precisely 9.53pm the gunmen appeared inside the pub door. Eddie Ryan was sitting with his back to them. Keane shouted in his direction: "You bastard, come out ya bastard." Keane and his accomplice remained standing in the doorway as they opened fire on their former partner and friend. The gunmen fired fourteen rounds at Eddie Ryan. Mary and Deirdre Reddan, who had nothing to do with the feuding gangs, were also hit in the hail of indiscriminate bullets. The noise of the shots was deafening and terrified customers dived to the floor for cover. The attack was over in ten seconds.

The gunmen ran back to the getaway car. Keane shouted, "Drive! Drive!" and Coffey sped away. As they left the scene, the killers fired seven more shots at the front of the pub, showing no consideration for innocent bystanders. Kieran Keane was delighted with his night's work. He kept shouting and cheering in the back of the car: "Eddie is dead, Eddie Ryan is dead – he's gone." Coffey dropped the killers at a nearby house. Then he dumped the car in a deserted lane and set it on fire.

In the pub there was a stunned silence as the customers slowly began to realise what had happened. The smell of cordite from the gunshots wafted in the air. Eddie Ryan had been hit eleven times at point blank range. Two rounds hit him in the right shoulder, seven in the back and one each in the hip and left arm. The bullets travelled through Ryan's chest penetrating both lungs. Another shot ripped through his spinal cord. Forensic examination would later show that some of the bullets which hit him were specially designed for the German police for use in shooting out car tyres. Eddie Ryan lay slouched down in his seat. A customer ran over and asked Ryan where he had been hit. "Everywhere," gasped the underworld hard man, slipping off his chair onto the floor. Blood oozed from his wounds as he gasped for his last breath. Seconds later Eddie Ryan was dead.

Mary and Deirdre Reddan had been seriously injured in the merciless gun attack. Mary Reddan was hit in the abdomen and lower chest and her daughter was also hit in the chest. Both women underwent emergency surgery for the life threatening wounds. Mary Reddan had to be airlifted by helicopter to be treated at Cork University Hospital. Doctors later said the women were lucky to survive.

Kieran Ryan had also been lucky. He was in the toilet when Kieran Keane walked through the door. If he had been with his father he would have been either killed or seriously injured. No doubt Kieran Keane would have considered that a bonus.

Gardaí said the shooting was one of the most callous and indiscriminate gangland attacks ever in Limerick. They commented that it had been "pure luck" that other innocent customers had not been killed or injured.

It didn't take long for detectives to nominate suspects. They were aware of the ongoing feud between the former criminal pals but knowing the perpetrators was a world away from bringing them before the courts. They got a lucky break, however, when an informant came forward and told them that Paul Coffey had been the driver of the getaway car. On December 7, a force of seventy armed Gardaí raided several houses in St Mary's Park arresting seven suspects, including Paul Coffey, Kieran Keane, the second gunman and Keane's nephew, Owen Treacy.

As the arrested gangsters were interrogated Coffey soon proved to be the weakest link. At first he denied that he had taken part in the hit, claiming he had been with his girlfriend at the time. But following a visit from his girlfriend, during which she urged him to tell the truth, Coffey changed his story. He came clean and admitted his role in the murder. In a statement Coffey named Kieran Keane and his accomplice.

On December 9, Detective Sergeant Jim Ryan formally charged Coffey with the murder of Eddie Ryan. The Gardaí now hoped that they could convince Coffey to testify against the killers. There was consternation in the Keane gang when they heard what had happened. They made several attempts to intimidate Coffey and his girlfriend. The getaway driver later retracted his statement through his legal representatives. Coffey's reluctance to testify meant that the State would not have enough evidence with which to charge Keane and his accomplice. Fear had once again worked in the gang's favour.

Eddie Ryan's murder sparked a major upsurge in violence. Over the following year there were at least thirty petrol bombs and gun attacks on John Ryan's house alone. And for each attack there was retaliation. In one incident, in May 2001, Owen Treacy's father Philip, a baker, suffered serious burns when two petrol bombs were thrown through the front window of his home in County Clare. Two associates of the Ryan family, twenty-five-year-old Noel Price from Kileely and nineteen-year-old Michael Stanners of Delmege Park were later charged with the attack. In May 2003, the two thugs were convicted of arson and were each jailed for twelve years. Price had more than ten previous convictions, including an arson attack on the car of an off-duty Garda, assault, possession of a firearm and drugs offences.

Three months after the attack on Philip Treacy's home the Gardaí had their luckiest break in many years. Detective Garda Ronan McDonagh was one of the sharp young officers who had learned his trade the hard way since leaving the Garda training college. He had been sent to Limerick city centre as a rookie and was familiar with every hood in the city. On August 21, McDonagh and two colleagues were chasing a handbag snatcher who ran into

St Mary's Park. After a search of the area they lost the thief and were resuming their patrol when McDonagh spotted Christy Keane walking across waste ground in the park. The drug baron was carrying a coal sack over his shoulder. As a result of the ongoing tensions in the area the Gardaí had a policy of stopping known gangsters for searches whenever they saw them. In many cases the searches had resulted in the recovery of knifes and firearms. This time McDonagh hit gold when he stopped Christy Keane.

When Detective Garda McDonagh searched the coal bag he found hashish with a street value of €240,000. Christy Keane, the most feared and untouchable godfather in Limerick, had been caught by pure chance. Keane looked stunned as he was being arrested. He couldn't believe that he had been busted so easily. When Keane was brought into Henry Street Garda Station for questioning in relation to the find, word flew around the city like wild fire that the gang boss had been nabbed. Detectives travelled from other stations around the city to see for themselves that their number one target had finally been caught red-handed. This time Christy Keane was going down.

A week later Christy Keane's seventeen-year-old son Liam also found himself in serious trouble with the police – as the prime suspect in a murder. Liam Keane, like so many of his peers, had been born into a life of crime and displayed an unhealthy propensity for violence from an early age. He was following in the footsteps of his father, his uncle and the other psychopaths who had filled his world from as far back as he could remember. This was the family business and Liam was being groomed to be godfather of the next generation of feared Limerick hard men. Liam Keane's first foray into violent crime however had nothing to do with the ongoing feuding. It all began as a seemingly innocuous row over a dog. It ended with the deaths of two young men.

On the night of August 27, twenty-one-year-old Jonathan Edwards, Liam Keane's friend from Abbeyvale in Corbally, visited the Lee Estate where he collected an Alsatian pup. Shortly afterwards Edwards bumped into a group of young men, that included nineteen-year-old Eric Leamy. The group had seen Edwards kicking the dog and they weren't happy about it. After some discussion Edwards brought the pup back to its original owner and left the area.

According to witnesses he went back to the Lee Estate later that night, this time in the company of Liam Keane where they ran into Eric Leamy. Leamy was unarmed and when a fight broke out witnesses later maintained that Eric Leamy urged Keane to put away the knife he had produced. Minutes later Leamy had been stabbed a number of times. He died a few days later from his injuries.

The day after the murder Leamy's best friend, Willie Moran Junior, met Jonathan Edwards in St Mary's Park. Moran would later tell Gardaí that Edwards had taunted him and threatened to kill him – like Leamy. Moran picked up an aluminium bar and hit Edwards over the head. He suffered a fractured skull and was rendered unconscious. Later, while still in a coma, Edwards developed pneumonia and died in hospital. In a subsequent trial the prosecution claimed that the killing of Edwards was in retaliation for the Leamy murder. Moran claimed that he had acted in self -defence and the jury acquitted him on those grounds.

Liam Keane was charged with Eric Leamy's murder, after seven people gave statements to the Gardaí saying they had witnessed the murder. The case was sent forward for trial to the Central Criminal Court in Dublin. Two years later Liam Keane's trial would lead to a serious crisis in the Criminal Justice system and make him a household name for all the wrong reasons.

In the meantime the feuding continued with more shootings and stabbings. In one incident the Army Bomb Squad was called in when a booby trap device was found under the car of a gangster associated with the Ryans. Gardaí suspected that the Keanes' associates in the INLA had made the device. The device failed to explode and was discovered when it fell off the car onto the road. Gardaí on the ground could see that it was only a matter of time before another murder occurred. As the violence and number of attacks escalated many of the victims had lucky escapes. The problem was getting so out of hand that Chief Superintendent Gerry Kelly ordered that an armed police cordon be placed around the Island area. After dark each night a Garda checkpoint, supported by armed squads, effectively sealed off the area making it impossible for the gangs and thugs to roam freely. As a result of the operation several criminals were arrested and arms and drugs were seized. But intensive operations are extremely expensive to run and after several weeks it was scaled down. As one officer revealed at the time: "These boys and girls have nothing else to do except sit and wait. They know that we can't keep something like this going indefinitely and we will have to pull out eventually. That's when they'll make their move. And you can not stop people who are determined to kill and maim each other."

The city's main court buildings are situated beside St John's Castle. They have always been a flash point for the various feuding factions in Limerick. The gangs have made use of their many appearances in the building to have a go at their rivals. Unlike anywhere else in the country the Gardaí regularly have to send heavy reinforcements, including armed detectives, to the courts just to keep the feuding clans apart. In January 2002 a confrontation between Kieran Keane and Eddie Ryan's widow, Mary, illustrated the blind hatred that now epitomised the war. The Keanes and their allies took pleasure in taunting the Ryans. "The maggots are atin' Eddie," they would shout across the street. Mary Ryan was walking from the courts one afternoon when she bumped into Kieran Keane. He began abusing the widow about her family and taunting her about her dead husband. She gave as good as she got. Then Keane head-butted Mary Ryan, twice, and shouted at her: "I got your husband. Now I'm going to get you." Gardaí moved in and arrested Keane for assault and he was jailed for three months.

On March 5, Eddie Ryan's son Kieran stabbed Christy Keane's son Liam as he walked through the city centre. Ryan was subsequently charged with assault and two counts of being in possession and producing a knife. Despite the arrests and the attempts to take the protagonists off the streets the Gardaí knew they would not be able to stop the war. The attacks continued unabated.

On Thursday, May 30, 2002, Christy Keane went on trial before a jury at Limerick Circuit Criminal Court, charged with possession and supply of illegal drugs. The ruthless godfather was determined to pull every trick he could think of to avoid going to jail. On the first day of the trial the presiding judge ordered one of Keane's henchmen out of court for acting in an intimidatory manner towards the jurors. Then, as part of his defence, Keane produced an incredible witness. Daniel Braddish claimed that he had been carrying the sack load of hash when Keane's arrest took place. Braddish stated that he had paid for the drugs with stolen money. When prosecution counsel put it to Braddish that he was being paid to take the rap for Keane he replied: "The State should reward me with money for owning up to this. I expect him [Keane] to go free because he is innocent." The witness was laughed out of court.

On Monday, June 3, the jury unanimously convicted Keane and the court sentenced him to ten years. It was a huge victory for the local Gardaí but the Keanes' drug business was far from over. Kieran Keane immediately took over the reins and he wanted everyone in town to know that he was calling the shots – there would be no let up in the violence.

On August 23, John McCarthy, Eddie Ryan's nephew, was sitting in the front garden of his house in Moyross when a car pulled up alongside. One of the occupants opened fire with an AK47 assault rifle, similar to the type used by the IRA. McCarthy and his family had a lucky escape and one round narrowly missed McCarthy's nine-year-old son. The gunmen were later identified as cousins, Ross Cantillon and Roy Woodland. Both of them were from St Mary's Park and associates of the Keanes. They had grown up amid feuding and killing. Woodland, who was nineteen, had already lost his right leg after being shot in cross-fire and on another occasion he nearly died when he was stabbed in the head. Twenty-year-old Cantillon had also suffered serious injury in a number of stabbing incidents. The two would-be assassins were disarmed and arrested by a passing Garda patrol as they made their escape. The incident caused grave concern to the authorities – half-baked thugs were now armed with deadly assault rifles and were prepared to use them. All this for a row that had begun with vandalism to a car and escalated with squabbles between school children. But things were going to get a lot worse.

On January 23, 2003, Kieran Ryan stood trial at Limerick Circuit Criminal Court on charges relating to the stabbing attack on Liam Keane the previous March. On his way to court Ryan was ambushed and beaten up by a number of youths, leaving him with cuts and bruises. The start of the trial was delayed by three hours while Ryan's injuries were looked after. Liam Keane, the victim and witness in the case, did not want to be in court either. Like all the other criminal families in Limerick the Keanes and the Ryans had nothing but contempt for the law. They had their own way of seeking justice: an eye for an eye and a life for a life. There was no room for courts or due process in their primitive world.

When the case finally started Liam Keane took the witness stand. He was asked who had stabbed him. "Kieran Ryan. Kieran Ryan stabbed me in the back," he replied casually. The prosecuting counsel then asked Keane to look around the court and see if he could identify his attacker. Keane looked around and then faced the judge and said "no" even though his sworn enemy was sitting a few feet away from him.

Judge Carroll Moran had no alternative but to direct the jury to find Ryan not guilty of the charge. "It is a very sorry state of affairs that this should happen and if this is going to persist we are going to live in a state of social chaos and anarchy," the judge remarked.

Within hours the judge's prophecy had become a grim reality. The continuous feuding of the past three years was about to reach a bloody climax. A chilling plot to wipe out the main players in the Keane/Collopy crime gang had been hatched. An apparent abduction was to provide the ruse to lure four men into a murder trap making the way clear for a third gang, the McCarthy-Dundons, to take control of the drugs trade in Limerick and the mid-west. It was to be the gangland equivalent of a political coup.

Between 10.30 and 11 o'clock that night Kieran Ryan, his older brother, Eddie Junior and Christopher "Smokey" Costelloe were walking on Moylish Road in Ballynanty on their way to the home of another friend. They were in high spirits celebrating Kieran Ryan's escape from justice earlier in the day. Later it would be claimed that a car or van pulled up alongside them and two armed and masked men jumped out on top of them. As they bundled the Ryan brothers into the vehicle Costelloe, it was later claimed, managed to break free and make a run for it. One of the 'kidnappers' fired a shot into the air as "Smokey" ran away. The vehicle took off and the Ryans vanished without trace for a week. A short time later Costelloe alerted the Gardaí who immediately launched a huge manhunt. As officers from across the city and surrounding divisions were being mobilised, experienced detectives expected the worst. The search, they feared, would be for dead bodies.

Over the next seven days the Gardaí, backed up by scores of soldiers, searched the Cratloe Woods and Woodcock Hill area, which is situated just across the Clare border outside the city. It was the most likely location for assassins to use to comfortably dispatch their victims without the fear of being caught in the act. In the meantime terror and apprehension gripped the city. If the Ryans turned up dead a major escalation in the ongoing violence appeared to be inevitable. Everyone expected the worst. A number of houses were shot at or petrol bombed, and there were serious street fights between men, women and children from both sides of the dispute, including a full scale riot at the city's gleaming new Circuit Court complex. Potential combatants in the simmering war began wearing bullet-proof vests and made no effort to conceal the fact that they were preparing for combat. Limerick had become a powder keg.

As the authorities continued their efforts to locate the Ryans and keep a lid on the impending mayhem the underworld plot was to take a dramatic and unexpected twist that no one could have predicted. What was about to happen next has become one of the most diabolical double crosses in gangland history.

Kieran Keane and the rest of his criminal mob had kept their heads down since the disappearance of the two brothers. Inevitably they were the prime suspects. The police were everywhere and keeping close tabs on their movements. Several homes had been searched and anywhere gang members went they were stopped, searched and questioned about the missing brothers. It is widely believed in both police and underworld circles that the McCarthy-Dundon gang convinced Kieran Keane that they had abducted the Ryans and were holding them hostage. It is also understood that Keane had offered the gang a bounty if they kidnapped the Ryan brothers for him. Keane feared that one day the hate-filled teenagers would be in a position to retaliate for their father's murder and he wanted the advantage of drawing first blood.

On the afternoon of Wednesday, January 29, Keane was visited by twenty-year-old Dessie Dundon and invited to meet with the gang holding the Ryan brothers. Dundon was well-known to the local Gardaí and was considered to be one of the city's most dangerous young thugs. Dundon was already a suspect in a number of attempted murders including a machine gun attack in which another criminal was shot fourteen times. At the time Dundon was just sixteen years old. Keane and Dundon arranged to meet the 'abduction gang' in the home of twenty-one-year-old Anthony "Noddy" McCarthy at Fairgreen in the Garryowen area of the city later that evening.

Around 6pm Owen Treacy and Kieran Keane left Treacy's home at St Munchin's Street in Keane's blue Passat car. Treacy would later claim he had no idea what the meeting was about or who had contacted his uncle. Keane employed anti-surveillance techniques, taking a circuitous route around the city, driving up one-way streets in the process, in order to lose a possible Garda tail. When they arrived at Fairgreen at around 7pm they met an unidentified member of the gang who would later be referred to in court as Mr X. Mr X told Treacy and Keane: "The lads are inside." In the sitting room they met Dessie Dundon and "Noddy" McCarthy. "Noddy" McCarthy produced a .38 revolver and ordered them to get down on the floor. Keane had expected to walk into a 'business meeting' – instead he had been lured into a death trap.

Dessie Dundon tied the two criminals' hands behind their backs and ordered them to sit down. Keane and Treacy were told that if they played along they would be released unharmed and everything would be "okay". At the same time two other gang members emerged from the kitchen wearing balaclavas. Treacy recognised one of them as thirty-one-year-old David "Frog Eyes" Stanners. Dundon demanded that Keane phone brothers Kieran and Philip Collopy and arrange to meet them "out the road". Keane and Treacy both refused to phone their associates. As ruthless criminals, they were both experienced enough to know that their captors had one plan for all four of them – murder. They were beaten and tortured but would not give in to the demand. Hoods were then placed over their heads and secured with duct tape.

After about an hour Keane and Treacy were led out to a waiting Nissan Micra car and pushed into the boot. "Noddy" McCarthy drove the car and Mr X was in the passenger seat. The kidnappers brought their captives to a house in Roundwood Estate, a middle-class area of Rosbrien on the outskirts of the city. They drove the car into the garage and ordered the uncle and nephew to get out. They were brought upstairs and their hoods were taken off. The hostages were again ordered to phone the Collopys to arrange to meet them outside the city. The two men still refused to make the call. Their captors had now been joined by twenty-four-year-old James McCarthy from Delmege Park in Moyross and Christopher "Smokey" Costelloe who had 'escaped' during the 'kidnap' of the Ryan brothers a week earlier. Treacy overheard Dundon talking to someone on the phone: "We've got them," he bragged.

Ten minutes later "Noddy" McCarthy led Treacy and Keane down the stairs at gunpoint. They were brought out to a green Hiace van. McCarthy pushed Treacy inside and Dessie Dundon forced Keane to follow him. Keane and Treacy were ordered to lie on the floor and blankets were thrown over them. "Frog Eyes" Stanners drove the van with James McCarthy in the passenger seat and "Smokey" Costelloe in the back. Costelloe was armed with the gun "Noddy" McCarthy had been using earlier.

The van drove for around thirty-five minutes and eventually stopped on a lonely road at an area called Drumbanna, five miles outside Limerick City.

"Frog Eyes" Stanners ordered Kieran Keane out of the van and pushed him to the ground. He stabbed Keane in the side of the head and then calmly shot the crime lord in the back of the head with a handgun. The gangland hard man slumped onto the cold wet road.

Costelloe and Stanners then turned their attention to Treacy. Costelloe began stabbing Treacy in the throat. Treacy cut the palm of his hand as he tried to wrench the knife from Costelloe's hand. Stanners then grabbed the knife and started to stab Treacy. Stanners stared into his victim's face and hissed: "This is the last face you're going to see." He then stabbed Treacy several times in the ear, neck and chest. A seriously injured Treacy fell to the ground and pretended to be dead. In total Owen Treacy suffered seventeen serious stab wounds in the attack. Treacy heard James McCarthy shouting to the others: "Come on, come on, he's dead, he's dead." The killers got into the van and drove back towards Limerick, convinced that the two men were dead.

Before the attack Treacy had managed to loosen the ties on his hands and when the van left he staggered to his uncle's side. He could hear Keane faintly breathing. Treacy struggled to his feet and stumbled to a house up the road to summon help. By the time help arrived Keane was dead. An autopsy would later find that he died from a single gunshot wound to the head. He had also suffered six stab wounds near his left ear. Owen Treacy was rushed to hospital where he underwent emergency surgery. The situation could have been a lot worse if the gang had managed to lure the Collopys to the same spot. If their heinous plan had been successful the road at Drumbanna would have been the scene of unprecedented slaughter.

Six hours later the Ryan brothers turned up near Athlone Garda Station. They looked remarkably well and unscathed for two teenagers who had been held hostage for seven days. On the day of their release the Ryans held a very public party in Kileely, drinking cans of beer and posing for photographers. Everyone was in jubilant mood and one even mooned for the cameras. It was hard to know whether they were celebrating their 'freedom' or the murder of Kieran Keane, or both.

Among those celebrating was one of Kieran Keane's killers, James McCarthy. "Smokey" Costelloe also turned up at one stage to take part in the impromptu festivities. The killers had two reasons to celebrate – the death of a deadly foe and the safe return of their pals. There was intense speculation as to whether the Ryans had in fact been kidnapped at all or whether it had been part of a complex ruse. Kieran Ryan stood smirking and laughing with his mates. When reporters asked him about what had happened to him and his brother he replied: "I got threatened not to talk to anyone. I don't know where I was held, I couldn't tell you. Our family had no hand, act or part in Kieran Keane's murder. We didn't do it."

The day after the Keane murder John Ryan made a rather ambivalent comment to reporters: "If they [had] left them [his nephews] go loose, or told us that they were dead. They told us nothing at all. They left us linger on the whole time, so we had to get revenge somewhere along the line."

Not long after Kieran Keane's murder his henchmen, Ross Cantillon and Roy Woodland, went on trial for the AK47 gun attack on Eddie Ryan's nephew, John McCarthy, the previous August. After initially pleading not guilty, on February 11, the two cousins changed their pleas to guilty. At a subsequent sentence hearing Detective Sergeant Jim Ryan told the court he believed the defendants were "acting under the influence of more sinister elements of the family feud" and that they were not "at the top of the tree in relation to the ongoing dispute". Cantillon and Woodland were each jailed for seven years.

At Kieran Keane's funeral the song *The Wind Beneath My Wings* blared out around St Mary's Church. The local Curate, Fr Donough O'Malley, talked about hatred, violence and death: "To have peace it is necessary to let got of prejudice and hatred. It requires a change of heart, attitude and behaviour." The priest's words of wisdom were falling on deaf ears.

Christy Keane applied for compassionate leave to attend his brother's funeral but Justice Minister Michael McDowell refused the request. The Prison Service and the Gardaí had advised him that Keane's presence at the funeral would create a major security risk and was very likely to escalate the already extremely volatile situation.

After the funeral the hard men and boys of the Keane family and their associates walked behind the hearse for the three miles to Kilmurray graveyard. "What are they trying to prove? That they still own the place," remarked one disgusted local who had seen enough of the thuggery and madness.

Within twenty-four hours of the Keane murder and the party, a lot of the Ryans, their associates and members of the third criminal drug gang had fled the city and gone to England and Spain. The killers decided to go into hiding when they learned that Treacy had survived the appalling attack although they hung on to the hope that he would succumb to his injuries and die.

Meanwhile back at the city's Garda HQ officers began the awesome task of unravelling the astonishing events of the past week. Limerick's feuding had suddenly become a National crisis. Scores of extra Garda resources poured into Limerick from Dublin and Cork to prevent an all-out bloodbath and to assist in the complex investigation. Limerick appeared to be spiralling out of control. Observers began comparing the city to some of the worst days in Belfast during the Troubles. At a press conference held in Roxboro Garda Station, the afternoon after Keane's murder, Chief Superintendent Gerry Kelly described the worsening situation as one of utter madness. For the first time ever, teams of the Emergency Response Units were deployed to man checkpoints and mount foot patrols on the streets of an Irish city while a police helicopter monitored events on the ground from the skies above. But the detectives were already secretly making progress in the case.

Despite his critical injuries Owen Treacy was able to identify his attackers within a few hours of the incident. Detective Garda John Nagle visited Treacy in the intensive care ward of Limerick Regional Hospital three hours after the shooting. Despite being very seriously ill he was coherent. "Who stabbed you and who shot Kieran Keane?" the detective asked. Treacy replied slowly "green Hiace". Then he whispered "David 'Frog Eyes' Stanners, James McCarthy, Moyross and 'Smokey' Costelloe."

Over the following weeks Owen Treacy gradually recovered from his injuries. He agreed to give the Gardaí a full statement of the events of the night of his uncle's murder. He could clearly identify six members of the abduction gang: "Frog Eyes" Stanners, "Smokey" Costelloe, James McCarthy, Dessie Dundon, "Noddy" McCarthy and Mr X, who cannot be named for legal reasons. Mr X is believed to be on the run somewhere in England and is still officially wanted by the Gardaí. Treacy was breaking with the accepted tradition among the gangs of never allowing the police to get involved in disputes. This was no ordinary situation. The opposition was clearly hell bent on wiping out as many of the Keanes and Collopys as they could get their hands on. It was a plot to commit mass murder.

As news leaked out that Treacy was making a good recovery and was prepared to testify against his attackers, he was placed under 24-hour armed Garda protection. The murder gang would make every effort to kill Treacy before he reached the witness stand. Both sides were hiring hit men from outside the city. While Treacy was under police protection his gang were getting help from associates in Dublin to prepare a counter-attack.

At the same time the Garda investigation was moving forward at a dramatic pace. By March 2003, thirty-four people had been arrested and questioned including the Ryan brothers who were quizzed about their alleged abduction. On March 23, three of the five men named by Treacy – James McCarthy, "Frog Eyes" Stanners and "Smokey" Costelloe – were charged with the false imprisonment of Treacy and Keane. The following Monday, March 31, "Noddy"

McCarthy and Dessie Dundon were also charged with two counts of false imprisonment.

In June 2003 the five killers were formally charged with the murder of Kieran Keane and the attempted murder of Owen Treacy. Gardaí had painstakingly built their case against the five men. The file on the case ran to over 5,000 pages containing 720 individual statements.

As a direct consequence of the ongoing investigation and the influx of high quality intelligence, the Gardaí scored several major successes against the gangs and began turning Limerick gangland upside down. The criminals' main source of income began to dry up as a result of the intense pressure from the police. Several individuals from both sides of the feud were arrested in operations in Limerick and Dublin. Among those arrested were hired hit men who had been brought in from the UK to carry out executions in Limerick. Gardaí also seized a large cache of sophisticated firepower including Uzi machine guns, assault rifles, grenades and car bombs. The investigation uncovered a link between the Limerick crime gangs and the sale of illegal firearms in Britain. This breakthrough came when Garda divers found a Czech-made handgun in a river at Annacotty in Limerick. The weapon had been used in the murder of night-club security manager Brian Fitzgerald in August 2002. It was discovered that the gun, which had originally been bought from a collector in Britain, had been "re-activated". This involves re-equipping decommissioned firearms with firing mechanisms. Other seizures of Uzi machine guns and a British Army sterling sub-machine gun were also traced to the same illegal dealer in the UK. The operation that followed allowed UK police to smash the underworld gun trade. Anti-terrorist police in the UK also uncovered a renegade IRA cell and a large cache of weapons near Manchester as a direct result of the Limerick investigation. The Continuity IRA had been selling the Limerick gangs firearms. In a search of a house at Mongret on the outskirts of the city four men were arrested when guns, drugs and a large car bomb were discovered. The bomb was primed and ready to be fixed on a gangster's car. The Gardaí also seized millions of Euro worth of drugs en route to the gangs and the Criminal Assets Bureau began a major trawl of the gangster's financial affairs.

The ongoing success of the operation had certainly saved lives but the feud had still not gone away. With so many gang members in custody awaiting trials for various feud-related crimes, prison security had to be dramatically stepped up in order to prevent the bloodshed continuing behind prison walls. The situation was treated so seriously that a total ban was placed on the use of razor blades in Limerick prison as they could be used to inflict injury. Instead prisoners were provided with electric razors. When prisoners first arrived they were carefully vetted to ensure they were not accidentally placed in cells with individuals from opposing sides. Despite these measures Dessie Dundon had to be moved between prisons after he was involved in a violent incident.

Outside the prison walls the trouble continued. On May 27, 2003, the people of Limerick were again reminded that the spectre of hate was still looming over their city when a ferocious full-scale battle erupted in the forecourt of a fast-food restaurant on the Ennis Road. The fight began when a member of one faction walked into Supermacs burger bar and spotted a large contingent from the opposing side. He contacted his associates and within minutes reinforcements arrived. Armed with snooker cues, baseball bats and iron bars the Ryan and Keane factions waded into each other. Luckily for the innocent men, women and children caught in the middle of the riot, a group of officers from the Garda Water Unit were also in the burger joint when the battle broke out. Along with reinforcements from around the city the 'water rats' soon brought the battle under control. Nine men were arrested and later charged with a variety of offences including assault, violent disorder and the unlawful possession of weapons. The combatants were remanded in custody before their trials so they were off the streets. Their absence was seen as a positive step towards returning calm to the city.

By Summer 2003 at least thirty serious criminals were in custody awaiting trial. However the ongoing crime wave and the success of the Garda investigations had created another major problem for the authorities. To relieve the sheer volume of murder cases waiting to be heard the Department of Justice took the landmark decision to locate the Central Criminal Court in Limerick for the duration. Moving the court to the city meant that dozens of Gardaí who would otherwise be required to travel to Dublin for the trials would have more time to participate in the ongoing crime investigations in Limerick. If the court had not moved then the backlog of cases would have caused a chronic personnel shortage and seriously hampered the continuous efforts by Gardaí to solve the various crimes and prevent further bloodshed. The Garda forces in Limerick were already stretched to the limit and suffering from a chronic lack of resources. The decision was historic as it was the first time the court had ever moved from its traditional base in The Four Courts in Central Dublin.

* * * *

John Ryan had been keeping his head down in the six months following Kieran Keane's murder but in July 2003 he dropped his guard. He went to help a friend put down a patio at the front of his house in Thomondgate. As Ryan was working a motor bike pulled up along the kerb. The pillion passenger got off and shot Ryan three times in the leg and abdomen. The bike sped off in the direction of St Mary's Park, the Keane's stronghold. John Ryan later died in hospital.

It was the Keanes turn to have a party that evening. The Keane faction even rang the Ryans to tell them that the grotesque celebration was underway. The suspects for the murder were teenagers of sixteen and seventeen. Again the word on everyone's lips was revenge.

A few weeks later Paul Coffey pleaded guilty to the manslaughter of Eddie Ryan in the Central Criminal Court and in November 2003 he was jailed for 15 years.

In the meantime the need to retaliate for John Ryan's murder had not been forgotten. The alarm bells began to ring on Friday, October 17, when two members of the McCarthy-Dundon mob, who had been unlawfully at large with jail sentences for minor offences, walked into Henry Street Garda Station to give themselves up. The police immediately knew that something was about to happen and desperate efforts were made to check with informants to find out what was brewing. No information came back so the cops had no choice but to wait and see. The two thugs, who would have normally stayed on the run until they were caught, had provided themselves with a cast iron alibi – occupying a cell in the local prison.

On Monday the police's worst fears were proved correct when the badly mutilated body of twenty-three-year-old Michael Campbell-McNamara was discovered on waste ground in Barry's Field near Southill. A member of the Keane crime gang, Campbell-McNamara was Christy Keane's daughter's boyfriend. He was lured to his death when he went to buy a firearm from criminals who were associated with the two hoods who had turned themselves in the previous Friday. He had been involved in a number of attacks on the Ryan/McCarthy-Dundon group. Several months earlier Garda surveillance had recovered a grenade in a car abandoned by Campbell-McNamara. He was also suspected of burning the homes of Ryan and McCarthy-Dundon family members who had fled the city in the immediate aftermath of the Keane murder.

It later emerged that when Campbell-McNamara arrived at the meeting he was abducted at gunpoint. He was tortured and questioned about the activities of the Keane gang. The kidnappers then tried to force him to lure Brian Collopy into the murder trap. Kieran Keane's killers had tried a similar stunt to lure Collopy's brothers, Kieran and Philip, into an ambush in January. Since then Brian Collopy has become one of the main movers in the Keane criminal empire and is now one of the opposition's main targets. Collopy had obviously learned from past experiences and wisely refused to meet Campbell-McNamara. When they realised that Collopy was not falling for the trap the kidnappers executed Campbell-McNamara by blasting him in the back and head with a sawn-off shotgun. Medical evidence later showed that the dead man was stabbed at least a dozen times after his execution. A few weeks later Brian Collopy was reluctantly forced to attend a different type of meeting. This time with officers from the Criminal Assets Bureau who had obtained a High Court order seizing his €250,000 home, on the outskirts of the city.

Meanwhile, at Campbell-McNamara's funeral, Father Donough O'Malley expressed his revulsion at yet another senseless murder and, like so many of his colleagues in the past, made yet another heartfelt plea for peace: "Now is the time to stop being unkind, selfish, fighting, vengeful. I ask you in the name of God to stop fighting, stop killing, you can do it, you will do it with God's help."

But heaven would be the last place Limerick's psychopaths would be looking for help. A week after the murder another crisis meeting was held at the local Garda HQ. Intelligence had been received that several murder contracts had been ordered on members of the three main gangs in the city. That weekend a senior Garda source in the city commented: "It is not an exaggeration to say the place is awash with blood money being offered to carry out murders. It is a thriving market for would-be assassins."

The volatile situation reached boiling point as the focus shifted to the city's court complex on King John's Island. On October 21 the Central Criminal Court sat for the trial of the five men accused of Kieran Keane's murder. As the case commenced a cloud of fear hung over the proceedings. Jurors had been summoned to attend the court from Limerick and the surrounding counties and a huge security operation had been put in place for the high-profile trial. A police helicopter patrolled the skies overhead while Garda snipers watched from the roof of the courts and a Garda boat patrolled the River Shannon that runs around the Island. Everyone entering the court complex was searched for weapons.

After two days the court found it impossible to empanel a jury of twelve people from a total selection panel of five hundred and twenty-nine people. The sense of fear was plain to see. The jurors felt that the gangs could get to them. Jurors presented medical certificates for myriad problems but mainly for "stress and anxiety".

In the end the decision had to be made to move the trial to Dublin. The failure to run the trial in Limerick was a major embarrassment to the State and a victory for mob rule. Critics of the landmark move to Limerick had declared that the Central Criminal Court would fail to effectively operate in the city because of the sense of fear and intimidation generated by criminal gangs – unfortunately this had proved to be the case.

Several months later, Mr Justice Paul Carney who had enthusiastically supported the court's move to Limerick, was critical of the security operation surrounding the Keane murder trial. He claimed that it had caused unnecessary anxiety among the jurors. But despite the problems in the Keane trial Justice Carney's defence of the court's move to Limerick was ultimately vindicated. By

Autumn 2004 the backlog of murder and rape trials had been cleared with juries returning guilty verdicts in at least fifteen cases. "The cupboard is now empty," a satisfied Mr Justice Carney remarked after the final case was heard.

Meanwhile as preparations were made for the transfer of the Kieran Keane murder trial to Dublin, Kieran's nephew Liam's trial for the murder of Eric Leamy opened in the Central Criminal Court in October 2003. The court heard that seven people would testify to witnessing nineteen-year-old Keane stabbing Leamy in August 2001. But on the second day of the trial serious problems began to emerge when the witnesses developed what Mr Justice Paul Carney described as "collective amnesia". David Murphy, the first civilian witness to be called to testify began shouting that he "seen nothing, knew nothing and heard nothing" as he approached the witness box. "I'm answering no questions," nineteen-year-old Murphy declared at which point the judge ordered Gardaí to "put him in the cells".

Two more witnesses, James Price and Paul Campbell, were also removed to the cells by the judge when they developed similar difficulties with their memories. Price claimed that he could not remember giving Gardaí a statement about the stabbing.

Mr Justice Carney asked him: "Why are you having all these memory problems?"

Price replied that he was on drugs – "pinkies, upjohns and other tablets".

The judge then asked Price if he had a doctor.

Price replied: "I buys them on the streets."

The judge enquired where he had got the tablets from and Price repeated, "I buys them on the street".

"Well I think we need a little help with this memory problem," the judge remarked as he ordered Gardaí to remove Price from the court. As he was led away the judge told Price that he would receive medical assistance to help him with his memory loss. Paul Campbell also claimed that he could not remember anything either "due to drugs and other matters".

Twenty-year-old Amanda McNamara had given a statement to the investigating detectives in which she alleged that she saw Liam Keane with a knife in his right hand on the night Eric Leamy was confronted. "Eric was saying 'put down the knife and I'll fight you.' Liam Keane was the only person I saw with a knife," she had told Gardaí. But as she sat in the witness box while prosecuting counsel Dominic McGlynn read out her statement, McNamara repeatedly claimed that it was either untrue or that she could not recall anything. "I was off me head on drugs the previous night," she replied, adding that she had a problem with alcohol and drugs. On the night Eric Leamy was murdered she said she was drinking and popping ecstasy pills.

Mr Justice Carney declared Campbell, Price and McNamara to be hostile witnesses. He warned David Murphy to seek legal representation and told him he would have to return to give evidence.

The following day the drama continued. There were exchanges between Mr Justice Carney and John Phelan SC, Liam Keane's counsel, over the way the judge had addressed the fifth witness, Stephen Blackhall. When Blackhall denied making a detailed statement to detectives in which he had said he saw Liam Keane stab Eric Leamy in the side, Justice Carney had warned Blackhall about the dangers of incriminating himself. Blackhall also denied that he had been at the scene of the attack at all. The judge had cautioned the witness about the consequences of perjuring himself in court. Mr Phelan commented: "Your lordship is attempting to intimidate the witness intro retracting what he said on oath." Keane's counsel also sought to have the jury discharged, adding that the judge's comments to Blackhall, such as "perjury, life imprisonment and five years", could prejudice them. However, Mr Justice Carney replied that it was his duty to issue a warning to Blackhall against self-incrimination and he felt it necessary that this be done. "There isn't a single word of admissible evidence against your client. I'm not going to treat the jury as simpletons," he said.

The sixth State witness Tony McMillan was also warned by the judge of the consequences of self-incrimination after he too denied making a statement to Gardaí that he had seen Keane stab Eric Leamy.

The final nail in the State's case came on Monday morning when the seventh witness, twenty-four-year-old Roy Behan from St Mary's Park, also denied making a statement to police identifying Liam Keane as the killer.

The case against Liam Keane lay in tatters. In the absence of witness testimony the DPP had no choice but to enter a *nolle prosequi* thus dropping the charge against Liam Keane. Mr Justice Carney could scarcely conceal his utter frustration at such a blatant attack on the fundamentals of law and order. "The likes of what has happened in this case has never, I can assure you, been encountered in this court before," he declared, as he released the jury.

Liam Keane, who had smirked throughout the farcical trial, was jubilant. As he left the court building he turned and gave the two fingers to waiting cameramen. His face, a frightening mix of hostility and aggression, appeared on the front pages of the next morning's newspapers. The picture sent a chilling message to Irish society. Nineteen-year-old Liam Keane was walking away a free man after his trial collapsed, amid an atmosphere of unmistakable fear and intimidation. That one disturbing photograph spoke more than a thousand words about the stranglehold of crime in general and about the situation in Limerick in particular. It was a clear message that the criminal justice system was under serious threat – the law of the underworld had neutered the rule of law.

Back in Limerick, the only people with cause to celebrate the outcome were Liam Keane, his cronies and his family. Eric Leamy's heart-broken parents were emotionally distraught and were comforted by counsellors from Victim Support before taking the train home. They were disgusted and incredulous that the justice system had been so completely undermined. News of the result was also greeted with universal dismay and consternation in the estates worst affected by the ongoing feud. Yet again the innocent people living in those areas, who had been hoping for an end to the madness, had to brace themselves for more violence and mayhem. Additional armed patrols were deployed on the streets of the potential flash points, as a police helicopter kept vigil from the darkness of the cold Winter sky. Members of the extended Keane gang and their allies also patrolled the streets near Keane's home, watching for gunmen.

Two days later Liam Keane was back in court in Limerick this time facing public order charges for using threatening and abusive behaviour and being drunk in a public place. The incident occurred on October 19, the same day that Michael Campbell-McNamara was murdered. On November 5, Keane received a three month suspended jail sentence and was allowed to go free.

On November 26, Gardaí again arrested Keane outside the same court building. He was shouting threats at a member of the rival faction. The following January he was jailed for four months on that charge and, two weeks later, Limerick District Court granted a Garda application to activate the three month suspended sentence imposed on November 5. Liam Keane had earned himself a short stint behind bars.

The disintegration of the Liam Keane trial, coming just two weeks after the failure to empanel a jury in his uncle's murder case, caused an unprecedented public outcry. Within hours of the collapse of the trial Justice Minister Michael McDowell held a number of crisis meetings with Garda management and officers from the offices of the Director of Public Prosecutions in a bid to work out a way of dealing with the crisis. The Minister announced that an extra two million Euro was to be made immediately available to Gardaí. It would boost Garda man-hours by providing extra resources for overtime in Limerick and also in Finglas, north-west Dublin, which had also experienced a dramatic increase in gangland bloodshed in the preceding months. Minister McDowell later told reporters: "It would be foolish to think the entire criminal justice system has broken down because of the collapse of one trial. But it would be even more foolish for people to believe that they can give the two fingers to the community they live in and not ultimately expect to face the wrath of the State." In the summer of 2004, as a direct result of the collapse of the Keane trial, Michael McDowell published legislation which will enable courts to accept as evidence witness statements made to the Gardaí which were later recanted in court. (By October 2004 this legislation had not yet been enacted. It is expected to be passed into law sometime in 2005.)

As the furore over the Liam Keane case raged the Limerick crime saga was set to continue to dominate the news. On the morning of November 5 the trial of the five men accused of Kieran Keane's murder opened in Cloverhill Court in Clondalkin, West Dublin. The court was deemed to be the most secure place for the trial because it is attached to Cloverhill remand prison. Prisoners can be brought to and from the courtroom through a secure underground tunnel linking it with the prison complex. There was tight security as the seven men and five women of the jury were driven under armed escort to the court complex. Everyone entering the court walked through electronic scanning equipment.

The five men: Dessie Dundon, David "Frog Eye" Stanners, James McCarthy, Christopher "Smokey" Costelloe and Anthony "Noddy" McCarthy filed into the court room accompanied by several prison officers and armed Gardaí. They appeared confident and cocky, smiling and waving to family and friends in the court and sneering across at members of the Keane family, including the murdered man's widow, Sophie Keane. The five gang members sat beside each other in a row behind their five individual legal defence teams. They denied all the charges against them.

Opening the case for the State, prosecutor Mr Denis Vaughan Buckley SC, told the jury it was the State's case that all five men acted as part of a joint enterprise and as such, were all involved in the abduction and murder. He said the prosecution case depended "wholly or substantially" on the evidence of Owen Treacy. Mr Vaughan Buckley then outlined the events of the night of January 29 as witnessed by Treacy. The prosecutor told the jury that the five men were no strangers to Owen Treacy, as he had known most of them for years. Mr Justice Paul Carney, who had also presided over the Liam Keane trial, warned the jury that "this case has attracted very, very extensive publicity" and that there "is a great deal of inaccurate material and casual material floating around".

Two days later, on November 7, Owen Treacy took the stand amid tight security. Two members of the Emergency Response Unit stood near Treacy as he sat in the witness box.

Mr John Edwards SC, representing James McCarthy, objected to the presence of the two detectives who were also wearing earpieces and whose firearms could be seen bulging from beneath their jackets. "I would like to know who they are," the lawyer said to Mr Justice Carney. One of the officers replied that he was attached to a special protection unit: "My responsibility is the protection of the witness and those are my instructions."

"It suggests that there is some threat to the witness from my client and the other accused in this case. Clearly this is not the case as the accused are flanked by prison officers. If this room can not be secured what kind of a fair trial can my client have?" asked Mr Edwards. However Mr Justice Carney said that he was not going to interfere with security operations and he instructed the prosecution to continue examining Treacy's evidence.

From the beginning Treacy proved to be a determined and coherent witness as he faced the men who had tried to butcher him. They regularly stared, smiled, winked and gestured at Treacy, giving him a clear message that he would be 'got at'. But throughout his evidence Treacy showed no fear and stared back at his uncle's killers. He refused an option to sit out of their view and often leaned forward to respond to their antics with his own gestures. Speaking in a clear voice, Treacy calmly told Mr Denis Vaughan Buckley SC how he had been abducted with Kieran Keane. He stated that they were hooded and had their hands tied behind their backs with duct tape on the night of the murder. He explained that they were met at the house in Fairgreen by a sixth member of the gang, described as Mr X, who was not before the court. "He told us that the lads were inside," Treacy recalled. He recounted how they went into the sitting room and met Dessie Dundon and Anthony "Noddy" McCarthy. McCarthy had a gun in his hand.

"Did you know Desmond Dundon?" the prosecuting lawyer asked.

"I know him all my life, My Lord," Treacy replied confidently and pointed to Dundon.

Treacy recalled that he and Keane had been ordered to lure the Collopy brothers "out the road" so the gang could kill them. "There was no way we could do that," he told the court.

Treacy then identified David "Frog Eyes" Stanners as the third man he encountered in the house in Fairgreen who, he said, walked into the room wearing a balaclava. "He is a man I know all my life," he said. He said he identified Stanners from his voice. "I knew his voice all my life," Treacy declared.

"Not a scintilla of doubt about it?" counsel asked.

"No doubt whatsoever, My Lord. I could identify David 'Frog Eyes' Stanners."

Later he told the court what happened when the gang brought him and Keane to Drumbanna. "I witnessed David 'Frogs Eyes' Stanners shoot my uncle in the back of the head," he said. "He pushed Kieran Keane to the ground like a dog and shot him like a dog with his hands tied behind his back." Treacy related how Stanners and Costelloe then came towards him: "'Smokey' stabbed me in the throat. I was stabbed seventeen times on the 29th January. David Stanners stabbed me in the chest a good few times My Lord. He kept stabbing me in the ear and the neck. I was stabbed twice in the lung with terrible force and pressure."

"Who stabbed you?" asked Mr Vaughan Buckley.

"'Frog Eyes", David Stanners. Stanners told me: 'this is the last face you're going to see' and he stuck the knife in me. I heard James McCarthy saying: 'He's dead; he's dead; he's dead.' I played dead, My Lord, because I knew it was the only way to get rid of these men," Owen Treacy replied.

Over the next eight days Treacy remained in the witness box and was subjected to intense cross-examination by the five defence teams representing the accused men. Cross-examined by Mr Blaise O'Carroll SC for Desmond Dundon, Treacy said that the night of the murder was the worst night of his life: "It has turned my life upside down. My life has ended since the 29th of January, My Lord." Treacy claimed that there had never been animosity between him and Dundon. When asked what conceivable motive could Dundon have had for the incident Treacy replied: "I don't know why he done it but he done it."

At one stage in cross-examination Treacy was asked by defence counsel was it not true that he and his uncle had been told they would be returned home safely to their homes on the night they were ambushed. Treacy replied: "My Lord, what these men had in their heads was to kill the four of us on the 29th of January. The four of us were going to be killed. If me or my Uncle Kieran made that call there was four of us going to be killed. At no time were we going to lure the Collopys out the road – at no time."

Defence counsel asked Treacy if he could have been mistaken about Dundon tying his hands. "My Lord, members of the jury, the man that taped my hands is Dessie Dundon and he also taped Kieran's. I remember him twisting our hands," Treacy replied, putting his arms behind his back to illustrate how it was done for the benefit of the jury.

At different stages in the trial the accused men let their masks slip as they discovered that Treacy's evidence was sinking them. On one occasion the hoods began openly arguing amongst themselves, berating "Frog Eyes" Stanners for failing to kill Treacy that night. Their view point seemed to be that if he had done things right then they wouldn't have a problem now.

When Treacy described what happened at Drumbanna defence counsel put it to him that he "magically did a Houdini act" by getting out of his binds. "I had no other choice my Lord, it was either life or death on 29th January," he replied.

"How did you manage to escape and Kieran did not?" counsel asked.

"That's correct my Lord he did not," Treacy replied.

"You did not go to any classes on Houdini or escapology?" counsel continued to enquire.

"Do you know who Houdini was?" Mr Justice Carney interjected.

Treacy said he didn't know Houdini. When it was explained to him Treacy replied: "My Lord, if you want to call me Houdini you can. I was just a bit luckier than Kieran on the 29th January – that's the way I put it."

Treacy denied that he or his murdered uncle had been involved in the drug trade. He also denied that they had gone to the house in Fairgreen for a "nefarious purpose", claiming that he was there for no purpose. He also denied that the purpose of the visit was for Kieran Keane to hire "some security or henchmen".

"There is no henchmen My Lord. Kieran was no drug dealer," Treacy stated. He added that he had no idea why they went to the house in Fairgreen.

Defence counsel put it to him: "Here you are an innocent breadman, the family man from St Munchins Street who knew nothing about crime, nothing about drugs, nothing about guns. Why did you not protest at the unfairness of the situation which you were in? Did you not round on Kieran and say 'what have you led us into'?"

"No my lord," Treacy replied.

The Kieran Keane trial lasted for thirty-one days and on December 18, 2003, the jury retired to consider their verdict. They deliberated for more than fifteen hours, over three days, and reached their decision on the evening of Saturday, December 20. The trial had moved to The Four Courts for the jury's deliberation and there was even tighter security than usual there. Armed members of the ERU ringed the court and formed a human barrier between the accused men and their families and Treacy and his supporters. Everyone was individually searched entering the courtroom. The tension in the court was palpable as the Gardaí and the people of Limerick gathered to hear the verdict they had been anxiously awaiting for a year. The five men were agitated and aggressive as the jury returned with their verdict. They unanimously found the five men guilty on the charges of murder, attempted murder and false imprisonment.

As the verdicts were read out members of the Keane family cheered and punched the air. Mr Justice Carney paid tribute to the jurors for their courage and sacrifice during the marathon trial. He sentenced all five men to the mandatory life sentence for murder and deferred sentencing them on the remaining three counts until February 3.

Keane's widow Sophie took the stand in order to tell the court how the murder had affected her and her family. "They are animals," she said of the five men who had just been convicted. "My life stood still and my life was finished the day they took my husband's life." She was then asked by prosecuting counsel what her husband had done to deserve such a death. Before she could reply one of his killers shouted: "He sold drugs and killed people. He killed Eddie Ryan."

As the five were led away in handcuffs to a convoy of prison vans, "Noddy" McCarthy shouted towards Treacy and the rest of the Keanes: "For every action there's a reaction – remember that. You'll be looking over your shoulder for the rest of your life boy." James McCarthy snarled at Treacy, calling him a bastard.

The outcome of the Kieran Keane trial was a welcome development in light of the controversy over the Liam Keane trial a month earlier. Later, in an interview with reporters, Chief Superintendent Gerry Kelly was candid about the ongoing situation. He said that the Gardaí in the city were determined to stamp out the murderous feuding but expressed his fear that if the situation deteriorated any further some of his own officers could also be murdered. In the weeks during the trial a number of officers had been attacked and threatened by thugs supporting the killers. As a result Chief Superintendent Kelly deployed armed officers to escort unarmed uniformed Gardaí as they patrolled the flash points in the city. This was the first time in the history of the Irish criminal underworld that the largely unarmed police force had been forced to take such precautions.

On Tuesday, February 3, 2004, Kieran Keane's five killers appeared in the Central Criminal Court for sentencing on the three outstanding guilty verdicts. The court returned to Limerick for the hearing. It was a symbolic gesture that sent an unequivocal message to the warring gangs in the city that they were no longer untouchable. Tight security reminiscent of the big Mafia show trials in Italy had become a regular sight around the Limerick court building and the surrounding area but security that day was even tighter than before. The five convicted men were now serving life sentences and there was little for them to lose if they orchestrated a major violent incident or a break out. Both sides had been shown to have access to bombs, high-powered weapons and professional assassins – the Gardaí were taking no chances.

Almost one hundred heavily armed officers backed up by uniformed colleagues and at least twenty prison officers were on duty for the ninety-minute hearing. Scores of supporters and family members from both sides of the bloodbath turned up to jeer, cajole and threaten each other. The killers' family and friends wore specially printed t-shirts with the words: 'Keanes are rats' emblazoned across them. In the courtroom sixty Gardaí stood between both sides and surrounded Kieran Keane's murderers. Owen Treacy and the rest of the Keane family were guarded in the public gallery as they awaited Mr Justice Paul Carney's arrival.

The five men, surrounded by a large group of prison officers and Gardaí, looked like they hadn't a care in the world. They laughed and waved to supporters in between shouting threats and gesturing to the family of the man they had so happily butchered. They looked like a bunch of high-spirited lads who were facing the court for a minor offence like jay-walking. Either the reality of the situation hadn't yet sunk in, even though it was almost two months since they were jailed for life, or, more likely, they were putting on a brave, unrepentant face for the world. Alternatively, since they had sacrificed their future for mindless hate, perhaps life really didn't mean much to them in the first place.

Before sentence was passed Superintendent Gerry Mahon, the officer in charge of the investigation summarised the background to the feud. "This feud started in the summer of 2000 when two families who were previously close associates had a disagreement which ultimately led in November 2000 to a murder taking place in The Moose Bar in Cathedral Place. Three further murders have occurred, all directly related to this particular feud," he said. Supt. Mahon listed the astonishing catalogue of serious crimes which had accompanied the murder spree: assaults, use of firearms, possession and use of explosives, the possession and use of high-powered weapons, intimidation and criminal damage. "The prime motivation in all this feud is the sheer and absolute hate by each side for each other. It is a hate that has not diminished to this day. The motivation and the objective of this particular gang was to murder both Kieran Keane and Owen Treacy and to lure two other people into the trap and I believe two other murders would have occurred had they been successful," the investigator continued. "The motivation was to eliminate those who stood in their way and those perceived to be their enemies with the objective of totally dominating Limerick City." As Superintendent Mahon gave his grim assessment the five men continued to smirk and laugh amongst each other, like bold children being reprimanded for stealing sweets.

Mr Justice Paul Carney sentenced Stanners, Costelloe, Dundon and the two McCarthys to fifteen years each on the count of attempted murder and a further seven years each on the two false imprisonment charges. Both sentences were to run concurrently. As sentence was passed the five men whooped with laughter, cheered and shouted threats at the Keanes but Mr Justice Carney had a stark warning for the ebullient thugs and their clans. "Life sentences have already been imposed on each of the accused in this case. I wanted to say primarily to the friends and supporters of the accused on the outside that each of them will die in prison unless there is intervention in their cases by the Parole Board. The Parole Board is entirely independent, but it seems unlikely to intervene while the feud is a live issue. This should be borne in mind by the friends and supporters of the accused outside and the accused themselves."

As the five men left the court for the last time it appeared Mr Justice Carney's warning had fallen on deaf ears. Their supporters cheered them on, as if they were war heroes. In the background both sides continued to hurl abuse and death threats at each other. Owen Treacy was photographed shouting abuse at his enemies as he left the court under armed guard. As the warring thugs began to disperse, under the watchful eye of an army of police officers, recriminations were exchanged between the families of the guilty men. One of them was heard to say of "Frog Eyes" Stanners: "If that fuckin' bollocks had done it right then we wouldn't have this shite goin' on. He made a complete fuckin' mess of it."

After the hearing Chief Superintendent Gerry Kelly said he hoped the feuding clans would listen to the judge's warning. He said: "This definitely draws a line in the sand and I hope that the families involved will take notice of this and the feuding will stop with this generation." He revealed that the local Gardaí had established lines of communication with the various warring families. Officers had been trying to persuade the gangs to stop killing and harming each other. But he still believed that his officers were at risk from the gangs: "An unarmed Garda in a car at night is a high risk and that is why they must be accompanied by an armed escort."

In the months that followed the trial several members of the feuding gangs were jailed, including four men for the Mongret arms seizure and a suspected hit man who had been caught in Dublin on his way to Limerick with an Uzi machinegun. One of the men arrested in connection with the bomb find at Mongret, Sean Smith from Brixton in London, was given twelve years. He had admitted to being offered €10,000 to plant the bomb in Limerick. Had it gone off, bomb squad experts said up to eight people could have been killed.

On June 29, the nine men charged in connection with the riot at Supermacs on the Ennis Road were also jailed for a total of thirty-eight years between them. 'Kidnap' victim Kieran Ryan was one of four men jailed for six years each. Twenty-four-year-old Philip Collopy, the man Kieran Keane's killers tried to lure into a murder trap in January 2003, was jailed for two years after he pleaded guilty to the unlawful possession of a weapon. The men were convicted after a thirteen-day trial. After passing sentence Judge Carroll Moran described the ongoing feud: "This problem has evolved over the past three to four years as an extremely serious problem and in fact it is the most serious problem in the city and it has to stop. I would be open to the most serious criticism and well justified criticism if I did other than try to bring an end to this mindless violence. It's going nowhere."

By the end of the summer of 2004 twenty-five people were serving a variety of jail sentences associated with the feuding. The crack down by the forces of law and order brought with it an uneasy peace. But after three years of gangland mayhem an uneasy peace is a welcome change in Limerick. With so many gangland killers and troublemakers behind bars there had been a noticeable decrease in the murder rate by Autumn 2004.

Following the conviction of the nine people involved in the Supermacs riot, Brian Collopy discussed a peace pact of sorts with the Ryans and the McCarthy-Dundons. The pact was not inspired by some new love for peace and tranquillity. The Limerick mobs had not suddenly found God in their pathetic lives. The pact was motivated by business. As long as the feuding continued the cops would keep up the intense pressure. The CAB was already crawling all over the criminals and the Garda National Drugs Unit was seizing millions of Euro worth of drugs. It was all starting to hurt in the most sensitive spot imaginable to the greedy gangsters – their pockets. If there wasn't a lull in hostilities then the crime rackets, especially drug trafficking, would continue to suffer big losses. If there was peace then the cops would ease up and forget about them. Then everyone could go back to making a good living. At the time of writing it appears that this glorified peace is holding.

But not everyone was happy with the 'peace pact' – particularly Christy Keane who has been closely monitoring the situation from his prison cell on the E1 Wing in Portlaoise Prison. E1 is home to the men considered to be the country's most dangerous organised crime figures. Despite the fact that it is the country's most secure prison many of the inmates still control their criminal empires from the security of their cells. Keane is kept fully informed of events in the outside world. He cannot comprehend the idea of any let up in the war against the Ryans. He wants vengeance for his dead brother and nothing less. Any kind of peace would be an insult to Keane's fallen sibling. Christy Keane decided to teach his 'peace-loving' partners-in-crime a salutary lesson.

In July 2004, through contacts made in prison, Keane organised a drug deal between the Collopys and a gang based in Finglas, in west Dublin. Like Keane the Finglas mob had connections on E1. When the Collopys travelled to Dublin to collect the drug shipment they were ripped off. The Finglas hoods had no fear of the hard men from Limerick. They stole €30,000 from the Collopys and advised them to "fuck off" back to Limerick before they got hurt. The Collopys could do nothing about the Finglas hoods without the help of Keane's associates in Dublin, who were connected to the INLA and a major cocaine dealer based in County Kildare. Furious about the 'peace pact', Christy Keane wasn't feeling helpful.

The incident caused a major rift between the two crime families. On August 19, 2004 Gardaí arrested two men as they travelled to Christy Keane's home. They found ammunition and a gun that they suspected was to be used in a gun attack on Keane's home. At the time of writing it is unclear if the two families have settled their differences. If they don't Limerick can look forward to a new twist in the bloody feuding.

By October 2004, Limerick was still enjoying a lull in the hostilities between the gangs. The small local Garda force have been spectacularly successful in challenging the mob head on but even they admit that this does not mean that a lasting peace is on the horizon. Owen Treacy, who refused to enter the Witness Protection Programme, is still very much a marked man. Almost two years after he first cheated death, Treacy and his family are still receiving full-time armed police protection. For many years to come he will remain at the top of Limerick's long list of dead men walking. Just in case he forgets the slogans daubed on walls around the working-class ghettos are a constant reminder that it is unlikely that he will die in his sleep as a contented old man. The hatred and thirst for vengeance is unquenchable.

In terms of the Limerick feud and the future it is fair to say that there are people who will be seeking murderous revenge in many years to come who have not even been born yet. A chilling prophecy of what is yet to come was uttered by the ten-year-old-son of one of the protagonists. "When I grow up I am going to get a gun and kill all the Keanes. I won't stop till they're all dead." The hatred is indiscriminate and ruthless. Not even childhood is safe from its poison.

Ten

The Westies

The dog-eared photograph portrays an image of absolute terror. The big burly thug glares through the holes in his balaclava. He hunches over a young woman: in one hand he clasps a large hunting knife to her throat; his other hand holds her head by the hair. His eyes, wide and mad, glare angrily into the camera. His pearly-white teeth are bared in a snarl. He looks like some kind of deranged monster. The cocaine-fuelled madman wears white gloves, combat trousers and a black t-shirt. His arms and chest bulge with muscles puffed up by steroids. This is the chilling face of crime in Ireland's new Millennium.

The image is horrifying. But what makes it even more sinister is the fact that this is the masked man's idea of a bit of fun. In a previous edition reference was made to this woman as his girlfriend. She was not his girlfriend, but his sister. She had no association with the gang and no involvement with its criminal activities. In other pictures from this extraordinary collection, taken sometime in 2000, the knife man poses with his closest friend and fellow psychopath. They push out their chests and flex their muscles, obviously proud of the terrifying image they project.

The hooded friends are among the most feared and dangerous criminals to emerge from the underworld in recent years. Their gang have come to epitomise a new generation – a ruthless gangland brat pack. During a five-year reign of terror in the sordid world of Dublin drug dealing they have terrorised, injured and tortured their way to dominance. They are armed and extremely dangerous and prepared to wipe out anyone, cop or criminal, who stands in their way. Their most prominent members are Shane Coates and Stephen Sugg and the gang itself is better known as The Westies.

One of the most chilling predictions ever made by an Irish criminal came from a member of the once notorious Dunne family in the early 1980s. After the police had successfully smashed the

Dunne family's powerful heroin empire Dunne was being led away to begin a lengthy jail sentence for drug trafficking. Before Dunne disappeared into a prison van, he shouted at the celebrating citizens who surrounded him, delighted that their lives would no longer be plagued by his family's business, and to the groups of reporters: "If you thought we were bad, just wait 'till you see what's coming next." It was probably the only truthful statement the drug dealer ever made.

By the late 1990s organised crime had become an integral component of contemporary Irish life. The young hoods emerging at this time were entering an underworld that had been in existence for twenty years. The public had become cynical about gangland violence and were no longer shocked by the levels of serious crime. In both the law-breaking and law-abiding societies, life had become cheaper than ever. It is the natural order of evolution in the underworld that gangs and godfathers are usurped, jailed and replaced. Current evidence clearly shows that during the past three decades there has been a direct correlation between growing profits from the drug trade and the dramatic increase in the number of gang-related murders. Each new mob has become more violent and callous than the one it blasted out of the way. The Westies gang are among the worst of all. The picture described above could be captioned: "Dunne's prediction was right... We HAVE arrived. Signed The Westies Gang."

* * * *

The man holding the knife in the picture was Shane Julian Coates from Hartstown, West Dublin. Born in 1972, Shane Coates was the second oldest of four brothers and six sisters. Coates' partner-in-crime was Stephen Sugg from the sprawling, working-class Corduff estate in Blanchardstown, also West Dublin. Sugg was five years younger than Coates and very much the second-in-command. The *Sunday World*, the first newspaper to expose the gang's reign of terror, christened them The Westies gang in 2000. In the days before Coates was named in the Irish media the *Sunday World* nicknamed him the 'New Psycho' because of his reputation for extreme violence. The nickname originated from Coates' notorious predecessor PJ Judge otherwise known as The Psycho. When a bullet entered the back of Judge's skull in December 1996 it brought an end to his unparalleled reign of terror. His rise to power had included some of the most gruesome murders in gangland history. Judge had controlled a huge drug dealing empire that stretched across West and North Dublin, supplying hashish, ecstasy, cocaine and heroin. The Westies gang quickly emerged as the most suitable heirs to The Psycho's vacant throne.

Coates and Sugg had been best friends since their early teens. The pair began their criminal careers together, stealing high-powered cars for lethal, so-called, joy-riding escapades. In the company of other young hoods, they began doing smash and grab raids throughout the country, stealing alcohol, cash and cigarettes from pubs and shops around Ireland. Then they moved into armed robbery. From the beginning former neighbours, criminal associates and police, recall that the pair had a natural predisposition to violence. Even as teenagers they had notorious reputations and were feared by other young criminals. One officer who knew the youthful terrors commented: "You could see then that they were both very close and Sugg was greatly influenced by Coates. They had very little fear of anyone and they were very violent."

It wasn't long before Coates and Sugg began to notch up extensive criminal records – for car theft, robbery and violence – and served a number of jail sentences. The pair showed contempt for the courts and the law. On several occasions they absconded while out on bail facing various charges. During a ten-year period from the late 1980s, at least sixteen arrest warrants were issued for Coates due to his failure to attend trials.

The Westies were also involved in a number of feuds with other gangs in which guns were used. In 1990, Coates was shot in the stomach and seriously injured. As a result of the attack he was forced to wear a colostomy bag. Former associates recall that after the shooting Coates was even more determined to prove himself as a ruthless gangster. He took up body-building and rarely drank alcohol. He also became a father in 1994 when his girlfriend had a baby boy. Coates and Sugg continued to operate together. "Coates led Sugg around by the nose. Without Coates, Sugg was nothing," recalled a former associate. Eventually, however, the deadly partners ran into serious trouble with the law.

In April 1995, Coates and Sugg were arrested during an attempted robbery at J and M Meats, at Huntstown Shopping Centre in west Dublin. Police arrested them in possession of sawn-off shotguns just as they were about to do the heist.

Coates and Sugg were convicted in June 1996 and sentenced to five and a half years each for attempted robbery, possession of firearms, ammunition and car theft. In January 1997, Judge Kieran O'Connor reviewed the sentences in the Circuit Criminal Court and decided to give the aspiring mobsters a chance to mend their ways. He suspended the final three years of their sentences. As a strict condition of their release Judge O'Connor ordered the pair to enter a bond not to associate with each other on the outside. This was a clear recognition from the law that Coates and Sugg were considered to be a very dangerous combination. Probation reports handed in to the court suggested that both men stood a better chance of going straight if they were separated. But the dangerous duo had no intention of either quitting crime or breaking up their deadly partnership.

The following July detectives at Blanchardstown Garda Station brought the two criminals back before the courts with proof that they had ignored the non-association order. This time their friendship cost them their liberty. Judge O'Connor re-activated their original sentences and sent them back to jail.

A year later, in July 1998, Coates and Sugg were released by the courts on condition that they be of good behaviour and did not associate. This time they were careful to continue their friendship out of sight of the police. The following December Judge O'Connor suspended the remainder of their sentences and lifted the ban on their association. The two friends were free men.

From the time of their first release from prison in January 1997, Coates and Sugg had begun to establish their criminal empire. By the end of 1996, the criminal underworld was undergoing a major transformation – John Gilligan's gang had been smashed and PJ Judge had been murdered. There was a huge vacuum in the drug trade and The Westies gang seized their opportunity. They used two devices to set up their business – extreme violence and fear. The gang literally took control of the scene with brutal force. Dealers and pushers who were not working for The Westies gang were severely beaten and threatened with death if they didn't shove off or become employees. Addicts were warned that if they didn't deal with The Westies gang then they would be dealing with no one. One addict would later recall: "If you wanted gear [heroin] then you got it from them. If you dealt with anyone else or pushed gear for another dealer then you were looking at a stint in intensive care." Several heroin dealers either moved out of Blanchardstown or began working directly for the gang.

On their release in July 1998, after a year long absence, Coates and Sugg had little difficulty re-establishing themselves in west Dublin. The gang already had good contacts in the UK who supplied their heroin. The two thugs assembled a large gang of young criminals and addicts to run their criminal empire on the streets. Some gang members worked at cutting up the heroin, breaking it down and bagging it into street deals; while other members of the gang acted as couriers and sellers; sellers in turn sold batches of deals onto street pushers.

The gang also did business with a number of other up and coming young drug gangs across Dublin. Gangs in the area who were involved in the distribution of cannabis or ecstasy were forced to pay "tax" to The Westies gang if they wanted to continue walking, breathing and dealing. Coates and Sugg had an inner-circle of other hardened hoods, including Sugg's younger brother Bernard "Verb" Sugg and armed robber Dylan O'Sullivan, who acted as the gang's enforcers. The operation was well-organised, well-equipped and very efficient. In the two years following Coates's and Sugg's release from prison in July 1998, the gang amassed a fortune.

Based on evidence gathered from a number of the gang's street dealers in 1999, Gardaí conservatively estimated that The Westies gang turned over one million pounds in their first year of operation alone. Throughout 1998 and 1999, the gang paid an average of IR£800 for an ounce of heroin. The following example, based on information from one of the gang's bagmen who prepared heroin for sale, gives an insight into how the racket operated. The bagman would cut up an ounce of heroin by diluting it down with other substances, including glucose and curry powder, to maximise profits. Each ounce usually made eighteen batches. Each batch contained fifteen 'Qs': each 'Q' provided a single 'fix', which an addict either injected or smoked. A typical addict would need up to five 'Qs' per day to feed his/her habit, depending on the purity of the heroin. The average street deal has a purity of between fifteen and thirty per cent. At the time a 'Q' sold for IR£20. The Westies gang paid their bagman IR£200 for cutting up the original ounce of 'gear'. Added to the gang's original outlay of IR£800 per ounce this brought their investment up to IR£1,000. An average one-ounce deal made the gangland brat pack over IR£4,000 profit. In the example above the bagman concerned was cutting an average of four ounces every week, giving The Westies gang potential profits of over IR£16,000 a week. This one small part of the operation was turning over almost IR£1million per year. At any one time the gang had six or seven people cutting heroin for them. Some of the bagmen were cutting an ounce every day. Business was booming.

The most prominent gang members split everything they made. Some gang members began buying and selling used cars to launder the money. And they got greedier as the money rolled in. They operated a strict "no credit" policy. A drug addict owing them as much as IR£50 was severely beaten or even mutilated. If a street pusher was suspected of stealing heroin or money for himself he got the same treatment. Anyone suspected of talking to the police got even worse. The Westies gang had no fear of being caught or charged. They were exploiting and terrorising the weakest and most pathetic members of society – young drug addicts.

In a short time the gang were responsible for an astonishing catalogue of brutal attacks on competitors, drug dealers and addicts, who were either encroaching on their turf or owed them money. In one case the gang attacked a thirty-eight-year-old drug addict who was also a mother of nine children. During the incident they used lighted cigarettes to burn the woman's breasts because she owed them IR£500 for heroin. Another female addict had her hair chopped-off, and her home and car were smashed up. In one horrific incident two members of the gang threw a young junkie from a fifth floor balcony in the Ballymun flat complex. He owed them IR£16. Somehow the victim survived the fall and limped away. One pusher had jump leads attached to his nipples while he was tortured and several other pushers were slashed with Stanley blades. On another occasion The Westies gang suspected that an eighteen-year-old drug addict, who sold their heroin to pay for his habit, had ripped them off and was selling drugs for himself. In revenge the gang burned down the home of his innocent parents. Several other pushers and addicts were injured in gun attacks, many of which were never even reported to the police. The Westies gang had brought sheer mayhem to the streets of their old neighbourhood.

The gang's ferocious violence and terror campaign had rendered them untouchable and they seemed to act with impunity. They employed clever anti-surveillance tactics to keep the police off their backs and rarely handled the drugs themselves. One victim, who suffered appalling injuries at the gang's hands, gave this writer an insight into the situation at the time: "Anyone who owes them as much as a pound is liable to be seriously injured or murdered. They are animals. They haven't been caught because everyone is too scared to talk. Most of their victims are just junkies anyway, like me, and they feel that no one gives a shite about them. These boys can do what they like." Drug pushers who worked for The Westies gang often gave information to detectives about the drug operation but none of them would testify in court. As one officer recalled: "Pushers preferred to face the music in court and be jailed rather than give up the gang. It is an example of just how much they are feared."

The Westies gang irrevocably established their fearsome reputation when one of the gang's associates, heroin-dealer Pascal Boland, decided to set up his own operation. The forty-three-year-old father-of-one had been mixed up in the drug business for many years and had been one of PJ Judge's associates. Boland and his gang of runners and pushers were already doing considerable business across Finglas and Ballymun. The huge profits being turned over by The Westies gang tempted Boland to go into business in Blanchardstown. He felt that there was room in the huge West Dublin market for everyone. He began dealing on the gang's patch. Other addicts and dealers warned him to be careful but Boland, who considered himself something of an elder lemon, laughed at The Westies gang. He told friends the gang were "nobodies".

Between October 1998 and January 1999, Boland and his partner, a drug dealer from Finglas, had successfully imported five large shipments of heroin. They had bought it from the same Birmingham contact used by The Westies gang. Like other drug traffickers, Boland used dispensable down-on-their-luck couriers to smuggle heroin concealed in their bodies. Typically the drug is carried in condoms and then either swallowed and excreted later, or concealed in the courier's anus or vagina. Boland operated from his house at Ashcroft Court in Mulhuddart – in the heart of The Westies gang territory.

It didn't take long for the gang to discover what was going on. By this time, beating and torturing debtors and competitors was an everyday chore for members of The Westies gang. With such a sustained level of violence and terror it was impossible for a new competitor to set up shop without them hearing about it. In January 1999 the brat pack found out about Boland's operation. His operation was the first well-organised incursion into their territory. Addicts who owed The Westies gang money began shifting their loyalties to Boland. The gang were having none of it.

Around January 20, 1999, a member of the gang ordered one of the bagmen to contact a drug pusher who was working for Boland. The bagman and the pusher were friends but The Westies' man was too terrified to disobey his bosses. At the time he was "working" for the gang to pay off a debt. One of the gang had threatened to cut his legs off if he didn't do as he was told. The bagman would later reveal: " I was afraid of the gang. They're off their heads. They're capable of chopping your legs off."

Around 8pm that night the bagman lured Boland's pusher into a meeting with The Westies gang. Two gang members took the pusher into a field opposite the graveyard in Mulhuddart, West Dublin. It was snowing and freezing cold. The bagman later told police that he believed his friend was going to be murdered: "I was afraid they were going to kill him [pusher]. They're head cases. They'd shoot you as soon as look at you, they are like wild things. I knew they were mad about him [pusher] selling gear on their patch for Boland. He was my friend but I was fucking terrified of them." The pusher was dragged into the field. One of the gang produced a baseball bat and began beating his victim. The two gang members threatened the pusher until he admitted that he was working for Boland. The pusher was begging for mercy and the beating stopped.

The gang decided to send Boland a message, through the terrified pusher. "Tell Boland that if he doesn't stop selling gear we'll blow his fucking head off," a gang member threatened. He gave the pusher a mobile telephone number and told him to give it to Boland.

The following day, January 21, Boland phoned a prominent member of The Westies gang. The violent young hood repeated his threat to kill Boland if he didn't stop dealing on the gang's patch. Boland was unimpressed and treated the dangerous young criminal with contempt. He told him to "fuck off" and asked him who did he think he was. One of Boland's friends, who overheard the conversation, later revealed that Boland had hurled abuse at The Westies gang: "You're fucking nobodies, now fuck off with yerselves." Pascal Boland had signed his own death warrant.

Over the following days Boland continued to run his operation as usual. In the last weekend in January 1999, Boland and a number of associates flew to Birmingham to buy a Stg£20,000 consignment of heroin. A member of the travelling community in west Dublin was paid to bring the stuff back into Ireland, secreted in his body. Meanwhile, two of The Westies gang were keeping tabs on Boland's movements. The gang wanted to have a word with Boland in person. The West Dublin brat pack had collected and stolen a large arsenal of shotguns and handguns to protect their operation and were known to arm themselves.

On the evening of January 27, Boland arrived back as his home at Ashcroft Court around 8pm. He was getting out of his car when a man stepped out from the shadows. The man confronted Boland and repeated the earlier warnings about dealing on The Westies gang's patch. Boland laughed in the man's face and a gun was produced. The two men began scuffling. Eleven shots were fired at Boland, seven of which hit him in the body. The man then ran to a stolen getaway car which drove towards Mulhuddart Village. Boland, who had been hit in the stomach and chest, collapsed and died at the front door of his home. The car was dumped and a failed attempt was made to set it on fire.

Within twenty-four hours of the murder, the Gardaí in Blanchardstown knew who their main suspects were – The Westies gang made no secret of their dirty work. They wanted people to know that they meant business. In Blanchardstown Garda Station a major murder investigation was set-up. The local detective units had been aware of the gang's existence but this was their first opportunity to launch a full investigation into The Westies gang's operation.

In an incident room at Blanchardstown Garda Station a section of the wall became a picture gallery of gang members. It also included graphs and tables that illustrated the connections between the various gangsters. Within a few months the wall was completely covered with material. "The sheer size of the operation and the number of people involved was unbelievable," revealed one of the investigating officers. Several members of the gang were arrested and questioned. During swoops, street pushers and bagmen were arrested and charged with drug offences. A large amount of heroin and other drugs were recovered. When detectives arrested one gang member, suspected of participating in the Boland murder, he was asked if he was afraid of the leaders of the gang: "Yeah everybody is. They're mental. They beat you and they'd kill you. They've no fear of anybody. They think they're bullet-proof." In interviews with investigators, the people arrested gave graphic and detailed descriptions of The Westies gang's operation. The Garda team began compiling a list of attacks that they could trace directly back to the gang. No one, however, was prepared to give a signed statement. A few years in a prison cell was a much better option than a plot in a nearby graveyard or a prolonged stay in an intensive care ward.

In the first few months following the Boland murder, the gang had scaled down their heroin dealing operation as they waited for the Garda heat to die down. But it hadn't dissuaded them from attacking and torturing people who owed them money or who they suspected of talking to the police. A young man and woman, both heroin addicts, had witnessed the attack on Boland and had openly told people that they could identify the killer. Over the following months, the couple were attacked and severely beaten by members of The Westies gang.

As the investigation continued the gang conducted witch-hunts among their dealers. In early March 1999, one gang member arranged to have a particular suspect lured to the home of another drug pusher. Shortly after the suspect arrived at the house members of The Westies gang appeared and brought the hapless addict into the kitchen. On previous occasions, this particular suspect had helped the gang attack other rogue dealers, including his friends. Now it was his turn for punishment. The Westies gang had no favourites. They accused the terrified addict of stealing heroin from them. "I didn't, I didn't," he pleaded. One gang member produced a pair of vice grips and grabbed two of the pusher's fingers with it. Then he tightened the grips, as the pusher screamed with pain and begged for mercy. The junkie denied that he had ripped them off. After a while they accepted his answer but the gang members then demanded that he get money for them. If he didn't produce cash within a few days then the next time he would not get off so easy.

The Westies gang were growing increasingly paranoid, as the police stepped up the heat on their operation. The drug addict, who had set up his friend for the 'vice grips' torture was next to fall foul of the gang. The addict had been spotted talking to a detective and members of the gang gave him a severe beating, smashing his teeth in the process. Sometime later when the addict was questioned, as part of the ongoing murder investigation, he told officers about setting up his friend for the 'vice grip' torture: "He was roaring with pain. When they took the vice grips off his hand you could see the marks of them on his fingers. I set him up. I told him later that I was sorry. He knows that I did it through fear. He did it to other mates for the same reason. Then they see me talking to a copper and they give me a terrible beating. That's why I want to get out of this fucking mess."

The Westies gang's campaign of terror continued. This time the unfortunate target was eighteen-year-old Paul Dempsey from Sheephill Green in Blanchardstown. Dempsey's 'crime' was that he had been going out with Stephen Sugg's younger sister, sixteen-year-old Frances. Dempsey had also gone out with one of Sugg's former girlfriends while the drug baron was doing time. The dangerous hoodlum had threatened to kill Paul Dempsey if he didn't stop going out with Frances. The threats were surprising considering Sugg was a close friend of Paul Dempsey's older brother, Robert. The two friends had gone to school together and had later served time together in prison.

In March 1999, Paul Dempsey approached Sugg and asked if he could resume his relationship with Frances. But Sugg was having none of it. "Will you fuck off out of my sight or I will blow your fucking head off," Sugg replied. The love-struck teenager was well aware that Sugg did not make idle threats and he stopped going out with Frances Sugg. The separation, however, did not last long and Paul Dempsey's heart overruled his sense of self-preservation. He later told police: "But after that we got back together because we were mad about each other. Since then Sugg has been looking for me." Dempsey was forced to go into hiding, as some of gangland's most dangerous men were hunting him. In an effort to lure Dempsey out of hiding, two members of The Westies gang abducted one of Paul Dempsey's friends. They dragged the friend from his van, wrapped jump leads around his neck, and bundled him into their car. They drove to a country back road and forced the friend to ring Dempsey. They told him to arrange a meeting with Dempsey near Dublin airport. The gang were planning an ambush. However, Paul Dempsey got suspicious and refused to go. The two gang members then dumped Dempsey's friend out of the car and tried to drag him along the road with the jump leads still wrapped around his neck. Fortunately the leads slipped off and Dempsey's friend survived.

Over the following months, as Dempsey remained in hiding, the investigation continued to uncover astonishing information about The Westies gang. The amount of information revealed prompted the man in charge of detective units in the Garda Western Division, Detective Superintendent Tony Sourke, to establish a specially designated team to target the notorious gang. Two vastly experienced serious crime investigators, Detective Inspector Todd O'Loughlin and Detective Inspector John Mulligan, assisted Detective Superintendent Sourke.

In October 1999, the special Garda unit was set up at Blanchardstown Garda Station to target the gang. Investigators working on Boland's murder had complied a list of forty serious attacks carried out by The Westies gang in just over a year. The gang had used guns, baseball bats, knives, broken bottles, batons, iron bars, jump leads and even vice grips on their victims. And these were only the incidents the cops knew about. Senior officers attached to the team acknowledged that there had been many more attacks. The victims were approached and asked if they wished to press charges. No one was prepared to make a complaint. The gang had successfully built a wall of silence around their operation. None of the terrified victims would dare to testify against them.

At the height of The Westies gang's unprecedented campaign of violence the Garda officer in overall charge of the police investigation, Chief Superintendent John McLoughlin, launched an equally unprecedented public campaign against them. Cops seldom speak publicly about their targets but in a newspaper interview Chief Superintendent McLoughlin summed up the police's frustration when he angrily declared: "They've been involved in stabbings, slashings and shootings. They put vice grips on a fella's thumb. They're unbelievable. They're evil. I would love to see them on a [charge] sheet with Garda evidence. We've got to nail them."

The Westies gang, however, were not offended by their growing reputation or even very worried by the increased attentions of the police. They revelled in it – seeing it as an achievement – and continued to operate as normal. Far from concerning themselves with the mounting Garda investigation in October 1999, the gang's main focus seemed to be pursuing the vendetta against Paul Dempsey. At 4.30am, on the morning of October 7, 1999, the gang made their next move. Sugg, Coates, Dylan O'Sullivan and the rest of the gang burst through the front door of the Dempsey's family home, armed with a sawn-off shotgun, an iron bar and a baseball bat. O'Sullivan had been living with the two gangsters since his release from prison the previous April. He had served just six months of a three-year stretch for two armed robberies. Inside the house Dempsey's father, Con, heard the noise first and confronted the thugs. He was beaten to the ground and kept prisoner by Sugg while the other gang members ran upstairs to find Paul Dempsey. Robert Dempsey, Sugg's old friend, came out of his room to see what all the commotion was about. O'Sullivan hit Robert with an iron bar, ordering him to "stay in the fucking room". He smashed one of Robert's knees. At the same time one of his accomplices was trying to break into Paul Dempsey's bedroom, shouting, "He's in here," as Paul Dempsey tried to keep him out.

The following is Paul Dempsey's account of what happened next: "I tried my best to keep them out. I caught a scaffolding pole they were using to open the door and held it so they couldn't swing it at me. Then the door swung open and I saw two fellas rushing in the door. One of them had a gun in his hand. When I saw the gun I jumped onto the bed. The guy with the bar stood holding it towards me. The fella with the gun loaded one bullet into the gun. When the fella with the gun put the bullet into the gun he closed it. Then he pointed it at me and told me to 'stay easy'. I was standing on my bed and screaming my head off. I was terrified; I thought I was going to be shot dead. Then the fella with the gun fired one shot which hit me in the back of my right thigh. I was jumping around the bed when he fired the shot. I was shouting, 'Please stop, please stop'. After he fired the first shot I fell onto the bed. Then he fired a second shot and hit me on my right calf muscle and blew my leg to pieces. I didn't move any more. I couldn't believe what was happening. I looked down at my leg and it was destroyed. The two fellas ran out of my room and downstairs. I was screaming, 'I'm shot, ring an ambulance'. I was in agony. I wasn't sure if me leg was gone or not."

Paul Dempsey suffered serious leg injuries in the attack and was hospitalised for several days. Despite the fact that their attackers were wearing balaclavas, the Dempsey boys instantly recognised them. They were adamant that Coates was involved and that O'Sullivan beat Robert with the iron bar. They gave detailed statements to the police and said they were willing to give evidence in court. It was a major breakthrough for the investigation team.

Meanwhile the violence continued. Two nights later two members of The Westies gang shot and injured two doormen at the Red Cow Inn on the Naas Road in Dublin. The incident resulted from a row in the nightclub, Club Diva, during which prominent members of the gang were thrown out. Neither of the doormen was seriously injured in the attack.

* * * *

Derek "Smiley" McGuinness from Corduff Park in Blanchardstown was a typical example of the addicts working for The Westies gang. By the time he was twenty-eight years old he had been a chronic heroin user for half his miserable life. McGuinness, who was also a father-of-three, was a habitual criminal. He carried out robberies and sold heroin to feed his habit. For two years he had been selling batches of 'gear' for the gang until they accused him of owing them IR£200. Members of The Westies gang had been haunting McGuinness for months, demanding the money. "Smiley" did his best to stay out of the gang's way. He later explained to this writer why he owed them the money: "It was for heroin I used myself instead of selling for them. The stuff they sold was so badly cut that you couldn't get a hit off it anyway. But I would have paid that money to them only for the fact that on my son's Confirmation Day they drove up and attacked me outside the church. On a point of principal after that I told them to fuck off because I could have paid them the money." When I asked "Smiley" McGuinness how he had planned to get the money he candidly replied: "I was going to steal it, how else do you think I was going to get it?"

Two members of The Westies gang, Andrew Allen and Herman "the Vermin" White were told to keep watch for McGuinness. They were instructed to find McGuinness and hold him until Sugg and Coates got there. Both Allen and White were aged twenty-one and in the same trap as practically every other heroin abuser in Blanchardstown at the time. They were effectively The Westies gang's slaves, 'working' to feed their drug habits and terrified of their two lethal bosses.

Around 2.30pm on the afternoon of October 20, 1999, "Smiley" McGuinness was walking through Corduff Park when he bumped into Allen and White. He knew the two men and had no reason to be afraid of them. McGuinness walked and talked with his fellow junkies. Suddenly, without any warning, White produced an iron bar and hit McGuinness hard across the head and face, knocking him to the ground in the process. White repeatedly hit McGuinness in the face with the bar as he lay on the ground, smashing his nose and his teeth. At the same time Allen phoned Coates on his mobile. Allen was delighted to be in a position to please his lunatic boss. "We have 'Smiley' here. Do you want to come up and deal with him now?" he asked the monster on the other end of the line. But the New Psycho could not make it to the park. Allen came up with another idea for his boss's entertainment. "Here listen to this," said Allen, as he placed the phone on the ground beside McGuinness' head. Then the two thugs began kicking and beating "Smiley" with the iron bar. Coates wanted to hear McGuinness scream for mercy.

In the meantime Stephen Sugg had arrived in the park, armed with a Stanley knife. He joined in the torture, slashing "Smiley's" ear, the back of his head and the full length of his left jaw. Sugg sliced his victim's left hand, from between his thumb and forefinger back up to his wrist. When they'd finally had enough the three men walked away, leaving McGuinness in a bloodied heap on the ground. Somehow McGuinness managed to make his way home where his girlfriend called an ambulance. The drug addict lost nine pints of blood in the attack and spent several days in intensive care: both sides of his jaw were broken, all his teeth were smashed and he received over sixty stitches for the appalling knife wounds. "The doctors told me that my jaw was so badly broken that it was literally held together by the skin. They nearly killed me," McGuinness told this writer, after the attack. After his miraculous recovery, however, "Smiley" had had enough of The Westies gang's brutality. He identified his attackers to the police and gave the Gardaí a full statement.

After almost nine months of intensive investigation it appeared that the team targeting the gang were making progress. They had successfully identified everyone involved in the organisation and knew the truth about several of The Westies gang's crimes. The unit had arrested and charged several of the gang's runners and dealers and seized large quantities of heroin in the process. Unfortunately, none of that was of any consequence when people were too scared to co-operate with the police to help put the main players away. But now, with the Dempsey family and "Smiley" McGuinness, it seemed that the two criminals, Sugg and Coates, had finally crossed the line. By October the spiral of violence was also making media headlines and the public were demanding action. The *Sunday World* published a two-page investigation into the gang's activities and it was followed by a number of public meetings organised in Blanchardstown by community groups. Coates and Sugg actually turned up at one of the meetings in an attempt to intimidate the people attending. Detective Superintendent Sourke and Detective Inspector Mulligan decided that they had enough hard evidence to bring serious charges against both men and Dylan O'Sullivan. If all three men were remanded in custody the Gardaí believed that they stood a real chance of restoring some sense of calm across West Dublin. In turn they thought this would help them to build other criminal cases against The Westies gang.

The Gardaí made their move a few days later. The investigation team, supported by the Emergency Response Unit, arrested Stephen Sugg, Shane Coates and Dylan O'Sullivan for questioning about the Boland murder and the attack on McGuinness. The three thugs were then charged with a number of serious incidents, including the McGuinness attack and the Dempsey shooting. They were remanded in custody to Mountjoy Prison. While O'Sullivan was being questioned, he admitted that he had taken part in the Dempsey shooting and he identified Sugg and Coates as his accomplices. The charges had come just in time. Members of The Westies gang had already begun intimidating the Dempseys and other potential witnesses to the Boland murder. Sugg, Coates and O'Sullivan were also charged with assaulting two addicts.

At the same time Allen and White were also arrested. During his detention Allen was asked why McGuinness had been attacked. "Listen that was his own fault," he replied. "He is a stupid cunt. He owed them for gear for ages. I told him ages ago to sort it out or he would be smashed up. I gave him one box, I didn't want to get the virus [HIV]." At the time of his arrest Allen was found in possession of around IR£2,000 worth of heroin. He later helped detectives locate a sawn-off shotgun and another quantity of heroin. He told officers that the drugs and the gun belonged to Coates and Sugg. Allen and White were charged with the McGuinness attack and Allen was also charged with possession of heroin.

In the meantime the investigation team continued their efforts to build a drug trafficking case against the notorious gang. Fourteen people had been arrested and questioned. With the hoods finally behind bars people were not as afraid of giving the police information. The success of the case depended on keeping Coates and Sugg off the streets and out of harm's way. Detective Superintendent Sourke sent urgent reports to the DPP's office urging that the State fight any attempts by the two criminals to get bail. He also urged the DPP to give priority to other investigation files on The Westies gang's criminal activities, with a view to preferring other charges. In one report the Detective Superintendent recommended: "I am fearful that should either Shane Coates,

Stephen Sugg or Dylan O'Sullivan gain release from prison that the safety of our witnesses will be severely jeopardised. My concerns are that should they be released, they will then flee the jurisdiction and more sinisterly, be in a position to organise and control the intimidation of our witnesses from abroad."

The investigation team also began exploring the prospect of placing some of their witnesses in the Witness Protection Programme or, at the very least, moving them to an undisclosed location where they could not be contacted. But the cops were fighting an uphill battle. Most of the victims and witnesses were drug abusers and could therefore not be relied on to see the case and their testimony through to trial. As one member of the investigation team explained: "We had compiled a huge amount of intelligence and hard evidence in the form of statements from victims and drug pushers working for the gang. But in the back of everyone's mind was the reality that all these people could be got at and easily intimidated. Drug addicts are more vulnerable than most people in society. In the end the only thing they really worry about in the world is where the next fix is coming from and it usually comes from people like The Westies gang."

At the same time the Criminal Assets Bureau (CAB) were called in to investigate the gang's money trail. Armed with the intelligence obtained by the Blanchardstown investigation and the various statements from pushers working for the gang, the CAB succeeded in obtaining interim tax assessments on Coates and Sugg for over IR£100,000 each. Even if the witnesses did not testify against the two thugs the CAB could still use their financial information to support the case. The figure was based on The Westies gang's drug earnings in the year 1998 to 1999. By Autumn 2003, together with interest and further assessments that figure had risen to around €500,000 each.

With the feared crime bosses still stuck behind bars the sense of peace and calm continued on the streets of West Dublin. That peace held even when Stephen Sugg was released on bail in March 2000. Dylan O'Sullivan also received bail but immediately went on the run for fear of his life. His former pals had discovered that he had co-operated with the police and had vowed to kill him. At the time of writing O'Sullivan is still in hiding and wanted by the police. Coates was not given bail and would spend fourteen months on remand. Without Coates, Sugg was considered relatively harmless. Together, however, they were still extremely dangerous.

But then, in October 2000, the investigating Gardaí discovered that their cases against Coates and Sugg were in jeopardy. The inevitable had happened. When the Dempseys were called to testify in the trial they developed sudden amnesia and said that they could not identify the attackers. "Smiley" McGuinness was also struck by memory loss and would not testify against Sugg. Coates was released from custody. The most prominent members of the Westies gang – one of the most dangerous mobs in gangland – were back in business.

"Smiley" McGuinness, however, did proceed with his evidence against gang members, Andrew Allen and Herman "the Vermin" White. On November 27, 2000, they both pleaded guilty to the attack in the Circuit Criminal Court. Allen also pleaded guilty to possessing IR£2,000 worth of heroin. Detective Sergeant Liam Kelly and Detective Garda John Baxter from Blanchardstown gave evidence of the attack and of the two gang member's backgrounds. Defence counsel told the court that both men had been forced to attack McGuinness because of their relationship with " a major drug dealer" and that the drug dealer had inflicted the worst wounds on McGuinness. Judge Elizabeth Dunne jailed White and Allen for four and a half years and said that the attack was " …as bad an offence as one could commit.". Allen received a concurrent four-year term for the heroin charge. Both men had declined to give evidence against Sugg in the case.

By the end of 2000, The Westies gang were in a jubilant mood. The gang's reign of terror had paid off. The photograph described at the beginning of this chapter was taken during a party to 'celebrate' the gang's victory over the law. Coates and Sugg were more confident than ever but they had been badly mauled by the police. The gang had lost at least IR£500,000 worth of drugs and also several firearms which had been seized in Garda swoops. Several gang members were behind bars and the CAB was on their tails. Plus, despite the setbacks, the investigation team stepped up the pressure. The Westies gang decided to hit back, by attacking a member of the investigation team.

In early 2001, the gang targeted one of the senior officers co-ordinating the ongoing investigation. The officer, who was based at Blanchardstown Garda Station was secretly followed to his home, his health club and to a number of social occasions. In the early hours of a March morning, a uniformed Garda patrol from Rathfarnham station stopped Sugg, Coates and another associate in a car not far from the officer's home where he lived with his wife and young children. Some time earlier a concerned neighbour had spotted the men acting suspiciously at the back of the Garda officer's home. The disturbing discovery sparked a major investigation. Senior officers told the media that they were treating the development "very seriously". The officer and his family were given armed protection for several months. The Westies gang had upped the stakes in their war with the police.

A week after the incident at the Garda officer's home, Coates was brought to Blanchardstown Garda Station, on suspicion of drunk driving. Coates was anxious to let the uniformed officers know exactly whom it was they had taken in. It was the first encounter the two young Gardaí had had with the hoodlum. The drink test proved negative. As Coates was leaving the station he asked the officers if they knew his reputation. The two cops, who had only recently been posted to the area, knew nothing about his criminal pedigree. Coates smirked and told them: "You'll get to know me all right... I am an evil bastard."

* * * *

Jeffrey Mitchell from Monasterboice Road in Crumlin, South Dublin, was an armed robber and drug dealer. Mitchell met Coates and Sugg while he was serving a sentence for armed robbery. When he was released from prison in 1999, at the age of twenty-seven, Mitchell got heavily involved in heroin dealing and worked closely with The Westies gang. But the relationship turned dangerously sour when the mobsters fell out over money. One of Mitchell's street dealers, twenty-two-year-old drug addict Neil Hanlon, from Crumlin, lost a consignment of Mitchell's heroin. The armed robber had bought the drugs on credit from a wholesale heroin supplier, who also supplied The Westies gang. The wholesaler demanded that Mitchell pay for the lost drugs and when he refused heroin supplier asked The Westies gang for help.

In June 2001, two members of the gang burst into Mitchell's home, armed with handguns, and tried to shoot their former partner. Mitchell managed to escape, uninjured, through a rear window, as two hoods fired a number of shots in his direction. In a fit of frustration the gangsters shot Mitchell's dog before leaving the house. Mitchell went to ground.

Two months later, in August 2001, the situation escalated. On August 11, members of The Westies gang raided a flat on Brabazon Square in south Dublin. Mitchell was using it as a safe house to count his drug money. A short time earlier Mitchell had actually left the flat with over IR£200,000 in cash which the gang had intended to steal. They interrogated one of Mitchell's associates who lived in the flat with his girlfriend. During the attack the victim was severely beaten and stabbed and he later he received forty stitches. A gun was also held to his girlfriend's mouth. In a subsequent interview the injured man admitted to Gardaí that he knew who had attacked him but that they had phoned him and apologised for the incident. They claimed that he had been beaten by "mistake" and their real target was Mitchell. The associate refused to make a formal complaint.

Following the incident, Jeffrey Mitchell accused Neil Hanlon of giving The Westies gang information about the flat and about his movements on the night of the attack. On the evening of September 29, 2001, Neil Hanlon left his family home at Downpatrick Road in Crumlin. The troubled drug addict, who had made several attempts to kick his habit, was never seen alive again. It wasn't until February 2002 that Gardaí discovered his remains in a shallow grave in a park in Crumlin. A medical examination later found that the tragic young man had been mutilated at the time of his death. Information was then received that Hanlon had been drugged and then murdered by two drug dealers associated with Mitchell's gang.

Back in Blanchardstown The Westies gang's campaign of terror continued unabated. In November 2001, the gang were again the suspects behind a horrific attack on a thirty-four-year-old woman who had been having an ongoing row with a gang member's sister. The woman, who also lived in Corduff Estate, was abducted and

beaten by three men using baseball bats. She suffered smashed
kneecaps, broken legs and ribs and extensive internal bleeding.
Armed Gardaí protected the woman while she was being treated in
intensive care. Later she informally identified her attackers but was
too terrified to make a complaint. She told officers she feared that
she would be murdered along with the rest of her family. The
investigation was dropped.

A few weeks later, as 2001 drew to a close, shots were fired
into the homes of two heroin addicts in the area who owed The
Westies gang money. Detectives intercepted and arrested three gang
members as they were about to carry out a third gun attack. The
intended target was a relative of the late General, Martin Cahill.
After they were arrested one of the men admitted that they had
been ordered to hold the drug addict down and "blow his feet off"
with a sawn-off shotgun.

The drug business continued to prosper and, for several months,
The Westies gang were busy and faded out of view. In addition to
their drug-dealing activities the gang began a lucrative "steal to
order" racket, robbing high performance cars and selling them to
corrupt car dealers. Their modus operandi was to break into houses
with high-powered cars parked outside and to simply steal the keys
and drive off. To avoid being stopped by police in the stolen car
gang members would drive ahead in a legally owned vehicle so
that they could warn the car behind if they saw the Gardaí. They
also used scanners to listen in on the Garda radio frequencies.

In November 2001, Gardaí in north Dublin were alerted to the
fact that The Westies gang were operating in their area. At the time
a bulletin circulated to all units in the region contained a stark
warning for officers coming into contact with members of the gang:
"These individuals are extremely violent and have access to firearms.
They will attack Gardaí if they think they can get away with it.
They are not to be approached if a member [Garda] is on his or her
own. Do not use radio contact with base," the bulletin warned.

The Westies gang were back in the news again in February
2002 when the *Sunday World* ran an interview with Jeffrey Mitchell.
After the discovery of Hanlon's body Mitchell admitted that he was
a suspect for Hanlon's murder but denied that he had anything to
do with it. He refused to talk about the attempt on his life by members

of The Westies gang in June 2001. Mitchell just wanted to put the record straight after another of his former partners-in-crime, twenty-two-year-old Dave McCreevy, was shot dead outside his home in Tallaght, on February 3. McCreevy had been arrested with over €150,000 worth of Mitchell's heroin the previous November. Dave McCreevy was suspected of admitting to detectives that he was involved with Mitchell. Ironically McCreevy was shot dead a week before the discovery of Hanlon's body. Mitchell commented at the time: "I may rob banks and sell drugs but I don't go around killing people, especially me friends." As the McCreevy murder investigation progressed detectives discovered that Mitchell and The Westies gang had "sorted out" their differences over the gun attack the summer before. The gang were among the prime suspects for carrying out the McCreevy murder. In gangland, relationships and allegiances are as changeable as the Irish weather. No one was ever charged with the murder. Mitchell has since been convicted of a number of serious crimes, including armed robbery.

As the unrelenting violence continued both underworld and Garda sources were even more amazed that no other gangs had taken on The Westies gang. The gang's brutal rampage to control the drugs trade had left them with no scarcity of enemies. But their record of immunity was about to change.

In April 2002, Bernard "Verb" Sugg, Stephen Sugg's younger brother, was admitted to hospital, suffering from a gunshot wound to the stomach. When Gardaí went to the hospital to investigate Sugg was aggressive and refused to co-operate. It later emerged that he had been shot in a laneway near Corduff Shopping Centre. No suspect was ever identified for the attack.

In late 2002, Shane Coates was convicted and jailed on a number of road traffic offences. While he was off the streets a rival gang decided to take on the dreaded Westies. On February 3, 2003, Stephen Sugg had a narrow escape as he got into his car at his home in Corduff. A hit man opened fire on him with a machine gun and a total of eleven shots were fired at Sugg in the assassination bid. A week later Sugg left the country and went into hiding in Alicante in Spain. He joined up with three other fugitive gang members who were living in a private villa.

A few weeks later, Coates was released from prison and the

shooting started again. He moved to live near Navan in County
Meath, from where he continued to control his criminal organisation.
Gardaí suspected that the dangerous thug and his mob had been
responsible for a post office robbery in Navan and the hi-jacking of
a van near Slane. Then in April a small-time drug dealer, Paul Ryan
from north Dublin, was shot in the back of the head as he relieved
himself on the side of a country road near Birr, County Offaly. Ryan
owed a dealer €30,000 for drugs that had been seized by the Gardaí.
In the subsequent murder investigation one line of enquiry suggested
that the drug dealer had "sold" Ryan's debt to The Westies gang. In
another feud with a rival drug gang in April one of the gang's drug
couriers was ambushed and shot in the foot. The following night a
member of the rival gang was shot in retaliation. More trouble was
brewing.

For the first time The Westies gang were being challenged by a
rival gang who had no intentions of backing down. This outfit were
every bit as ruthless as the West Dublin thugs. They sent word to
the gang that the tit-for-tat shootings would continue. The Westie
gang's response was to tool up for war by re-stocking their arsenal
of firearms.

On the morning of May 16, 2003, a gang of four armed and
masked men broke into the home of a registered firearms dealer in
Coney Hill near Balbriggan in north County Dublin. A gun was
held to the dealer's head as his terrified family were bundled into a
room, where they were tied up and locked in. The raiders made off
with twenty-six shotguns and stole the family's four-wheel drive
jeep.

Garda intelligence had already located a vacant holiday home
near Virginia, County Cavan, that The Westies gang were using as
a base to stockpile their weapons. Undercover officers and members
of the Emergency Response Unit (ERU) were sent to the area to
back up officers investigating the Balbriggan robbery case. On
searching the house they found an arsenal of twenty-one handguns,
shotguns, rifles, sawn-off shotguns and more than 1,000 rounds of
ammunition hidden throughout the house. Gardaí later described
the cache as "frightening". A digital camera, recovered at the scene,
contained photographs of the gang members posing for pictures
with their firearms. When it came to cameras the gang could not

help themselves. The ERU slipped back out of view and lay in wait for the gang to turn up. Unfortunately cutbacks in Garda overtime dictated that by Monday, May 19, most of the ERU and surveillance officers were pulled out of the area and brought back to Dublin. The various units involved could not agree whose budget would be used to pay for the operation. It was a typical example of the ludicrous cutbacks in Irish law enforcement and their impact on day-to-day policing.

Shortly after 10pm on May 19 a member of the public, who had spotted suspicious activity near the house, alerted the Gardaí in Virginia. Subsequent events seem to suggest that the local officers were unaware of the ongoing undercover operation. A lone unarmed Garda went to investigate the neighbour's report. He noticed a broken window at the rear of the house and moved in to have a closer look. While he was investigating five gang members arrived and demanded to know who he was. When it emerged that he was a Garda and he wanted to know who they were, the men tried to bundle him into the back of their car at gunpoint. As Garda reinforcements arrived one member of the gang opened fire. An armed detective returned fire, hitting Coates twice in the leg. But in the darkness the feared gangster managed to escape across the fields. It was later understood that his injuries were treated by a doctor before he slipped out of the country to join Stephen Sugg in Spain. Gardaí have since confirmed that they wanted to interview Coates about the arms cache, the shooting in Cavan and the raid on the gun dealer's home in Balbriggan.

In a number of follow-up searches detectives in County Meath and Dublin recovered five stolen high performance cars, computers and camera equipment. In a search of an apartment used by Coates in Navan, they found evidence that he had even been involved in the theft of four rare parrots from Grove Gardens mini-zoo, near Navan, two weeks earlier. Two of the birds were recovered in the search and a third, a cockatoo called Cocky, was later found in Kinnegad, County Westmeath. Coates had released Cocky into the wild.

With Shane Coates and Stephen Sugg holed up in Spain, Bernard "Verb" Sugg took over the reins of The Westies gang's operation. Although "Verb" Sugg had no serious convictions for crime he was well-known to the Gardaí and local people also knew him well, as one of the gang's main enforcers. He was, in the words of one detective who knew him: "Violent, monosyllabic, thick and full of himself." Sugg did not drink much and was into body-building. He was a violent thug who helped to control the drug, robbery and protection rackets across West Dublin. He collected around €1,500 in protection money in Blanchardstown each week. He was also involved in several attacks on rival gangsters and errant drug addicts. Police suspected that it was a rival drug gang who had shot and injured "Verb" Sugg in April 2002. The feared mobster had no scarcity of enemies. It was almost inevitable that he would be targeted by hit men a second time around.

The twenty-three-year-old hoodlum worked as a doorman at the Brookwood Inn around the corner from his home in Corduff. He was the perfect bouncer as the locals were all afraid of him. One drinker later recalled how Sugg even dominated the TV in the pub, insisting that it was on MTV when he was there. "Nobody was allowed or would dare to change it," the drinker said. Around 10.30pm, on Sunday, August 17, 2003, a masked man calmly walked into the Brookwood Inn and headed for the area where Sugg was sitting with his friends. It wasn't hard to locate him. He always sat with the rest of The Westies gang and their hangers-on, to the left just inside the front door. At the time there were about 140 people in the pub. The hit man pulled a pistol from his jacket and fired nine shots at Sugg as he sat at a table. Two bullets hit "Verb" Sugg in the chest before he dived to the ground. Screaming customers fled for cover as Sugg crawled along the floor to escape but he was too late. He was pronounced dead an hour later. The gangland murder was well-planned and efficient. The hit man had been covered by at least two other armed men, who had stood inside and outside the main entrance, and a fourth man who was waiting in a dark-coloured getaway car. The prime suspects for the murder are a gang centred on "The Penguin's" former protégé from Donaghmeade in North Dublin, who is now a major drug baron.

Death had finally come to The Westies gang and the only people who seemed surprised were the gang members themselves. Stephen Sugg turned up in Blanchardstown for his brother's funeral which took place on the following Thursday morning. It was a relatively small affair with only close associates and family members present. Even some of The Westies gang's victims turned up pay their respects. One wag reckoned that they really came to make sure that "Verb" Sugg was dead. The Gardaí, who had been on the trail of the gang for the past five years, turned out in large numbers to keep watch in case Coates turned up at the graveside. He didn't. But a week later an off-duty Garda spotted him in Dunshauglin, County Meath. Coates was definitely back in Ireland.

In the days after the murder of "Verb" Sugg the talk in west Dublin was of revenge. There was no doubt that more blood would be spilt on the streets of gangland. By August 2003, "Verb" Sugg was the sixteenth gangland murder victim in Ireland that year. Sugg's death, and the retaliation that follows, will inevitably push the chilling death toll even higher. A detective working on the case certainly believes that the killing isn't over. "I have been investigating these guys for a long time and there is no way they will take this lying down. The only question now is when will the next murder take place," he said.

On the streets of Corduff even the young children know that the story of The Westies gang is far from over. A thirteen-year-old boy, who was standing at the police cordon around the scene of the crime, excitedly exclaimed: "It's going to be like World War Three around here now."

Six months later, in January 2004, while speculation continued about what would happen next there was to be a totally unexpected twist in the story of the Westies.

The sun-kissed province on the Costa Blanca has, through the years, become the main European hub for several of Europe's toughest criminal organisations. The Mediterranean paradise had become particularly popular with Irish criminals and terrorists who preferred it to Marbella and the Costa del Sol. Coates and Sugg had had no difficulty establishing a criminal base in Alicante when they fled there in 2003. The two violent partners loved the place and at that stage planned to stay put. From the town of Torrevieja several major Irish criminals organised huge drugs and arms shipments to Ireland and the UK. Behind the peaceful appearance of the area, criminals had made it their corporate headquarters in the sun. The Westies worked closely in Alicante with UK crime gangs, Northern

Ireland Loyalist gangs, INLA and IRA members, Moroccans and the Russian Mafia. Hundreds of millions of Euro in drug cash were ploughed into property and bars in Alicante where few questions were asked by the authorities. From there it was easy to set up major deals and organise transport home without taking any major risks.

In December one of the Westies' main partners, Liam Judge, the drug trafficker boyfriend of John Gilligan's daughter Tracy, had suddenly died from a heart attack. There is speculation that as a result of Judge's death the Westies decided not to pay over money they owed Judge for a shipment of drugs. The drugs had originated from Moroccan and Russian gangs but Sugg and Coates showed no fear of the "foreign" hard men. They had forgotten one thing – in Dublin they were big fish in a small pond where they could terrorise everyone including police but in Alicante they were nobodies. Sugg and Coates were operating in a very large pond with people whose reputations were notorious throughout the world for causing pain and death; people who, when it came to violence, could make the Westies gang look like a pack of choirboys.

On the evening of January 31, 2004, the two thugs told their girlfriends they were going to a meeting and would be back later. They drove off in a €140,000 Mercedes. Later that night the apartment they had been renting was broken into and a Porsche car one of them owned was taken away. By the time of writing this updated edition of *Crime Lords* there has not been any further trace of either of them.

The disappearance of Sugg and Coates has become one of gangland's blood-curdling mysteries and there has been much speculation about what has happened to them since they vanished, particularly in the media. For many news organisations it was the first time that they were prepared to actually name the pair although they, and their activities, had been exposed in the *Sunday World* and in *Crime Lords*. Speculation and gossip have also been rife in the criminal world about their fate. There are four likely scenarios in relation to what happened. The first is that both of them were taken away, possibly by a Moroccan or Russian gang who were not impressed by their bully boy tactics, murdered and then buried in unmarked graves. The second popularly held belief is that they were kidnapped and then one of them, Coates, was later murdered and buried somewhere in Spain. Sugg, according to the same theory, escaped and is now in hiding somewhere in North Africa, Spain or Britain, depending on who is telling the story. The third theory is that both of them ran into trouble with international crime gangs and decided to go into hiding. They couldn't come back to Ireland as by that stage their Irish operation had been effectively taken over by the rival gang responsible for the murder of "Verb" Sugg the previous August. The Gardaí were also looking for Coates to arrest him in relation to the incident in Virginia and other armed robberies. So if they had decided to return to Ireland they would have found themselves between the cops on one side and the rival gangs on the other. The fourth theory is that they are living with new identities in a foreign clime and not even their families know their fate.

These theories aside, by November 2004 there had been dozens of reported sightings of Coates and Sugg in Dublin, London, Manchester and Marbella. There have been reports that they are living in either Tunisia or Algeria. None of the so-called sightings have been found to be true. The two criminals have quite literally vanished without trace. One of the reasons why it is most likely that they were murdered is the fact that neither of them had the sophistication or ability to actually go into hiding for the rest of their lives. Sugg and Coates were brutal thugs with little education. They were only really comfortable on the turf they dominated in Dublin or hanging out with their own kind in the bars around Alicante. Like a lot of other Dublin criminals they could not exist without getting in contact with their families. Their families still say they believe the pair to be dead. If the two thugs had had any kind of contact with other criminals or their families in the eleven months since they vanished information would have inevitably leaked to the police or to the media. Further proof that they are no longer living may be the fact that on the streets of their original fiefdom, Blanchardstown, their drugs' patch has now been completely swallowed up by the criminal gang responsible for "Verb" Sugg's murder. If the Westies were alive they could not have resisted coming home to seek revenge. Initially it was thought in police circles that the pair had purposely faked their own disappearance in order to mount a surprise attack on their enemies in Dublin. There has been no surprise attack and, by the end of

2004, the only surprise would be evidence that Shane Coates and Stephen Sugg were actually alive.

In September 2004, Alicante became the Irish gangland equivalent of the Bermuda Triangle when another major crime figure, Sean Dunne, also vanished without trace. The thirty-two-year-old father of two from North Dublin had been part of a major Irish drug trafficking syndicate but most significantly he was also heavily involved in VAT fraud rackets on behalf of Sinn Féin and the IRA. In November 2003, Dunne had narrowly escaped death when he was shot five times by the IRA in a row over money that was missing from the fraud racket. Along with a number of former key members of Sinn Féin and the IRA, Dunne also had extensive property interests in Alicante. At the time of his disappearance Dunne was facing a huge tax demand from the Criminal Assets Bureau. It is now feared that Sean Dunne has also been murdered in Spain, possibly by his former business partners in the Republican movement. Another theory, suggested by criminal sources, speculates that he is alive and well and in hiding somewhere in the USA. But there are many who disagree with this theory on the grounds that Dunne had extensive property interests in Alicante and no real reason to run. He was also close to his young children and would not allow a day go by without contacting them. There does not appear to be a direct link between Dunne's disappearance and the disappearance of Coates and Sugg. However, as a result of enquiries into Sean Dunne's disappearance, a Dublin criminal living in Alicante informed this writer that a major Russian crime figure has claimed that it was his associates who took the two thugs away. He claimed that he is satisfied that they are dead and will not be coming back. In any event, if Sugg and Coates ever turn up alive again the only group of people happy to see them will be their families.